This book offers an extended reinterpretation of English policy in Ireland during the sixteenth century. It seeks to show that the major conflicts between Tudor governors and native lords which characterised the period were not the result of a deliberate Tudor strategy of confrontation as conventional interpretations have assumed, but argues that they arose from a failed experiment in legal reform and cultural assimilation which had been applied with remarkable success elsewhere in the Tudor dominions. The book seeks to explain the course of this exceptional failure, and it identifies a distinct administrative style which evolved in Irish government during the middle of the century under a complex set of pressures acting on the would-be reformers both in Ireland and at the Tudor court. It argues that it was this distinctive, highly centralised and intensely activist mode of government that inadvertently undermined the aims of reform policy and provoked the alienation and hostility that was precisely the opposite result to that which was originally intended.

Cambridge Studies in Early Modern British History

THE CHIEF GOVERNORS

Cambridge Studies in Early Modern British History

Series editors

ANTHONY FLETCHER
Professor of Modern History, University of Durham

JOHN GUY
Professor of Modern History, University of St Andrews

and JOHN MORRILL
*Reader in Early Modern History, University of Cambridge, and
Fellow and Tutor of Selwyn College*

This is a series of monographs and studies covering many aspects of the history of the British Isles between the late fifteenth century and the early eighteenth century. It includes the work of established scholars and pioneering work by a new generation of scholars. It includes both reviews and revisions of major topics and books which open up new historical terrain or which reveal startling new perspectives on familiar subjects. All the volumes set detailed research into broader perspectives and the books are intended for the use of students as well as of their teachers.

For a list of titles in the series, see end of book.

THE CHIEF GOVERNORS

The rise and fall of reform government in Tudor Ireland 1536–1588

CIARAN BRADY

Trinity College, Dublin

CAMBRIDGE
UNIVERSITY PRESS

PUBLISHED BY THE PRESS SYNDICATE OF THE UNIVERSITY OF CAMBRIDGE
The Pitt Building, Trumpington Street, Cambridge, United Kingdom

CAMBRIDGE UNIVERSITY PRESS
The Edinburgh Building, Cambridge CB2 2RU, UK
40 West 20th Street, New York NY 10011–4211, USA
477 Williamstown Road, Port Melbourne, VIC 3207, Australia
Ruiz de Alarcón 13, 28014 Madrid, Spain
Dock House, The Waterfront, Cape Town 8001, South Africa

http://www.cambridge.org

First published 1994
First paperback edition 2002

A catalogue record for this book is available from the British Library

Library of Congress Cataloguing in Publication data
Brady, Ciaran.
The chief governors: the rise and fall of reform government in
Tudor Ireland, 1536–1558 / Ciaran Brady.
p.   cm. – (Cambridge studies in early modern British history)
Includes bibliographical references and index.
ISBN 0 521 46176 6 (hc)
1. Ireland – Politics and government – 1172–1603.   2. Great Britain –
Politics and government – 1485–1603.   3. British – Ireland –
History – 16th century.   4. Tudor, House of.   I. Title.
II. Series.
DA935.B69   1994
941.505–dc20   93-43767   CIP

ISBN 0 521 46176 6 hardback
ISBN 0 521 52004 5 paperback

CONTENTS

Preface   *page* ix

Acknowledgements   xvi

Abbreviations   xvii

Prologue: Ireland in the wake of the Kildare rebellion, 1536   1

Part 1 The course of reform government, 1536–1578   11

1   Reform as process: the viceroyalties of Lord Leonard Grey
    and Sir Anthony St Leger, 1536–1547   13

2   Ireland and the mid-Tudor crisis, 1547–1556   45

3   Reform by programme: the viceroyalties of the earl of Sussex,
    1556–1565   72

4   Reform on contract: the viceroyalties of Sir Henry Sidney,
    1566–1578   113

Interlude: Government in Ireland, 1536–1579   159

Part 2 The impact of reform government, 1556–1583   167

5   Reform government and the feudal magnates   169

6   Reform government and the community of the Pale   209

7   Reform government and Gaelic Ireland   245

Epilogue: Reform in crisis: the viceroyalty of Sir John Perrot,
1584–1588   291

Bibliography   301

Index   317

*In memory of
my mother
and
my father*

PREFACE

Mankind, in following the present sense of their minds, in striving to remove inconveniences, or to gain apparent and contiguous advantages, arrive at ends which even their imaginations could not anticipate, and pass on, like other animals, in the track of their nature, without perceiving its end . . . and nations stumble upon establishments, which are indeed the result of human action, but not the execution of any human design. (Adam Ferguson, *An essay on the history of civil society, 1767*)

This is an old-fashioned book, concerning relatively well-known events, written in the main as a conventional interpretive narrative. It was not meant to be that way. At the outset (a setting out that took place far too long ago) the study was intended to serve as a contribution to the recently revitalised topic of the Tudor conquest of Ireland. By that time the traditional account of sixteenth-century Irish history as an era in which the last bastions of 'the Celtic fringe' gradually collapsed in face of the superior armed strength of a centralised Tudor state was already being superseded by interpretations of considerably greater sophistication. A number of historians, notably David Quinn, Nicholas Canny and Brendan Bradshaw, were then drawing attention to important developments within the Tudor attitude towards Ireland, and were suggesting that such alterations could be related to significant ideological shifts that were taking place in English political culture throughout the sixteenth century.

Thus the recounting of the wars, rebellions and foreign intrigues of the period which had been the stock in trade of earlier historians had begun to be displaced by more subtle, if more speculative, enquiries as to the forces at work in shaping the course of Tudor policy for Ireland from the optimistic days of Henry VIII to the dark final years of Elizabeth. Already a wide range of possible ideological influences on changing policy options had been suggested by historians, among which the effects of Spanish–American colonial writing, late Renaissance ethnology and an increasingly pessimistic Calvinism were the most strongly favoured. Thus my original intention was simply to explore how such a constellation of general influences operated in practice, in the formulation and execution of particular policies by successive Tudor administrations in Ireland.

All too superficially acquainted with the work of Max Weber and C. Wright Mills, I proposed to compile a collective biography of all of those individuals who held middle to high office in the Tudor administration in Ireland in which the social background, educational training, political allegiance and religious affiliation of each official would be discovered and correlated. By these means the shared and opposing interests of various groups involved in the making of policy would be laid bare, and the way in which one group succeeded and another failed to exploit the instruments of government in the best interests of their ideological objectives revealed. It gradually became clear that such a quest was futile. The surviving sources were scarce, and those which survived refused to yield to such predetermined questions. Thus, after many months of research, I was left only with shoe-boxes of index cards crammed with esoteric prosopographical data and an ability to name the second chamberlain of the exchequer at any date in the century.

The results of this preliminary study of the structure and personnel of the Irish administration were not, however, entirely fruitless: for the obstacles which they raised obliged me to pursue a number of alternative avenues of approach. The first concerned the curious evolution of English administration in Ireland during the sixteenth century. It became clear that while my initial, exploratory questions concerning the operations of competing groups had some significance in the 1530s and again in the 1590s, they remained largely irrelevant for the bulk of the period in between, because in these intervening years the business of making and executing policy had been concentrated in the hands of one central figure, the Irish chief governor.

For, despite the brief initiative taken by Thomas Cromwell in the early 1530s and the occasional formal declarations of the conciliar nature of Irish government which were enunciated thereafter, the Irish council never proved capable of assuming the central role in the management of policy that might have been assigned to it. Certain individual councillors acquired a great personal authority in policy matters from time to time, and others, on occasion, were able to exert a more negative influence in working to undermine the reputation of their governor. But the standing of the former was at all times dependent on the confidence placed in them by the viceroy; while the effectiveness of the latter was activated only by the intervention of other figures with more influence at court than a viceroy could match. The limited capability of its most senior offices, and the political insignificance of the majority of its personnel underlined the subordinate character of the Irish council and the central administration during the crucial period of

Tudor rule. The decision of Richard Bagwell, that doyen of nineteenth-century Tudor scholars, to divide his history into chapters corresponding with the periods in office of the major viceroys, it then appeared, reflected not merely a Victorian preoccupation with the deeds of great men, but a clear appreciation of the fact that the high sixteenth century could justifiably be classified as the age of the viceroys.

In tandem with this first, unexpectedly old-fashioned, discovery, there emerged a second and even more disturbing one. Neither the great viceroys nor their closest confidants were, it appeared, powerfully articulate ideologues, willing to provide detailed defences of their actions in the light of clearly stated assumptions. Such opinions as they were prepared to express concerning the character of the native Irish and the nature of their customs were few, and invariably took the form of brief *obiter dicta* most of which had already been thoroughly 'source-mined' by previous researchers and allowed of little further development. What typically concerned them in their voluminous correspondence and in their carefully structured memoranda were matters of a practical and technical character, proposals for administrative reform, institutional innovation and requests for the increase and alteration of personnel in government office. Only rarely were they distracted by speculations on the nature of the Irish and their destiny; and when they did reflect upon history, it was merely to puzzle over the fate of all earlier attempts to establish English rule in Ireland.

It took some time to recognise that behind these ostensibly dry and routine preoccupations there lay indeed an ideology: not some exotic form of renaissance anthropology or reformation ontology, to be sure, but the traditional English ideology which can be loosely described as common-law thought. The governors' obsession with administrative and jurisdictional details reflected, not their intellectual limitations, but their implicit conviction that English political culture could be revived in Ireland through the reform and extension of the institutions and procedures of law and administration which had maintained a stable and peaceful polity in England rather than by radical measures. For them the value of military conquest, leaving aside its very great risks and difficulties, was inherently limited; and whatever purpose it served had already been discharged when the Anglo-Norman conquerors demonstrated the corruption and inferiority of the Gaelic culture which they had vanquished.

That the English lordship thus established had itself decayed demonstrated only the inadequacy of a simple military solution and the necessity of a vigorous campaign of cultural conquest to follow it up. The descendants of the Anglo-Normans had failed in this obligation, abandoning the forms of law for the violent ways of bastard feudalism; and it had now fallen to the Tudors, who had themselves only recently rescued England from the brink of anarchy, to fulfil that task in Ireland. Thus it was no accident that the writings of the principal governors should have been so taken up with the *minutiae* of legal and administrative mechanics. For these were nothing less than the grammar and syntax by which the language of traditional English constitutionalism was articulated in Ireland.

Such discoveries might have made for little more than a rather negative critique of the unquestioned assumptions underlying the concept of 'the Tudor conquest' had they not been accompanied by a further and most powerful impression derived from that same large corpus of public and private writing: that is, the overwhelming sense of desperation and failure with which it was suffused. From the bitterly frustrated letters of Lord Lieutenant Sussex's last years, to the cold disillusion of Sir Henry Sidney's masterly memoir of service, to the baroque rancour of Sir John Perrot's allegations and self-justifications, almost all of those who held the chief governorship expressed deep disappointment with their tenure of office. All had indeed suffered grievously on account of their time in Ireland: each had grown heavily in debt in his term of service; some had been ruined. All were to provoke deep hostility during their time in office, most were to suffer at least temporary disgrace after their resignation, and two were ruined by trumped up charges of treason. In the sixteenth century, as in later times, Ireland was indeed the graveyard of aspiring English statesmen.

This pervasive sense of failure posed a particularly acute problem when viewed in relation to the other discoveries noted above. Had these been aggressive, tough-minded individuals determined to initiate a new military conquest in the island, then their experience of confrontation, disappointment and defeat would have been readily enough accounted for. But they were not: they were instead conservative constitutionalists, seeking to revitalise a political culture that had once existed in most parts of the island by reform, persuasion and the minimum of coercion. This determined gradualism only made the universal hostility which they confronted, and their failure to overcome it, all the more difficult to explain.

In approaching this difficulty I began to notice that, from about the middle of the century, an important distinction was to be drawn between the overall aims of these governors and the immediate techniques which many adopted as a means of obtaining them. Beginning with the governorship of the earl of Sussex, it became the habit of reforming viceroys to establish their own agenda of priorities before entering office, to isolate the particular problems they regarded as of immediate importance, to propose specific solutions for such problems, and to provide detailed estimates of budgets and time scales within which they would be resolved. The advantages of this programmatic approach to government were considerable: it seemed to offer at least temporary relief from the instinctive royal tendency to disavow the undertakings of subordinates and to deprive them without notice of adequate funding. But the long-term consequences of this refusal to engage with the warp and woof of Irish political processes were, as a review of the Elizabethan administrations' dealings with the different political communities of the island clearly revealed, disastrous. In each case the rapid deterioration in relations between Dublin and the other *foci* of power in Ireland could be explained not in terms of fundamental ideological conflict, but simply on the grounds of the administration's failure to respond sensitively to the needs and fears of those social and political interests with whom it dealt.

For some time it seemed sufficient to leave the argument there: the series of confrontations known as the Tudor conquest was not the result of some irrepressible conflict, but of a simple, yet disastrous executive innovation adopted unthinkingly by English administrators in their efforts to accelerate progress towards modest and quite conventional ends. But doubts remained. Why, it had to be asked, did successive governors persist in applying such an administrative technique when its nefarious effects were becoming so obvious throughout the country? And why should an apparently superficial alteration in managerial style have of itself provoked such a universally hostile reaction from the country in the first place? These problems suggested the need for yet a further look at the nature of the administrative changes that had occurred after 1556, to see how radically they departed from the character of previous governments and to see also how they represented a profound alteration in the attitude of the governors towards the office of viceroy itself.

At the outset my view of the government of Sussex's predecessor, Sir Anthony St Leger, was influenced largely by the opinions of those who had unseated him. That St Leger had indeed been corrupt and venal as they had charged was demonstrable; and the verification of their allegations did something to dim the somewhat roseate reputation which he had acquired over time. Yet I began to see that, whatever its initial motivation, St Leger's apparent corruption was highly functional, and that it supported his far larger attempt to shape a coalition of support for his government throughout the country. As I investigated the breadth of St Leger's ambition and the very great risks which it entailed I was driven further back towards an examination of the short and disastrous viceroyalty of his predecessor, Lord Leonard Grey; for it was the cluster of problems which had ruined Grey that St Leger had determined to overcome by a series of constitutional, political and simply personal initiatives. Such problems were not of either man's making; but their origins were not hard to trace. They arose directly from the sudden disruption of Tudor plans for Ireland which occurred upon the wholly unexpected rebellion of the Kildare Geraldines in 1534. It now became clear that the Geraldine rebellion had profoundly disturbed the structures of Irish politics in ways generally unappreciated. It had disturbed political relationships that had been in place for more than half a century, introduced new volatile factors into Irish politics and forced the English governors to assume a pre-eminence in Irish affairs far beyond that anticipated in the original reform schemes of the early 1530s, simply in order to survive.

The massive risks entailed by such a highly political role were made all too clear in Grey's sorry career, and its fundamental weaknesses were more thoroughly exposed by the decline of St Leger. But the abandonment of his strategy by St Leger's successors entailed considerably more than the introduction of a more stable and defensible executive technique. It represented also their implicit if inadvertent rejection of the analysis of the problem of Irish governance which had been adopted by earlier reforms in the wake of the disastrous commencement of the initial reform project itself. Thus while the object of the constitutional reconstruction of Ireland remained the same, the means by which it was to be achieved was for the second time in twenty years radically altered in a way that would make its realisation more than ever difficult to attain. Afflicted by some dire Heisenbergian principle, the Tudor attempts to reform Ireland seemed of themselves to have redefined the nature of the problem they aimed to resolve.

The structure of the present book is designed to elucidate this paradox. The prologue aims to present a brief analytic overview of the principal problems facing the English government in Ireland after the débâcle of the Kildare rebellion. The four chapters in Part 1 provide a chronological account of the means by which successive administrations sought to preserve the objectives of reform in the aftermath of this defeat and in the face of a host of additional and extraneous pressures which came to bear upon them. An Interlude, placed at the end of this chronological section, seeks to offer an analysis of the essential characteristics of the new administrative mode which came to predominate in Tudor Irish government after mid century; and to trace the implications that necessarily arose from its altered assumptions and- techniques. It is intended to serve as a bridge between the largely chronological chapters of Part 1 and the thematic chapters of Part 2. This section contains a series of case studies in confrontation between the Dublin government and the major political forces of the island. The conflicts themselves are relatively well known, and have been variously explained. But in each case it is shown that the interpretations conventionally proffered have been mistaken or seriously inadequate; and it is argued instead that the sources of these violent collisions lay in no predetermined, ideologically rooted antagonisms, but in the inadvertent provocations and disappointments of the new administrative style. Finally, an epilogue draws the subject matter of both parts together in a brief consideration of the viceroyalty of Sir John Perrot, a man who by his fierce determination to bring the reform project to completion, precipitated instead its mortal crisis.

The ironies inherent in the account that follows are not, it should hardly need saying, intended to obscure the ultimate tragedy of Ireland's history in the sixteenth century. The horrific suffering and brutal expropriation amidst which the century closed cannot be erased from the record; and that these evils in company with the countless other instances of cruelty and injustice in the Elizabethan period were directly the end result of so many failed experiments in reform is a central contention of this book. The implicit arrogance of the entire reform project – its unearned and wholly unquestioned claims to cultural superiority – should also be registered now. But the compulsion to bear witness and to apportion praise and blame in particular cases should not blind the historian to the greater revelation of the human condition which the encounter between Englishmen and Irishmen in the sixteenth century purveys: that is the perennial incapacity of individuals to comprehend the inner logic of their actions, to grasp their implications or to control their consequences. That the vanity of the chief governors' vision, their personal ambition and their quick and superficial intelligence did indeed introduce some element of predetermination in the events of their time, as the traditional accounts of 'the Tudor conquest' have always insisted, may finally, therefore, be granted. But the forces driving men towards confrontation were far more complex and more subtle than any which even the most sophisticated versions of that venerable interpretation have supposed – and they were all the more ineluctable for that.

ACKNOWLEDGEMENTS

The bibliography records in a formal manner the very substantial debts to archivists, librarians and scholars which I have contracted during the course of this work. But I should like to acknowledge here my personal gratitude to the institutions that have supported me and individuals who have stimulated, sustained and distracted me through long years of research and writing. To the editors of this series, and in particular to John Morrill, I owe a special debt for their patient and persistent efforts to force me to get this study into print. From Bill Davies of Cambridge University Press and the Job-like Sheila McEnery, whose fund of goodwill I must well-nigh have exhuasted, I can only beg forgiveness. I am indebted to the Grace Lawless Lee fund of Trinity College for generous support in preparing this book for publication. To many colleagues I owe much thanks. Though it might often seem otherwise to outsiders, the school of early modern Irish historians is an intensely enjoyable place in which to ply one's craft. For years it has been my privilege to share the same curiosity, engage with the same problems and occasionally even to agree with scholars whose help it is now a pleasure to acknowledge: Nicholas Canny, Steven Ellis, Alan Ford, Ray Gillespie, Colm Lennon, Hiram Morgan, Ken Nicholls, Mary O'Dowd and Tony Sheehan. Three close friends and colleagues, Brian Jackson, Bill McCormack and Michael Quigley deserve my particular gratitude. Their help in the closing stages of this work has been invaluable. But throughout they have supplied a tonic which has dissolved unwarranted depressions and dispelled unreal enthusiasms. My principal intellectual obligations remain, as ever, to two teachers, Brendan Bradshaw and Aidan Clarke, whose contrasting styles and common commitments have been my lode stars for almost twenty years. Nothing will inhibit them from dissociating themselves from what has been done here; but neither can they evade responsibility for the inspiration and encouragment they have lent me in the doing of it. My deepest debt, ineffable as such things always are, is to Aoife Nic Reamoinn.

ABBREVIATIONS

Add. MSS	Additional manuscripts (British Library)
AFM	Annals of the Four Masters
ALC	Annals of Loch Cé
Anal. Hib.	*Analecta Hibernica*
APC	Acts of the Privy Council
Archiv. Hib.	*Archivium Hibernicum*
BL	British Library
Bodl.	Bodleian Library, Oxford
Cal. Car. MSS	*Calendar of Carew Manuscripts*
Cal. pat. rolls	*Calendar of patent and close rolls in Chancery*
Hen. VIII and Eliz.	*(Ireland) Henry VIII to Elizabeth I*
DNB	*Dictionary of National Biography*
EHR	*English Historical Review*
Fiants, Henry VIII	*Calendar of fiants (Ireland)*
GEC Peerage	GEC (Cockayne) *The complete peerage*
HJ	*Historical Journal*
IER	*Irish Ecclesiastical Record*
IHS	*Irish Historical Studies*
JEH	*Journal of Ecclesiastical History*
Jn Kildare Arch. Soc.	*Journal of the Kildare Archaeological Society*
Jn. of Kilkenny and	*Journal of Kilkenny and South-East of Ireland*
SE Ireland Soc.	*Archaeological Society*
JnRSAI	*Journal of the Royal Society of Antiquaries of Ireland*
Lib. Mun.	*Liber Munerum Publicorum*
LP (1519–23)	*Letters and Papers of Henry VIII*
NAI	National Archive of Ireland
PRO	Public Record Office, London
Proc. RIA	*Proceedings of the Royal Irish Academy*
s.a.	*sub anno*
SP	Public Record Office, State Papers (MSS)

SP Hen. VIII	*State papers of Henry VIII*
Studia Hib.	*Studia Hibernica*
Trans. Am. Phil. Soc.	*Transactions of the American Philosophical Society*
Trans. R. Hist. Soc.	*Transactions of the Royal Historical Society*
TCD	Trinity College, Dublin
UJA	*Ulster Journal of Archaeology*

Prologue: Ireland in the wake of the Kildare rebellion, 1536

(I)

The Kildare rebellion of 1534 was an accident, a débâcle anticipated by few and one from which no one was to emerge without loss. In this simple but frequently misunderstood fact all of the major issues which would plague Irish politics for the rest of the sixteenth century had their origin. For the rebellion and destruction of the house of Kildare let loose a series of problems both for the English government and for the native communities of Ireland which neither side could resolve and which would ultimately result in their unwilling but irreparable estrangement. The year 1534, then, deserves its place as a date of crucial importance in the Irish historical canon, but not as tradition would have it, as the starting point of an ever more triumphant Tudor conquest; it marked rather the beginning of a long series of misunderstandings, miscalculations and failures which were to constitute Ireland's political tragedy in the sixteenth century.

In one important respect the traditional view of the event retains its point. The rebellion did indeed bring about the end of the Kildare ascendancy: the power of the Fitzgerald family was smashed, its leadership all but annihilated, its vast possessions confiscated. The collapse was so sudden and so complete that it seems strange the Kildares should have raised any resistance to Tudor power in the first place. Yet their decision to rebel was based on two perfectly realistic assumptions. The first was the confident belief that no Tudor government could hope to replace the essential network of connections and alliances which they had carefully constructed throughout the country over the previous century. The second, building on this, was the assumption that any attempt to persevere in a policy to which the Geraldines were opposed would soon be revealed as impracticable. Thus when the Geraldines were confronted with a royal request for moderate reforms which might in the long term lead to a reduction of their national influence as currently exercised, they decided to give early notice of a refusal to co-operate. They rebelled, that is, in full confidence, not in desperation.

1

In the event, as we know, the second of these assumptions proved to be false. In the dangerous times of the 1530s, King Henry and his minister, Thomas Cromwell, were determined to suppress all demonstrations of dissent no matter what the consequences; and in despatching a large campaign army to Ireland, they displayed unprecedented resolution which the Geraldines could not have expected. The Kildare bluff was called and the rebellion collapsed.[1]

The Geraldines, then, had fatally misjudged the larger international context within which their action was perceived. Yet despite this error their initial suppositions concerning the domestic consequences of rebellion remained sound. The great Geraldine network had not been fully activated in the rebellion, and in its suppression the government could take action only against a handful who had committed themselves unequivocally to the Kildare cause. Thus throughout the country, among the O'Neills and O'Donnells in Ulster, the Anglo-Irish of Lower Connacht, the Fitzgeralds of Desmond, the O'Connors and O'Mores in the midlands and even within the Pale itself, there existed large numbers of Geraldine clients who had been more or less supportive of the Kildare cause but against whom the government was incapable of proceeding. Though leaderless now, and vulnerable to exploitation on an individual basis, they remained nevertheless sufficiently numerous and powerful to threaten the authority of any administration which provoked their opposition. Their sense of party unity remained strong, kept alive by the survival, despite repeated government attempts to capture him, of the direct heir to the house of Kildare, Lord Offaly's younger brother, Gerald.

The political disposition of these former Geraldine allies was not, however, uniformly hostile. For though they might continue to hope for the restoration of the house of Kildare, each had in the meantime to make the best available accommodation with the government which had left them leaderless. The need for compromise with the crown varied considerably among the Geraldine ranks. Palesmen suspected of involvement in the rebellion were prepared to pay large fines in order to escape further investigation. But more powerful and remote figures, like Conn Bachach O'Neill, expected to be paid off instead. Others, like Cahir O'Connor, Manus O'Donnell and James Fitzgerald of Desmond, wanted government

---

[1] For a general account see Laurence Corristine, *The revolt of Silken Thomas* (Dublin, 1987); important interpretive essays are Brendan Bradshaw, 'Cromwellian reform and the origins of the Kildare rebellion', *Trans. R. Hist. Soc.*, 5th ser., 27 (1977), pp. 69–93; S. G. Ellis, 'The Kildare rebellion and the early Henrician reformation', *HJ* 19 (1976), pp. 807–30 and 'Thomas Cromwell and Ireland 1532–1540', *HJ* 23 (1980), pp. 497–519, and 'Tudor Policy in the Kildare ascendancy in the lordship of Ireland, 1496–1534', *IHS* 20 (1976–7), pp. 235–71.

recognition of their claims to their respective lordships as the price of obedience. But the characteristic common to all of these attitudes was that they were all conditional. Each was premissed upon the assumption that the government would be willing and able to guarantee the support or protection required. Should the government refuse or fail in these conditions, then these groups would swing radically towards the only available alternative means of rescuing their positions – foreign intrigue and restoration by force.

The highly volatile state of the leaderless Geraldines in the years after 1534 was complemented and exacerbated by the agitated condition of their factional rivals, the Butlers of Ormond and their followers. Within the Butler group, which drew its support from most of the anti-Geraldine interests in the country, the effects of Geraldine rebellion were profoundly ambiguous. Butler acceptance of the royal reform proposals had always been tentative. In the light of their own failure to compete with the Geraldines as national political leaders, agreement to a plan which seemed to promise them equal status was attractive in principle.[2] But the rebellion and the subsequent dislocation of the Geraldine group overturned their original estimations of the balance of power and presented the Butlers with a disturbing combination of opportunities and dangers. The opportunities of the post-rebellion environment were obvious. This was the time to settle old scores with their fallen rivals, to reopen old land disputes, to force new dynastic settlements in the lordships. Yet this sudden alteration in the balance of power significantly altered the status of the Butlers in the wake of the Geraldine ascendancy. For the government no longer had need of the Butlers as a useful ally against a common enemy. Rather, as the surviving part of the factional system, the Butlers began to appear as a smaller but hardly less troublesome example of the over-mighty subject than the Geraldines themselves, who ought to be treated with a similar caution and mistrust. The fall of the Kildares, therefore, threatened the Butlers with a consequent loss of their own political status in London, even as it seemed to herald an indefinite extension of their interests at home. Enmeshed in this web of ambition and fear, Butler political conduct thus became highly inconsistent and erratic; as at once they promoted the view that the crown should exploit Geraldine discomfiture in every possible way, while they jealously defended their own privileges and those of their followers against any encroachments from royal government.[3] Far from simplifying the Irish

---

[2] See in particular Bradshaw, 'Cromwellian reform'.
[3] The Butler case in this period was advanced primarily by their agents Robert and Walter Cowley; see (*inter alia*) *SP Hen. VIII*, II, 249–56, 323–40, 445–52; III, 20–3

political scene, then, the rebellion of 1534 rendered it even more intricate and complex, leaving the government to deal with two powerful but unstable groups upon whose allegiance no trust could be placed and without whose agreement no government directive could take effect. The Geraldines, then, had been right: without them the Tudor attempt to govern in Ireland would be an awesomely difficult business.

(ii)

The government's bewilderment was further confounded by the fact that it was its own deliberately moderate reform programme that had produced such an unexpectedly violent reaction. The proposals submitted to the earl of Kildare in 1533 were neither particularly novel nor immediately threatening.[4] Kildare and Ossory were both required to endorse a series of measures which would lead to the restriction and eventual abolition of various feudal and bastard feudal practices known collectively in Ireland as 'coyne and livery'. Kildare himself was to surrender his jurisdictional liberty in Co. Kildare and relinquish government into the hands of an English governor, Sir William Skeffington. Such demands might seem to have constituted a serious challenge to the Geraldine ascendancy but in reality they were quite mild. The reform of 'coyne and livery' proposed in the *Ordinances for the government of Ireland* had all been previously submitted to Kildare and received his approval in the past. There was no suggestion now that his renewed acceptance of these conventional aims should lead to the abolition of his privileges or that, in undertaking to implement reform, his position should be weakened in relation to other magnates practising the same methods. Moreover, the Geraldines' claim to a palatine jurisdiction was no more than thirty-five years old. It had never been accepted by the crown and had already been challenged by an act of the Irish parliament in 1531.

It is doubtful, however, whether the suppression of this claim would have entailed any noticeable loss of authority for the Geraldines in their own country. For the man nominated to act as the crown's representative in Ireland himself offered no real challenge to their influence in the country as a whole. Sir William Skeffington was neither a dangerous nor a prestigious man. He did not come, like the earl of Surrey in 1520, as commander of a powerful force, equipped with the resources to implement an independent policy. On the contrary, during his previous brief term in office Skeffington had shown himself incapable of surviving without the co-operation of the

---

[4] Ellis, 'Thomas Cromwell', pp. 500–4.

great magnates; his reappointment thus served as a deliberate sign from King Henry and Cromwell as to the moderate character of their intentions, showing that they wished to renew reform, not in opposition to the great lords but with their co-operation.[5]

Yet if the substance of the reform proposals was limited, the larger conceptual context within which they were formed was, as Brendan Bradshaw has argued, quite novel.[6] The *Ordinances* heralded the inauguration of a campaign to revive English government in Ireland and eventually to make the powers in the island answerable and obedient to English law. This new commitment to long-term reform derived from three very different sources. The first was Henry's and Cromwell's acute awareness of the threat posed to England's security by the exposed and highly unstable condition of Ireland. As England's isolation from Europe became more pronounced, and as the crown's concern with the enforcement of conformity to religious change grew more intense, so Ireland's quasi-autonomy and susceptibility to foreign intrigue became less tolerable. A second, related element in this new concern with reform was the recognition that the urgent necessity of making Ireland secure could not be met simply by launching a new military conquest. Over a decade before the crisis of the early 1530s the earl of Surrey had examined and rejected the strategic possibility of a lengthy campaign in Ireland. A new attempt at conquest, he had concluded, would be immensely expensive, would be of indefinite duration, and would remain wholly uncertain in its outcome. In the light of Surrey's analysis, Tudor policy towards Ireland in the later 1520s had drifted uncertainly through a number of unsatisfactory experiments in government without Kildare. But as the crisis of the 1530s mounted, so a third element in the new perspective on Ireland began to gain prominence. This final element was an understanding of the country's problems and potential as perceived by a number of reformist thinkers within Ireland itself.

The outlines of Anglo-Irish political thought, particularly as expressed by a number of Palesmen in a set of treatises and memoranda addressed to the English government has of late received considerable attention from

---

[5] Ellis, 'Tudor policy', especially pp. 244–54; Philip Wilson, *The beginnings of modern Ireland* (Dublin and London, 1912), pp. 105–8; see also the entry on Skeffington in *DNB*.

[6] Bradshaw, 'Cromwellian reform', and *The Irish constitutional revolution of the sixteenth century* (Cambridge, 1979), chs. 1–3; the general context of Henrician reform thinking has been the subject of a number of major studies since W. G. Zeeveld, *The foundations of Tudor policy* (Cambridge, MA, 1948); among many see A. B. Ferguson, *The articulate citizen and the English renaissance* (Durham, NC, 1965); A. Fox and J. A. Guy, *Reassessing the Henrician age* (Oxford, 1986); T. F. Mayer, *Thomas Starkey and the commonweal* (Cambridge, 1989); see also Bradshaw's critical review, 'The Tudor commonwealth: reform and revision', *HJ* 22 (1979), pp. 455–76.

historians.[7] Attempts have been made to identify the authors of these tracts as representatives of particular schools of thought. Elaborate taxonomies have been devised in which a wide range of positions have been discerned from the conservative, which sought merely to maintain a defensive *status quo*, through the radical which aimed at reviving the conquest, to the revolutionary which proposed the abandonment of the ancient opposition between English and native Irish, and their peaceful integration. Such exercises in categorisation, however, can be seriously misleading. A heterogeneous body of writing which included formal treatises, private memoranda, working briefs, letters written to different recipients at different times over twenty years does not yield easily to analysis. So it is not surprising that inconsistencies and overlaps have been found within these analytic frameworks. What is more important than the substance of these texts, however, is the fact that they were written at all. Though they frequently bewailed the decay and degeneration of the old Anglo-Norman colony, these writings in themselves constituted an implicit declaration that the origin and momentum of the old conquest had not been entirely exhausted. The richness and occasional novelty of these proposals, that is, were eloquent testimony that the aim of anglicising Ireland remained alive in a small but particularly self-conscious element of the colonial community who, despite their rhetorical pessimism, still believed that the situation could be salvaged. By their very appearance, then, these writings implied that the problem of reasserting English royal authority in Ireland, though formidable, was not essentially different from that then being addressed in the northern and western parts of England and Wales.

This diverse body of reform writing made a second and more specific contribution to the shaping of Tudor thought on Ireland. Though they offered a great variety of proposals for the reform of Ireland, they displayed a striking degree of agreement on the causes of the colony's decay. The corruption of the Anglo-Normans, they affirmed, was rooted in their adoption – in collusion with the Gaelic Irish – of an elaborate system of extortion, intimidation and protection which they termed 'coyne and livery'. This composite term, embracing both the Gaelic exaction of *coinmeadh* (which connoted the great lord's right to demand hospitality for his person) and the English livery (which connoted similar claims for his horses) was employed to summarise and indeed to symbolise the extent to which both ethnic groups had joined in establishing an informal mode of government throughout the island which consolidated their power in their respective

---

[7] Most particularly by Bradshaw whose discussion in *Constit. rev.* provoked some debate; see reviews by Brady in *Studia Hib.* 19 (1979), pp. 177–81; Canny in *HJ* 24 (1981), pp. 1023–6; and Ellis, *IHS* 22 (1980–1), pp. 78–81.

areas and negated the influence of English law. The abolition of this pernicious system was the primary objective upon which all reform texts, whatever shape they took, agreed.[8]

This initial assumption allowed for a second but quite often implicit agreement on the stages through which the attack on coyne and livery should proceed. Whether they were concerned with immediately urgent problems or with the elaboration of long-term proposals, all of them assumed that reform should commence in the Pale through the improvement of its military and defensive facilities or through the reform and revival of its social and royal institutions. Though some memoranda restricted themselves to these immediate issues, such an assumption cannot be categorised as the position of any particular school, it was simply a fundamental starting point of all reform thinking. On the question of the further advance of reform, however, differences of opinion became more marked. Yet consensus continued to prevail on two central points. First, it was accepted that the task of furthering English law could not be delegated solely to either of the great magnates, Kildare or Ormond; but secondly, it was understood that no reform could take effect without first securing the agreement and co-operation of the widespread diplomatic networks which the great lords had established. Thus the two groups were neither to be excluded from the enterprise nor allowed to take it over; both were to work under the supervision of a respected English governor.

Those writings which dealt with the further phases of reform, particularly in relation to the Gaelic Irish, displayed, not surprisingly, the greatest differences of opinion. Yet a significant inverse relationship can be discerned between the severity of the proposals advanced and the space devoted to a consideration of the problem. The two surviving texts which devoted any considerable attention to the problem of Gaelic Ireland concluded by advocating a moderate, gradualist policy of peaceful assimilation under the common law.[9] For the more practical-minded men of the Pale, however, the matter of coming to terms with Gaelic Ireland was a relatively distant problem for which traditional military solutions could be

---

[8] See, for example, 'Report on Ireland, *c.* 1515', *SP Hen. VIII*, II, 1–31; 'Memorandum', *c.* Mar. 1520, *LP (1519–23)*, no. 670; 'Discourse on Ireland', *c.* 1528, BL, Lansdowne MS 159, fos. 2–14; 'Instructions to John Alen', 1533, *SP Hen. VIII*, II, 162–6; 'Report on Ireland', *c.* Mar. 1534, ibid., pp. 182–92; Patrick Finglas' 'Breviate of the getting of Ireland and of the decay of the same' (full version), SP 60/2/7; on the development and systematisation of coyne and livery in the later middle ages, see C. A. Empey and Katharine Simms, 'The ordinances of the White Earl and the problem of coign in the later middle ages', *Proc. RIA* 85 (1975), sect. C, pp. 161–87.

[9] 'Report on Ireland, *c.* 1515'; 'Discourse on Ireland', *c.* 1528; see also Archbishop Rokeby's 'Memorandum', 1520, *LP (1519–23)* and Thomas Finglas' 'Report', 1534, *SP Hen. VIII*, II, 182–92.

briskly restated and then be deferred until more urgent issues had been resolved.

Thus, despite the varieties of perspectives from which they were written and despite their differences on specific issues, these reform writings collectively offered a distinct scale of priorities as to what should be attempted first in Ireland and how. Thus when Henry and Cromwell came to look at Ireland, deeply aware of the need for positive action, and the impossibility of launching a new conquest, they had ready to hand a large body of opinion which, whatever its internal inconsistencies, provided a clear prospectus for the commencement of reform. They should begin by reconstructing the civil administration and local defences of the Pale and then proceed further by securing the agreement of the Anglo-Irish magnates to a set of reforms which would eventually lead to the voluntary abolition of coyne and livery. In a sense, therefore, Dr Bradshaw and his critics have both been right; the reform plans of the 1530s were neither original nor radical; but in the hands of Thomas Cromwell they were, as Bradshaw has claimed, moulded into a coherent and progressive programme of reform which would enable the government to deal with Ireland in the manner in which it was now coping with the problems that confronted it in England.

(III)

The origins of this reform policy are ultimately of less importance than the Geraldine reaction to it. For their rebellion not only destabilised the Irish political system, it also undercut the central assumption upon which Cromwell's reform plan had been based. For now the exploitation of the magnates' networks to advance the gradual progress of reform was no longer possible: Cromwell's programme remained frozen in its earliest stages. Moreover the rebellion and its aftermath gave rise to a further set of political requirements which had hitherto played a relatively unimportant role in the process of policy formulation. The suppression of the rebellion alone had cost something in the region of £40,000 (st.), and continued insecurity thereafter compelled the crown to maintain a standing army in Ireland of far greater size than had ever been contemplated. The business of reforming Ireland, it was now clear, would be a far more difficult and far more expensive undertaking than anyone had led the crown to expect. From this late apprehension arose a further demand that the Dublin administration should be made to function with maximum efficiency, that savings be made in every department, that existing sources of revenue be exploited to the utmost, and every effort be made to find new ones. In the short term, then, financial retrenchment and economic enterprise came to assume a place of greater priority than the larger objectives of political reform.

Finally, the rebellion decisively changed the London government's view of the role of the English official who was to have primary responsibility for the extension of English rule in Ireland. The estrangement of the Geraldines, and the emergence of the Butlers as a dangerously ambitious interest, undermined the complacent assumption shared by Cromwell and by so many of the Anglo-Irish writers that the governor should function in a conciliar manner, managing and mediating between powerful indigenous groups whose strength could be harnessed to the cause of reform. From henceforth it was clear that the governor must be a far more formidable figure, an independent power possessing the capacity to establish the crown's authority in its own right. Yet even as he was required to assume a more active and aggressive political role, the reverberations of the rebellion had seriously disturbed the offices of the administration from which he was supposed to derive support. The factional rivalries which had long been inherent within the Dublin administration had now become intensely active, as Butler clients, most notably Robert and Walter Cowley, pushed vigorously in the interests of their clients, and Geraldine appointees, compromised by the rebellion, eagerly pressed their services on any who would offer them protection. Between these groups even the small cadre of recently appointed English officials was itself divided. There was a circle, centered upon the Master of the Rolls, John Alen, who still hoped to advance reform by means of a conciliar government, but one in which the Anglo-Irish would play a distinctly subordinate role. And though this group were willing to support any governor in the assertion of royal authority, they were markedly suspicious of one who would make himself anything more than *primus inter pares* among the English. But there was also to be discerned, particularly among the military men, a second group led by the vice-treasurer, Sir William Brabazon who were, for reasons of their own, quite satisfied with Sir William Skeffington's lax management of financial affairs, and despite being more than happy to support a strong military governor, were deeply hostile to any efforts he might make towards financial reform.[10]

The prospects facing an English governor in the wake of the Geraldine rebellion were, therefore, daunting. Plunged into an extremely volatile political situation, he was to assert his authority in the country without showing any dependence upon either the Butlers or the Geraldines, or yet becoming a mere cipher in the closet intrigues of the Dublin administration. And he was to maintain this lofty role while responding promptly to the demands for economy and retrenchment from a government in London

---

[10] For Brabazon's early attitude see Brabazon to Cromwell, 30 June 1536, *LP (1536)*, no. 1224.

that was now unprecedentedly vigilant. From the beginning, therefore, the English chief governor in Ireland moved, in a phrase that would often be applied thereafter, within a dark and dangerous labyrinth. The first man to experience these fearsome conditions was Lord Leonard Grey.

Part 1

THE COURSE OF REFORM
GOVERNMENT, 1536–1578

Reform as process: the viceroyalties of Lord Leonard Grey and Sir Anthony St Leger, 1536–1547

'Poor Leonard Grey', as he began to sign himself soon after his appointment as lord deputy in February 1536, has been as harshly treated by historians as he was in his own times. Recalled in disgrace after barely four years in office and executed in 1541 on groundless charges of treason, his sad fate has conventionally been seen merely as the result of his own intemperate and somewhat obtuse conduct as viceroy. A bungling militarist who placed too much confidence in agreements exacted under duress, a relentless self-seeker inattentive to advice and intolerant of criticism, he has been adjudged to have contributed greatly to his ruin by failing to appreciate the extraordinary opportunities for the reform of Ireland that had been made available to him after the fall of the Geraldines.[1]

Grey's slender reputation has been easily overshadowed by those of two of the most formidable figures of the period, his superior, Secretary Thomas Cromwell, and his successor as viceroy, Sir Anthony St Leger. Modern assessments of these two have left little for Grey to claim as his due. Such credit as had been given for the limited reforms introduced during his time in Ireland has been accorded to Cromwell, while his failure to establish his authority over the native lords has been contrasted with the great diplomatic successes for which St Leger has received so much praise. Such judgements would seem, however, to be both unfair and misleading. They are unfair because they ignore the massive difficulties which Grey was compelled to face in the aftermath of the Kildare rebellion; but more importantly, they are misleading because they underestimate Grey's not inconsiderable achievement in re-establishing the authority of an English governor in Ireland. No one can deny that Grey was ultimately a failure, but the circumstances of his ruin should not obscure the boldness of his experiment

---

[1] The style first appears in Grey to Cromwell, 7 May 1536, *SP Hen. VIII*, II, 315, and recurs regularly thereafter; typically unflattering treatments of Grey are Bradshaw, *Constit. Rev.*, pp. 123–34; Ellis, *Tudor England*, pp. 135–6; and the sketch in *DNB* by J. T. Gilbert.

in viceregal government and its importance for the subsequent development of reform in Tudor Ireland.

(I)

Thomas Cromwell's attempt to reorganise the government of Ireland before and after the Kildare rebellion has now received due acknowledgement. He is said to have confirmed the English crown's authority by stage-managing the Irish parliament of 1536–7, securing the smooth passage of the act of supremacy and related legislation. He is said also to have resuscitated the central administration, increasing its revenues through the confiscation of Geraldine and some monastic lands, and introducing procedural reforms by which the crown's revenues might be better accounted. And he has been credited with the most ambitious aim of subordinating the government of Ireland to direct control from London through his own regular involvement in Irish policy-making and through the appointment of a series of special commissioners who reported directly to him.[2]

The reconstruction of a coherent programme of Cromwellian reform for Ireland is consistent with what, until recently, was the conventional view of his methods in England. In the Irish context, however, such a conclusion seems somewhat forced. Though Cromwell played an active role in the preparation of the parliament of 1536–7, the central pieces of legislation then devised, such as the attainder bills and the constitutional changes required by the reformation, were simple necessities clearly dictated by events. Other items, most notably the act against absentees, had long been advocated by reform writers in Ireland, while many more were simply matters of local interest. The proficiency of the secretary's management of parliamentary affairs, moreover, should not be exaggerated. Between them Cromwell and the commissioners he appointed to direct business for him in Ireland were responsible for a number of embarrassing errors and delays. The replacement of one act of succession (declaring the legitimacy of Anne Boleyn's progeny) by another (denying it), the error specifying the time for the collection of the annual subsidy, and the disregard of the residential conditions imposed on members by a statute of 1477 which rendered the bulk of the parliament's legislation technically invalid, all testified to a certain lack of care.[3] Such mistakes do not seriously question Cromwell's

---

[2] Bradshaw, *Constit. rev.*, chs. 4–6; for a different emphasis see Ellis, 'Thomas Cromwell'.
[3] For a detailed reconstruction of the parliament's proceedings see R. D. Edwards, 'The Irish reformation parliament of Henry VIII, 1536–7', T. W. Moody (ed.), *Historical Studies* VI (1968), pp. 59–84; and for important corrections Brendan Bradshaw, 'The opposition to the ecclesiastical legislation in the Irish reformation parliament', *IHS* 16 (1969), pp. 285–303.

genuine concern; but they raise doubts about the extent of his concentration on Irish matters. The secretary's routine correspondence with Ireland further suggests the intermittent character of his engagement. It was by and large spasmodic, reactive and infrequent; even in his most active period between August and December 1537, it was not particularly impressive: of the nineteen letters known to have been despatched by him in that time, only three related in any way to matters of policy while the remainder, as might be expected, were concerned with the recommendation of private suits. For the following year, not a single letter from the secretary survives.[4]

None of this detracts from Cromwell's reputation as an administrator. As a man burdened with an extraordinary range of responsibilities, Ireland generally assumed a place of secondary importance in his scale of priorities, to be given close attention only when its affairs appeared to impinge upon larger issues closer to the centre of power. For this reason Cromwell's attention to Ireland following the defeat of the Geraldines was both intermittent and inconsistent: yet two fundamental principles may be seen to have determined the secretary's attitude in these years.

The first was a concern with public finance, with the increase of revenues and more emphatically with the reduction of costs. In the matter of raising revenue Cromwell's achievements were distinctly limited. Though the newly acquired crown lands promised an increase of £5,320 and though the clerical and lay taxations sanctioned by parliament promised further substantial gains, none of the administrative innovations established by Cromwell to exploit such resources in England were introduced into Ireland. The new business proved too great for the traditional offices of the Dublin administration to manage and, as arrears and bad debts mounted, crown revenues in Ireland stagnated in the later 1530s, yielding an average of less than £4,500 p.a. Since revenue improvement demanded more attention than Cromwell was prepared to give it, the secretary concentrated instead on the less complex matter of reducing government expenditure. To cut costs he had the royal garrison halved from 700 to 340 in September 1537, and even then he continued to press for further reductions in the numbers in service. The costs of maintaining the army drove him to look with increasing interest at ways of delegating the defence of Ireland once again to acceptable Anglo-Irish lords and even to pay serious attention to Butler proposals to launch a private colonising enterprise in south Leinster.[5]

This willingness to consider farming out the defence of English interests

---

4 Bradshaw, *Constit. rev.*, pp. 141–2; for Cromwell's patronage correspondence during the period see *LP (1537)*, nos. 414, 456, 457, 468, 472, 486, 500, 575, 591, 734, 735, 763, 782, 826, 838, 991; for political letters, nos. 485, 1189, 1207.

5 Ellis, 'Thomas Cromwell'.

in Ireland is closely related to the second principle of Cromwell's post-rebellion Irish policy: his concern with the establishment of a patronage network. Cromwell's exploitation of patronage, the recommendations for grants of land, office and private suits which swell his correspondence, has sometimes been explained as part of an effort to encourage a dependable reformist group within the Dublin administration. Certainly, he was anxious to buttress the position of his men in office, but he was happy also to further the suits of several Anglo-Irish lords, whose interests were by no means identifiable with the promotion of reform. It is unlikely in any case that deep political considerations underlay his support of the merchant Edward Beck, the adventurer Francis Herbert and a host of more obscure souls like Hugh Lynn and Mathew Skeyn with whom he concerned himself. Instead, Cromwell, like so many of his contemporaries at court, was simply determined to establish widespread bonds of dependence wherever the opportunity arose.[6]

Cromwell's involvement with Ireland in the years after the Kildare rebellion, therefore, hardly amounted to anything like a coherent pro-gramme of reform. On review it seems simply to reflect the basic *desideratum* of all Tudor governments in their dealings with Ireland: that of defending England's interests in the island in the cheapest possible manner. Such a conservative intent was, in the wake of the disorders of the early 1530s, quite understandable; yet it presented a most serious obstacle to the English official charged with the daily management of the crown's affairs in the island. Seen from London, where Ireland was regarded as a potentially dangerous but intermittent problem, it seemed reasonable to eschew expensive and possibly troublesome initiatives in favour of more cautious, occasional interventions. From the closer perspective of Dublin, however, such complacency appeared to be highly irresponsible. In Dublin it was clear that the conditions prevailing in every province of post-rebellion Ireland were by no means so settled as to allow for an easy withdrawal to financial retrenchment and inaction.

Within the sprawling Desmond lordship of the south-west, the crown's nominee to the vacant earldom, James Fitzmaurice, was openly challenged by his uncle James FitzJohn, an active supporter of the Kildare Geraldines whose claims to succession had already been denied by the government. To the north of Desmond, the Gaelic lordship of Thomond remained unreconciled to the Kildare defeat, offering sanctuary to Geraldine refugees

---

[6] On the concern with patronage at the Henrician court see David Starkey et al., *The English court from the wars of the roses to the civil war* (London, 1987), ch. 3; Starkey, 'Court and government' in Christopher Coleman and David Starkey (eds.), *Revolution reassessed* (Oxford, 1986), pp. 29–58.

and refusing entry to government forces. Throughout Connacht pro-Geraldine elements among the MacWilliam Burkes, the O'Connors of Sligo and the O'Malleys placed the anti-Geraldine Clanrickard Burkes and their supporters under constant pressure. In Tyrconnell, the ambitious Manus O'Donnell then seeking to displace his father as chieftain adopted a pro-Geraldine stance, while O'Neill, the most powerful Geraldine figure in Ulster, remained hostile. In Leinster itself the government faced more immediate threats from Geraldine allies among the O'Connors, the O'Mores and the Kavanaghs who seemed poised to attack the Pale at the earliest opportunity. For the governor in Dublin, the outlying Geraldine areas were not, as Cromwell and some later commentators seemed to assume, isolated long-term problems which could be dealt with at some point in the future. They were the essential elements of a national network of disaffection which threatened his administration with imminent danger and required immediate action.[7]

The unreconciled Geraldines were not the only powerful interest threatening the English governor: the Butlers of Ormond presented a quite different but equally dangerous challenge of their own. At court Ossory's agent, Robert Cowley, was pressing strongly for a thorough campaign against Geraldines in all parts of the country which Ossory himself was to lead with the support of his allies in each province, while pro-Butler counsellors in Dublin were castigating the deputy's failure to establish his authority by military means.[8]

The new English governor thus faced a simultaneous challenge to his authority from two different directions both of which required a finely judged response. To assert himself with the Geraldines he would have to operate not on a local but on a national level, ranging up and down the country as the Kildares had done assuring potential allies and enemies of his ability to offer powerful friendship and to inflict fearful punishment. Yet in assuming such an assertive stance, he had also to separate himself from the Butlers, avoiding identification with their interests and dependence on their resources lest he be seen as a pawn of the house of Ormond. Thus, simply in order to maintain the independence of his office, the viceroy was from the beginning compelled to adopt a strategy that was directly contrary to the restrictive, conservative axioms laid down by his superiors in London. This

---

[7] Ossory to Cromwell, 2 June 1536, *SP Hen. VIII*, II, 297–9; Thomas Fokes to Cromwell, 22 Mar. 1536, ibid., p. 308; Grey and council to Cromwell, 1 June 1536, ibid., pp. 318–21; Grey to Cromwell, 7 May, 24 June, 10 Aug., ibid., pp. 314–15, 324–6, 353–7; council of Ireland to Cromwell, 9 Aug., ibid., pp. 349–53.

[8] Walter Cowley to Robert Cowley, 29 Apr. 1536, *SP Hen. VIII*, II, pp. 311–14; Robert Cowley to Cromwell, June 1536, ibid., pp. 323–30; Walter Cowley to same, 10 June, *LP (1536)*, I, no. 1112.

tension between the needs of the governor and the outlook of the ministers in Whitehall became evident even within a year of Lord Leonard Grey's appointment to office.

(II)

During the first months of his service Grey seemed more than willing to be guided by Cromwell and his agents. He was happy to allow the management of parliamentary business by special commissioners and to take the advice of two of Cromwell's *protégés*, the master of the rolls, John Alen, and the chief justice of common pleas, Gerald Aylmer. Throughout 1536 both men remained close to Grey, supporting him strongly against the allegations of another of Cromwell's special agents, William Body. By the middle of 1537, however, relations between Grey and the two counsellors had become strained and by the end of that year Alen and Aylmer had become open opponents of Grey, identifying themselves with a Butler effort, which they had previously denounced, to secure the viceroy's recall.[9]

The causes of their disillusion with the deputy were, according to Alen and Aylmer, all too simple: Grey, they alleged, had abandoned reform and the English interest in general and was seeking through factional alliances and intrigues to establish himself as the new leader of the dispossessed Geraldines. The evidence which they produced in support of this charge was indeed persuasive. From the beginning of 1537 Grey, they claimed, had launched a systematic campaign to rehabilitate the Geraldines. In Desmond he disowned the anglophile James Fitzmaurice, supporting the case of the disreputable James FitzJohn and even acknowledging the latter's claims to a suzerainty over MacCarthy More and the Fitzmaurices of Kerry. In Thomond he made his peace with the Geraldine Cormack O'Brien. He befriended the Geraldine claimant to the lordship of MacWilliam Burke and rejected his Butler supported rival. In Ulster he made peace with O'Neill and furthered the chieftain's provincial ambitions by recognising his son-in-law as the rightful Magennis and by launching an unprovoked attack on the independent-minded O'Reillys. In Leinster he gave the lordship of the O'Connors to Ferganim, a brother-in-law of the rebel Lord Offaly, and even lodged with him on a journey into Munster leaving troops and ordnance with the new chieftain for his own use. He released a son of the O'More who had been detained in Dublin Castle for his part in the rebellion and covertly tolerated the raids which O'More in alliance with the Kavanaghs was

---

[9] Grey to Henry VIII, 23 Feb. 1536, *LP (1536)*, I, no. 317; same to Cromwell, 29 May, 24 June, 24 Nov., ibid., nos. 988, 1194; II, 1157; Thomas Alen to Cromwell, 17 July, ibid., II, no. 101; John Alen to Henry VIII, 6 Oct., *SP Hen. VIII*, II, pp. 383–8.

making on Butler territories in the midlands. Grey had even carried his divisive strategy into the halls of the Dublin administration, openly antagonising English officers like Alen and Brabazon, restoring favour to figures like Chief Justice Howth and Attorney General Bathe who had been compromised in the rebellion, and, most seriously of all, surrounding himself with shadowy, unofficial counsellors like James and Richard Tuite who were well known to have been active Geraldine agents in the past.[10]

In seeking to explain the viceroy's conduct historians have tended to take Grey's detractors very much on trust. Grey, they have concluded, was a crude political adventurer who badly miscalculated both his own strength and that of those who were led to oppose him.[11] Yet this simple tale of a greedy and reckless fool is in the end unconvincing for two important reasons: first, it ignores the very real pressures which forced Grey to adopt his hazardous pro-Geraldine attitudes and, having done so, it fails, secondly, to see how close the deputy came to making his strategy work.

Given the realities of political conditions throughout Ireland, the restrictions imposed from London left Grey with little choice but to attempt a *rapprochement* with the Geraldines. The crown's directives to keep the peace and to increase the revenues while cutting costs and reducing the garrison were deeply contradictory, and had he attempted to meet them the governor would soon have found himself embattled in Dublin, incapable of asserting his authority in the island or even of defending the Pale. He might, of course, have compensated for this weakness by employing the services of the Butlers, but such a reliance would have entailed the loss of the independence which the Dublin government had won only so recently and at such a great cost.

Faced with this dilemma, Grey's decision to look toward the Geraldines had considerable merit. Unexpectedly jolted from their ascendancy and vulnerable now to attack from many sides, the Geraldines were urgently in need of a protector who could limit their exposure and perhaps restore them to some measure of influence. At the same time they continued to enjoy elaborate networks of connection far more extensive than the English governor or even the Butlers could hope to acquire. With Geraldine co-operation the viceroy could expect to have royal directives transmitted

---

[10] Alen's reports to the commissioners, 1537, *SP Hen. VIII*, II, pp. 480–501; Alen's charges against George Paulet, Mar. 1538, ibid., pp. 551–3; his memo to Wriothesley, Mar. 1538, *LP (1538)*, no. 641; Alen and Aylmer's accusations against Grey, June 1538, *SP Hen. VIII*, III, pp. 36–43, and letters to St Leger and Cromwell, July, ibid., 46–8, 55–7; the names of Grey's closest Geraldine supporters are supplied in Agard to Cromwell, 1 July 1536, *LP (1536)*, II, no. 1, and W. Cowley to Cromwell, Apr. 1538, *SP Hen. VIII*, III, pp. 12–14.

[11] See note 1 above.

and enforced with the same effectiveness and economy as those of the earls of Kildare. The establishment of a sound understanding with the surviving leaders of the group thus seemed to allow the English government to retain the authority which it asserted in 1534, while at once meeting the financial restrictions required since then, and avoiding a dangerous dependence upon the Butlers.

This was, of course, a high risk strategy. The Geraldines, it was clear, would not become steadfast allies overnight to the man who had once promised their leaders pardon and reneged upon his word: they would have to be educated gradually through a mixture of persuasion and coercion to value his good-will. But more immediate trouble was to be expected from the disappointed Butlers and from the anti-Geraldine reformers within his own administration who would see in the viceroy's conduct only a betrayal of the aims for which they had already risked so much.

The inevitable consequences of Grey's strategic decision followed almost immediately. Ossory's son, Sir James Butler, and his closest advisers Robert and Walter Cowley, began their assault on the deputy's character as soon as his independent attitude became clear. And though their allegations originally savoured of party interest, their claims were considerably reinforced by the unrelated criticisms levelled by the disillusioned Alen and Aylmer. The campaign against Grey grew more intense when King Henry despatched Sir Anthony St Leger to investigate, among other things, the grounds for the charges against his viceroy. St Leger appeared to sympathise with Grey's enemies, encouraging their allegations and their propositions for an alternative approach to government; and when he concluded his commission in April 1538, Alen, Aylmer and Lord Butler returned with him to London. Given the standing of his critics, the gravity of their charges and their access to influence at court, Grey's removal seemed inevitable. Alen, indeed, was so confident of the outcome that he presumed to offer Cromwell advice as to how it should be most smoothly effected.[12]

But despite all this, no order for Grey's recall was received from the king upon St Leger's return. Instead both parties were simply directed to resolve their differences and to join together in the execution of the king's business. The much anticipated coup had failed to materialise. By the end of the year, moreover, Grey's credit at court appeared to have recovered remarkably, and his critics were on the defensive as Cromwell began to investigate the

---

[12] Cowley to Cromwell, R. Cowley to Cromwell and to Norfolk, 10 June 1536, 14 Oct. 1536, 20 Jan. 1538, *LP (1536)*, I, no. 1112; II, no. 709; *LP (1538)*, I, no. 114; Ormond to St Leger, 12 Mar. 1536, June 1538, ibid., II, 556–8; III, 20–3, 55; Lord James Butler to Cromwell, 11 Aug. 1536, and to Cowley, June 1538, ibid., II, 357–9; III, 32–4; Agard to Cromwell, 4 Apr. 1538, ibid., II, 567–8; Alen's memo to Wriothesley, Mar. 1538, *LP (1538)*, no. 641, and to Cromwell, 29 Nov. 1538, *LP (1538)*, II, no. 937.

counter-allegations which Grey had made against them. At the same time, Grey's own supporters were busy reporting his military and diplomatic successes to Cromwell and urging his requests for additional supplies of men, munitions and money.[13] King Henry was also reported to have approved of Grey's work and of his plans for an impressive progress through the country, and, as a token of his renewed confidence in the viceroy, he sent Grey a goshawk early in 1540.[14] By then, in any case, the coalition against Grey had all but broken up. Ormond wrote to Cromwell in December 1539 renouncing his earlier hostility, as an unworthy scheme fomented by others 'more to please our affections than to have regard for the commonwealth'.[15] Walter Cowley now wrote recommending the governor for reward as enthusiastically as he had once demanded his dismissal; and Treasurer Brabazon now renewed good relations with Grey, leaving Alen and Aylmer virtually isolated on the Irish council. Far from having succumbed to the criticism which he himself had provoked, Lord Deputy Grey seemed not only to have survived the attack with remarkable ease, but to have established at last a firm control over his own administration. And when his long pressed suit to report to the king in person was at last answered, it was granted on the express understanding that he should return promptly to commence the great campaigns in Ulster and Munster which he had proposed.[16]

The reasons for Grey's success in confounding his critics are not hard to find. Despite the gravity of their charges and the urgency with which they were pressed, the coalition against Grey was not invulnerable. The motivations which lay behind the Butlers' resentment of Grey were obvious to Henry and Cromwell, as were the more narrow ambitions of those administrators who sought to establish a position of influence for themselves in government. And so while King Henry might have been willing to check the overweening stratagems of his viceroy, he was hardly willing to do so to advance the aims of the more ambitious and more dangerous Butlers or still less the notions of obscure political figures like John Alen. The coalition itself, moreover, had never been solid: though St Leger had feigned sympathy with Grey's critics, his fellow commissioner George Paulet openly declared his support for the deputy. Later Thomas Cusacke, that weather-

---

[13] Francis Herbert to Cromwell, 20 Mar. 1538, Mathew King to Cromwell, 26 Apr., *LP (1538)*, I, nos. 559, 849; Irish council to Cromwell, 12 Dec. 1538, 16 Feb. 1539, *SP Hen. VIII*, III, 108–11, 118–21; James Bathe to Cromwell, Nov. 1539, *SP Hen. VIII*, III, 157–62; William St Loe to Cromwell, 21 Apr. 1540, *LP (1540)*, no. 558.

[14] Grey to Henry VIII, 10 Mar. 1540, *SP Hen. VIII*, III, 187–9.

[15] Ormond to Cromwell, 20 Dec. 1539; Cowley's 'Memo', 5 Feb. 1540; council of Ireland to Henry VIII, 16 Jan. 1549, *SP Hen. VIII*, III, 164–7, 179–84, 174–5.

[16] Henry VIII to Grey, 1 Apr. 1540, *LP (1540)*, no. 441.

vane of Anglo-Irish politics, who travelled to court with Grey's critics, underwent a sea-change, and announced his support for the embattled governor. These defections considerably weakened the strength of the case against Grey. But a far more important defence lay in the viceroy's own hands: for in spite of the influence his opponents may have hoped to exert at court, he still retained the power of initiative in Ireland.[17]

Whatever suspicions may have been raised by Grey's pro-Geraldine policy, its practical results were, in the short term, quite satisfactory. Despite ever-more limited military resources, Grey turned out to be a surprisingly active and effective governor. He made several tours of the country, conducting a progress through each province on at least two occasions, settling territorial and dynastic disputes and securing formal bonds of good behaviour from the principal lords in each province. Grey's favoured mode of reply to his critics thus took the form not of defensive rejoinders, but of detailed accounts of his progresses through the island accompanied by copies of the agreements which he had secured from the lords.[18] It could not be assumed, of course, that such treaties would prove durable in themselves; yet they provided evidence of Grey's ability to establish respect for the royal presence in several important areas with the minimum of force. By means of sharp punitive campaigns in Connacht and Leinster he compelled O'Brien, O'Flaherty and O'Connor to confirm their submissions. In Ulster he forced MacMahon to make good his agreements by seizing his herds until he had paid compensation for his disorders. He made several surprise raids upon O'Neill, and finally inflicted grievous injury on the great chieftain in a daring attack on his forces at Bellahoe in Farney late in 1539. In these ways Grey signalled the conditional nature of his friendship towards individual Geraldine followers: for though he was clearly anxious to attach many of them to his cause, he recognised also that the most powerful figures in the group would follow him only if they could be convinced of his ability to overwhelm them. It was for this reason that at the end of 1539 Grey pressed so strongly for permission to follow up his victory against O'Neill and further to reinforce his authority over the restless James FitzJohn of Desmond through a well-supported military progress.[19] And it was the manifest success of his strategy in the previous four years that persuaded

[17] Articles by Alen and Aylmer against Paulet, Mar. 1538; Thomas Alen to St Leger and to Wriothesley, 10 Aug. 1538; Lord Butler to Cromwell, 27 Aug.; Anthony Budgegode to Cromwell, 26 Sept. 1538, *LP (1538)*, II, no. 471; nos. 65, 66, 196, 433.
[18] Grey and council to Cromwell, 8 Oct. 1538, 18 Jan. 1539, 9 May 1538, 30 June 1539, *SP Hen. VIII*, III, 99–101, 111–15, 126–7, 135–6, 154–6; 'Treaties between Grey and the Irish', ibid., pp. 169–73.
[19] R. Cowley to Cromwell, 8 Sept. 1539; Grey to Cromwell, 21 Oct. 1539; Ormond to Cromwell, 20 Dec. 1539, *SP Hen. VIII*, III, 145–7, 154–6, 164–6; *AFM*, sub anno 1539.

Henry and Cromwell to discount his critics and summon Grey to court to plan the new offensive.[20]

The evidence of Grey's remarkable recovery between the summer of 1538 and the spring of 1540 must qualify the traditional view of his viceroyalty as a period of continuous wrangling and failure. Perforce, however, it makes his eventual fall seem all the more sudden. Yet that, like so many other coups at the court of King Henry, is precisely what it was. On arrival at court in April Grey was, to the dismay of his Irish enemies, warmly received, and the matter of his summer strategy was referred directly to the privy council. A letter from that body to the Irish council early in June did not mention the deputy but showed continued support for his proposal to launch a new campaign. Then suddenly, on 12 June, the council baldly announced to Dublin the viceroy's arrest and imprisonment on a charge of treason. The written record offers no further evidence.[21]

Some circumstantial developments, however, provide a basis for explanation. Sometime in May, Alen and Aylmer followed Grey to court to renew their allegations: their list of charges had grown, but their case was essentially the same as that which had failed two years before. If anything, their position was weaker, for they came now without Butler support, and Alen had been summoned only to answer the counter-charges which Grey had levelled against him.[22] A more serious occurrence was the unrest among the O'Connors whose raids on the borders of the Pale were attributed by Grey's enemies to his own covert intrigues. The restiveness of the O'Connors, however, was related to a more ambiguous development which had occurred in Grey's absence: the dissolution of the Geraldine league and the flight of the Kildare heir to sanctuary in France. Again, Grey's enemies claimed that the escape of Gerald Fitzgerald was evidence of the deputy's incompetence, of his bemusement by the Geraldine faction; but it could equally be reported as a direct result of Bellahoe, a recognition on the part of the Geraldines in Munster and Ulster that it was time to come to terms with the governor.[23] These Irish issues were not in themselves decisive, but they gained considerably in importance when related to a far more important event which took place at the English court: on 10 June, two

[20] Grey to Cromwell, 30 Dec. 1539, 13, 15 Feb., 10, 17 Mar. 1540; Henry VIII to Grey, 1 Apr., *SP Hen. VIII*, III, 167–8, 182–4, 185–6, 187–9, 193–4, 194–5.

[21] Richard Cox, *Hibernia Anglicana* (2 pts., London, 1689–90), II, 264–6; Brereton to Cromwell, 17 May 1549, *SP Hen. VIII*, III, 204–6; Henry VIII to Brereton, June 1540; privy council to Irish council, 12 June, *LP (1540)*, nos. 723, 775.

[22] Alen to Wriothesley, 20 Apr. 1540; Alen's 'Allegations and defence', June 1540, *LP (1540)*, nos. 550. 830.

[23] On the collapse of the Geraldine league compare Wilson, *Beginnings of mod. Ire.*, pp. 171–226, with Bradshaw, *Const. rev.*, pp. 132–8, 174–85; Grey and council to Henry VIII, 18 Jan., 13 Feb., 17 Mar. 1540, *LP (1540)*, nos. 82, 199, 355.

days before Grey's arrest, Thomas Cromwell was accused of treason at the council board by the duke of Norfolk and immediately sent to the Tower.[24]

Grey and Cromwell had established strong personal links over many years. Cromwell began his career in the household service of Grey's father, the earl of Dorset, and he was to return the favour by employing Grey's nephew in his own household in 1539.[25] It was Cromwell who had secured Grey's appointment as viceroy, and though he was initially unhappy with the deputy's pro-Geraldine strategy and rebuked him for his treatment of the Butlers, the secretary gradually became convinced of the merit of Grey's management of affairs in straitened circumstances. It was Cromwell who shelved the allegations against Grey in 1538, who brought about a reconciliation between Grey and Ossory in the same year and who finally convinced the king of the virtues of Grey's plan for a new offensive.[26] By 1540, then, Cromwell had become an advocate and defender of a formerly controversial policy. To his enemies, therefore, it was equally important that his decisions concerning Ireland should be discredited along with all the other projects with which he had been identified.

In part, then, Grey's fate was simply like that of the Viscount Lisle and a handful of other figures who were innocent victims in the fall of Thomas Cromwell. But the link between Grey's ruin and the palace revolution of 1540 was sealed when Sir Anthony St Leger, one of Norfolk's closest associates in court politics and one exceptionally qualified for the Irish office, declared himself willing to succeed Grey as deputy. St Leger's own plan for Ireland was, as we shall see, ambitious and subtle: but an essential precondition of its success was the ruin of his predecessor. Thus more than two years after his special commission which had reached no conclusions, issued no report and made no recommendations, St Leger at last broke silence and formally endorsed all those charges which Alen, Aylmer and the Butlers had unavailingly raised against the viceroy for so many years. Powerless to influence affairs in Ireland and defenceless at court in face of a determined high-level intrigue to unseat him, Grey's position was hopeless. Just twelve days after his committal to the Tower he was succeeded as

[24] On the circumstances of Cromwell's fall see B. W. Beckingsale, *Thomas Cromwell, Tudor minister* (London, 1978), pp. 138–43; Muriel St Claire Byrne (ed.), *The Lisle letters* (6 vols., Chicago, 1981), VI, pp. 135–77; G. R. Elton, 'Thomas Cromwell's decline and fall', *HJ* 10 (1951), pp. 150–85.

[25] On Cromwell's connections with Grey see *LP (1521–23)*, no. 2437; *LP (1524–26)*, no. 3053; *LP (1538)*, I, no. 136, and II, no. 1184. I am grateful to Dr Mary Robertson of the Huntington Library, San Marino, for these references.

[26] Council of Ireland to Cromwell, 16 Feb. 1539; Grey to Cromwell, 6 Nov. 1538; Ormond to Cromwell, 20 Dec., *SP Hen. VIII*, III, 118–21, 163–4, 164–7; Cromwell's 'Remembrances for Ireland', Sept. and Nov. 1538, *LP (1539)*, II, nos. 287, 494.

king's deputy in Ireland by the man whose dogged pursuit of the treason case eventuated in Grey's execution in the following year, Sir Anthony St Leger.[27]

(III)

Though it accords closely enough with his rather ambiguous contemporary reputation, St Leger's role in the fall of Grey contrasts sharply with modern estimations of his character.[28] Indeed, like Cromwell, his standing among historians has improved steadily over time and is now, thanks largely to the major work of Brendan Bradshaw, at its highest. After Bradshaw, St Leger is now credited with initiating a period of unparalleled, and sadly truncated, amity in the history of Anglo-Irish relations.[29] The centrepiece of his radical initiative was, according to Bradshaw, an act introduced in the Irish parliament of 1541 recognising Henry VIII as king of Ireland. The 'act for the kingly title' formally dissolved the old ethnic distinctions in Ireland between the king's English subjects in Ireland (who were to be defended and encouraged) and his Irish enemies (who were to be conquered and subjugated) simply by declaring the old conquest to be complete, and by recognising all of the island's inhabitants as constitutionally equal subjects of the same monarch. It was under the *aegis* of this 'constitutional revolution' that St Leger undertook a major series of negotiations which aimed, as Bradshaw has put it, at the gradual transformation of their legal and social infrastructures while leaving their political superstructures intact.[30]

Here was a reform initiative of remarkable boldness: yet it was to prove, according to Bradshaw, of exceptionally short duration. St Leger's policy, he concedes, soon encountered unexpected difficulties, provoked serious opposition in several quarters, and was 'forced into passivity' within two years of its official inauguration in 1541.[31] Such an early demise would seem to raise serious doubts about the strength of the policy's original conception and about the commitment of St Leger and his advisers to its success. Yet this acceptance of the abortive character of the enlightened strategy is

---

[27] Henry VIII to Irish council, 24 June 1540, *LP (1540)*, no. 805, and to St Leger, 26 Sept., *LP (1540–1)*, no. 77.

[28] See, for instance, Campion's assessment: 'a discrete gentleman very studious of the estate of Ireland, enriched, stout enough, without gall', *Two bokes of the histories of Ireland*, ed. A. F. Vossen (Assen, 1963), p. 136; also the 'Book of Howth' in *Cal. Carew MSS*, V, 195.

[29] St Leger's greatest modern defender is Brendan Bradshaw; see in general his *Constit. rev.* and 'The beginnings of modern Ireland', in Brian Farrell, *The Irish parliamentary tradition* (Dublin, 1973), pp. 68–87.

[30] Bradshaw, *Constit. rev.*, p. 195.

[31] Ibid., p. 258.

based largely on a misconception concerning both the circumstances within which the policy was devised and the manner in which it subsequently developed.

Bradshaw's own account of the origins of the reform policy is attractive but somewhat speculative. Its roots, he suggests, are to be found in an increasingly optimistic attitude towards the possibility of social and moral improvement which a number of Henrician statesmen began to adopt under the influence of certain political and philosophical writings of the late Italian and northern renaissance. 'Civic humanism', according to Bradshaw, came late to Ireland; but its arrival was all the more propitious for that. For it began to inform the thinking of Anglo-Irish and English administrators at the very time when the beleagured English government was becoming urgently aware of the need to do something about Ireland, and was consequently more receptive to new strategic initiatives.[32]

This is a fascinating claim though it lacks the extensive evidential support necessary to sustain it. The discreet St Leger never gave any indication of the intellectual forces which guided him. His correspondence is typically concerned with particular or personal matters, and seems on occasion deliberately to evade discussion of broader principles. In marked contrast to most of his successors, no general statement or justification of his reform objectives is known to have issued from his pen. More importantly, the range of ideas which emanated from Ireland in the 1520s and 1530s, and from which St Leger is said to have formulated his ideas, were of such diverse provenance as to make the demonstration of prior intellectual influence impossible.[33] Ironically, one unmistakable sign of renaissance influence, calligraphy, seems to suggest a humanist training for only one of St Leger's most vigorous subsequent critics, John Alen.[34] Such objections, like the case against which they are directed, rest of course on an argument from silence: it remains possible that the ideas of civic humanism did indeed influence the formulation of Irish policy, but their precise role cannot be identified let alone claimed as predominant. More seriously, however, speculation concerning the possible intellectual origins of reform distracts attention from more immediate and more pressing conditions within which the strategy was formulated and which it was designed to withstand.

As a policy, St Leger's reform through peaceful persuasion certainly invited trouble from the beginning. It threatened in the first place to give

---

[32] Ibid., ch. 2, *passim*, and pp. 189–96.
[33] For a further elaboration of this view, see the reviews of Bradshaw, *Constit. rev.*, by Brady in *Studia Hib.* 19 (1979), pp. 177–81, and by Ellis in *IHS* 22 (1980–1), pp. 78–81.
[34] See for instance Alen to Wriothesley, 23 Aug. 1539, and to Cromwell, 12 May 1539, SP 60/7/37, 8/15; his penmanship remained distinctive throughout his career: see Alen to Cecil, 16 Dec. 1558, SP 63/1/7.

rise to deadly dynastic struggles among all of those lordships where the succession was uncertain and where the application of the English principle of primogeniture would therefore be divisive. Again, it tended to produce serious disputes over rights, liberties and territorial boundaries between the lords and their subjects and between neighbouring lordships. Finally the obligation to pay homage to the new Irish king, which the formal diplomatic agreements required, threatened to become an irritant and an embarrassment to lords concerned with the assertion and defence of their own highly unstable authority.

Such difficulties were doubtless unfortunate; but it is unlikely that they were regarded by St Leger and his Irish advisers as either unexpected or insurmountable. On the contrary, St Leger's early agreements with the Gaelic lords display a refined understanding of the complexities and uncertainties of Gaelic politics. The deputy, for instance, was fully alive to the danger of conceding more authority to the lord of a territory than he could practically lay claim to. Thus the agreements remained resolutely vague as to the extent of the lord's hegemony in each country. A chieftain was to enjoy only 'those castles, manors and lordships which he formerly possesses'.[35] He was to acknowledge the freeholders in his territory as independent subjects of the king and his right to exact military and other services from them was to be subject to the will of the king's deputy. Yet no immediate steps were to be taken to establish the precise extent of the lord's tenurial and feudal rights or the status of the country's freeholders. This was to be established by inquisition only at a later stage of the reform process, and the government declared its willingness to have the most difficult issues determined by the deliberations of the clansmen themselves.[36] Similarly, St Leger and his advisers were sensitive to the problems likely to arise from the imposition of succession by primogeniture in the lordships. Thus among the O'Briens, the O'Tooles and the Kavanaghs the institution of *tanaiste* was formally recognised and the rights of the incumbents to succeed as chieftain accepted.[37] Again, among the O'Neills and the O'Briens the interests of powerful dynastic segments who were to be excluded from the chieftaincy by primogeniture were explicitly protected by separate agreements.[38] Finally, while the payment of an annual rent to the crown was included in

[35] *Cal. pat. rolls, Hen. VIII–Eliz.*, pp. 85–7.
[36] For the O'Briens see ibid., p. 87; the agreement with the O'Tooles is printed in P. L. O'Toole, *History of the Clan O'Toole* (Dublin, 1890), pp. 258–63; for the Kavanaghs, see H. F. Hore, 'The Clan Kavanagh, temp. Henry VIII', *Journal of Kilkenny and South East Ireland Archaeological Society*, new ser., 2 (1858–9), pp. 73–92; for the O'Neill indenture see Lambeth, Carew MS 603/38.
[37] *Cal. pat. rolls Hen. VIII–Eliz.*, p. 87; Hore, 'Clan Kavanagh'; O'Toole, *Clan O'Toole*, pp. 258–63.
[38] *Cal. pat. rolls Hen. VIII–Eliz.*, pp. 86–7; Lambeth, Carew MS 608/39–45.

most agreements, St Leger openly precluded the prospect of collecting any revenue until the reform had been well advanced.[39]

The responsiveness to prevailing circumstances revealed in these early agreements was to be seen also in St Leger's subsequent dealings with the lordships. When original agreements ran into trouble, the viceroy's characteristic response was not to accept defeat, but rather to commence fresh negotiations. Thus when his initial plans for the settlement of the O'Tooles were wrecked by the assassination of the chieftain, St Leger responded simply by recognising the internal division of the territory, accepting the right of the chief's opponents to secede while continuing to allow the heir apparent, Brian O'Toole, to enjoy the crown lands granted to his father and even granting him office as sheriff of Dublin.[40] When Cahir MacArt Kavanagh reneged on his treaty with the crown, St Leger prepared to make war; yet he accepted Cahir's renewed submission in 1550 and even licensed him to repair to court to effect a reconciliation.[41] The deputy was even prepared to renegotiate the carefully drafted 1542 settlement in Thomond when it became clear that the third nominee as earl was unable to assert his authority over all of the O'Briens.[42]

The most serious obstacle to the advance of reform arose in Ulster when Con O'Neill's injudicious choice of an heir, Mathew, the baron of Dungannon, proved too weak to maintain against his half-brother, Shane. But once more St Leger's response was finely calculated: while continuing to uphold Dungannon's formal rights, he quietly ignored the depredations of his rival and even granted Shane a government pension as a token of good-will.[43]

St Leger's conduct in these instances was certainly statesmanlike. Yet it is hard to see how he could have acted in any other way had he genuinely expected his declared strategy to take root. The reform of Ireland could not possibly be attained overnight: it required rather a protracted process of initiation, familiarisation and education which could be carried out only through years of political, administrative and personal interaction. Constitutional declarations and diplomatic agreements provided only the formal channels through which the substance of reform could pass; and to assume that St Leger had placed his faith in them alone and abandoned all hope of reform when they failed to deliver early results is to attribute a level of

[39] St Leger to Henry VIII, 31 Mar. 1542, *SP Hen. VIII*, III, 362–5.
[40] List of sheriffs (GO, MS 200); St Leger's 'Reply to Alen', Aug. 1546, *LP (1546)*, no. 917.
[41] Edward VI to Crofts, 17 Aug. 1551, SP 61/3/48; *Cal. pat. rolls Hen. VIII–Eliz.*, p. 342; Hore, 'Clan Kavanagh', pp. 79–82.
[42] Cusacke to Northumberland, 8 May 1662, SP 61/4/43; 'Ordinances for Thomond', Lambeth, Carew MSS, 603/25–30.
[43] Shane O'Neill to Elizabeth, 8 Feb. 1561, SP 63/3/14.

naïvety to the wily deputy which most of his contemporaries would have found highly unlikely.

Yet if the policy of surrender and regrant was a far more sophisticated and far more hardy undertaking than its most ardent apologists have so far claimed, a difficulty then arises concerning the outlook of its originator. For all the recent concern with intellectual influences, one central question remains yet to be addressed: namely, what made St Leger and his advisers believe that such a difficult policy was at all practicable, and how, given the inescapable problems which it faced, did they plan to put it into effect?

St Leger, it is true, assumed the viceroyalty under broadly favourable circumstances. As the man who had finally brought Grey down, he enjoyed immediate popularity with all who had opposed his predecessor. The Butlers looked expectantly towards him as did the English administrators in Dublin Castle. The Geraldines, whose bluff had been called in 1540 as in 1534, were without either a leader or a surrogate, and were once again discomfited. But beneath these superficial advantages, the fundamental problems of the viceregal office with which Grey had long struggled remained unresolved. Despite their failure to drive a hard bargain with Grey, the Geraldines remained intact, their local positions undisturbed, and their potential leader safe in exile. At the same time the threat posed by the Butlers had significantly increased; for they had not only withstood a Geraldine recovery in the later 1530s, they had also helped ruin a governor who had tried to resist them. In the same way, the apparent victory of Grey's opponents on the Irish council had reinforced their conviction that the viceroy should not act independently of their advice and consent. Finally, in repudiating the new expenditures sought by Grey and agreed to by Cromwell in 1540, St Leger undertook to reduce the costs of the Irish administration to the point of self-sufficiency.[44] Thus whatever the novelty of his policies and the intellectual influences that inspired them, St Leger had taken office under the same rigorously restrictive conditions with which Grey had wrestled until the very last months of his administration and which had, with St Leger's help, finally ruined him.

In view of this, St Leger's attempt to introduce a radical change of direction may appear to have been foolhardy in the extreme. But on closer analysis the new policy may be seen to have been formulated not in blissful ignorance of the forces which had brought Grey down, but as part of a deliberate and finely calculated attempt to withstand and overcome them. The extent to which St Leger's Irish policy was conceived as a careful revision of the strategy originally devised by Grey can be seen on a number of levels. Though they were quite similar in the manner in which they were

[44] Cusacke to privy council, *SP Hen. VIII*, III, 327–30.

reached, St Leger's agreements with the lords marked a considerable advance on Grey's in an important respect. Formally, the new agreements were made not between the governor and the local lord, as Grey's had been, but between the lord and the new king of Ireland. The lords were expected to renounce their traditional titles and assume new English ones to be conferred on them in person by the king himself at Westminster. Thus it would be made clear that the new Irish king was no mere distant overlord, demanding occasional homage, but the personal sovereign of a new Irish nobility.

The constitutional significance of this protocol has already been sensitively analysed by Bradshaw,[45] but it also entailed a number of practical political advantages. By involving the king directly in the deputy's proceedings, the formula helped to protect St Leger's position at court, freeing him from the suspicion of ambition and favouritism which had plagued and ultimately destroyed his predecessor. But it served an even more important purpose in Ireland itself. For it made clear to the lords that the relationship which they were now being invited to enter was of a different order to the factional alliances created by the Butlers and the Geraldines and replicated by Grey. St Leger was intent on constructing a new form of political alignment in Irish politics which would transcend the factional structures of previous decades and fashion from among the ranks of Geraldine and Butler clients a new association which would have as its head neither a magnate nor a viceroy, but the king of Ireland. What St Leger sought to create, in effect, was an entirely new phenomenon amidst Ireland's political structures: a king's party.

The benefits of such a new relationship with the king have long been recognised. Those who accepted it could look forward to dynastic and political stability in their own territories and to the support of the Dublin government in defending their rights against their neighbours.[46] In the long term St Leger's project promised more permanent gains than Grey's personal bonds of fealty, and so it is not surprising that so many native lords found it more attractive. Yet a prematurely positive response to the governor's overtures was clearly dangerous for any chieftain uncertain of his ability to suppress opposition to the change among his own people. Thus St Leger was urgently in need of incentives to persuade a sufficient number of lords to make their first tentative commitments to reform despite its risks.

---

[45] Bradshaw, *Constit. rev.*, pp. 196–212.
[46] For general discussions see W. F. T. Butler, *Gleanings from Irish history* (London, 1925), ch. 3; K. W. Nicholls, *Land, law and society in sixteenth-century Ireland* (O'Donnell Lecture; Cork, 1976); C. Brady, 'The O'Reillys of East Breifne and the problem of surrender and regrant', *Breifne* 6: 23 (1985), pp. 233–62.

In this matter also St Leger revealed the extent to which he had learned from Grey and had advanced beyond him. The dissolution of the Geraldine league offered him much the same opportunities as their earlier crisis had given Grey in 1536. Thus he renewed the conciliatory attitude which had been abandoned by Grey in 1540 and offered terms to leading Geraldines, most importantly promising recognition to James FitzJohn as earl of Desmond.[47] But as Grey's experience had made clear, St Leger could never hope to depend solely upon a Geraldine alliance. Thus from the beginning St Leger showed that there were clear limits to his friendship: he was not, for instance, willing to defend Geraldine interests in Leinster against Butler and English interference, nor to support the claims of Geraldine contenders in north Connacht. But most importantly of all he was not prepared to allow his own administration to become dominated by counsellors of Geraldine sympathy. Indeed, it was in the offices of central government in Dublin that St Leger determined to lay the foundations of his own suprafactional political movement.

St Leger has often been praised for his sensitivity to local interest. But while the establishment of formal links between his government and local elites was central to his project, his personal dependence on figures of local influence was remarkably limited. The Palesman, Sir Thomas Cusacke, was his closest Irish adviser. The possible author and most able defender of St Leger's reform strategy, Cusacke advanced rapidly under St Leger's patronage, eventually becoming lord chancellor in 1550 and crowning his career by appointment as lord justice in 1552. Cusacke's attachment to St Leger, however, was not exclusive. He had entered political life as a servant of Lord Deputy Skeffington, changed his allegiance to Grey unexpectedly, and equally quickly to St Leger. Cusacke was to recover also from his involvement in St Leger's disgrace in 1556, attaching himself to the earl of Sussex and to the man who displaced him, Sir Henry Sidney.[48] Cusacke, moreover, was an exception in St Leger's camp: most Anglo-Irish counsellors remained at a distance, some, like Walter Cowley, were overtly hostile, while St Leger himself was happy to boast that with the exception of Cusacke he trusted no other Irish-born official.[49]

In fact the figures with whom St Leger associated most closely were Englishmen who, like himself, were of relatively recent arrival. John Parker

---

[47] Bradshaw, *Constit. rev.*, chs. 7, 8; G. E. Cokayne, *The Complete Peerage of England, Scotland and Ireland* (8 vols., Exeter, 1887–98, rev. edn, V. Gibbs, 13 vols., London, 1910–49), under Desmond.

[48] On Cusacke generally see *DNB*; F. E. Ball, *The judges in Ireland, 1221–1921* (2 vols., London, 1926), I, pp. 200–2, for evidence of his earlier political manoeuvrings, *LP (1536)*, nos. 993, 1149, 1157; *(1537)*, I, no. 1027; *(1538)*, II, no. 66.

[49] St Leger to Wriothesley, 26 Feb. 1545, *LP (1545)*, I, no. 273.

and John Goldsmith both came to Ireland with St Leger in 1540, the former as his private secretary, the latter as the recently established clerk of the Irish privy council. These were St Leger's closest confidants; agents whom he sent on diplomatic missions in the country and to defend him against intrigues at court, they were detested by St Leger's Irish critics as 'men of liberal speech and character', who would 'take no scruple to cloak men's actions'.[50] Another of St Leger's close associates, Thomas Agard, was even more distrusted. Sent by Cromwell to enquire into the affairs of the Dublin administration of 1535, Agard soon attached himself to the vice-treasurer, Sir William Brabazon, and used his influence with the secretary to discredit first Skeffington and then Grey in order to serve his new master's ambitions. As deputy to the treasurer, Agard acquired an evil reputation as 'a sharp receiver and a slow payer' and it was openly alleged that he had exploited his position to advance his own fortunes at the expense of the crown. But while St Leger's investigations as a royal commissioner had undoubtedly made him aware of Agard's repute, the new viceroy appointed him accountant to his household. He employed Agard also as an agent in England, enthusiastically supporting his suits for further reward: in 1547 it was on St Leger 's recommendation that Agard was appointed to the highly lucrative position of treasurer of the mint newly established in Dublin to undertake King Henry's policy of debasement.[51]

Agard was not the only dependant shared by the treasurer and the viceroy. Cusacke had been a client of Brabazon in the 1530s, and his later attachment to St Leger entailed no loss of the treasurer's friendship. Lesser figures also supported the bridge of alliance. Sir William Wise, an alderman of Waterford was a useful agent of both men in the south. His son Andrew, whose preferment Wise had committed to St Leger, married Brabazon's daughter, Mary, becoming deputy to the treasurer, then joint holder of the office and eventually succeeding to the treasury in full on Brabazon's death in 1552, the only Irish-born figure to hold the position in the century.[52] The merchant, Walter Peppard, who with Brabazon's help had bought his way into monastic properties, also lent his services to St Leger, both by surrendering leases in Dublin for distribution as residences for the provincial magnates whom St Leger wished to reward, and by providing

[50] Ormond to privy council, 20 Feb. 1546, *LP (1546)*, I, no. 247.
[51] Agard to Cromwell, 15 May 1535, SP 60/2/44; Grey to Cromwell, 31 Oct. 1536, 5 Feb. 1537, 26 May 1539, *LP (1536)*, no. 933; *(1537)*, no. 382; *(1539)*, no. 1027; R. Cowley to Norfolk, 6 July 1540, *LP (1540–541)*, no. 849; St Leger to Henry VIII, 4 June, 10 Sept. 1543, *LP (1543)*, I, no. 646; II, 165.
[52] Wise to Cromwell, 21 Mar. 1540, BL, Harl. MS 35, f. 270; Wise to St Leger, 22 Apr., 1 Nov. 1544, 5 Jan. 1545, *LP (1544)*, I, no. 378; II, no. 531; *(1545)*, I, no. 20; St Leger to Cecil, 23 Mar. 1551, SP 61/3/18, *Cal. pat. rolls Hen. VIII–Eliz.*, pp. 459–60.

direct financial support to his administration.[53] Other individuals like Francis Herbert, John Travers and even John Parker can be shown to have enjoyed the friendship of both men. Thus it is not surprising that St Leger and Brabazon were regarded by contemporaries not as separate forces but as allies, united, their enemies alleged, in a common conspiracy to advance themselves at the expense of the crown and the commonweal.[54]

The basis of their alliance was in part political in the narrowest sense. Both had been active enemies of Grey; and though it was said that Brabazon had coveted the viceroyalty for himself, he acquiesced in St Leger's appointment and continued to accept the role of second in command with ease. For his part St Leger only spoke well of Brabazon and specifically recommended his preferment over Chancellor Alen as lord justice during one of the deputy's absences.[55] Historians have noted an apparent difference between the two over policy in the midlands. But there is no evidence that Brabazon's decision to attack the O'Connors during his time as lord justice gave rise to any serious rift between the two men. The real strength of their connection was founded, however, not on political strategy, but on a more fundamental agreement as to how the fruits of the Irish revenues were to be employed. Brabazon and St Leger were for reasons of their own at one in believing that the crown's wealth in Ireland should be used for purposes other than the maintenance of the establishment.

Sir William Brabazon had acquired an unhappy reputation as a dubious husband of the royal finances from the beginning of his Irish career. Within two years of his appointment as vice-treasurer his conduct in office had already aroused the suspicions of some of his colleagues on the Irish council, and prompted King Henry to write to him in warning.[56] Cromwell's friendship enabled him to survive these charges, and the first audit of his accounts was carried out in 1538 without remark. A second audit in 1540, however, revealed some startling abuses. Brabazon, it appeared, had kept no formal record of the several large subventions he had received from England nor of their expenditure in Ireland. His account appeared to balance, but with only the personal letters of Cromwell to show in his support, there could be no external check upon the treasurer's figures. At the same time allegations were made that Brabazon had sold off the chattels of several dissolved religious houses at prices well below their real value, but since no

[53] *Fiants Henry VIII*, nos. 384, 386, 400–1, 446, 464; Brabazon to Cromwell, 16 Feb. 1540, SP 60/9/11; St Leger and council to Henry VIII, 16 June 1543, SP 60/11/31.
[54] See, for instance, R. Cowley to Henry VIII, 17 Oct. 1541, *LP (1541)*, no. 1268.
[55] St Leger to Henry VIII, 4 June, 10 Sept. 1543, *LP (1543)*, I, no. 646; II, no. 165.
[56] Walter Cowley to Cromwell, 10 June 1536; Grey to Cromwell, 24 June, *LP (1536)*, I, nos. 1112, 1195; R. Ap Powell to Cromwell, 1 July 1536, *LP (1536)*, II, no. 2; Henry VIII to Irish council and Brabazon, 25 Feb. 1537, *LP (1537)*, I, nos. 503–4.

formal record of these transactions had been kept either, there remained only the figures which Brabazon himself produced. But for all the suspicion that hung over him, no definite proof of fraud could be brought against the treasurer, and his account, after all, was not in debt. Thus with some prompting from St Leger, the king chose to put the best interpretation on affairs, and after some sharp words to the treasurer, let the matter drop.[57] When such striking instances of misconduct went unpunished, it is not surprising that less demonstrable charges – that he engrossed, underleased and selectively distributed crown lands – went uninvestigated. From then on, despite a rather slip-shod audit carried out in 1548, Brabazon was allowed to remain undisturbed in office until his death in 1551. It was only three years later that the first full investigation of the Irish finances revealed the full extent of his maladministration.[58]

For almost twenty years, then, during a period when the Irish revenue was greatly augmented by the confiscation of monastic properties and the attainder of Geraldine lands, the financial administration received no significant attention from England, and the Irish treasurer was left free to take whatever advantage he might from the windfall. He appears to have made the best of his opportunities. For though the monastic and Geraldine confiscations alone were expected to bring in an additional revenue of almost £9,200, and though other sources of revenue were estimated to amount to around £5,000 pa, annual revenue in the years 1541–7 averaged only a little over £11,000 and showed an overall fall. As the expenses of the administration mounted steadily, domestic revenues not only stagnated, but displayed an alarming tendency to decline.[59]

Receipts wavered uncertainly throughout the 1540s simply because the amounts due were not being collected. Between 1540 and 1547 arrears of £18,640 were allowed to accumulate on crown leases alone. Responsibility for the short-fall lay with Brabazon who, as general receiver, was supplied with a troop of horse for the specific purpose of collecting and destraining for arrears. The soldiers, however, were redundant; for Brabazon, it was said, was accustomed to lie 'at Dublin . . . not calling for any more than has been brought to him already'.[60] It is clear, however, that reasons other than

---

[57] St Leger to Henry VIII, 24 Oct. 1540, *LP (1540–1)*, no. 191; privy council to St Leger, 25 Mar. 1541, no. 655; Mynne and Cavendish to privy council, 11 June 1542, *LP (1542)*, no. 499; Henry VIII to Irish council, 5 Mar.; Irish council to Henry VIII, 15 May 1543, *LP (1543)*, I, nos. 245, 553.

[58] The Browne–Rouse report is titled 'Statement of the revenues and suggestions for its improvement', BL, Add. MSS, 4767, fos. 73–9.

[59] N. B. White (ed.), *Extents of Irish monastic possessions, 1540–1541* (IMC, Dublin, 1943); survey of the Geraldine attainder, SP 65/3/2; 'Expenses and revenues 33 Henry VIII to 6 Ed. VI', SP 61/4/75; 'Statement of the revenues', BL, Add. MSS, 4767, fos. 73–9.

[60] 'Statement of the revenues', BL, Add. MSS, 4767, fos. 73–9.

laziness underlay this inaction. Several of his closest colleagues figured in the list of debtors with payment that had been outstanding since the first gale date. Nor were the debtors poor men: they were rather enterprising speculators with extensive interests in crown properties.[61] The arrears were thus a symptom of a booming speculative market in which crown holdings were being bought and leased at a remarkable rate.

The demand for crown land was not simply due to its unusual availability; it was also being offered at prices far below its real value. The low prices at which crown lands were being placed on the market in the 1540s were ostensibly the result of administrative confusion. But again it seems that a smoke-screen of incompetence was being used to obscure proceedings of a more dubious nature. Despite the surveys carried out by the commissioners in 1540–1, no formal procedure for the management of the royal estate had been established. A crown surveyor was salaried from the civil list, but though he inspected a number of individual holdings, his position was in large part irrelevant because he enjoyed no official relationship with the officers of the exchequer. He was not commissioned to make a survey on the issuing of every new lease, and any new survey which he conducted was not communicated directly to the exchequer. Conversely, the exchequer did not communicate its own records, the surveys taken in 1540–1, for periodic revision in the surveyor's office, but continued to make out new leases on the old surveys. Thus there existed two types of survey record in the 1540s and 1550s, one up-to-date and of no practical importance, another quite obsolete but in everyday use.[62]

Apart from their growing obsolescence, the exchequer extents contained two major defects as survey records. First they did not essay an estimate of the potential value of the property to the lessees, but offered only an assessment of the current use-value of the lands. Valuations were, therefore, systematically conservative, and lands of considerable potential value which had recently been allowed to go to waste were frequently valued as nil. A second defect arose directly from the first. As accounts drawn up for the immediate purposes of the crown in 1540, the extents offered as the total annual value of each holding the sum remaining after the deduction of clerical pensions and annuities which the crown had agreed to pay. But though the crown remained responsible for the payment of pensions, it

---

[61] 'Arrears outstanding on ministers accounts', 1548, SP 65/5/1–2; 'Statement of the revenues', BL, Add. MSS, 4767, fos. 73–9.

[62] Walter Cowley was appointed surveyor-general in 1548 for the specific purpose of surveying the confiscated territories in the midlands; his successor, Michael Fitzwilliams, attempted without success to operate more generally (see SP 61/4/65 and enclosure). This account of exchequer practices is based on 'Statement of the revenues', BL, Add. MSS, 4767, fos. 73–9.

was to these *net* totals that the exchequer officials referred when issuing a lease. In fact these figures were extracted from the extents and entered into an account book which became the basic reference work of the exchequer: the provenance of the valuations and their true significance were thus lost.[63]

Such persistent administrative misconduct could not have been sustained without the active encouragement of the vice-treasurer. From the initial survey of crown lands, through the issuing of leases to the collection of rents and the final making up of revenues actually leviable, Brabazon was deeply involved at every stage by which the new crown holdings were placed on the market. No one got rich on crown lands in Ireland without his good-will. Brabazon looked first, of course, to his own interest. He held a number of crown leases and from each he derived a substantial profit. He took a lease of the Cistercian Abbey at Mellifont for £316 13s 4d, though it had been conservatively estimated in the extents to be worth £324 19s 6d. He procured a grant in perpetuity of the site of St Thomas' Abbey near Dublin for 18s 5d pa, though it had been surveyed to be worth £14 12s 0d, and he paid no entry fine. He received leases of rectories of Baltinglass Abbey and St John's Hospital for £88 p.a. under the figure of their combined survey value, together with some leases of the Kildare attainder for a total of £12 6s 8d under their estimated worth.[64]

In turn, Brabazon's activities could not have been sustained without the connivance of the officers of the exchequer; but their co-operation seems to have been cheaply bought. The chief baron secured a discount of at least £8 16s 8d on his leases; and though the chief remembrancer appears to have deserved his later reputation as an honest servant his discretion seems to have been secured by the grant of far more leases than an official of his status would normally have expected.[65] Bigger risks were taken by Brabazon's close associates. Thomas Agard acquired leases of two

[63] 'Statement of the revenues', BL, Add. MSS, 4767, fos. 73–9; *Extents Ir. mon. possessions*; 'Survey of the Geraldine attainers', SP 65/3/2; the preliminary nature of the surveys is obvious from the frequency with which land of considerable potential value is accounted 'nil', as it had been recently allowed to go to waste; on the progress of the survey see Bradshaw, *The dissolution of the religious orders in Ireland under Henry VIII* (Cambridge, 1974), chs. 7–9.

[64] This and all subsequent differentials are derived from a comparison of values fixed in the surveys with the rents set in the leases. Monastic lands were rarely leased whole; it has therefore been necessary to check individual lands named in each lease against the extents in detail. For Brabazon see *Fiants Henry VIII*, nos. 254, 543, 547; *Fiants Ed. VI*, nos. 774–8; *Extents of Irish monastic possessions, 1540–41* (IMC, Dublin, 1943), pp. 26, 62–6, 125–7; Geraldine attainder, SP 65/3/2.

[65] *Fiants Henry VIII*, nos. 450–1, 466; *Fiants Ed. VI*, nos. 34, 106, 731, 906; *Extents Ir. mon. possessions*, pp. 26–9, 32–6; Bathe's other leases were either at survey value (*Fiants Henry VIII*, nos. 480, 513, 539) or are untraceable.

monasteries in Meath for £30 below the survey value; Walter Peppard enjoyed the farm of St Mary's Abbey in Dublin for about half its estimated worth, a priory in Kilkenny for £10 below survey and the Geraldine manor of Kilkea for about £15 below its conservatively estimated value.[66]

Sir Thomas Cusacke also speculated heavily in his native county Meath. He received a lease of the priory of Lismullen for £5 below the survey, fell into arrears and apparently used the capital thus saved to make a purchase of other religious lands for a sum of £168 13s 4d which was only 77 per cent of the twenty-year valuation which was conventionally charged for grants in perpetuity. In 1547 he received a grant of the abbey of Multyfarnham for little more than half the expected twenty years' purchase.[67] John Parker, another close associate of St Leger and Brabazon, entered the market comparatively late, but he too rapidly acquired a series of interests in monastic properties in Wexford and Dublin again at prices below the surveyed value, crowning his investments by a purchase of the vast lands of Selsker Abbey for the ludicrously low price of £285 15s 5d.[68] Even the viceroy's brother, Robert, turned a profit from his purchase of the manor of Kill for £271.[69]

It is impossible that St Leger was unaware of what was going on around him. It was from his own work as commissioner in 1537 that the recommendation to confiscate all monastic properties first arose; it was during the first months of his administration that the survey of monastic extents was actually carried out, and it was under his authority that the great bulk of the underrated grants and leases were actually issued. Despite the widely voiced suspicions of Brabazon's management of affairs which St Leger both as commissioner and as viceroy had been directed to investigate, he refused to institute any serious inquiry. Instead he wrote repeatedly to Westminster supporting the treasurer's pleas for increased subventions from England and

---

[66] For Agard: SP 65/4, fo. 15; *Fiants Henry VIII*, no. 318; *Extents Ir. mon. possessions*, pp. 267–70, 302–6; for Peppard: Bradshaw, *Dissolution of religious orders in Ire.*, pp. 88, 190; SP 60/8/25, 9/11; *Fiants Henry VIII*, nos. 386, 400, 401, 446; *Cal. pat. rolls Hen. VIII–Eliz.*, pp. 86–7, 104–5; *Fiants Ed. VI*, nos. 643, 728; *Extents Ir. mon. possessions*, pp. 1–24, 374–5. I have been unable to trace all the Geraldine lands listed in the lease in the Geraldine attainder and have accepted all current evaluations of waste land; this is, therefore, a conservative estimate.

[67] *Fiants Henry VIII*, nos. 96, 309; *Fiants Ed. VI*, no. 18; *Extents Ir. mon. possessions*, pp. 255–60, 54, 506–7; NAI, RC 1/1–6, nos. 41–56; Multyfarnham was first granted to Cusacke's agents and then transferred to him, *Cal. pat. rolls Hen. VIII–Eliz.*, p. 123.

[68] *Fiants Henry VIII*, nos. 343, 370; *Fiants Ed. VI*, nos. 19, 370, 771; *Extents Ir. mon. possessions*, pp. 53, 87, 207–8, 298, 321, 367–70; Parker's grant of Rosbercon priory was not accompanied by a survey, but N. B. White (ed.), *Irish episcopal and monastic deeds 1200–1600* (IMC, Dublin, 1936), p. 283, indicates that it was worth considerably more than the purchase price of £44.

[69] *Fiants Henry VIII*, no. 465; twenty years purchase on a valuation of £15 13s 1d should have been £313 1s 8d.

furthering the private suits of Agard, Peppard, Parker and Cusacke for the leases and grants which made them rich.[70]

He did so because he himself was deeply implicated in the whole conspiracy. Some of his purchases were set only modestly below the estimated price; but others, like his grant of the demesne lands of St Mary's Trim, were won for £160 below the conventional twenty years' purchase. He acquired the nunnery of Grane, worth at least £67 p.a., for a rent of £3 6s 8d held the abbey of Mullingar for £43 13s 2d under the survey, and the friary of Louth and the abbey of Balliboggan for a combined £97 below the official estimate.[71] The viceroy was one of the chief holders of undervalued crown lands in Ireland. He was also among the slowest of debtors: in 1556 the total sum due on all his Irish leases amounted to almost £5,000.[72]

Only a handful of the most influential figures in the Irish government involved in this widespread corruption have been examined here; a host of lesser examples might also have been cited. Almost every grantee or lessee who appeared in the patent rolls or fiants of the period profited to a greater or lesser degree from St Leger's and Brabazon's deliberate abuse of the crown revenues. The inquiry of 1554 which was by no means exhaustive estimated that the crown was losing more than £2,100 p.a., merely on leases issued below the survey value: it made no effort to assess the loss on properties granted away altogether.[73]

The profits to be made out of the lavish distribution of crown lands moreover extended well beyond Dublin and the Pale. Ormond, Desmond, Thomond and Clanrickard all made killings in the market at this time. As no proper surveys were made of a large number of monastic holdings in their territories and as much was simply granted away without any attempt to gain a return for the crown the full extent of their profits cannot be accurately gauged. But some indications are suggestive. A later review of Desmond's leases revealed that he had received lands for at least £142 p.a. below the survey value.[74] Ormond was subject to no such inquiry and he acquired grants of several monasteries even before the first surveys were

[70] St Leger and council to Henry VIII, 24, 27 Aug., 7 Dec. 1542; 15 May, 4 June, 10 Sept. 1543, *LP (1542)*, II, nos. 664, 668; *SP Hen VIII*, III, 432–40; *LP (1543)*, I, nos. 554, 646; II, no. 665; St Leger to Paget, 11 Aug. 1545, *LP (1545)*, II, no. 98; Irish council to privy council, 5 Jan., 27 Aug. 1546, *LP (1546)*, nos. 17, 1512.

[71] *Fiants Henry VIII*, nos. 304, 325, 340; *Extents Ir. mon. possessions*, pp. 125, 303, 308.

[72] 'Estimation of St Leger's debts', PRO, E 101/248/22.

[73] 'Statement of the revenues', BL, Add. MSS, 4767, fos. 73–9.

[74] 'Book of the debt of the old earl of Desmond', May 1562, SP 63/6/14, enclosure (i); on the treatment of the great magnates generally, see Bradshaw, *Dissolution of religious orders in Ire.*, ch. 10.

carried out; but we know that from St Leger he received a lease of Kells Abbey for a full £100 below the survey.[75] But more important than the acquisition of specific pieces of property was the very great influence and discretion which each of the magnates was allowed to exert over the surrender and survey of monastic sites in their territories: Ormond, Desmond and Thomond were each appointed commissioners for the surrenders in their respective regions, while in Gaelic Ulster the question as to whether and how the monastic lands were to be disposed was left entirely to the great lords themselves. Nor was the lavish distribution of crown lands confined to the great lords alone. Lesser figures among the Butlers, like the lords of Dunboyne and Cahir, among the Geraldines, like the Berminghams of Carbery and among the Gaelic septs like Fitzpatrick and Magennis were all granted a share in the takings.[76]

Evidence exists to show then that a very large group shared directly in the great sale of crown lands in Ireland. But an even larger group of beneficiaries must remain, for the present, unknown. Many of the great speculators like Brabazon, Parker and Agard we know did not retain their many holdings, but resold or sublet them in great and small parcels. There is evidence of a brisk trade in leases in Dublin from mid-century on, but how widespread the process was has yet to be established.[77] The extent to which the new landlords chose to pass on a portion of their profits in the form of more favourable rents is also inestimable. Certainly the margin of their own profits was sufficiently wide to enable them to act generously without incurring serious loss. And generosity too had its political advantages: for newly arrived servitors anxious to gain acceptance in the settled community, it bought popularity and respect. All of the new men discussed above gained such acceptance, all were integrated into the community of the Pale; some, like John Parker and Francis Agard, even became its spokesmen.

The uncovering of this large conspiracy to swindle the crown for personal profit should not be seen simply as yet another example of pervasive Henrician political corruption.[78] The active self-interest of St Leger and his followers is undoubted; but it served also some rather more important political purposes. The discretion granted to the great lords served, as

75 *Fiants Henry VIII*, no. 161; *Extents Ir. mon. possessions*, pp. 188–93.
76 Bradshaw, *Dissolution of religious orders in Ire.*, pp. 187–98; *Fiants Henry VIII*, nos. 197, 384; St Leger and council to Henry VIII, 7 Dec. 1542, SP 60/10/86.
77 Ciaran Brady, 'The distribution of monastic lands in Co. Dublin, 1540–1640' (unpublished paper given to the conference of Irish social and economic historians, Sept. 1986).
78 Nicholas Canny has assumed erroneously that such is 'the essential thrust' of my argument concerning St Leger's administration, Canny, *Kingdom and colony* (Baltimore, MD, 1988), p. 10.

Bradshaw has written, 'to show that admission to the crown's jurisdiction was likely to redound to the[ir] benefit rather than to the[ir] loss'.[79] But the great land distribution served also to resolve one of the viceroy's most serious and most immediate strategic problems. By this means St Leger laid down practical foundations for that new movement, the king's party, on which his reform project depended. He was able, that is, to form throughout the island a new interest made up of Palesmen and English *arrivistes*, of Anglo-Irish and Gaelic Irish lords, of Butlers, Geraldines and neutrals all of whom shared in the benefits of the government's generous land policy and all of whom owed consequently their loyalty and support to the governor and his associates who had made these gains possible and who promised to protect them. Loyalty of this kind, of course, was neither uniform nor indefinite: among each of these elements some were closer to (or owed more to) St Leger than others. In time, as the benefits of the policy were exhausted, so the credit of the man who brought them would decline. Yet in the crucial initial stages of the reform process, before its eventual benefits became clear in their own right, the policy served to generate a broad fund of good-will and to create a more select group of committed advocates which enabled St Leger to maintain credit and support in the country at large amidst the many compromises, revisions and reverses which his policy was fated to meet. St Leger's almost universal popularity and the remarkable era of good feelings between the government and the local communities were founded in the first place not on some vague aspirations towards long-term cultural transformation, but on widespread fraud and a conspiracy of remunerative silence.

(IV)

The success of St Leger's strategy of survival became clear in the closing years of King Henry's reign. Like Grey before him, St Leger toured the wilder parts of Munster, Connacht and Ulster with only a small retinue and secured the submissions and promises of allegiance of the great lords. The agreements he made were more far-reaching than Grey's and the seriousness with which they were regarded by the great lords is evident in the ease with which they were prevailed upon without coercion to make their submissions personally to the king. The extent of St Leger's advance over Grey is instanced also by his success in persuading both Gaelic and Anglo-Irish lords to send a joint expeditionary force of 1,000 men to help with Henry's wars in France and in the extraordinary testimonials which he carried with him in 1546 when he left to make report of his six years government in

---

[79] Bradshaw, *Dissolution of religious orders in Ire.*, ch. 9, especially p. 180.

Ireland.[80] Yet St Leger's greatest achievement in this time was at heart negative: for during his first period as governor he succeeded not only in evading but in wholly defeating the same combination of forces that had ultimately ruined Grey.

Even the most lavish distribution of monastic lands could not have been sufficient to deflect the resentment which St Leger's national policy, like Grey's less developed effort, inevitably provoked among those whose interests it threatened. Within a year of his assumption of office St Leger had begun to encounter trouble from predictable quarters. In the autumn of 1541 Robert Cowley, the then master of the rolls in the Dublin administration and close counsellor to the earl of Ormond, presented a series of all too familiar charges against the new viceroy. St Leger, he claimed, was deeply hostile to the loyal Ormond and was intent on establishing 'a new Geraldine breed'. But Cowley went further. In collusion with Brabazon and other accomplices within the administration, St Leger was engaged in a conspiracy to defraud the crown: 'Every of them seek their own profits and fleeces from his majesty, making their hands his hands thinking all one ware.' Even at this point, as we have seen, such charges might have been easily verified. But Cowley could get no further. The Irish council, including John Alen, proffered no corroboration, the commissioners for the monastic survey, while criticising Brabazon's accounting procedures, rejected them, and Ormond determined to remain silent. Thus isolated, Cowley was condemned at court as 'a seditious and contentious man' and summarily dismissed from office. Cowley's fate made it clear that challenging St Leger was a more dangerous undertaking than attacking Grey, and that the old coalition between Butlers and discontented administrators could not be revived at will. But over time, the very advance of St Leger's government tended to bring about such an alliance by force.[81]

Though his coming to office had been greatly facilitated by his association with the Butlers, St Leger realised as had Grey that it was vital for the preservation of his own authority that the influence of this ascendant faction be curbed. Thus, like Grey, he set about containing Butler interests in Leinster and Munster by rejecting their offers for military enterprises in the south and by encouraging possible opponents like the Fitzpatricks of Upper Ossory, the Kavanaghs and, of course, Desmond. At the same time St Leger

---

[80] Brabazon to Henry VIII, 7 May 1544, SP 60/11/43, 44, and enclosures; St Leger and council to privy council, 6 May 1545, SP 60/12/8; testimonials from the Irish council and native lords, 20–3 Mar. 1546, SP 60/12/38–41; for an account of the Irish expedition see D. G. White, 'Henry VIII's Irish kerne in France and in Scotland', *Irish Sword* 3 (1957–8), pp. 213–25.

[81] 'Allegations against St Leger', Dec. 1540, *LP (1540)*, no. 304; R. Cowley, 'Statement', 26 Aug. 1541, SP 60/10/28–9; St Leger to Henry VIII, 8 May 1542, *LP (1542)*, no. 340.

penetrated into the Butler lordship itself, allowing his brother Robert to revive old claims of the St Legers in County Kilkenny. The old family relationship which might have been expected to sustain ties between the governor and the earl was thus itself becoming a source of contention. In the wake of the Cowley affair Ormond remained calm, preferring for the moment not to become implicated in yet another intrigue against an Irish viceroy. But by late in 1545 he had become so convinced of St Leger's determined hostility that he wrote to the council claiming that the viceroy was plotting his assassination.[82]

By the time he made them, Ormond's complaints against St Leger had been supplemented by a further set of apparently unrelated charges already sent to court by Grey's old enemy, Lord Chancellor Alen. At the outset Alen had been a strong supporter of St Leger; a close adviser during the 1537 commission, Alen had risen to the chancellorship under St Leger's recommendation and was speaker of the house in St Leger's parliament. But as he had grown disillusioned with Grey so he became estranged from St Leger; and for exactly the same reasons. To Alen both men had fallen victim to the same failing; both, he believed, had deserted their principal responsibilities as defenders of the king's interests in Ireland, both had shared the ambition of asserting their personal influence in the regional and local politics of the whole island and both had deliberately discounted the advice of their fellow English councillors who had warned them against such temptations. In criticising the deputy, Alen concentrated, however, on the specific failures of government. St Leger, he claimed, had failed to advance his policy of surrender and regrant beyond its most rudimentary stages; he had made false friends and in doing so had disheartened the king's true subjects, and the royal revenues had not been increased but rather depleted through St Leger's prodigal distribution of rewards and gifts to his followers.[83]

The combined complaints of Ireland's lord chancellor and Ireland's premier peer appeared to pose a threat to St Leger no less serious than that which Grey had confronted. Yet the success of St Leger's strategy was to become clear in the marked difference between the fate of the two viceroys. St Leger defended himself at length against Alen's charges, but in each case his answer came down to the simple assertion that none of his critics could improve on his performance. They deplored his political and military inaction, but he had established an unprecedented period of peace in the land. They charged him with favouritism. Yet Alen, whose past associations were well known and whose current claims were now being presented to

---

[82] Ormond to Lord Privy Seal Russell, 15 Nov. 1545, SP 60/12/24 and enclosure.
[83] Ibid., Alen and Aylmer to Henry VIII, 27 Feb. 1546, SP 60/12/34; Alen's 'Charges', c. Aug., ibid., nos. 42, 47.

court by Walter Cowley in tandem with Ormond's wild allegations, could hardly deny his own factional connections. They hinted at personal corruption, but Alen, Cowley and above all Ormond had each taken a share in the great dispensation of crown lands. In reply St Leger hinted strongly that none of his critics was above reproach; and there the matter ended.[84] In such a dangerous area neither side was prepared to call the other's bluff.

In the face of St Leger 's stonewalling and the apparently solid support which he received from the great lords, from the Palesmen and from the rest of the Dublin council, the revived coalition against the governor crumbled. Under interrogation at Westminster his critics divided sharply among themselves. Ormond disowned Walter Cowley as he had once disowned Cowley's father, alleging that he had been duped by his evil advisers. Cowley, under pressure, made a complete confession, exonerating St Leger from all of the charges and declared that the intrigue had been mastered from the beginning by Alen who, he said, had been jealous of the deputy's success. Both were disgraced, sent to the Tower and immediately dismissed from office. Just weeks later Ormond who had professed reconciliation with St Leger, mysteriously fell victim to food poisoning while dining at the bishop of Ely's residence at Holborn. The rout of St Leger's enemies was complete.[85]

By the autumn of 1546, then, St Leger's ambitious and extremely risky political strategy seemed to have been completely vindicated. And to capitalise on his success, he embarked on a second, even more audacious, phase of his strategy of political reconstruction through generous land distribution. In October 1546 he secured King Henry's agreement to dissolve the cathedral of St Patrick's in Dublin, and back in Ireland, he worked over the next six months to complete the hasty pensioning off of the prebendaries and the leasing out of the cathedral's extensive properties in Dublin and elsewhere to chosen favourites in the manner that he had disposed of the monastic and the Kildare properties years before.[86]

---

[84] St Leger's 'Reply', c. Aug. 1546, SP 60/12/46; Alen himself received a grant in perpetuity of the priory of St Wolstan's (Co. Kildare) for a mere £10, though its real value was estimated to be £30 pa; Cowley had leases of at least £69 under the survey value (*Fiants Henry VIII*, nos. 57, 151, 155, 175, 349; *Extents Ir. mon. possessions*, pp. 176, 184, 60, 64, 178–80, 43).

[85] *APC (1542–6)*, pp. 523–4; Walter Cowley to privy council, Oct. 1546, SP 60/12/49–53; Alen to Paget, 21 Apr. 1549, SP 61/3/32; Stanihurst in *Holinshed's Irish Chronicle*, Dublin, 1978, L. Miller and E. Power (Dublin, 1979), pp. 307–8; for a full treatment of the mysterious circumstances surrounding the poisoning, see David Edwards, 'Malice aforethought: the poisoning of the ninth earl of Ormond', *Jn. Butler Soc.* 3: 1 (1986), pp. 30–41.

[86] *Fiants, Edward VI*, nos. 32–111; on this occasion St Leger's leases were set much closer to the official valuation, but, as in the case of the monks, it was the Crown rather than the leaseholders which assumed responsibility for paying the clergy's pensions. I am very grateful to James Murray for information in relation to this affair, a fuller account will be found in his forthcoming doctoral thesis, 'The administration of the diocese of Dublin in the sixteenth century' (University of Dublin).

The urgency with which St Leger launched this second speculative boom in Crown lands was in itself an indication of the demanding nature of the political strategy to which he had committed himself. But in the heady months of early 1547 such doubts were wholly obscured by the apparent brilliance of his recent success. In the previous seven years he had constructed a nationwide support for the establishment of a new political system under the framework of an Irish kingdom and by the practical authority of a viceroy based in Dublin. During that time he sustained the confidence of that following through the extension of tolerance and flexibility and through the generous provision of many royal gifts most of which were unknown to the king. And finally he had succeeded in destroying the most serious of challenges to his long-term political objectives. In the power vacuum left by the collapse of the Kildare Geraldines, St Leger had crafted an alternative form of political association based neither upon coercion nor upon factional considerations, but on the demonstration of common social and political interests. St Leger was not the conquering lord for whom some of the Anglo-Irish had hoped, nor yet the surrogate Kildare whom the Dublin reformers had feared, but a unique political leader whose authority and influence throughout the country was based upon his position as the creator and chief representative of a united Irish interest. His position at the beginning of 1547 seemed impregnable. Yet it rested on the central assumption that the Irish king would continue to regard his Dublin viceroy as precisely that, as his proxy endowed with the same authority to preserve the new Irish kingdom as the monarch himself defended the kingdom of England. This was an exalted view of the Irish office and the conditions which sustained it were rapidly to be undermined in the years that followed.

2

Ireland and the mid-Tudor crisis, 1547–1556

(I)

Until recently a deep but generally unnoticed contradiction has existed in the ways in which English and Irish historians have viewed the reigns of Edward VI and Mary. For English historians the years between the death of King Henry and the accession of Elizabeth have traditionally been seen as years of profound instability and almost unrelieved crisis. It was a time when the fragile consensus of the English political nation was fractured by the eruption of radical political and religious divisions, when the stability of the commonweal was undermined by economic crisis, made worse by personal incompetence, greed and corruption, when narrow self-interest, factional intrigue and rebellion reduced the government of England to a state of chronic powerlessness and, in Pollard's daunting phrase, 'sterility'.[1]

All of this has contrasted sharply with the way in which Irish historians have traditionally understood the significance of the period. To them these were years not of indecision and ineffectualness but of radical innovation, in which the English government broke away from its long dalliance with diplomacy and procrastination and launched instead into a determined campaign to gain control of Ireland by the establishment of plantations and firm military government throughout the whole island.[2]

The recall of St Leger as deputy in May 1548 is conventionally understood to mark the inauguration of this radical change of policy. Though he was to

[1] W. R. D. Jones, *The mid-Tudor crisis 1534–63* (London, 1973), provides a critical survey of traditional views of the concept. A characteristic expression of the older interpretation can be found in J. D. Mackie, *The earlier Tudors 1485–1558* (Oxford, 1952); A. F. Pollard's magisterial judgement was applied specifically to the reign of Mary (*History of England, 1547–1603* (London, 1910), p. 172), but it is also the organising concept of his treatment of the previous reign.

[2] For the argument that the mid-Tudor period witnessed the turning point in English attitudes toward Ireland see (*inter alia*), Bradshaw, *Constit. rev.*, pp. 258–63; Ellis, *Tudor Ireland*, pp. 228–37; D. G. White, 'The reign of Edward VI in Ireland', *IHS* 14 (1964–5), pp. 197–211; Wilson, *Beginnings of modern Ire.*, ch. 7; D. B. Quinn, 'Ireland and sixteenth-century European expansion', *Historical Studies* 1 (1958), pp. 20–32.

return on two further occasions, St Leger's influence over Ireland is adjudged to have declined precipitately from that date, and political initiative in Ireland is seen to have passed to a set of new, tougher men bent on securing the subjugation of the native lords by force. The first of this new school of martial men, Sir Edward Bellingham (May 1548–Dec. 1549), is credited with setting the agenda for each of his successors in reopening the war against the O'Mores and in laying the foundations of a plantation in the territory which became an increasingly important preoccupation of every subsequent governor. Bellingham was also responsible for the first steps in establishing military garrisons in the country at large; and under the rule of his successors Sir James Crofts (May 1551–Nov. 1552) and the earl of Sussex (app. Mar. 1556) old castles were reconstructed in Ferns, Leighlin Bridge, Athlone and Carlingford; new forts built in Maryborough and Philipstown, and the important ports of Cork, Waterford and Dungarvan refortified.[3] Following Bellingham the mid-Tudor viceroys are said to have adopted a markedly aggressive attitude in dealing with the country's political leaders. Powerful local figures who had hitherto enjoyed a relative immunity from royal authority now felt the weight of unexpected government interference in their affairs. Con O'Neill, the first earl of Tyrone, was arrested and held in the Pale first in 1552 and again in 1556; Cahir MacArt Kavanagh was proclaimed a traitor, and even the earl of Desmond (whom St Leger had done so much to reconcile) was forced to accompany Bellingham under constraint to Dublin.[4] The same forcefulness is said to have characterised the governors' approach towards the enforcement of religious change. St Leger's generally *politique* approach was disowned by Bellingham and Crofts whose zealous pursuit of conformity estranged at once the clergy and the hitherto indifferent laity.[5]

This traditional account of mid-Tudor Irish policies is not, of course, uncritical. It has been argued that the turn toward coercion and plantation was far more expensive and hardly more successful than earlier conciliatory attitudes. It is agreed also that the insensitive handling of particular Gaelic lords created unnecessary problems for the future, and that the over-ambitious pursuit of religious change led to a hopeless polarisation of

---

[3] For general surveys see Richard Bagwell, *Ireland under the Tudors* (3 vols., London, 1885–90; reprint, London, 1963), I, chs. 16–18; Wilson, *Beginnings of modern Ire.*, chs. 6–7; and the biographical sketches of Bellingham and Crofts in *DNB*.

[4] The unlikely story of Desmond's arrest is found only in John Hooker's 'Chronicle of Ireland' in R. Holinshed, *Chronicles of England, Scotland and Ireland*, 6 vols. (1807–8 edn), p. 100; there is no supporting contemporary evidence.

[5] Brendan Bradshaw, 'The Edwardian reformation in Ireland', *Archiv. Hib.* 34 (1976–7), pp. 83–99; R. D. Edwards, *Church and state in Tudor Ireland* (Dublin, 1935), pp. 131–40; for a more critical view see S. G. Ellis, 'John Bale, bishop of Ossory, 1552–3', *Jn. Butler Soc.* (1984), pp. 283–93.

government and community and ultimately to the failure of the reformation. Yet even in acknowledging all its inadequacies, Irish historians have continued to regard the mid-Tudor period as a time when radically aggressive ideas about the nature of England's problem in Ireland which were to dominate strategic thinking until the end of the century first made their appearance.[6] This sharp dichotomy in the way in which Irish historians have continued to regard the mid-Tudor years and the rather more sombre attitudes of English historians towards the same period raises a curious interpretative problem: how can these highly contrasting perspectives be applied to the same historical epoch?

This apparent problem has now been somewhat eased by the work of English historians who, over the past few decades, have successfully dismantled the idea of a pervasive mid-Tudor crisis. In the sphere of high politics the image of the duke of Somerset as a sincere if naive reformer tricked and supplanted by ruthless, hard-faced men has been replaced by a new view of the Protector as a conservative pragmatic administrator, responding (not always successfully) to a complex series of challenges to his rule.[7] His successor, Northumberland, has been more positively rehabilitated, being seen now as a highly efficient, perceptive and successful political manager whose unhappy reputation is merely an unearned result of the harsh decisions he was forced to make.[8] More generally, scholars have rescued the Edwardian and Marian councils from the charges of factionalism and incompetence traditionally levelled at them and have revealed them to be far more united and far more hard-working than they have previously been seen.[9] Re-examinations of parliament, in particular the workings of the house of Lords, in this period have produced similarly creditable results.[10] But, most importantly of all, the investigations of several researchers into the mid-Tudor financial administration have demonstrated the remarkable achievement of reformist efforts in the midst of the most serious inflationary pressures of the century.[11] The cumulative effect of these revisions has

[6] See note 2 above.
[7] M. L. Bush, *The government policy of Protector Somerset* (London, 1975).
[8] D. E. Hoak, 'Rehabilitating the duke of Northumberland: politics and political control 1547–1553', in J. Loach and R. Tittler, eds., *The mid-Tudor polity c. 1540–1560* (London, 1980), pp. 29–51.
[9] D. E. Hoak, *The king's council in the reign of Edward VI* (Cambridge, 1976); Ann Weikel, 'The Marian council revisited' in Loach and Tittler (eds.), *The mid-Tudor polity*, pp. 52–73.
[10] J. Loach, *Parliament and the crown in the reign of Mary Tudor* (Oxford, 1986) and 'Conservatism and consent in parliament' in Loach and Titler, *Mid-Tudor polity*, pp. 9–28.
[11] W. C. Richardson (ed.), *The report of the commission of 1552* (Morgantown, W.VA, 1974); J. D. Alsop, 'The structure of early Tudor finance', and Christopher Coleman, 'Artifice or accident; the reorganization of the exchequer of receipt' in Christopher Coleman and D. Starkey (eds.), *Revolution reassessed* (Oxford, 1986), pp. 135–62, 163–98; see the reviews of Loach and Titler, *Mid-Tudor polity*, by David Starkey and Joel Hurstfield respectively in *History* 66 (1981), pp. 509–10, and *EHR* 97 (1982), pp. 359–65.

been to demonstrate that the much vaunted success of the Henrician and Elizabethan regimes in establishing and then reviving the reform of Tudor government were greatly exaggerated and that the real credit for preserving and extending the authority of the central administration amidst unprecedented problems belongs rightly to the mid-Tudor period.

The new emphasis has not sought entirely to revise the problems of these years out of existence. Few of the revisionists have argued that this was a period of radical innovation or dramatic new departures. Most have been content to conclude that the political measures and administrative procedures which were applied in this period were designed to withstand the varied dangers of dynastic instability, foreign invasion, social unrest and economic recession then immediately threatening England. The real achievement of the mid-Tudor governments was not revolutionary but conservative: the ability to maintain continuity in the midst of crisis.[12]

The discovery of a strong element of continuity in mid-Tudor government suggests in turn the need for a revision of the traditional view of its character in Ireland. For here, despite the alterations, innovations and disruptions too often associated with them, the regimes of mid-century can be seen to have been concerned above all with the maintenance of order and with the preservation of as much continuity as possible with the Henrician strategies of St Leger.

A notable element of continuity in these years was indeed provided by St Leger himself. For despite his recalls St Leger was repeatedly reappointed to office and served as viceroy for a total of fifty-one months between April 1547 and his final dismissal in April 1556. As such he was by far the longest-serving governor of the mid-Tudor period; and even during his absence from Ireland he continued to exercise a significant influence over the administrations of Sir James Crofts (twenty months) and the Lord Justices Cusacke and Aylmer between December 1552 and October 1553. Even when not in office St Leger continued to enjoy favour in government: he served on diplomatic missions and retained his place on the privy council. But his continuing importance in Ireland was acknowledged in the most practical manner in the Edwardian government's decision to allow him to retain the grants and leases which he had acquired in Ireland as viceroy.[13]

It is perhaps unnecessary to emphasise St Leger's continuing influence over Irish policy, for his successors in office, Bellingham and Crofts, soon

---

[12] Croft to privy council, 28 July 1551, Edward VI to Croft, 17 Aug. 1551, SP 61/3/38, 48.

[13] The exact periods of service of St Leger and his successors are listed in T. W. Moody, F. X. Martin and F. J. Byrne (eds.), *A new history of Ireland*, IX (Oxford, 1984), pp. 486–98; for St Leger's continued property interests see PRO, E/248/22.

came to appreciate the importance of the reform strategy which he had promoted. Bellingham's rigorous suppression of the midland stirrings and his brusqueness with recalcitrant subjects has led to his portrayal as a severe and unbending martinet. Cultivated in part by the trenchancy of his prose, the impression is, however, greatly exaggerated. He was, to be sure, abrupt in manner; but in its essentials his approach to the government of Ireland was surprisingly close to St Leger's. Though he was determined to suppress disorder, Bellingham urged that surrender and regrant be further extended through the entertainment and ennoblement of more Gaelic lords at court. He wanted all remaining restrictions on intermarriage lifted, and argued that trade with Gaelic lordships should be encouraged. He proposed that the importance of the 1541 legislation be reinforced through a general grant of English liberties to all the native Irish, and, most interestingly, he sought to have St Leger's national political system strengthened by the erection of a number of viceregal residences which were to be sited in each of the provinces.[14]

In practice, moreover, Bellingham continued St Leger's habit of arbitrating among disputing septs in a particularly energetic manner. He supported Teig O'Carroll of Ely against the contending claims of his nephew Calough, temporarily settled the dispute between Manus O'Donnell and his son Calough, and displayed an unexpected tact in dealing with Cahir MacArt Kavanagh in his feud with the Wexfordmen. In June 1549 Bellingham summoned Tyrone, Phelim O'Neill, Maguire, MacMahon and several other lords of Ulster to Dublin in an attempt to settle all the disputes in the province, and he undertook similar arbitrations among the Burkes of Clanrickard, the O'Brennans and the Ryans.[15]

Despite the ruthlessness with which he pursued the O'Mores and the O'Connors, Bellingham's proposals for the midlands were relatively modest. He wanted the general inhabitants disturbed as little as possible, and proposed that the confiscation of land be restricted to those strategic areas where the new forts were to be established: he was even prepared to concede restricted rights of residence to the very leaders of the midlands rebellion. Bellingham's close counsellor, Walter Cowley, underlined the moderation of

---

14 Privy council's reply to Bellingham's 'Remembrances', 24 June 1549 SP 61/2/46; see also John Alen's criticisms of Bellingham's moderation, Apr. 1549, SP 61/2/32.
15 On Bellingham's dealing with the O'Carrolls see his correspondence of Nov. and Dec. 1548, SP 61/1/137, 138, 146, 147, 153; on his dealings with O'Donnell, see Calough O'Donnell to Bellingham, 4 Jan. 1549, SP 61/2/2 and his arbitration with O'Connell, O'Neill and other Ulster lords, July, Dec. 1549, see Lambeth Palace, Carew MSS, 603/6–16, 47–54, and SP 61/1/164; on his treatment of Cahir MacArt Kavanagh, SP 61/1/104, 144, 167–8; for instances of his other arbitrations see Cowley to Bellingham, 25 June 1549, SP 61/2/47 and Bellingham's correspondence with Clanrickard, Aug. 1548, 61/1/68–72.

the governor's midlands policy in a treatise devoted to the issue. The new garrisons, Cowley explained, were to serve as instruments for the ordering and containment of the native inhabitants, not as the beachheads for a general confiscation. The Irish chiefs bordering on the affected territories were to be assured of the government's intentions and encouraged if possible to contribute to the construction and supply of the forts.[16]

All of this conflicts with Bellingham's reputation as a severe and bellicose governor, but this traditional view is derived in good part from an uncritical acceptance of the viceroy's own self-image. Bellingham, for instance, frequently proclaimed his determination to deal mercilessly with all resistance and dissent. Yet the chancery records of his period in office are crammed with pardons for felony issued by the governor to all levels of society from noblemen to kerne.[17] Similarly he was disposed to write in a rather brutal manner to those from whom he required material sustenance; yet he became renowned in the Pale as one of the most generous and unexacting governors of the century.[18] The manner of his address, it should also be noted, was equally terse whether he was directing back-sliding Gaelic chieftains, indolent but loyal Palesmen, or his own subordinates. For in each case the assumption justifying his peremptory commands was the same: in Bellingham's eyes each shared a common obligation as subjects of the Irish kingdom to obey the royal deputy in Ireland as fully and as willingly as English subjects obeyed the king himself.[19] This was perhaps a rather premature reading of the constitutional significance of 1541, yet it made clear that Bellingham accepted every bit as much as St Leger that the act for the kingly title constituted not a mere change of nomenclature but the cornerstone of a radically new political entity.

It is not coincidental in this regard that the only serious objections raised against Bellingham during his period in office emanated neither from the Gaelic Irish nor the Palesmen, but from that inveterate enemy of every viceroy who sought to encompass all the island's political interests under their influence, Sir John Alen. To Alen, Bellingham was a man to be distrusted, like Grey and St Leger before him, as a man too concerned with impressing his personal stamp of authority over the indigenous powers and

---

16 Privy council's reply to Bellingham's 'Remembrances', 24 June 1549 (SP 61/2/46); Cowley's 'Device', 14 Mar. 1549, SP 61/2/25, enclosure (i).

17 See, for example, a sample of pardons issued in 1549 alone in *Fiants Ed. VI*, nos. 223–33, 248–8, 250–94, 305–43, 345–73, etc.

18 Compare Bellingham to the Irish council and to the mayor of Dublin, Aug. 1548, SP 61/1/67, with his reputation recorded in the Book of Howth, *Cal. Carew MSS*, VI, 195, and in Hooker's 'Chronicle' in Holinshed, *Chronicles* (1808), p. 100.

19 Compare Bellingham's letters to the Pale nobility, English captains and the Gaelic chieftains O'Molloy and O'Carroll, SP 61/1/25, 75, 134, 138; for Bellingham's distinctly cordial relations with St Leger's closest Irish adviser see SP 61/1/61, 76.

too quick to disregard the advice of those who sought to share the responsibilities of government in Dublin.[20]

Sir James Crofts' rather more phlegmatic temperament has allowed him to escape the easy characterisation which has befallen Bellingham. Yet once again the degree of his commitment to the long-term aims of reform has been generally overlooked. Crofts himself initiated surrender and regrant agreements with MacCarthy More and with a number of lesser lords in Munster who had not been approached by St Leger. He completed the reconciliation of Cahir MacArt Kavanagh begun by Bellingham and furthered by St Leger during their previous governments and furthered Kavanagh's suit to be ennobled as a baron at Westminster.[21] It was Crofts who revived an old reform proposal once espoused by St Leger and others to have established in each of the provinces judicial councils on which the local magnates would occupy a place. And it was Crofts who succeeded in establishing an informal type of regional administration in Munster by appointing the earl of Desmond to head a commission of peace in the province.[22]

Elsewhere Crofts continued St Leger's and Bellingham's earlier efforts at conciliation and arbitration. He held a series of formal consultations with the Anglo-Irish lords of the Pale to improve their relations with the government.[23] Late in 1551 he toured Ulster, persuading Tyrone and Dungannon to agree to the establishment of a garrison at Armagh, and organising an impressive hosting against the Scots (then settling in large numbers along the north-east coast) in which Tyrone, O'Donnell, O'Neill of Clandeboy and several other Ulster lords took part. At Carrickfergus he worked out a series of complicated agreements and drafted an elaborate scheme for the maintenance of good relations between the lords of the province which was to be enforced by a sheriff and the small garrison at Armagh with the co-operation and support of the lords themselves.[24] He displayed, it is true, rather less confidence in the stability of Tyrone than Bellingham; and, on the advice of Sir Thomas Cusacke, he persuaded the earl to withdraw from the lordship to a form of protective detention in the Pale, while the baron of Dungannon attempted to assert his will

20 Alen to Paget, 21 Nov. 1548, 21 Apr. 1549, SP 61/1/129, 2/32.
21 Crofts to privy council, Crofts' 'Instructions to Thomas Wood', 28 July 1551, SP 61/3/38–39; Edward VI to Crofts, 17 Aug., SP 61/3/48.
22 Crofts to privy council and 'Instructions to Thomas Wood', 28 July 1551, SP 61/3/38–39; further 'Instructions' to Wood, 29 Sept., SP 61/3/54; Croft to Cecil, 22 Dec. 1551, SP 6/3/79 and enclosure.
23 Crofts to Northumberland, 22 Dec. 1551, and to privy council, 27 Jan. 1552, SP 61/3/80 and enclosure (i); SP 61/4/5, and enclosures (i), (ii).
24 Cusacke to Warwick, 27 Sept. 1551, Bagenal to Crofts, 27 Oct.; Crofts to privy council, 18 Nov., SP 61/3/52, 56, 65.

independently in the country.[25] Each of these efforts to stabilise Ulster, to extend surrender and regrant in Munster and to establish the institutions of English government wherever possible reveal Crofts' continued commitment to the reform policy's objective of transforming the existing social and political structures of the island by patient diplomatic and administrative effort.

It is clear, therefore, that, despite the apparent disruption for which they have been held to account, St Leger's recalls in the late 1540s and early 1550s heralded no real discontinuity in the general aims of Tudor government in Ireland. Nor did his final displacement by the earl of Sussex in 1556 entail a drastic change in approach. Like Bellingham, Sussex's reputation as an unbending authoritarian is to some degree deserved. The issues with which he concerned himself all involved a measure of confrontation and he was to spend the bulk of his nine years in office relentlessly attempting to attain them. The repression of Shane O'Neill, the establishment of order among the O'Briens, the expulsion of the Scots and the settlement of a plantation in the midlands all embroiled Sussex in a web of increasing violence. Yet it is important to separate the ends for which Sussex aimed from the means by which he pursued them. Sussex's principal objectives in government were wholly consistent with the reform policy. Like St Leger, he sought to put an end to all of the illegal extortions of coyne and livery, seeking as he affirmed in his very first Irish state paper 'to have every man live of his own'.[26] Thus his interventions in Thomond and in Tyrone were undertaken not as part of some campaign of conquest, nor even to weaken the position of the local lords, but simply to reinforce the terms of the surrender and regrant agreements negotiated in the early 1540s and to bolster the position of those who had then been nominated as dynastic heirs.[27]

Sussex's determination to establish an elaborate plantation scheme in Laois and Offaly has generally been seen as a radical departure from St Leger's policies. But even in this regard qualification is necessary. The first effort at a midlands plantation, it is important to recall, was begun not by Bellingham, whose plans were quite limited, but by St Leger himself who issues the first leases for attainted lands in 1550.[28] The 1550 scheme,

---

[25] Crofts to Northumberland, 22 Dec. 1551, SP 61/3/80; Cusacke to Northumberland, 8 May, 22 Dec. 1552, SP 61/4/43, 69.

[26] 'A present remedy for the reformation of the north and the rest of Ireland', *c.* Apr. 1556, SP 62/1/13.

[27] See ch. 3 below.

[28] 'Instructions to St Leger', July 1550 SP 61/2/57; 'Offers of Gerald Aylmer, etc.', 1550, SP 61/2/69; *Fiants Ed. VI*, nos. 599, 661, 724; Edmund Curtis (ed.), 'The survey of Offaly in 1550', *Hermathena* 45 (1930), pp. 312–52.

moreover, was in a sense even more radical than that envisaged by Sussex in that it was to remain exclusive to English and Anglo-Irish planters. It was indeed drafted as a further phase of the great distribution of crown lands which St Leger had supervised a decade before; and many of the speculators in monastic lands featured prominently in the first plantation schedule.[29]

St Leger's involvement in this first (and ultimately abortive) plantation project was not inconsistent. He himself had shown an interest in a number of smaller schemes; but personal considerations apart, settlements of this kind were a valuable support to his general policy. They were strategically necessary in certain difficult or vulnerable areas, and politically important as an exemplary reminder to the Irish lords that the crown expected them to take seriously the obligations which they assumed under the Irish kingdom. But they were valuable finally as an example to neighbouring natives of the material and cultural benefits which were to be derived from the adoption of English laws and customs which they were now being persuaded to undertake. Though it was rather more energetic and sustained, Sussex's efforts after 1556 to re-establish a settlement in the midlands thus constituted no radical departure from the varied considerations which motivated St Leger. Unlike his equally forceful actions in Tyrone and Thomond they were intended not to undermine but to affirm the aspirations of the kingdom of Ireland.[30]

The generally conservative character of the mid-Tudor viceroys, their desire to maintain the momentum of reform while supplying a judicious element of coercion when particular circumstances required, thus places the Irish experience firmly within the pattern established by recent English historiography. That odd contradiction between English and Irish views of the period noted at the outset may appear, therefore, to have been resolved, and the mid-Tudor period can be seen to have been neither as disastrous as older English historians nor as decisive as their Irish counterparts have portrayed it, but simply a time of determined efforts to maintain order and continuity in the midst of extraordinary difficulty on both sides of the Irish sea.

Such a conclusion is accurate enough in so far as it goes; but it is not ultimately convincing. For despite the best efforts of the mid-Tudor politicians and of modern sympathetic historians, the political divisions, dynastic uncertainties and economic disruptions of the period can not be willed away; they remained as persistent problems, forcing rulers into

---

[29] 'Offers of Gerald Aylmer', SP 61/2/69; D. B. Quinn (ed.), 'Edward Walshe's "Conjectures" concerning Ireland', *IHS* 5 (1946–7), pp. 303–22.

[30] On St Leger's earlier view on colonisation, see St Leger et al. to Cromwell, 2 Jan. 1538, *SP Hen. VIII*, II, 534–9; Bradshaw, *Dissolution of religious orders in Ire.*, pp. 168–9. The continuity of Tudor colonisation schemes is discussed in ch. 7 below.

radical changes of direction, sudden decisive actions and unwonted procrastinations that profoundly influenced the character of their administration. And they did so, moreover, in a particularly acute way in Ireland.

At the core of the mid-century's troubles lay the accidental but inescapable fact of dynastic uncertainty. Edward VI was indisputably king in 1547 but he was also a boy of ten who was already showing signs of the ill-health which was to consume him within six years. The doubts surrounding the young king's future were to provide a rich breeding ground for personal, political and ideological intrigue among the most powerful interests at the English court which threatened to undercut the normal routines and concerns of government for most of his reign. Queen Mary was likewise the rightful monarch in 1553, and it is probable that had she lived longer she would have succeeded in consolidating her authority over her subjects. But the initial uncertainties which overshadowed her accession, the unpopularity of her marriage to Philip II, the resentment provoked by the radical religious and foreign policies, and the growing perception that she too would die without issue ensured that her reign also was to be afflicted by faction, intrigue and even insurrection.[31]

Persistent dynastic uncertainty created wider ramifications as each new reign brought with it the question of marriage alliances, and dragged England, on the whole unwillingly, into the marketplace of European diplomacy. Protector Somerset sought to release England from the entanglements which resulted from King Henry's agreement to have his heir betrothed to the Scottish princess Mary. But his efforts to do so led him into a war with France and Scotland which dominated and finally destroyed his administration. Northumberland's efforts to extricate England from the worst effects of Somerset's war brought about a temporary peace, but only at the price of further costly concessions and of strengthening the French influence in Scotland. Queen Mary's all too enthusiastic acceptance of a Hapsburg alliance which her marriage entailed involved her government in yet another international debacle which issued finally in the loss of Calais. A direct result of mid-Tudor dynastic uncertainty was England's entrapment in a series of desperate foreign adventures which produced not only a loss of credit and territory on mainland Europe, but, more alarmingly, in the emergence of a threat to England's own coasts and borders.[32]

At the same time as they faced these diplomatic and military difficulties,

---

[31] For a balanced view of the reigns of Edward and Mary see A. G. R. Smith, *The emergence of a nation state* (London, 1984), pp. 52–97; J. A. Guy, *Tudor England* (Oxford, 1988), chs. 7, 8.

[32] On the problem of the Scottish war see Bush, *Government policy of Protector Somerset*, passim.

mid-Tudor governments were confronted with a separate but not unrelated economic and financial crisis. Whether it was due to Spanish silver, a slump in trade, mounting population pressure or Henrician monetary policies, an unprecedentedly severe inflation was another of the period's persistent and inescapable problems. It has been shown that Northumberland's and the early Marian administrations coped remarkably well with the crisis; yet despite their efforts the royal finances suffered severely throughout this time. As both the chief *rentier* and chief consumer in the land, the royal treasury was doubly exposed to inflation. Heavy losses in relative income and expenditure exacerbated the absolute increases in costs brought on by the war, and forced successive administrations to resort to large-scale currency debasements which in turn stimulated inflation and deepened the crown's fiscal difficulties. Once again the success of the mid-Tudor administrations in avoiding the worst consequences of the inflation deserves due credit; but the fact remains that for much of the period the energies of government reformers were consumed in a ceaseless struggle to avoid bankruptcy.[33]

Dynastic, foreign and financial difficulties combined to present the mid-Tudor governments with one further problem: they forced them to make policy. Few Tudor regimes approached the matter of policy-making with much enthusiasm. Henry VIII, driven to it in the critical years of the 1530s, sought to rid himself of the troublesome obligation after his despatch of Cromwell. Elizabeth after some necessary initiatives was also to reduce her responsibility in the area to a minimum. Policy initiatives were regarded as inherently disruptive: they encouraged argument and intrigue, promoted the formation of factions and alliances of dissent. For this reason Tudor governments sought generally to avoid innovation and to introduce change only when they were assured of a broad base of support. Yet the mid-Tudor regimes, which enjoyed the least capacity for the shaping of a policy-making consensus, had also the most urgent need of doing so. Again the success of the governors in fashioning general support should not be discounted, but there remained some essential issues on which disagreement proved unavoidable. Under Edward it arose, for instance, through increasing dissatisfaction with Somerset's wilful foreign policy and in reaction to Northumberland's espousal of a radical religious position. It could be found also in a rising antagonism spearheaded by Northumberland toward Somerset's fiscal practices and his lukewarm support of commonwealth reform and again in a deep dissatisfaction with Northumberland's handling of the crown's finances. Under Mary, the closing down of access to government and the gradual dissolution of consensus within the political nation led

---

[33] Ibid.

to the formulation of policies without support and, more frequently, to the suspension of the policy-making process altogether.[34]

The consequence of all this was a general deterioration in the quality and efficiency of the policies devised and put into effect. Though most of the regimes survived most of the challenges posed to them, each experienced chronic difficulty in responding effectively to the problems they faced. The mid-Tudor period presented therefore not a fundamental crisis of government, but a crisis in policy-making. Though the latter did not threaten the existence of all political order in England, it steadily corroded all attempts to devise and implement adequate responses to urgent and divisive political problems. And so it threatened to subvert in a particularly intense manner the momentum of the most ambitious, intricate and most dangerous of policies with which the Tudors had burdened themselves, the constitutional reconstruction of Ireland.

The manner in which the multiple problems of Edwardian and Marian England influenced affairs in Ireland was neither uniform nor direct. It cannot as yet be shown to what extent England's inflation was imported into the underdeveloped Irish economy; nor can it be presumed that the radical religious policies of the later Edwardian period exercised any significant influence whether positive or negative on the state of the church in Ireland. The endeavours of a few enthusiasts like Bishop John Bale may have provided some indication of the significance of the doctrinal changes yet to come; yet as the latest research seems to show, the alterations of personnel and procedures of the Church of Ireland even in the diocese of Dublin were far too limited to provoke any significant response among the laity.[35]

England's dynastic difficulties, however, exercised a far more marked influence on Irish affairs if only in an indirect and somewhat accidental manner. The accession of King Edward coincided with the most serious insurrection among the midland septs of O'Connor and O'More since the 1530s. The origins of this renewed outbreak are obscure; historians have been content to assume that it was deliberately provoked by St Leger's enemies to damage his administration. The assumption is speculative, and the fact that Brabazon, who had been nominated by St Leger as his deputy, was given charge of quelling the stirs renders it dubious. But more likely sources of the disorders can be traced to the occurrence of another dynastic crisis, albeit a local one.[36]

---

[34] On the mid-Tudor administrations' difficulties in relation to policy-making in general, see the works of Bush, Hoak, and Loades cited in notes 7, 8, 9 and 31 above.

[35] Ellis, 'John Bale, bishop of Ossory', pp. 283–93; Colm Lennon, *The lords of Dublin in the age of reformation* (Dublin, 1989), chs. 2, 4.

[36] There is no contemporary evidence to support the view that the war was precipitated by Sir William Brabazon; the immediate background to the outbreak is sketchy, but for Butler–

The mysterious death of James, earl of Ormond, in October 1546 created a sudden power vacuum in Irish politics almost as serious as that which had attended upon the fall of the Kildares a decade before. With many of his closest counsellors dead along with him and with a fifteen-year-old heir who was to be kept as a ward of court in England, Ormond's lands and claims to lordship in Leinster and north Munster were now exposed to imminent danger; and the opportunity was immediately seized by his Geraldine enemies determined to repay the scores of the 1530s. Thus the Geraldines came out again in Leinster among the O'Byrnes, the O'Tooles and the O'Mores and, most importantly, among the Kildares' chief Gaelic allies, the O'Connors of Offaly, who had already been fighting an intermittent war with the Butlers throughout the mid-1540s. This renewed Geraldine adventure constituted a threat to St Leger's alternative system similar to that which the Geraldine league had once presented to Grey. It was by no means as serious, however, and St Leger seems to have wished to deal with it quietly by means of a limited military expedition. Yet this was not how his new superiors in Westminster, ignorant of its local and historical sources, were disposed to view the unrest. Perceiving them in the wider context of the worsening international situation, the Edwardian council concluded that St Leger and his council were failing to treat the matter with the seriousness it deserved.[37]

In its closing years the Henrician council had grown increasingly concerned about the possibility of foreign and specifically French intervention in Ireland. According to the council's detailed but highly speculative intelligence, powerful lords in Ireland including O'Neill, O'Donnell, MacCarthy More and Desmond were engaged in active negotiations to secure French support for a Geraldine restoration. At the time France was far less interested in Ireland than in the prospect of strengthening its position with England's rather more dangerous neighbour, Scotland. But in late 1549 and early 1550, as the confrontation between France and England grew sharper and the Dublin administration's difficulties in suppressing unrest among the Geraldines became known, Henry II of France began to take a more positive attitude towards a group of Geraldine exiles who were attempting to persuade the king to launch a diversionary operation in Ireland. It is unlikely that the French ever seriously considered an invasion, and the Geraldine scheme did not advance beyond a secret negotiation with O'Neill and O'Donnell in which, they claimed, the Gaelic chiefs promised to

O'Connor rivalry see Upper-Ossory to St Leger, 11 Nov. 1545, SP 60/12/1, enclosures (i), (ii); Rory O'More to St Leger, June 1544, SP 60/11/49.

[37] On the changing mood of the late Henrician and early Edwardian council, see privy council's 'Instructions', 24 Sept. 1546, SP 60/12/48; 24 Oct., 2 Nov. 1547, SP 61/1/7, 8, *APC (1547–8)*, p. 496; Edward VI to St Leger, 7 Apr. 1547, SP 61/1/3.

offer their allegiance to the French sovereign. Yet the Geraldine intriguers were entertained for a time at the French court, sufficient to convince English observers in Paris and their superiors in Westminster that the French were indeed in the process of launching a determined intervention.[38]

Fears that a large-scale incursion on the southern Irish coast was about to take place were fuelled by the fact that a smaller but far more significant one was actually under way in the north-east. This settlement of the Scots from the western isles in the Glens and the Route in Antrim was again the subject of some misapprehension. It was not, as English observers feared, the result of a Franco-Scottish intrigue, but arose primarily from local conditions. Significant Scottish migration into the north had resumed in the early 1530s and was a source of some alarm to the Dublin administration by the end of the decade. In the early 1540s, however, after the failure of James MacDonnell to revive his authority as lord of the isles in the face of opposition from the earl of Argyle, the MacDonnell exodus began in earnest. In essence, therefore, the migration was little more than a further example of the lateral mobility induced by pressure from above which was characteristic of all Gaelic lordships and which would probably have occurred regardless of international conditions. But its sudden acceleration was doubtless encouraged by Argyle and the queen dowager of Scotland as yet another way of increasing the pressure on the embattled Edwardian government.[39]

These challenges to Tudor rule in Ireland were each of a different order, and might have been dealt with by different techniques. The midland disorders were a result of a renewed disturbance of factional alignments and might have been coped with by moves to restore the earlier balance. This was what the Dublin government actually attempted to do through the appointment of Sir Francis Bryan (an influential courtier who had hurriedly married the dowager countess of Ormond) as chief military authority in south Leinster and briefly as lord justice.[40] The Scottish migration might have been stemmed through the organisation of an alliance of opposition

[38] James Hogan, *Ireland in the European system* (London, 1920), pp. 74–155; St Leger to Henry VIII and council, 14 Apr., 15 May 1534, SP 60/12/5, 6, 8; St Leger to Paget 11 Mar. 1534, SP 60/12/28; George Dowdall to John Alen, 22 Mar. 1550, Brabazon to privy council, 26 Mar. 1550, SP 61/2/51, 52, and enclosures; *Memoirs of Sir James Melville*, pp. 1–10; Sir John Mason to privy council, 14, 29 June 1550, *Cal. SP Foreign (1547–52)*, pp. 48–50; privy council to St Leger and 'Instructions' 7, 26 Jan, SP 61/3/2, 4.

[39] See in general, G. Hill, *An historical account of the MacDonnells of Antrim* (Belfast, 1873, reprint Ballycastle, 1976); D. P. Dorrian, 'The cockpit of Ulster' (BA dissertation, University of Dublin, 1985), ch. 2; privy council to Bellingham, 6 Jan., 24 June 1549, SP 61/2/3, 46; Cusacke to Warwick, 27 Sept. 1551, SP 61/3/52.

[40] On Bryan see *DNB*; M. King to W. Wyse, 5 Sept. 1548, SP 61/1/89; privy council to Bellingham, 25 June, SP 61/1/47.

among the Gaelic lords of Ulster; and this again is how, belatedly, Sir James Crofts sought to cope with it.[41] Finally, the threat of a French invasion never approached the point of imminent probability and French attitudes remained throughout amenable to observation and manipulation through conventional diplomatic methods.

Yet to the beleaguered Edwardian government, acutely aware of its own vulnerability, each of these Irish developments was seen to be intimately related both to one another and to the even greater problems faced by the regime at home. It seemed imperative therefore that the problems in Ireland be confronted in as urgent and decisive a manner as the threat to England itself. Thus the method chosen to defend Ireland was the same as that then being applied to maintain England's own territorial security, that is the construction of coastal fortifications and strong internal garrisons. Both for Somerset and Northumberland the construction of a series of strong places around Ireland's coasts and within its most troubled areas became the central priority of government before which no other issue could take precedence. Both Bellingham and Crofts were initially sent to Ireland not as viceroys, but as commissioners to oversee the establishment of new wards and the renovation of old ones; even when they became viceroys the discharge of these prior responsibilities remained the central element in their instructions. Fort building thus became the defining characteristic of mid-Tudor rule in Ireland.[42]

This concern with defence in nowise entailed an abandonment of gradual reform or a lurch towards simple coercion. Bellingham and Crofts alike struggled manfully to continue and even extend St Leger's policies, and both Crofts and St Leger affirmed that the forts could survive only by cultivating the good-will of the neighbouring lords.[43] Yet over time this continuing preoccupation with strategic defence subtly influenced the character of the viceroyalty itself. Though each governor continued to demonstrate a commitment to peaceful constitutional reform in the long term, they were in the short term busily engaged on a project which, though not contrary to that end, tended inevitably to disrupt it. The establishment of military outposts in the country had always been envisaged as a necessary support to the reform process, but now under the imperatives of the Edwardian regime

---

[41] Cusacke to Warwick, 27 Sept. 1551, SP 61/3/52.

[42] Bellingham to privy council, Aug. 1548, SP 61/1/84; 'Instructions for Bellingham', *Cal. pat. rolls, Hen. VIII–Eliz.*, 197–8; 'Notes for Mr. Bellingham', c. Jan. 1549, BL, Lansd. MS 159, no. 5; Cowley to Bellingham, 25 Jan. 1549, SP 61/2/12; 'Articles for Ireland', 7 Jan. 1551, SP 61/3/2; 'Instructions' for Crofts, 25 Feb., 11 May 1551, 61/3/14, 23; Bush, *Government policy of Protector Somerset*, chs. 1, 2 and 6.

[43] St Leger to Warwick, 27 Sept. 1550, SP 61/2/60; 'Articles for the expedition to Ireland', 7 Jan. 1551, 61/3/2; Crofts to Warwick, May 1551, 61/3/27, and to privy council, 28 July, 61/3/38/

it became the first object of government, an end in itself. This alteration in priorities, placing narrow strategic objectives above the broader aims of constitutional reform also produced an important change in the way in which the viceroyalty itself was perceived. No longer to be seen as the manipulator of great factional connections, as Grey had sought to be, and still less as the architect of a new political structure such as had been St Leger's ambition, the mid-Tudor viceroys appeared primarily as military executives, engineers bent upon the completion of a specific, technical brief designed to serve the immediate requirements of the government in London. This did not imply that the Irish viceroy had been transformed into a coercive military governor; merely that in having its aims so redirected, the status of the Irish viceroyalty was correspondingly reduced. The reforming chief governor who had once been given responsibility for the creation of a new political community within the island was now displaced in fact if not in person by a far more inferior figure maintaining a holding operation in Ireland at the will of his superiors in London.

The deflection and consequent decline of the viceroy's role was further accentuated by a more direct attack upon the status of the office itself. The party struggles within and between the Edwardian and Marian regimes produced severe reverberations within the Irish administration. As Somerset rose to prominence, so the influence of old Henricians at court declined and so the standing of that distinctly Henrician figure St Leger began to fall. St Leger was thus replaced by a more dependable servant, Bellingham, but as Somerset in turn began to fail so, in his turn, Bellingham began to lose the confidence of the Edwardian privy council. Northumberland's attempt to re-establish political consensus by making friends among the old Henricians led him to seek St Leger's service again, and to retain him thereafter in a position of influence. But even Northumberland preferred his own defence priorities in Ireland to be discharged by a closer acquaintance, and so St Leger's tenure of the office was again briefly interrupted by Crofts. The pattern persisted. It was a concern also to establish continuity with the past that prompted Mary to confirm St Leger in his appointment in 1553 but once again it was a lingering mistrust of Edwardian servants that provided the basis for official criticism of St Leger and for his final displacement by younger men making their careers at the Marian court.[44]

---

[44] 'Notes for Mr. Bellingham', BL Lansd. MS 159, no. 5; *APC 1547–50*, p. 500; Edward VI to mayor of Galway, 12 Apr. 1548, SP 61/1/15; on Alen's recovery, *APC 1547–50*, pp. 173, 452; Alen to Paget, Apr. 1549, SP 61/2/32; Cantwell to Bellingham, 4 Oct. 1549, HMC, *Cecil MSS*, I, 75–6; on St Leger's return to favour, *APC 1547–50*, p. 342; his 'Requests' and 'Remembrances', July 1550, SP 61/2/54, 55; St Leger to Cecil, 5 Dec. 1550, 19 Jan., 23 Mar. 1551, 61/2/67, 3/3, 18, and his 'Devices' of early 1553, 61/4/83; the circumstances of his final recall are discussed below.

These periodic interruptions in viceregal tenure produced further dis-
locations in the lesser offices of the Irish administration. St Leger's triumph
over Ormond in 1546 led, as we have seen, to the dismissal of Lord
Chancellor Alen, Walter Cowley and even to the removal of lesser fry like
the midlands pensioner William Cantwell. Bellingham's appointment,
however, saw the rehabilitation of Alen, Cowley and Cantwell and the
consequent eclipse of those like Sir Thomas Cusacke and John Parker who
had displaced them. St Leger's return in 1550 saw a further reversal and
though his group was to retain influence under Crofts they were each to
suffer dismissal upon St Leger's fall from grace under Mary. Similar
fluctuations occurred in the ranks of the military establishment, first, when
captains in favour under St Leger, like John Wakely and Francis Herbert,
were pushed aside by Bellingham's dependants, and later, when all lost place
to Sussex's new command.[45]

The significance of these alterations can be easily misstated. They were
not, it is important to note, comprehensive; for most civil administrators and
many captains continued to serve without difficulty under every viceroy.
Nor did these matters of personnel signal any fundamental change of
attitude toward the now conventional Tudor reform policy. Yet they
inadvertently produced a serious obstruction to the process by which this
reform was to be brought about. For Grey and more importantly for
St Leger the aim of constructing a model English polity in Ireland was
predicated upon the prior creation of an active national interest group in
support of the policy. But the fashioning of this national following, as St
Leger more than Grey had realised, was itself dependent on the establishment of a small but influential group of promoters and facilitators whose
task it was to broadcast the attractions of the reform project to the country
at large. Yet it was precisely this liaison group whose credibility and
efficiency were most seriously threatened by the alterations of mid-century.
In the wake of their repeated displacement from positions of influence, men
like Cusacke, Parker, Agard and Peppard could no longer function as
authoritative promoters of a policy whose future success seemed vouchsafed; while others like Cowley, Alen and Cantwell who were themselves so
easily discredited could not bring serious weight to their own alternative
strategies. The ability of those connected with government to exert influence
in the country in favour of their viceroy's policy was therefore seriously
reduced.

---

[45] On Alen's fortunes, see *APC (1542–7)*, pp. 403–4, 497, 517; *APC (1547–50)*, pp. 173, 452;
HMC, *Cecil MSS*, I, 88, 89, 91; Alen to Cecil, 5 Apr., 27 May 1551, SP 61/3/19, 26; Alen
to Cecil, 16 Dec. 1558, SP 63/1/7. Cusacke's career is briefly summarised in Ball, *Judges*, I,
pp. 285–7; for Cantwell, SP 61/1/3, 2/46, 3/48; for Cowley, SP 61/2/12; HMC, *Cecil MSS*,
I, 91.

The clearest example of the declining influence of St Leger's agents was presented by the career of his most important provincial ally, James, earl of Desmond. Raised to the high honorary office of lord treasurer by St Leger and employed by him to prepare the ground for the spread of reform in the south-west, Desmond found himself suddenly out of favour with Bellingham and regarded as a dangerous Geraldine leader suspected of involvement in foreign intrigue. Under Crofts, Desmond was again admitted to political influence but even though Crofts had entertained greater hopes for his service, his practical role in those years was limited to providing support for the fortification of the coastal havens which was the major preoccupation of Crofts' administration. For Desmond, therefore, the principal advantage of a close association with the Dublin government was fast disappearing in the mid-Tudor period: far from being seen as the chief agent of a national reform policy from which all of the indigenous powers were expected to gain, he was now being regarded at best as a mere instrument of a policy over which he could exert no influence, and at worst as a potential enemy to that policy. And when Sussex reverted to treating the earl with undisguised suspicion, his estrangement from the Dublin administration was complete.[46]

There remained, however, a further and more central area in which the concerns of the English government threatened the status of the Irish viceroyalty – finance. The reconstruction of Ireland's defence infrastructure necessarily entailed a major increase in government spending. But the cost to the crown was far greater than anyone had supposed. Thanks to Brabazon and St Leger, Irish revenues remained low and even began to show signs of decline in the early 1550s. The increased pace of government activity had therefore to be supported by unprecedentedly large subventions from England. In the closing years of Henry VIII payments from England averaged around £8,000 (st.) a year. But under Edward they rocketed suddenly from £12,877 (st.) in 1546–7, to £18,450 (st.) in 1547–8, to £24,637 (st.) in 1548–9 and following a slight decline to £18,060 (st.) in 1549–50, they reached a massive £39,598 (st.) in 1550–1.[47] These figures provide a clear indication of mounting financial difficulty, but even so they are unrepresentative; for the treasury's subventions did not come in large evenly spaced instalments but were granted in irregular parcels and only when the Dublin administration's finances were truly critical. As a result

[46] *APC (1542–7)*, p. 421; Simon Geffrey to Bellingham, 8 Aug. 1548, SP 61/1/54; Bellingham to privy council, Aug. 1548, 61/1/84; Alen to Somerset, 21 Nov. 1548, 61/1/129; Alen's 'Instructions', Feb. 1550, SP 61/2/50; St Leger's 'Remembrances', July 1550, SP 61/2/55; 'Instructions to the earl of Desmond', 1 July 1551, SP 61/3/38, enclosure (i); Crofts to Cecil, 27 Dec. 1551, SP 61/3/79; Northumberland to Cecil, 25 Nov. 1552, SP 61/4/64; Desmond to Queen Mary, 1 Mar. 1557, SP 62/1/25.
[47] 'Accounts of Sir William Brabazon', SP 61/3/55.

Dublin was always in debt and the governors were obliged to repay pressing creditors out of their private funds. Bellingham did so generously and as a result died heavily in debt; Crofts resigned early to avoid a similar fate; St Leger characteristically demanded a 50 per cent increase in his stipend.[48]

In addition all of the viceroys were required to find other means of supporting their administrations. Bellingham exploited the traditional military obligations due from the community of the Pale to have workmen, horses, carts and supplies collected for his building of the midlands forts. St Leger did likewise, but introduced also the conversion of these services into cash payments which was to have serious implications for the future. All three were forced either to borrow from the country officially or to allow the soldiers to lodge in the countryside without pay. In either case the debt went unpaid.[49]

This unwilling but persistent exploitation of the countryside's resources dealt a further blow to the declining status of the viceroy as the herald of a great process of constitutional reform, but the governor's credibility was even more severely damaged by a further policy forced on each in turn by their superiors in England: a desperate experiment in currency debasement. A favourite panacea of the late Henrician and early Edwardian governments in England, the debasement of the Irish currency began to be employed by the mid-Tudor regimes with increased prodigality even as they began to apprehend the results which it had produced at home. The original aim of creating a special base currency for Ireland as presented to King Henry in the 1530s seems merely to have been to preserve the traditional exchange rate between the two countries (2 English: 3 Irish) which at that time was in danger of running against England's advantage. The first experiments in debasement with coin of around 10 oz fine were, therefore, modest enough. In the later 1540s, however, as the government's troubles deepened the currency issued for Ireland decreased sharply in quality while increasing greatly in quantity. In the last year of his reign Henry despatched some £100,000 of a mere 3 oz fine. But systematic debasement got under way only thereafter. Between 1548 and 1552 a mint established for the purpose in Dublin issued coins of 4 oz fineness with a face value of £62,000 and a further £32,400 of 3 oz fineness.[50]

---

[48] Crofts to privy council, 30 Aug. 1551, 27 Jan., 28 Feb., 14, 22 Mar., 16 Apr. 1552, SP 61/3/50, 4/5, 13, 27, 31; St Leger's 'Requests', July 1550, SP 61/2/54 and his 'Instructions', Oct. 1553, SP 62/1/2; *APC (1547–50)*, p. 305, *APC (1552–3)*, pp. 312–13; privy council to St Leger, 10 June 1554, SP 62/1/60.

[49] 'Extracts from the council books of St Leger and Crofts', BL, Add. MSS, 4763, no. 6; 'Devices for the cess', Feb. 1577, SP 63/57/18, enclosure (iii). See ch. 6 below.

[50] Michael Dolley, 'Anglo-Irish monetary policies 1172–1637', in J. C. Beckett (ed.), *Historical Studies* VII (1969), pp. 45–64; C. E. Challis, 'The Tudor coinage for Ireland', *British Numismatic Journal* 40 (1971), pp. 97–119; BL, Harl. charter 57/H.4; assays made by W. Williams, 15 Jan. 1552, SP 61/4/2–3.

By these means the government's mounting debt to the soldiers, the artificers and the carters was at length discharged. But the consequences of this activity for the Pale as a whole were economically disastrous. There and in all areas where it was dispensed the debased currency initiated a galloping inflation. By the end of 1551 Lord Deputy Crofts reckoned that prices had risen by 400 per cent and in some cases 600 per cent in the year. Inflation induced a sharp decline in real income not only for all government pensioners and stipendiaries but for the country in general which was charged with billeting and feeding his soldiers for a mere 2d per day. The debasement gave rise in addition to a sudden dearth of money and of agricultural produce in the Pale's markets as merchants withdrew fine moneys for export to the continent or to England and the husbandmen abandoned trade and resorted to barter. A general clamour from the Pale and from the coastal towns, where money was in use, supported by Crofts' eloquent pleas for relief persuaded the Edwardian council to agree to a devaluation of the face value of the Irish currency. Yet an accompanying promise to commission a large issue of respectable 9 oz coins was not honoured.[51]

As in other spheres the currency reforms contemplated but deferred under Northumberland were belatedly introduced under Mary and in September 1553 some £20,000 of 7 oz coins were minted for Ireland.[52] But by then the worst consequences of the crisis had already been registered there. For through its duration and extent this government induced inflation served to deepen the conviction that for all its claims of commitment to the construction of a new constitution for Ireland, the Dublin administration could in reality produce nothing of the sort. It was instead a well-meaning but helplessly exploitative agency, a means by which the English government maintained a hold on its western dominion in the cheapest manner possible regardless of the welfare of its inhabitants.

By thus transforming the viceroy into a financially repressive agency, by undermining its capacity to maintain a following in the country at large and by diverting it from its long-term reform commitments to apparently more urgent matters of defence, the Edwardian regimes were steadily if unwittingly undermining the Irish viceroyalty as the centrepiece of a new political system which St Leger (and in a lesser way Grey) had tried to make it. Thus while the aspiration to the constitutional reform of Ireland remained alive in principle, the possibility of its eventual attainment was now gravely

---

[51] Crofts and council to privy council, 30 Aug., 22 Dec. 1551, 27 Jan. 1552, SP 61/3/50, 80; 4/5; privy council to Irish council, 29 May 1552, 61/4/48; Edward VI to Crofts, 7 June, *APC (1552–3)*, p. 274.
[52] Challis, 'Tudor coinage for Ireland'.

threatened by the slow subversion of the very office by which it was to have been put into effect. The consequences of these varied pressures upon the Irish office were to large degree unrecognized by the London government; but there remained a final area in which Whitehall's assault on the Irish viceroy was both deliberate and ultimately decisive.

As the cost of governing Ireland rose markedly in the late 1540s and as Irish revenues signally failed to respond to these increased charges, so Westminster became increasingly concerned at the Irish treasury's failure to approximate the long-promised and long-awaited ideal of self-sufficiency. In 1548 in response to Alen's renewed innuendos concerning St Leger's and Brabazon's methods, Somerset despatched an auditor, Richard Brasier, to take the treasurer's seven-year account and to report on the Dublin government's methods of expenditure and receipt. Brasier's researches revealed serious deficiencies in Brabazon's records which again raised doubts about the propriety of his dealings. But the auditor's criticisms were silenced through St Leger's and Brabazon's usual method, the grant of an extensive piece of crown property at a bargain price.[53] The duke of Northumberland, however, was not to be so easily appeased. He was suspicious from the beginning of the operations of Thomas Agard in the Dublin mint, and when his inquiries uncovered the extraordinarily high costs of the projects he closed it down.[54] More importantly, as part of his campaign to reform the bases of Tudor finances as a whole, he established a central commission of inquiry in London to which sub-commissions on the administration of the royal finances in Berwick, Calais and Ireland were to report.[55]

The preliminary investigations of Northumberland's council in preparation for the general commission in themselves revealed the real extent of the English government's spending in Ireland and the failure of the Irish revenues.[56] In the short term this discovery convinced the council of the need of retrenchment and of reappointing St Leger. But the same concern also underlay the council's decision, confirmed by the Marian government late in 1553, to despatch two agents empowered with full authority to inquire into every aspect of the management of the Irish

[53] Brasier to Somerset, 14 Nov. 1548, SP 61/1/22; 'Answer of Mr Brasier to the articles of account found faulty', SP 66/Case A, no. 4; *Fiants Edward VI*, nos. 319, 613.
[54] Privy council to Bellingham and council, 24 June 1549, SP 61/2/46; Challis, 'Tudor coinage for Ireland'.
[55] Joel Hurstfield, 'Corruption and reform under Edward VI and Mary', *EHR* 58 (1953), pp. 22–36; W. K. Jordan, *Edward VI: the threshold of power. The dominance of the Duke of Northumberland* (London, 1970), pp. 440–66; Hoak, *The king's council*, pp. 203–13; privy council memoranda Jan., Feb., Sept., Oct. 1552, SP 10/14/7–9; 15/4, 14; S. Haynes, *Letters of state*, pp. 141–8; privy council to Crofts, 29 Nov. 1552, HMC, *Cecil MSS*, I, 104.
[56] Hatfield House, Cecil MSS, 151/60–61; Haynes, *Letters of state*, pp. 141–2.

government's finances over the previous decade.[57] The commissioner's first report which was presented to the privy council in April 1554 was cautious in tone but startling in its discoveries. It revealed for the first time the degree to which crown properties in Ireland had been undervalued and how the maladministration of the exchequer and the surveyor's office had allowed this undervaluing to continue unreported. They demonstrated moreover how these fundamental losses had been exacerbated by the chronic non-collection of rents and the piling up of arrears. Their findings led to the immediate dismissal and imprisonment of the vice-treasurer, Andrew Wise, Brabazon's son-in-law, who had succeeded to the office in 1551.[58]

But the commissioners at this point made no further recommendations. They did not specify which lands had been undervalued, nor even the extent to which particular holdings were held under value. They did not name the beneficiaries, nor did they implicate the viceroy or any other figure in his administration. They made no charges of corruption. Their report's moderation can be explained in familiar terms. By the time it was submitted the senior commissioner, Sir Edmund Rouse, had already succeeded to Wise's office, inheriting in addition to the conventional perquisites of the treasury, Brabazon's lease of the town and castle of Athlone. He had become involved also in a new colonising scheme in Ulster in partnership with St Leger's ally, John Parker.[59] By the middle of 1554, then, Rouse was no more serious a threat to St Leger than Brasier had been.

The Marian council's doubts persisted, however. Rouse's rapport with the viceroy aroused suspicions and late in October he was replaced as commissioner by a young but influential courtier, Sir William Fitzwilliam. Fitzwilliam's credentials were a clear indication of how serious the Marian council regarded his task in Ireland. He came armed with instruction directing the deputy to appoint him as a senior councillor, he was to have the especially created office of deputy chancellor and he was to be the senior member on the royal commission to issue leases.[60]

Unlike Brasier and Rouse, therefore, the new commissioner was not to be so easily bought off; he was moreover to prove directly hostile to St Leger himself. In collaboration with Rouse's junior, auditor Valentine Browne, he

[57] 'Certain questions touching Ireland', Jan. 1553, SP 61/4/75; Edward VI to Tyrone, May 1553, SP 61/4/80; APC (1552–4), pp. 312–13; 'Instructions to Sir Edmund Rouse', Cal. pat. rolls Hen. VIII–Eliz., pp. 349–50.

[58] 'Statement of the revenues and suggestions for their improvement', BL, Add. MSS, 4767, fos. 73–9; APC (1554–6), pp. 4, 5, 18; 'Order of the Irish Council', 8 May 1554, SP 62/1/5.

[59] For Rouse's delegation of his office, Cal. pat. rolls Hen. VIII–Eliz., p. 321; for his grants of land, pp. 338, 434; Fiants, Mary, no. 70; 'Petition for the fishing of the Bann', APC (1554–6), p. 183.

[60] APC (1554–6), pp. 13, 158; Mary to Wooton, 29 Apr. 1554, Cal. SP Foreign (1553–8), 81; commission to Fitzwilliam et al., Cal. pat. rolls (England) Philip & Mary, II, 103–4.

produced a series of reports which clearly demonstrated St Leger's direct involvement in the scandal of the public finances and revealed the extent to which the viceroy himself had profited from the operation.[61] Fitzwilliam's pursuit was accompanied by a more general attack on St Leger's closest associates in government. Late in 1553, Nicholas Bagenal was dismissed as marshal of the army and replaced by George Stanley, a new man who remained aloof from the viceroy and attached himself to Fitzwilliam.[62] In June 1554 St Leger was instructed to readmit Sir John Alen to the Irish council and to grant him a twenty-one year extension on all his leases.[63] In July 1555, following Fitzwilliam's revelations of his involvement in land sales, Chancellor Cusacke was sequestered from office and replaced as keeper of the seal by Fitzwilliam himself.[64] Along with John Parker, Walter Peppard and Richard Aylmer, Cusacke was summoned to London and imprisoned.[65] By early 1556, then, with Brabazon and Agard dead and Cusacke, Wise, Parker and Peppard in custody, St Leger was isolated in Dublin facing a hostile investigation into his finances as viceroy in Ireland.

Fitzwilliam did not confine himself to the criticism of the viceroy's financial misdoings. He corresponded secretly with London detailing the deputy's military and diplomatic failures.[66] His plantation effort in the midlands had been completely overrun by resurgent O'Mores and O'Connors who now even threatened the Pale itself. In the west the O'Briens of Thomond were embroiled in a vicious internal war which had destabilised the entire region. In the north Shane O'Neill had crushed any hope that the baron of Dungannon would succeed peacefully to the earldom of Tyrone, while St Leger had proved incapable of stemming the invasion of the Scots which had now reached alarming proportions. All of these problems were reported on by Fitzwilliam in a tone of urgency and alarm which the laconic St Leger had never employed. And when they were juxtaposed to Fitzwilliam's revelation of the viceroy's indolent and corrupt

[61] 'Note of divers superfluous charges', BL, Add. MSS, 4767, fos. 82–3; 'Brief estimate of the charges', SP 62/1/14; 'Memo of charges', SP 62/1/15; 'Memo of debts', SP 61/1/18; 'A book of wages', BL, Add. MSS, 4767, fos. 80–1; Archbishop Muzzarelli to Cardinal del Monte, 28 Oct. 1554, Archivio Vaticano, II (extract on NLI microfilm, p. 2526).

[62] *Cal. pat. rolls Hen. VIII–Eliz.*, p. 300.

[63] Ibid., p. 337.

[64] Commission to Fitzwilliam, 2 July 1555, *Cal. pat. rolls (England) Philip & Mary*, II, 344; table of red council-book, HMC, *Haliday MSS*, p. 282.

[65] Fitzwilliam's 'Commission', 2 July 1555, *Cal. pat. rolls (England) Philip & Mary*, II, 344; *Cal. pat. rolls Hen. VIII–Eliz.*, pp. 342–3; APC (1554–6), pp. 182, 189; NAI, Ferguson MSS, V, memoranda rolls, Philip & Mary, no. 13; 'Note of divers superfluous charges', BL, Add. MSS, 4767, fos. 82–3.

[66] St Leger to Petre, 18 Dec. 1555, SP 62/1/8 and enclosure (i); 'Reason for St Leger's repair to England', c. Apr. 1556, SP 62/1/18.

financial management, they pointed to one inescapable conclusion: that the current viceroy was both unfit and incapable of governing Ireland. In July 1556 he was dismissed from office, summoned to answer a full inquiry into his conduct in office and replaced as viceroy by another young man who was also a close associate of Fitzwilliam, Thomas Radcliffe, Lord Fitzwalter, later earl of Sussex.[67]

The causes and significance of the collapse of St Leger's long reign have been variously interpreted. His own account was simple, accurate and quite insufficient. Fitzwilliam and his friends, he asserted, had been motivated only by malice and ambition. They had slandered him, misinterpreted his actions and exaggerated his failures merely because they coveted his office.[68] There was doubtless truth in this; yet it does not explain why these ambitious young careerists should have chosen the Irish office as a vehicle for their advancement and having done so should have opposed themselves so implacably to an ageing viceroy who had shown himself to be so accommodating to newcomers in the past. Modern explanations go deeper: Sussex, it is sometimes said, represented a new style of political administrator who had been influenced by Spanish methods of government in Europe and in the Americas. His opposition to St Leger then was not simply personal but ideological.[69] Such an explanation is, of course, highly speculative. Though Sussex was indeed an agent at King Philip's court during the negotiations for Queen Mary's marriage, there is no evidence to show that he had become personally influenced by any of the (often conflicting) political arguments he may have encountered there. On the contrary, his earliest plan for the reform of Ireland, presented before his appointment was finalised, clearly reveals the moderate nature of his ideas.[70] Designed simply to contrast with the deficiencies of St Leger's performance as outlined by Fitzwilliam. Sussex's plan merely promised more action, more honesty, more results. Thus the expulsion of the Scots, the resettlement of the midlands plantation and the overhaul of the financial administration were his main points of emphasis. Behind them lay no deep determination to alter the government's attitude toward the Gaelic Irish or the Anglo-Irish, merely a reiteration of the conventional aim of his predecessor, to reform Ireland so that 'each man would live of his own'.

---

[67] Campion, *Histories*, ed. Vossen, pp. 135–6; 'Reasons for the repair of St Leger', *c.* 1556, SP 62/1/10; 'Instructions for Fitzwalter', Apr. 1556, (a) Lambeth MSS, 628/53–63; (b) BL, Cotton MSS, Titus B XI, no. 241.

[68] St Leger to Petre, 18 Dec. 1555, SP 62/1/8 and enclosure (i).

[69] Quinn, 'Ireland in sixteenth-century European expansion', in T. D. Williams (ed.), *Historical Studies* I (1958), pp. 25–6; and N. Canny, *The Elizabethan conquest of Ireland* (Hassocks, 1976).

[70] 'A present remedy for the north'; 'Notes for remembrance for Radcliffe', *c.* Apr. 1556, SP 62/1/13, 11.

The only other evidence relevant to Sussex's early interest in Ireland pertains to matters other than intellectual or ideological debate. In 1555 his father, the second earl, had finally rid himself of his 'unnatural and unkind wife' by divorce.[71] The earl's ostensible complaint against his wife was sorcery, but there is reason to believe that more earthly matters had intervened between the earl and his countess. At any rate when the divorced and widowed countess next appears in the records in 1559, it is as a distressed wife suing for the release of her second husband, the unlucky former Irish treasurer, Andrew Wise.[72] If we may discount the possibility that the countess began her liaison with the broken and indebted Wise after his imprisonment in 1554, we must conclude that it had begun sometime before the earl secured his divorce. This would certainly have made the old earl aware of the Irish administration and of the great gains to be made therein; but did the young Fitzwalter first learn of St Leger's dark doings in Ireland from the braggings of his step-mother's paramour?

This, too, is speculation. At best such a personal encounter would have provided a sharper focus for the more general opinions about the Irish administration that had been forming in the young courtier's mind throughout the mid-Tudor years. For as their concern with defence, internal order and financial retrenchment had grown, so the mid-Tudor governments had become increasingly unhappy with the quasi-autonomous kind of viceregal government that had emerged in Ireland since the reign of King Henry. In turn each of the mid-Tudor priorities had become a source of discontent with the Irish office itself. The problem of military defence was a persistent cause of worry: St Leger was reproved for being insufficiently energetic, Bellingham for being too hasty, Crofts for being too cautious. Religion too proved troublesome: Bellingham and Crofts were admonished for being too anxious in their concern to advance the reformed liturgy, while St Leger was condemned by the Edwardian government as a crypto-Catholic and by the Marians as a secret Protestant.[73] And throughout, finance had been a disappointment: Bellingham and Crofts had increased expenditure enormously without achieving any substantial results; and the substantial revenue gains much vaunted by the advocates of reform now looked further away than ever. Few of these criticisms were particularly accurate; nor were

---

[71] I have been unable to trace any record of divorce proceedings, but see *Lords' Jn.*, I, 449–50; Northumberland to Lord Darcy, 30 May 1552, SP 10/14/33; Winchester to Cecil, 23 June 1559, SP 12/4/58; the phrase quoted is from Sussex's will, quoted in GEC, *Peerage* (rev. edn), XII, pt 1, p. 107.

[72] Winchester to Cecil, 23 June 1559, SP 12/4/58; see also Luke Dillon to Cecil, 18 Mar. 1569, SP 63/27/47.

[73] Compare *Chronicles and political papers of Edward VI*, ed. W. K. Jordan (London, 1966) with Campion, *Histories* (ed. Vossen), pp. 135–6.

they in themselves ruinous to those against whom they were directed. But when, thanks to Fitzwilliam's investigations, they were linked to the exposure of the Irish exchequer's incompetence and corruption they became fatal not merely to St Leger but to the very concept of the viceroyalty for which he stood.

On looking at Ireland in the mid-1550s the young Marian courtiers saw a number of salient political and military problems which the current administration seemed incapable of solving. On looking again, they saw that the same administration's dealings with the country had been both highly compromising and morally dubious as well. And from these two observations they reached a clear and seductively simple conclusion: with a little more effort and a little more integrity the decline of Tudor authority in Ireland could be halted and the pursuit of reform resumed. Beneath the clear and apparently unoriginal proposals of Fitzwalter's first 'Remedy' for Ireland there lay, then, an unspoken but highly significant assumption concerning the nature and role of the Irish viceroyalty. The problem of reforming Ireland, it assumed, had entered a difficult but not insurmountable phase. A number of specific difficulties had arisen which required immediate and exclusive attention if further progress was to be made. Yet once these had been confronted, the obstacles which had paralysed reform in recent years would be removed. Then a model administration, which eschewed the murky manipulative techniques which had brought such dishonour on St Leger and his regime, could be erected, which would consolidate the authority of the crown and oversee the extension of English culture throughout Ireland by the same means that had brought peace and order to the outlying parts of England itself.

Its simplicity apart, the particular appeal of this neatly staged scheme of reform lay in the personal advantage which it seemed to offer anyone willing to undertake the initial campaign of action. It offered an ambitious young politician a remarkable opportunity to implement a wide-ranging reform policy comprehensively and conclusively, and without the risk of becoming embroiled in dangerous alliances in Ireland. The initial programme could moreover be easily conceived and expounded. The primary problems to be faced were quite obvious; and the means of resolving them close to hand. The time needed to remove the old obstacles and lay the foundations for the new order could be readily estimated and an assessment of the costs of clearance and reconstruction easily made. And at the conclusion of every set of proposals the same promise could be advanced with confidence: this done and the government of Ireland would cease to exist as a problem and become a matter of routine administration. Such an approach, that is, seemed not only to offer glory to its undertakers when the task had been completed, it seemed to grant them also the greatest possible autonomy from influence either in Ireland or at court during the period when their work was under way.

Yet the attractions of this novel administrative approach were deeply deceptive. For in their uncritical assault on St Leger's faults, the young Marians had themselves failed to grasp the subtle political understanding implicit in the old viceroy's system. St Leger's conduct in office was not simply a matter of personal preference or moral weakness: it had been carefully and deliberately fashioned to cope with particular features of the Irish political environment. His acceptance and furtherance of financial malversation, his careful construction of a political following throughout the country, his tolerance of dissent and his general unwillingness to engage in prolonged military actions were each integral parts of his larger project to bring about the formation of a new political community in Ireland under the framework of the act for the kingly title. For the ideal of the Irish kingdom, St Leger had recognised, could never be made a reality simply by legal and administrative reforms alone, it could be brought about only by the intense engagement of the Irish viceroy with the existing political and social forces in the island. The chief governor could not distance himself from the community he had come to reshape; he had to seek rather to accommodate, manipulate and represent its interests.

By the time they looked toward Ireland, however, such insight was lost to the Marians; because this delicate and highly ambitious role which St Leger had cast for the king's deputy had already been damaged beyond repair by the multiple pressures placed upon the office in the crisis years of mid-century. And the newcomers in observing merely the circumstances of its demise had no occasion to consider the more fundamental forces under which St Leger's system had originally taken shape. Thus in May 1556 as Fitzwalter entered upon the government of Ireland with his clear, honest and apparently straight-forward proposals, there occurred a change of profound consequence for the future of reform in Ireland of which no one was fully conscious.

3

Reform by programme: the viceroyalties of the earl of Sussex, 1556–1565

(I)

However insensitive and ill-informed he may have been at the outset, Sussex's* appreciation of the complexities of Irish government deepened and matured in time. As early as 1557 his understanding of what needed to be done in Ireland had broadened considerably and he was busy badgering Queen Mary to approve a general plan for the reordering of the realm through a revival of surrender and regrant and the establishment of a number of colonial settlements.[1] By 1560 he was able to present Queen Elizabeth with detailed recommendations for Irish reform based upon a shrewd analysis of the strength and ubiquity of faction.[2] The Butlers and the Geraldines, he now realised, exercised sway over all parts of the land; there were few local powers who were not aligned in some way with either group. But within this web of faction and the conspiracy of lawlessness which sustained it, Sussex could detect some rays of hope. There existed within both camps a number of subordinate powers who had already demonstrated their dissatisfaction with the system and were ready to embrace the laws and governance of the crown in return for a recognition and defence of their independence of the great lords. The effect of their desertion, Sussex was certain, would be cumulative; the example of one would lead another in the same direction until the factions would eventually wither away.

Sussex's confidence was bolstered by the additional certainty that one of the great factions would not resist this self-immolation, but would, under certain conditions, actually welcome it. The Butlers were 'for the most part of English blood or name, or of the Irish that continue in their obedience and

---

* Though he did not succeed to the earldom until his father's death in May 1557, I shall for simplicity's sake and because this chapter is not entirely chronological in organisation, refer to Thomas Radcliffe, Lord Fitzwalter as Sussex throughout.
[1] Fitzwalter to Mary, 2 Jan. 1557, SP 62/1/22, and enclosures; 'Articles . . . to be explained to the Queen', 15 Apr., 62/1/31: 'Articles touching the state of Ireland', 27 May, SP 62/1/38.
[2] 'The opinion of Sussex touching the reformation of Ireland' 11 Sept. 1560, Lambeth MSS, 614/271–80, incompletely calendared in *Cal. Carew MSS (1515–74)*, pp. 300–4.

at present seek to receive their estates from the queen majesty and to be reduced to English government'.[3] The earl of Ormond was willing to relinquish his authority over his factional subordinates if his special position within the realm could be acknowledged by the crown in some other way. Only the earl of Kildare and the Geraldines seemed to pose any serious challenge. But their power would soon be eroded if the crown would extend independent recognition to selected members of that group, 'making some to be viscounts, some to be barons' and encouraging all of them 'to give over their Irish ways and to receive their estates from the queen's majesty and to depend upon the crown'.[4]

The process of anglicising the Gaelic Irish and de-gaelicising the Anglo-Irish would, Sussex realised, be a long one. Yet its mechanism was essentially simple. A spurt of energetic activity on the part of the crown which would demonstrate its seriousness of purpose, its genuine benevolence towards those who would offer obedience and its determination to root out those who would not, would be sufficient to set the process in motion. Momentum would thereafter be self-sustaining. During this same crucially important initial period, Englishmen were to be planted in strategically chosen waste or confiscated lands both as a means of defending the new settlements and of providing the Irish with an example of the benefits that awaited them when their assimilation had been completed. Sussex himself offered to establish and to furnish one of these exemplary colonies. But his interest once again lay in the early phases of the plan, for the colonies, like the arrangements of surrender and regrant, were expected to be self-sufficient once they had been securely established.

The ideas outlined in 1560 were more fully developed in a magisterial treatise in which the lieutenant summarised his seven years' experience of Ireland at the end of 1562.[5] This time the focus of his analysis was narrower. The existence of faction and the means of its dissolution were presumed, and Sussex concentrated instead on a detailed exposition of the actual means by which the assimilation of the Gaelic and gaelicised regions was to be engineered. The government's chief instrument of operation was to be the presidential council. Two regional councils, enjoying approximately the same legal powers and physical strength as those currently in operation in Wales and in the marcher lands of the north of England, were to be established in Munster and Connaught. For the troubled province of Ulster, however, the character of the presidency was to be significantly different.

---

[3] Lambeth MSS, 614/272.
[4] Ibid., fo. 274.
[5] 'The opinion of the earl of Sussex, Lieutenant-General', c. Dec. 1562, Lambeth MSS, 609, a folio volume of forty-three pages, vellum, with several blank sheets; incompletely calendared in *Cal. Carew MSS (1515–74)*, pp. 330–44.

The president was to have a greater entertainment and a greater retinue with a budget five times as large as those allowed to his colleagues in other provinces. His civil and military authority and his powers of discretion were correspondingly larger. Leinster septs and the Gaelic countries surrounding the plantation in Laois and Offaly were to be the responsibility not of a president, but of an English captain whose powers of discretion were even wider than those allowed to the Ulster president and who was to be permitted to accept Gaelic modes of procedure in certain circumstances. Some territories, like O'Reilly's country, were to be excluded from any president's or captain's jurisdiction and were to be answerable to the chief governor alone, a sign of the government's good faith.

The political flexibility which these different approaches implied was further advanced by the concept of interim 'constitutions' which Sussex proposed for the use of his regional officials.[6] These legal codes that were to be applied amongst the Gaelic Irish by the presidents and captains alike, were composed of a blend of English and Gaelic legal procedures. The English mode of trial, sentencing and punishment was to be employed for the most serious offences, but lesser offences – and among these Sussex included the exactions of coyne and livery – were to be determined in accordance with Gaelic custom. Brehons were to be admitted to plead in such cases and were to be allowed fees from the courts for their attendance. The content of English practice within these constitutions was to be increased only gradually. Even in predominantly Anglo-Norman areas Sussex was prepared to be patient. He wished to revive the Kilkenny Statutes and the other laws prohibiting the adoption of Gaelic customs, but he also desired to see them moderated before being put into execution. Penalties for offenders were to be greatly reduced and the presidents were enjoined to use tact in the interpretation of their duties, lest they should unnecessarily estrange the magnates. By way of conclusion, Sussex anticipated the argument that only a pure and severe execution of English law could bring peace to Ireland: such harsh dealing, he replied, would only dispel the great store of good-will toward the crown which he knew already existed and would in any case be both expensive and unsuccessful.

The unoriginality of Sussex's memos on grand strategy is striking. Indeed in their grasp of complexity, their moderation and flexibility, and in their conviction that the process of acclimatising Ireland to English rule would be a gradual one, they seemed little more than a systematic articulation of the views that had guided his predecessor. Yet there is no reason to suppose that they were merely passing concessions to conservatism. For the earl continued to hold his views long after he had left Ireland. In his

---

[6] They begin at fo. 17.

correspondence with Lord Deputy Fitzwilliam in the early 1570s, he frequently counselled the viceroy 'to follow the old course and enter not into any new actions'.[7] If anything, his insistence that the government should establish a close rapport with the leading native powers increased. The Irish nobles, he argued, were neither as orderly nor as obedient as their English counterparts, but they were fundamentally loyal; and Fitzwilliam should not provoke them unnecessarily, lest by ruining them, 'a worser sort of people shall have their way'.[8] On this basis Sussex not only defended his old ally, the earl of Clanrickard, against the allegations of President Fitton, but argued that tolerance be extended to his old enemy, the unruly earl of Desmond. He was even prepared to recommend the once-hated earl of Kildare for high office.[9] In the late 1570s he was the sole member of the privy council to defend the continuing exploitation of coyne and livery by the Irish magnates; and the case he advanced on that occasion was based on the same gradualist and tolerant arguments he had employed in 1560 and 1562.[10]

By the early 1560s, then, Sussex's strategic thinking had already progressed a long way. No longer the overconfident neophyte who had assumed that all of Ireland's ills could be blamed on the corruption and negligence of St Leger's administration, it was Sussex who now articulated the insight which more subtle men like St Leger had simply taken for granted. Like St Leger, Sussex now realised the pervasive influence of factional alliance on Irish political culture, like St Leger also he recognised that it was necessary to dissolve these connections by the sustained application of government patronage, and like St Leger finally he understood that the best way of cutting through the old alignments was through the construction of an alternative political framework based upon a general if gradual acceptance of the procedures of English common law.

Sussex's intellectual progress was doubly impressive. His propositions, the interim constitutions apart, were not particularly original, but they displayed an unexpected ability to respond to specific problems of bewildering complexity. Where St Leger's approach had been informal, expedient and highly personal, and subject to the weaknesses that accompanied such characteristics, Sussex attempted to draft a programme of reform that was both systematic and impersonal which yet seemed to retain the essential flexibility which the government of Ireland demanded. But his unexpectedly acute perceptions are remarkable in a second and less

---

[7] Sussex to Fitzwilliam, 14 Dec. 1571, Bodl., Carte MSS, 57/190–1.
[8] Same to same, 6 Apr. 1572, Bodl., Carte MSS, 57/357–8.
[9] Bodl., Carte MSS, 57/357–8; see also same to same, 24 Aug. 1572, 57/410–11, 8 Jan. 1574, 56/284, 22 May 1574, 56/420.
[10] 'Coyne and livery and other exactions in Ireland', 1 Apr. 1578, BL, Add. MSS, 48015, fos. 291–6.

happy way: they make a sharp contrast with the earl's reputation as lord lieutenant in Ireland. They hardly appear to be the creations of that forceful but unthinking and unsuccessful viceroy who has become known to posterity.[11]

(II)

Sussex's viceroyalty thus heralded no qualitative change in the Tudor understanding of the Irish problem. Yet his appointment in 1556 has nevertheless appeared in retrospect to mark a decisive turning point. Thereafter the crown's intent to secure control over the whole island seems to have acquired a rapidly accelerating momentum leading the Dublin government towards increasing coercion and confrontation. The sources of this impression are in part accidental: in contrast to the spare and intermittent documentation of St Leger's administrations, the evidence of Sussex's Irish service is rich in detail. We know much more about what the lord lieutenant set out to do, when and how he did it, and what results he actually achieved, than we do about any previous viceroy. Sussex's image, then, as a restless, hyper-active governor may in part be an historian's chimera founded upon the accidental survival of sources.

But it is much more than that. We know so much about his activities because Sussex himself was anxious that his superiors and indeed everyone interested in Irish affairs should be fully informed about his achievements. Thus in addition to his normal state correspondence, Sussex commissioned a number of formal accounts of his doings and appointed a personal herald to compose them.[12] These formal narratives which bore a resemblance to the *res gestae* of medieval knights were designed to broadcast the glory of the lieutenant's service, recounting his travails and eulogising his successes in a tone wholly incongruous with their real significance. Sussex himself contributed energetically to the fabrication of his own reputation, composing countless newsletters which greatly exaggerated the significance of the actions reported. The account he sent to King Philip in April 1557 of the planting of Laois–Offaly is a good example.[13] Directed at a reader who was hardly in a position to check the facts, it contrived to give the impression

[11] Good examples of the conventional view of Sussex can be found in R. Bagwell, *Ireland under the Tudors*, 3 vols., London, 1885–90, II, chs. 19–21 and in R. Dunlop's sketch in *DNB*, sub Thomas Radcliffe.

[12] Original accounts of the viceroy's progresses in 1556, 1557, 1558 and 1563 have been collected together in TCD, MS 581; other copies in Lambeth MSS, 621, calendared in *Cal. Carew MSS (1515–74)*, pp. 257–62, 265–9, 274–8, 349–51.

[13] Sussex to Philip and Mary, 4 Apr. 1557, French abstract prepared for King Philip, SP 62/1/28.

that no plantation had ever been established in the area before, and that Sussex had single-handedly carved out the settlement from the chaos inhabited by the O'Mores and the O'Connors.[14] It claimed also that the plantation was now fully secured, an aspiration toward the future that proved no more accurate than Sussex's account of the past. In 1562 the lieutenant drafted a detailed account of his service since his first arrival which reached the satisfying conclusion that 'all the rebellions which I found in Ireland be now subdued, the knots and maintenances broken, the principal persons of the realm brought to acknowledge such obedience as heretofore they have not done, and all the realm remains in quiet'.[15] In 1565 his final state paper on Ireland was yet another long account of his own achievements which, while decrying the efforts of those who succeeded him, reached the same gratifying conclusions.[16]

Such tributes to Sussex's glory, however, were frequently accompanied by a rather more urgent tone in his personal correspondence. Almost anything, it appeared, that the lieutenant wished to attempt was of pivotal importance. The security of everything achieved thus far depended upon it; the surety of all that was yet to be done was guaranteed by it. Through this kind of rhetoric the two queens and their councillors found themselves frequently browbeaten and even blackmailed into giving their assent to the viceroy's latest schemes. Queen Mary was promised that if she would assent to the major outlay of treasure and munitions necessary for the plantation of the north-east coastline, then the whole realm would be quieted by the example of her gracious action, 'her laws would be executed and her commandments obeyed; she shall be feared as a sovereign and her great subjects shall no longer be as princes, but shall gladly follow the laws of their sovereign'. But if the queen could not be brought to act, then Sussex professed to see no course available to him other than to resign rather than see 'Her Majesty's treasure so consumed . . . and myself impoverished in vain'.[17] If the queen would allow Sussex to determine the succession in Thomond as he saw fit, then Sir Donnell O'Brien, 'The only stay of all the rebels in those quarters', would be banished and the rule of the crown would be established throughout the territory; but if she would not, 'Her Majesty's authority will forever be cast out of those quarters.'[18]

---

14 Sussex imposed a similar interpretation on events in the preamble to the act establishing Laois and Offaly as shires, see White, 'Tudor plantations', I, pp. 384–6.
15 'A relation of the earl of Sussex', *c.* Apr. 1562, SP 63/5/101.
16 'Brief memorial of service', SP 63/19/83.
17 'Articles . . . to be explained to the queen', 15 Apr. 1557, SP 62/1/31.
18 Sussex to Sec. Boxoll, 26 Apr. 1558, SP 62/2/37; for other expressions of the same rhetoric during the Marian period, see Fitzwalter to Mary, 2 Jan. 1557, SP 62/1/22. Sussex to Mary, 13 Sept. 1558, SP 62/2/69.

Queen Elizabeth was subjected to other pressures. Ably supported by his
deputy Fitzwilliam and his brother Sir Henry Radcliffe, Sussex mounted a
powerful campaign to persuade the new queen to maintain her predecessor's
commitment of government policy in Ulster, Thomond and the midlands,
and to ignore mounting criticisms of the viceroy in Ireland. Sussex's work,
they urged, was on the point of fulfilment; only the subversive conspiracies
of the Geraldines could forestall it. If Elizabeth would but extend to her
viceroy support sufficient to complete his stated aims, the factional
opposition would be disheartened and dissolve.[19] And once again the threat
of resignation was appended. For if Elizabeth withdrew her confidence,
Sussex could see no other way to rule the country, 'but to give the government thereof to the earl of Kildare; for it is certainly true that an English
governor and an earl of Kildare do so ill agree in this land as during both
their abodes here there can be no increase of revenue or diminution of
charge'.[20] The best examples of Sussex's methods of persuasion are to be
found in frequent attempts to secure Elizabeth's assent to his determination
to destroy Shane O'Neill. On each occasion the argument he advanced was
familiar. The eyes of the whole country were fixed upon Shane's challenge
to the crown's authority. If his impudence was severely chastised, then all
rebellious conspiracies would be scotched; but if Elizabeth flinched from
strong action, the whole realm would be consumed in revolt. Shane's
destruction was, as everything else had been, 'a matter all making or marring.
If Shane settle all be overthrown; if Shane be overthrown all is settled'.[21]

These notes upon the rhetoric of Sussex's viceroyalty may seem superficial; yet they reveal a number of curious contradictions which afflicted the
earl's attitude towards his Irish service. The intimidating tone of urgency
with which he pressed his demands is, for instance, curiously at odds with
the patient flexibility he appeared formally to prescribe in his treatises. Or
again, his practical emphasis upon the efficacy of the unique achievement
is hard to reconcile with the gradual processes which his more detached
analysis seemed to espouse. The discrepancies are more than implicit; they
appear openly in the pages of the viceroy's grand treatises. Each was
prepared and submitted in the context of a campaign currently being waged
for the implementation of some specific, immediate policy, and each was
explicitly premised upon the successful completion of that action. In 1560
all depended upon the removal of the earl of Kildare from Ireland; in 1562

---

[19] Fitzwilliam to Cecil, Mar. and Apr. 1560, SP 63/2/9, 11, 12. Radcliffe to Cecil, 3 May
1561, SP 63/3/63, Sussex's memorials for . . . reform, May 1560, SP 63/2/20–21.
[20] 'The earl of Sussex's opinion', 11 Sept. 1560, Lambeth MSS, 614, fos. 271–80; incompletely calendared in *Cal. Carew MSS (1515–74)*, pp. 300–4.
[21] Sussex to Cecil, 19 Aug. 1561, SP 63/4/37, see also same to same, 8, 14 Aug., 23 Oct., 3
Nov. 1561, 21 Sept. 1562, SP 63/4/31, 35, 62, 66 and 7/16.

everything was to follow upon the destruction of O'Neill. In both cases it was assumed that the government's difficulties arose directly from some elemental cruxes or 'knots' whose dissolution would allow the business of government to flow freely once more. In neither case was this assumption examined. The treatises contained, moreover, yet another paradoxical characteristic: each had a timetable and a detailed costing attached to them. In 1560 the process of establishing obedience to the crown throughout the entire country was expected to take three years, by which time the initial outlay would have already begun to be recouped. In 1562 the timetable was reduced to a mere year and a half, though the estimated outlay had been substantially increased.

Such puzzling contradictions point to a novel element which Sussex, despite his apparently whole-hearted adoption of St Leger's strategy, introduced into the government of Ireland. The problems of Irish governance were, it appeared, capable of being organised in a ranking order. A set of primary problems existed, and no extension of English influence could be achieved until they had first been confronted. But once they had been discovered and resolved, the long impeded progress of anglicisation would take its course smoothly. These primary problems were not necessarily of a single type: different circumstances generated different problems. But they shared one common characteristic. Each constituted, both in practical and in symbolic terms, a test case of the crown's determination to fulfil the long-term aims implicit in the kingship act of 1541. The most pressing task which faced the government in the immediate future, therefore, was to locate these issues within the dense web of the Irish polity, to resolve them and to institute the appropriate arrangements for the great process of assimilation that was expected to follow upon their resolution. This was the task which Sussex reserved for himself. By presenting his selection of primary problems within the context of a systematic programme of reform, and then by getting rid of O'Connor, or of Kildare, or of Macdonnell, or of O'Neill, Sussex could claim to be performing the most crucial service for English government in Ireland. What remained would be epilogue. The administration of the gradual process of anglicisation was a secondary task to be performed by inferior officers in accordance with the overall plan which Sussex had already drafted. His successors would merely be the executors of a general strategy which he had first conceived and had through his own campaigns made possible.

Sussex gave little thought to problems which might arise after his foundations had been laid. He simply assumed that none would be of sufficient import to disturb the inexorable pattern which he had set in motion, and none should be allowed to divert his successors from the plan which he had laid down for them. What the government needed above all, he insisted, was fixity of purpose, 'a resolution of a settled government to be directed to a certain end whereby every governor might keep on course . . . [and] whereby the matter intended might take effect, and not by tossing to and fro be entangled in a labyrinth, losing one year what was holden in another'.[22] For Sussex, the formulation of a programme, its initiation and its rigorous implementation was of such great importance as to overrule the cautious fear that any single plan for the government of Ireland might cease to be relevant or useful. Content was subordinate to form; ultimately the substance of a programme counted for less than the appearance of the programmatic style.

The sources of Sussex's silent strategic innovation are not difficult to discern. They lay partly in the case made by his supporters against St Leger. With apparently little effort on the latter's part, the majority of the Irish lords had remained at peace with the crown for most of his regime; it spoke well of their intentions. Yet St Leger had signally failed to suppress serious disturbances in the north, in the midlands and in Munster in the last years of his service. His failure had discredited the crown in the eyes of many and had endangered the general good-will toward the crown that existed throughout the country. The impression that this degenerating situation was the result of administrative incompetence and negligence was strengthened by the knowledge that St Leger and his associates had despoiled the crown in their own interests. St Leger was simply not doing his duty; he was corrupt. If this was so, then it needed only a little honesty and a little energy to recoup what dishonest stewardship had let go to waste. Once a determination for reform was again made the hallmark of English government, the rest of the work would be easy. Sussex's Irish service took on something of the air of a moral crusade.

Confidence in the accuracy of this analysis was strengthened by its very great desirability. To the newcomer, unknown in Ireland and unwilling to stay overlong, the two-tiered approach to the government's problems had undoubted practical advantages. It provided Sussex with a simple schedule of duty which enabled him to cut clean through the complicated skein of Irish political life. It offered ample opportunity for his ambition: to him would belong the honour of laying the foundations of a new commonwealth in Ireland through strategic skill and daring military endeavour. He might, moreover, achieve all this relatively quickly and go on to greater and more glorious exploits elsewhere. After all, Sussex was not, as he frequently observed, made for Ireland.

---

[22] 'The earl of Sussex's opinion', 11 Sept. 1560, Lambeth MSS, 614, fos. 371–80, fo. 280; the labyrinthine metaphor was commonly adopted by Sussex, see Sussex to Cecil, 3 Nov. 1561, SP 63/4/66 and same to same, 4 Dec. 1562, 63/7/53.

The programmatic approach brought with it one further advantage: it greatly simplified the governor's administrative problems. Since the targets he set himself were clearly defined, discrete and essentially military, Sussex had no need to concern himself with the long-term problems of establishing an effective power-base in Ireland which had so exercised St Leger. Because his problems were preselected and limited, he had no cause to seek further counsel from others and no desire to divert himself by listening to additional problems or grievances. He needed neither an influential native advisory group nor a broad basis of support amongst the population in order to lend authority to his policies. He required simply a tightly organised executive group who understood his plans and shared his fortunes to give effect to his will. In the long term an administration so impervious to outside influence ran the risk of alienating the loyal community. But its operation in Ireland was designed to be short lived, and any estrangements could expectedly be made good in the period of patient assimilation that was to succeed it. Thus the urgency of Sussex's rhetoric and the premature trumpetings of his achievements were not simply gratuitous; they were the stylistic symptoms of an apparently temporary, but drastically novel approach to Irish government.

(III)

One clear sign of a change in the disposition of the government in the years after 1556 was a virtual disappearance of political thinking as such. With the exception of Sussex himself few attempted to gain the attention of the crown by a political treatise. Some of the old policy-makers were, like Sir Thomas Cusacke, silenced for political reasons; but many more found themselves out of favour for no reason other than that they were theorists. Edward Walshe who had been highly critical of St Leger and had looked hopefully to Sussex was disagreeably surprised by the earl's attitude. His ideas were ignored and he himself excluded from favour: even a complaint to Cecil early in the reign of Elizabeth failed to improve his standing.[23] Walshe's experience was shared by a far more eminent figure, John Alen, who after a brief rehabilitation in 1556 was also excluded and died before a similar suit to Cecil could bear any fruit.[24] Rowland White, another framer of political propositions whose view on the settlement of the north-east coast corresponded closely to Sussex's also

---

[23] Edward Walshe to Cecil, 23 Aug. 1559, SP 63/1/71; for Walshe's criticism of St Leger, see his 'A detection of errors', BL, Cotton MSS, Titus B XII, no. 48.
[24] Alen to Cecil, 16 Dec. 1558, SP 63/1/7.

found himself out of sympathy with the viceroy and soon joined the ranks of his critics.[25]

Advice acceptable to Sussex was of a different character. The counsel tendered by Alen during his brief hey-day was strictly practical. It concerned the means by which the midlands plantation could be constructed and supplied, how the Pale was to be defended from attack, how the soldiers were to be billeted and how the viceroy's household was to be victualled.[26] The advice provided by Alen's brother Thomas at the same time was of an equally practical nature.[27] James Barnewall the attorney general also confined himself to matters of logistical detail.[28] Building materials, transport facilities, barrels, beeves and pipe-staves were his stock in trade. Only once, in preparation for the 1559 parliament, did he presume to discuss more general issues, and then his advice was not heeded. The decline in strategic thinking was a direct consequence of Sussex's methods of operation. Whether it was contained in the crude sketches of 1556 or in the sophisticated formulations of 1562, the programme which the earl intended to enact in Ireland was prearranged and unalterable. All further discussion on the matter was redundant, and only immediately relevant advice designed to facilitate the aims of the given plan was acceptable.

This severe pruning of his advisory group was but one aspect of Sussex's desire to construct a clear and disciplined chain of command. His appointment was the occasion of a major alteration in personnel at all levels of the Irish administration. Displacement was greatest, naturally, in the highest levels of government. St Leger's dismissal was accompanied by that of Cusacke from the lord chancellorship and of the discredited Sir Edmund Rouse from the treasury.[29] A new master of ordnance Jacques Wingfield, joined the recently appointed marshal, George Stanley, at the head of the military establishment.[30] And on the council only four of Sussex's regular attenders had served under St Leger.[31] Real power on the council, and on the

---

[25] For an early treatise by White, critical of Sussex's government, see 'Book of the waste and decay of the English Pale', SP 62/2/77. My attribution to White of these unsigned notes is based upon the recurrence of identical passages in White's later books, see SP 63/1/72–3.

[26] Alen's 'Advices', c. Sept. 1556, BL, Lansd. MSS, 159, nos. 3–46.

[27] Ibid., nos. 16, 20, 21.

[28] Ibid., nos. 23, 24, the attribution to James Barnewall is tentative. The writer was clearly experienced in matters of law and routine government administration. He makes frequent mention of the special suits of one Patrick Barnewall. James Barnewall was appointed attorney-general on Sussex's recommendation around the time the papers were drafted. Patrick Barnewall was a first cousin.

[29] *Lib. Mun.*, I, pt. 3, p. 43. Rouse had delegated the office to deputies since March 1554.

[30] *Cal. pat. rolls Henry VIII–Eliz.*, p. 389; Mary to Sussex, 13 July 1558, SP 62/2/60. A new clerk of ordnance also made his appearance in Ireland at this time, HMC, *De Lisle and Dudley MSS*, I, p. 364.

[31] Attendances recorded in Irish council book, HMC, *Haliday MSS*.

commissions which it authorised, was concentrated in the hands of a select few who were either relations of the earl on closely associated with him: his brother, Henry, his two brothers-in-law Sidney and Fitzwilliam, Marshall Stanley and Archbishop Curwen.

Changes of lesser import were registered at lower levels of the civil administration. John Goldsmith, St Leger's clerk of council was replaced by Ralph Coccerell.[32] In chancery a personal servant of Fitzwilliam's, Lancelot Alford, became clerk of the hanaper.[33] On king's bench Gerald Aylmer was removed for senility and replaced by John Plunket;[34] on common pleas, St Leger's chief justice was dismissed and replaced by a protégé of Sussex's, Robert Dillon.[35] In 1559 Barnaby Scurlocke was dismissed as attorney-general for insubordination and his place given to that useful counsellor, James Barnewall.[36] Numerous changes took place in the exchequer where almost all of the major offices changed hands.[37] Most importantly, Auditor Jenyson who had been implicated in the scandal of 1556 was dismissed and replaced by a client of Sussex's, Gabriel Croft.[38]

The same pattern occurred in the ranks of the military establishment. In addition to the appointment of new senior executive officers there were further changes in high command. The earl of Kildare was removed from authority in Laois–Offaly and Sir Henry Radcliffe appointed as lieutenant of the forts there in his stead.[39] Lord Howth was replaced as defender of the borders of the Pale by Marshal Stanley.[40] Edward Larkin, appointed to Carrickfergus by St Leger, surrendered his position to William Piers.[41] The fort at Stradbally was newly occupied by William Portas,[42] Henry Sidney took up residence at Brabazon's castle at Athlone and Henry Stafford replaced James Walshe as constable of Dungarvan.[43] Lower down replacement was even greater. Though the number of captains entertained by the

---

[32] 'Accounts of Sir Henry Sidney, 1556–9', HMC, *De Lisle and Dudley MSS*, I, p. 371; *Lib. mun.*, I, pt. 1, p. 83.

[33] *Lib. mun.*, I, pt. 2, p. 24.

[34] Ibid., p. 30; Ball, *The judges in Ireland*, I, p. 196.

[35] *Lib. mun.*, I, pt. 2, p. 35; Ball, *The judges in Ireland*, I, p. 206.

[36] Sussex's 'Instructions', 16 July 1559, SP 63/1/60; Fitzwilliam to Sussex, 15 Mar. 1554, BL, Cotton MSS, Titus B XIII, no. 3.

[37] *Fiants, Eliz.*, nos. 108, 111, 112; 'Accounts of Sir Henry Sidney 1556–9', HMC, *De Lisle and Dudley MSS*, I, p. 387; *Cal. pat. rolls Henry VIII–Eliz.*, p. 418.

[38] Sussex's 'Instructions', 28 Apr. 1556, Lambeth MSS, 628/63–73. Croft was auditor in 1560, Croft to Cecil, 21 Nov. 1564, SP 63/11/104.

[39] *Fiants Eliz.*, no. 288; 'Account of Sir Henry Sidney, 1556–9', HMC, *De Lisle and Dudley MSS*, I, p. 366.

[40] HMC, *De Lisle and Dudley MSS*, I, p. 366; Irish council book, HMC, *Haliday MSS*, p. 281.

[41] 'Account of Sir Henry Sidney', *De Lisle and Dudley MSS*, I, p. 366; *Lib. mun.*, I, pt. 2, p. 119.

[42] 'Account of Sir Henry Sidney', HMC, *De Lisle and Dudley MSS*, I, p. 366.

[43] Ibid., p. 370, *Lib. mun.*, I, pt. 2, p. 123.

crown increased greatly under Sussex, the proportion of experienced officers dropped significantly: only nine of a total of twenty-eight captains known to have served under St Leger continued under Sussex.[44]

It would be wrong however to assume that Sussex was engaged on a systematic purge of Anglo-Irish or older English elements in the Dublin government. The Palesmen suffered most from the shuffling of positions but they were by no means excluded from places of influence. Several like the new justices Plunket and Dillon, James Barnewall, James Dowdall and John Travers remained trusted executives of the viceroy and outside the exchequer the majority of clerical offices were retained by Palesmen without dislocation.[45] Nor was a consistent effort made to exclude St Leger's old adherents. Army captains like Nicholas Heron, Francis Cosby, and Henry Colley retained their commissions; and in the civil administration, respected figures like the remembrancer, Henry Draycot and the surveyor, Michael Fitzwilliam continued to enjoy the governor's confidence.[46] Sussex even offered to extend good-will towards John Parker, but his overture was soon rebuffed.[47]

These administrative changes were made therefore for neither ethnic nor ideological considerations: rather then were made to emphasise that retention of office depended upon the personal loyalty of each servitor to the viceroy. By dismissing unfriendly or insubordinate officers, by placing his own favourites in senior positions, and by ostentatiously renewing the patents who already held office under good behaviour, Sussex made it clear that it was through personal allegiance to him and through the obedient execution of his directives that a successful career in the Irish administration was to be pursued.[48] There was some managerial efficiency in all this: it made for a smooth flow of policy from the level of decision-making to that of executive action. Yet it constituted also a considerable withdrawal from the broader techniques of political manipulation which Grey, and most successfully, St Leger, had employed to link their governments with political interests in the country at large. In general terms therefore Sussex's managerial methods threatened to make his administration dangerously insensitive to the needs of the community in which it operated. Even before it began to implement any of its policies Sussex's government was in

---

[44] Estimated from a comparison of St Leger's and Sussex's early army lists, BL, Add. MSS, 4767, fos. 80–1; HMC, De Lisle and Dudley MSS, I, p. 387.
[45] For several commissions of a military and civilian nature on which they served, see Fiants Eliz., passim.
[46] 'Irish council book', HMC, Haliday MSS, p. 18; Fiants Eliz., no. 224; Cal. pat. rolls Henry VIII–Eliz., pp. 390, 438; Sussex to Sec. Boxoll, 10 June 1558, PRO, SP 62/2/51/
[47] 'Journey of the earl of Sussex', 30 Oct. 1557, TCD, MSS. 581; Ball, The judges in Ireland, I, pp. 205–6.
[48] See, for instance, regrants in Cal. pat. rolls (Ire.) Henry VIII–Eliz., p. 343.

danger of alienating much good-will by its organisational structure alone. The risk was made even more serious by the fact that several of these policies entailed the imposition of a number of onerous demands upon the very community which the administration was now less able than ever to accommodate.

(IV)

Whatever promises he held out for a balanced Irish budget in the near future, Sussex's plans always entailed a substantial immediate increase in government expenditure. The settlement of Laois–Offaly, the expulsion of the Scots, the reduction of Shane O'Neill all involved a considerable enlargement of the garrison and a corresponding increase in the money, munitions and victuals necessary to maintain it. At the beginning of 1556 St Leger had attempted to make do with 500 men, but immediately on his arrival Sussex doubled the garrison. By the middle of 1557 there were 1,500 men on active service in Ireland, and by the middle of 1558 the number had risen to 2,500.[49] In 1559 the garrison was reduced to 1,000, but the campaigns against O'Neill necessitated further increases.[50] Between 1560 and 1563 an average of 2,000 men were in pay each year in Ireland.[51]

The cost of maintaining this enlarged garrison was immense. Between 1556 and 1558 it amounted to almost £73,000.[52] The wage bill in the year ending December 1563 amounted to over £23,400.[53] The total cost of Sussex's administration between 1556 and 1565 amounted to over £322,000, almost half of which was accounted for in the first three years.[54] Throughout this period, however, revenue yields failed to attain the levels which Sussex had anticipated. In 1560 he estimated that revenues would net over £12,000 pa; and in 1562 he was confident that they would soon yield some £18,000.[55] But the total domestic receipts for the years between 1556 and 1565 inclusive amounted to no more than £43,000, an annual average of less than £4,500.[56] Sussex was therefore forced to rely heavily on subvention from England to meet his ordinary running costs. The crown's contribution was generous. During the same ten-year period some £272,000 (st.) of royal treasure was transported to Ireland to support the viceroy's

[49] 'Numbers retained in garrison', BL, Add. MSS, 4767, fos. 196–8.
[50] Ibid., *Fitzwilliam accounts*, ed. A. K. Longfield (IMC, 1960), pp. 40–4.
[51] *Fitzwilliam accounts*, pp. 48–54, 59–70.
[52] 'Account of Sir Henry Sidney, 1556–9', HMC, *De Lisle and Dudley MSS*, I, pp. 364–71.
[53] *Fitzwilliam accounts*, pp. 54–70.
[54] 'A brief note of the Queen Majesty's charges . . . April 1555–Oct. 1565', Lambeth MSS, 628/108; 'Book of receipts, 1555–81', SP 65/10.
[55] Lambeth MSS, 614/279; 609/22.
[56] 'Book of receipts', PRO, SP 65/10 gives a total of £32,460 (st.).

needs.[57] But in spite of the crown's ultimate acceptance of financial responsibility, actual instalments of treasure were irregular and inadequate. Sussex's apparently large receipt was thus spread out in a series of piecemeal and sometimes useless payments. It came in thirty-six instalments half of which were under £200 each, only eleven amounted to £1,000 or more. Only five were in excess of £5,000.[58]

In practical terms, therefore, Sussex's government was always in arrears to its own servitors and to the country. Between March 1560 and September 1562, for instance, the viceroy owed more than £20,700 to his own soldiers; and at the close of his government in May 1565 he was (despite recent large issues of treasure) still £32,200 in their debt.[59] In the absence of regular and adequate subvention from London, Sussex was obliged to find short-term ways of easing his predicament. One possible alternative was wholly orthodox, and indeed had been a declared objective of his first Irish programme. This was the thorough reform of the corrupt Irish financial administration. In 1556 Sussex had come with a separate set of instructions concerned entirely with the reform of the Irish exchequer.[60] Further commissions were issued in 1559 and in 1560, but their reports, which echoed the findings of the Browne-Rouse inquiry, merely revealed how little progress had been made under Sussex.[61] In 1560 the commissioner Gilbert Gerrard introduced the order book of the English exchequer into the Irish court and directed the Irish officers to comply with its procedures.[62] But any benefit it may have brought was not registered in the official figures; for annual revenues showed no increase and arrears continued to mount. In 1563 Auditor Croft estimated that the crown was owed some £30,000 – or more than six times the annual receipt – by its lessees.[63]

For this failure to carry out the reformist pledges of 1556 Sussex must take chief responsibility. The governor and his two treasurers were far too busy with the military priorities of his programme to bother over-much with tedious administrative reforms. They continued the old practice of delegating their charge to unpatented deputies, and the abuses that went with the habit continued. There was in any case nothing particularly glorious about the dogged pursuit of financial retrenchment, and the results of any improvements could be expected to appear only long after Sussex and

57 Lambeth MSS, 628/108.
58 Calculated from 'Certificate of money issued out of the exchequer to Sir William Fitzwilliam', SP 63/16/66.
59 Fitzwilliam accounts, pp. 48–58, 81–90.
60 Sussex's 'Instructions', 28 Apr. 1556, Lambeth MSS, 628/63–73.
61 BL, Add. MSS, 4767, fos. 84–6, 106–7, 127.
62 Sussex's 'Instructions', 16 July 1559, SP 63/1/60.
63 'Book of arrearages of the queen's revenues to Michaelmas 1563', SP 63/11/71.

his group had left Ireland. For these reasons, Sussex, having made some show of concern in the early months of his service, relegated administrative reform to the category of second-order problems to be coped with by his successors. Instead he turned toward more direct and less troublesome means of meeting his current financial requirements.

One expedient which he employed was not of his own devising at all. Debasement of the currency, as we have seen, wreaked havoc with the finances of the government and the economy of the Pale under Crofts and St Leger. In response to the latters' complaints, Northumberland and Mary seem to have intended genuinely to call a halt to the practice. But under Sussex it accelerated once again. Between March 1556 and April 1558 a total of £85,000 of 3 oz coins were shipped to Ireland: it was an unprecedented achievement. Worse, even while she disgorged base coins in vast quantities into Ireland, Mary was careful to bring Northumberland's plans for revaluation to fulfilment in England. As a result the exchange rate between the two kingdoms deteriorated drastically: in the last months of her reign it reached an unprecedented ratio of two to one.[64]

By then Sussex had become alarmed at the worsening state of the Irish currency and its effects upon the Pale. In the early months of Elizabeth he appealed to the new government to undertake a massive recoinage of the Irish currency, and was greatly disappointed with the half-hearted efforts which the crown eventually decided upon.[65] But it was only when it became clear that his own presence in Ireland would be longer than he had originally supposed that Sussex became particularly agitated about the problem. Before then the base moneys had been shipped to Ireland directly in response to Sussex's demands. Unlike Crofts, who had been especially sensitive to the long-term economic consequences of the policy, Sussex accepted the debased currency without demur. Its side effects were again a secondary problem to be met after the foundation of the great reform as outlined in his own programme.

Sussex's disregard for the needs of the local community in matters which concerned his own primary objectives is even more clearly evident in the steps he took for the victualling and the billeting of his troops. Some obligation to subsidise the governor's retinue had been conventionally acknowledged by the country. But the nature and extent of this obligation remained uncertain. It was generally accepted that the viceroy had

---

[64] Challis, 'Tudor coinage for Ireland', pp. 97–119. F. C. Dietz, *English government finance, 1485–1558* (2 vols., Urbana, IL, 1920; 2nd edn, London, 1964), ch. 16. Articles submitted to privy council, May 1558, SP 62/2/44, lord justice and council to Sussex, 7 Apr. 1558, SP 62/2/32 (i).

[65] Conyers Read, 'Profits on the re-coinage of 1560–1', *EHR* (1936), pp. 186–93; Sussex to Cecil, 24 Oct. 1560, SP 63/2/39; Challis, 'Tudor coinage for Ireland', pp. 114–15.

some share in the prerogative right of purveyance, and sheer military necessity was sometimes allowed to be sufficient reason for the governor to make extraordinary demands on the community. But equally, the governor had been expected to take up provisions at normal market prices when occasion permitted or to make good any losses sustained by the country through compulsory purchase. So his rights in the matter of supply remained vague. Significantly, the governor and the countrymen chose not to employ the explicit term 'purveyance' but had resorted to a much more general and ill-defined word 'cess'.[66] Most English governors seemed to have exploited some part of the cess during their sojourn; but since their use of the power was occasional and moderate, the issue remained politically insignificant.

For Sussex, however, whose presence in Ireland was uniquely expeditionary, the exploitation of cess was not simply to be an occasional expedient, it was an integral part of his administrative method. He was, from the outset, fully aware of the great advantages which the taking up of victuals for his army at purveyance prices offered him. Sir John Alen, for one, had drawn his attention to it and had provided him with detailed instructions as to how it might best be exploited. Cess early, was Alen's advice, 'that men knowing their charges may have it in readiness . . . and rather cess too much than too little and perhaps then an augmentation can be made'.[67] Sussex took the advice. Barely a fortnight after his arrival he proclaimed a cess for the supply of the midlands forts. Four months later, he cessed again, this time on a grand scale. In the following March he ordered more victuals to be taken up for the forts, and in October he proclaimed yet another general cess upon the whole of the Pale. This was the pattern which Sussex was to follow throughout his stay in Ireland. Between 1556 and 1563 he commandeered over 41,500 pecks of grain from the country in this fashion.[68] These general cesses, for which figures alone survive, were, moreover, only the most obvious and least onerous portion of the total supply burden which Sussex's expanded garrisons placed upon the country. The obligation to board and lodge the soldiers, their dependants and their animals was a good deal more continuous and more oppressive.

The total long-term cost of the cess in all its ramifications is extremely difficult to estimate, and the response of the Palesmen to the maintenance of

---

[66] On purveyance generally, see A. Woodworth, 'Purveyance for the royal household under Queen Elizabeth', *Trans. Am. Phil. Soc.*, new ser. 35 (1945), pp. 1–86; S. G. Ellis, 'Taxation and defence in late medieval Ireland', *Jn. RSAI* 107 (1977), pp. 5–28; the issue is discussed in more detail in ch. 6 below.

[67] Alen's 'Advice', c. Apr. 1556, BL, Lansdowne MSS, 159, no. 3; Sussex's 'Instructions', Apr. 1556, BL, Cotton MSS, Titus B XI, no. 241.

[68] Calculated from John Chaloner's collection of data from the council books relating to cess, NAI, MS 2753; a similar but not identical collection is in BL, Add. MSS, 4763, fos. 106 ff.

soldiers whose presence in the country was for purposes other than their defence is a question yet more involved. Both problems will be considered in a later chapter.[69] In the long term, cess helped alter fundamentally the attitude of the Palesmen towards English government in Ireland. In the short term however, the ubiquitous presence of Sussex's soldiers, and their manifold oppressions, provided the clearest indication to the Palesmen that an ominous change had occurred in the disposition of the government in the years after 1556. The cess became the symbol of Sussex's single-minded and exclusive administrative style; it became the focus of protest for all who opposed it.

(v)

The first signs of resentment within the Pale did not take long to emerge. One of Sussex's earliest proclamations on the cess acknowledged that tension and acrimony had already arisen between the soldiery and 'the people [who] in many places rather flee the towns when they see them coming, than minister any reasonable aid to them'.[70] There was trouble, apparently, in the parliament of 1557, where one lawyer was arrested and imprisoned for denying the viceroy's prerogative powers,[71] and Attorney-General Scurlocke's dismissal seems to have been due to the support he gave to a protest against the cess.[72] There were protests of a more violent nature also: 'the people be weary and irk of us', wrote Sidney in February 1557, and he adduced instances of soldiers who had already been killed in affrays with the citizenry.[73]

Sussex's response to the rising tension was minimal. He issued a proclamation urging calmness, and during a time of poor harvest he imposed export control upon grain.[74] But he took no direct steps to ease the burdens of the countrymen, and his refusal to act provoked a spate of protests to the crown against the viceroy's government in general. The strategic thinkers, Edward Walshe and Rowland White, made their feelings known; 'the soldiers', Walsh complained bitterly, 'have done more harm to the country than ever the Irish did.'[75] Far more weighty protests, however,

---

[69] Ch. 6 below.
[70] Proclamation of 27 Mar. 1557, HMC, *Haliday MSS*, p. 33.
[71] Mary to Sussex, 13 May 1557, BL, Cotton MSS, Titus B XI, no. 243.
[72] Sussex's 'Instructions', 16 July 1559, SP 63/1/60; Fitzwilliam to Sussex, 15 Mar. 1560, BL, Cotton MSS, Titus B XIII, no. 3.
[73] Sidney to Privy council, 8 Feb. 1558, SP 62/2/10, and to Sussex, 7 Apr., SP 62/2/32, enclosure (i).
[74] 'Irish council book', HMC, *Haliday MSS*, p. 6.
[75] Walsh to Cecil, 23 Aug. 1559, SP 53/1/71; White's 'Book of decay of . . . Pale', *c.* 1558, SP 62/2/77.

came from the most powerful members of the Anglo-Norman community. At the end of Queen Mary's reign both the earl of Desmond and Archbishop Dowdall of Armagh submitted formal complaints to the privy council about Sussex's conduct in government.[76] The substance of their grievances was similar. Both expatiated upon the extent of the oppression which the soldiers visited upon the country and the willing complicity of the viceroy in their actions. Dowdall, who had witnessed the sack of his cathedral city by Sussex's soldiers was particularly enraged. 'The realm', he declared, 'was never in my remembrance in worse case than it is now'. Prices were never so high; goods were never so scarce. The country was so bereft of its own food supplies as to be on the brink of famine. Already, Dowdall testified, people had died of starvation.[77]

Both Dowdall and Desmond, however, pressed their case further. Sussex's army was not only oppressive, it had failed also in its principal duty to protect the loyal subjects of the crown from attacks by the Irish rebels. Far from reducing the number of incursions suffered upon the Pale, Sussex's government had actually escalated the level of violence. Both the official policy of the viceroy and the unofficial freebooting of the soldiers had provoked a number of Gaelic septs who had hitherto remained at peace. And they had exacted their revenge upon the Pale. The borders of the Pale had been wasted in parts by their ravages. The loyal community, Dowdall declared, had never been so besieged since the time of the Kildare rebellion. This universal waste and oppression was all that the queen's great outlay of treasure had procured. 'It sorely grieves all the queen's friends', the archbishop concluded, 'to see what her government doth spend daily on Ireland, and it every year rather worse than better – though you be otherwise informed.'[78]

On the basis of this general criticism of Sussex's administration Dowdall and Desmond proferred an alternative policy of their own. What they recommended, in effect, was a return to the old gradualist methods of St Leger. The idea that permanent gains could be achieved by sudden and forceful action, Desmond argued, was false and unproductive. It simply put the Gaelic Irish on their guard and made any progress towards anglicisation impossible. It was necessary rather to delegate responsibility for this policy into the hands of local powers whom the clansmen already respected and who would be capable of exerting a continuous supervision over them. He recommended that the earls be appointed presidents in the regions in which

---

[76] Desmond to Mary, 23 Feb. 1558, SP 62/2/11, and 'Declarations of . . . Desmond's chaplin', 62/2/12; Dowdall to Archbishop Heath, 17 Nov. 1557, SP 62/1/61; 'The effect of a book exhibited by the archbishop of Armagh', May 1558, SP 62/2/45.
[77] 'Effect of a book', May 1558, SP 62/2/45.
[78] Dowdall to Heath, 17 Nov. 1557, SP 62/1/61.

they were already powerful influences and the lesser lords in the area be appointed to the presidential councils. In all major matters of policy, of course, the presidents would remain at the bidding of the viceroy.[79] Dowdall professed to be personally sympathetic to Sussex's attempt to put an end to Ireland's rebelliousness by military action. But as a policy he believed it was simply unrealistic. It was too expensive and it provoked unnecessary trouble. Considering 'the nature of that country and the rudeness and frowardness of that barbarous people', it was wisest to proceed only with the utmost caution and patience, 'for who so ever would take the rule of Ireland in hand, he must according to the gospel forgive until seventy times seven'. His case was nothing more than the conventional wisdom which had underpinned the original policy of surrender and regrant, and it is not surprising that Dowdall suggested that St Leger be recalled to court to consider his argument.[80]

Of the two submissions, that of the venerable archbishop made the greater impression. Dowdall was summoned to court to substantiate his claims, and Sussex was sufficiently alarmed to return to defend himself in person. The archbishop's case, he claimed, was shortsighted and sectionally interested. It concentrated only on immediate difficulties and ignored the great work currently in progress in Ireland. It was blind to the higher interests of the crown and unwittingly served the interests of those who would subvert the state. This was a reasonable case for the viceroy to make. But it was immeasurably strengthened by entirely fortuitous events: within months of each other Dowdall, Desmond and Queen Mary died. By a quirk of fate the respectable foundations of the Anglo-Irish protest had been undermined in a trice.[81]

Yet, despite the collapse of opposition, Sussex, with the support of his subordinates in Ireland, continued to press his case upon the new Elizabethan government. His work in Ireland, he affirmed, was at every turn subverted by a small group of conspirators whose end it was to have all power in Ireland for themselves. They would not rest until Sussex's government had been destroyed, and he in turn would not resume office in Ireland until he had authority to crush them. At the core of this conspiracy were the Geraldines and at its head the earl of Kildare. It was Kildare, Sussex claimed, who was behind all attempts to thwart his efforts in Ireland, and his motives were patent: for the earl had declared himself ready to

---

[79] 'Declaration of . . . Desmond's chaplain', SP 62/2/12.
[80] 'Archbishop of Armagh's opinion touching Ireland', July 1558, BL, Harl. MSS, 35, no. 4.
[81] Dowdall died on 15 Aug. 1558, Desmond on 14 Oct., *DNB* sv Dowdall; GEC, *Complete Peerage*, IV, p. 252.

banish all the English from the island by force and to have himself crowned king of Ireland.[82]

Kildare had good reason to be unhappy with Sussex's government. It had entailed his exclusion from high political favour, and Sussex, the earl was well aware, had been responsible for forestalling his suit to regain certain lands and rights omitted from the grant restoring his patrimony.[83] The idea that Kildare should be made governor in Ireland remained, moreover, a popular one amongst the Anglo-Irish.[84] Kildare, however, showed no overt antagonism to Sussex in the years after 1556. He took no part in the formal presentation of complaints against the governor, and he accepted the crown's ruling on his suits without complaint. It would be naive to assume that the earl was cowed simply because no direct evidence has survived to the contrary. He almost certainly used his wide influence within the Pale to foment opposition to the viceroy's proceedings. But whatever resentment he may have harboured, it is highly unlikely that it went as deep as Sussex and Fitzwilliam alleged. Neither then nor later did it appear that Kildare entertained ambitions for the governorship; indeed his later compliance under Sidney seemed to indicate quite the contrary. Sussex's hard evidence for the conspiracy consisted, in fact, of the dubious testimony of an English soldier whose Irish wife claimed that her brother heard talk to the effect amongst the retainers of the earl of Desmond, and the third-hand bragging of a Scottish mercenary.[85] Still, the fact that Sussex should have deemed it useful to create such a storm over the rumours is in itself significant.

His allegations might partially be explained as a form of paranoia; a symptom of the degree to which his administration had become detached from local realities. But the consistency with which he promoted the rumours suggests that Sussex's motives were more deliberate. The espousal of a conspiracy theory simplified matters greatly. It conveniently fused opposition to Sussex's administration with opposition to the government's general aims, and thus implied that there was no difference between the aims which Sussex set himself and the means by which he set about achieving them. This fusion of aims and means also helped establish a clear-cut and

[82] Sidney to Sussex, 26 Feb. 1558 enclosing W. Piers to Sidney, 15 Feb., SP 62/2/14, enclosure (i); Sussex to Cecil, 25 Mar. 1558, SP 63/1/25; Fitzwilliam to Cecil, 11, 20 Apr. 1560, SP 63/2/111–12; Sussex, 'Memorial', May 1560, SP 63/2/20.

[83] Petitions of Kildare and answers thereto', *c.* July 1557, BL, Cotton MSS, Titus B XII, no. 32; Kildare's requests, July 1558, BL, Cotton MSS, Titus B XI, no. 254. Sussex to Boxoll, 4 July 1557, SP 62/1/48.

[84] 'Treatise on the disorders of the Pale', *c.* 1556, Hatfield House, Cecil MSS, CP 201/116–23; 'Device for the better government of Ireland', *c.* 1553, SP 61/4/82.

[85] Fitzwilliam to Sussex and to Cecil, 15 Mar. 1559, BL, Cotton MSS, Titus B XIII, no. 7, SP 63/2/9; Piers to Sidney, 15 Feb. 1558, SP 62/2/14, enclosure (i).

rather invidious set of alternatives: if the queen would not accept Sussex and his methods, then she must settle for the government of Kildare with all the evil that it implied.[86] The men and the methods were inseparable. And as Sussex made clear in his memorandum of 1560, Kildare and himself would never co-exist happily in Ireland. Finally, the transformation of general discontent with his administration into one grand conspiracy paid a subtle compliment to the viceroy, for only a programme of the most decisive character could engender such a response. The existence of a conspiracy acted as a confirmation of the significance of Sussex's work. Thus, far from persuading the crown to caution, opposition in Ireland should have the effect of increasing its determination to execute its own or – more correctly – Sussex's declared aims. It was with this persuasive psychological appeal that Sussex won the support of the cautious Elizabethan councillors to his aggressive administrative methods. In the autumn of 1560, he returned to Ireland as lord lieutenant, his enemies worsted and his own plans for action endorsed, enjoying as much support under Elizabeth as ever Queen Mary had shown him.[87]

A satisfactory result indeed; but in reality Sussex's tactics were futile. For heeded or not, resentment in Ireland continued to rise and to spread, until it grew to resemble one of those primary problems which needed immediate treatment before anything else could be done. Yet it was precisely the kind of problem with which Sussex's finely honed administrative machine was unable to deal. The lieutenant could stifle Anglo-Irish criticism abroad, but he could not suppress rising resistance at home. This was a cost which Sussex seemed willing to bear. Should he succeed as planned in the execution of his designated tasks, then his stay in Ireland would be short and the bitterness he provoked would be swallowed up by the glorious memory of his grand achievements. It was unfortunate, therefore, for Sussex that the same chronic intractability mainfested itself in the very issues which he had taken it upon himself to solve.

Yet it was almost inevitable that it should have been so. For the more accurate his initial selection – the more, that is, the issues he chose were indeed the primary ones he supposed them to be – the more they reflected the complex interlocking nature of the Irish polity, and the less they lent themselves to Sussex's simple individuating administrative techniques. The steady spread of general resentment and the growing intractability of specific problems, thus, closely paralleled each other, each bearing testimony that the lieutenant's understanding of how to operate in Ireland

[86] Memorandum by Sussex, May 1560, SP, 63/2/20–21; Sussex, 'Opinion', Sept. 1560, Lambeth MSS, 614/271–80.
[87] Elizabeth to Sussex, 15, 21 Aug. 1560, SP 63/2/30–1.

was simply wrong. But Sussex's response to these ominous warnings was entirely negative. Encouraged by the short-term tactical success of his embattled self-justifications, he continued to insist that the solution to each selected problem was singular and that only malice and subversion made it appear otherwise. But the more he urged his simple, energetic solutions, the less relevant they became to the real issues at stake. Increasingly, Sussex became embroiled in a series of pointless attempts to enforce his will by military action which obscured and ultimately obliterated his original intent to find genuine solutions for real problems. This was to be his experience with every major problem he tackled in Ireland from 1556 on.

(VI)

In 1556 the most promising and the most outstanding of the problems which Sussex set himself to solve, was the re-establishment of a plantation in Laois–Offaly. Reconstruction of the midlands plantation was crucial in a number of ways. The crown had already committed itself to establishing an English colony in the midlands, and its plans had been upset only by the continuous rebellion of the O'Mores and the O'Connors.[88] The resettlement was, therefore, a test case of the government's determination to enforce its declared aims. In more practical terms, the failure of the earlier effort at plantation had incurred a substantial loss of investment, and the rebellion which ensued continued to inflict mounting losses upon both the crown and the community of the Pale. For considerations of finance and local defence, then, as well as for reasons of grand strategy, the implementation of the government's earlier commitment in the midlands was imperative. It was one of these primary problems whose practical and symbolic significance were of equal import.

Sussex's plan for Laois–Offaly, however, envisaged no bloody conquest. His 'Instructions' of 1556, and the 'orders for the consignation' of the two countries drawn up around the same time, made it clear that his central aim was the speedy construction of an integrated and self-sufficient community.[89] Despite their outlawed status, the Gaelic clans were assigned to a relatively generous portion of the territory to be planted. Allotments were to be made to the head of each extended family group who was to

---

[88] R. Dunlop, 'The Plantations of Leix and Offaly, 1556–1622', *EHR* 6 (1891), pp. 61–96: D. G. White, 'Tudor plantations in Ireland to 1571', unpub. Ph.D. (University of Dublin, 1967), chs. 5–6.

[89] Sussex, 'Instructions', May 1556, BL, Cotton MSS, Titus B XI, no. 241; 'Orders for Leix", c. Dec. 1556, SP 62/1/19–21 and for Offaly, SP 63/7/62 placed c. Dec. 1562, but probably of the same date as the other three documents.

be allowed to administer further subdivisions after the Gaelic fashion. Provision was made for the gradual extension of English law amongst the clansmen and for the construction of schools and churches within their territory. It was expected that the process of anglicisation could commence within a year of founding the plantation. The core of the new settlement, however, was to be formed by a group of English planter-captains whom Sussex had recruited with the express intention of regaining and defending the territory. The captains were each to be allotted a strategically selected site from which they could exercise surveillance over the surrounding countryside.[90] But their function was to be of short duration. They were not *conquistadores* who would wield permanent authority over a subject population, for the integration of the clansmen into this model English community was clearly envisaged in the 'orders'. They were, rather, a vital element of that tightly knit executive group upon whom Sussex depended to do his bidding and to uphold his authority in the crucial period during which the foundations of the new order were being laid. Thereafter, their military utility was expected to become redundant. Sussex's ends, that is to say, were orthodox: he aimed at assimilation rather than repression. His method of execution was his sole innovation. Yet it was to be a decisive one.

Sussex moved to implement his plan with deliberate speed. By the end of 1556 an impressive progress through the two countries had been sufficient to persuade the leaders of both clans to submit without a major confrontation, and Sussex had returned to Dublin to draft the legislation organising the territories as shires of the crown.[91] His hopes, however, were soon dispelled. Almost immediately after his departure, Connell O'More and Donough O'Connor broke their pledges. They refused to answer the viceroy's summons and began joint preparations to repulse his attack. Disillusioned, Sussex proclaimed them traitors; the hope of establishing Queen's County and King's County cheaply, speedily and peacefully had gone forever.[92] The campaign that followed yielded no satisfactory result. Sussex besieged and captured the O'Connors' major stronghold at Meleek, forcing them to withdraw to their fastnesses on the banks of the Shannon; and in Laois his captains captured and executed Connell O'More. But the clansmen were far from beaten. On its march homeward, Sussex's

---

[90] For the captains and their allotments, see White, 'Tudor plantations', I, p. 378, and II, ch. 12.

[91] 'Proceedings of the earl of Sussex', Oct. 1556–Feb. 1557, TCD, MSS, 581; Philip and Mary to Sussex, 13 May 1557, BL, Cotton MSS, Titus B XI, no. 243.

[92] Dunlop, 'Plantations of Leix and Offaly"; 'Proceedings of the earl of Sussex', July 1557, TCD, MSS 581, 'Proclamation of O'Connor and his allies, HMC, *Haliday MSS*, pp. 39–41.

expeditionary force was harassed by the resurgent O'Connors right to the borders of the Pale.[93] And in the territories themselves, the infant settlements were plagued by the raids of outlawed woodkerne, battening upon the support and protection of the native inhabitants who had nominally accepted the terms of the new order.[94] Though the parliament of 1557 had passed all the necessary legislation, the new shires existed at the close of Queen Mary's reign merely as legal fictions; not a single deed had been issued granting title to land in either.[95]

The new reign brought no improvement. Sussex himself, disheartened by the failure of his original plan and the futility of his attempt to impose it by force, lost interest; Laois–Offaly was delegated to his brother who was equipped to maintain only a holding action against the continual raids of the clansmen. In the early 1560s, therefore, the guerrilla war deepened and grew more bloody. Not until 1563 did Sussex again turn his attention to the beleaguered plantation, and by then the gap which separated the optimistic prognostications of 1556 from the prevailing reality had become clearly evident. Though the fiants of that year contained conditions of residence in accordance with the spirit of the 'orders', the original ideal of creating a model English community had been brought no nearer to realisation in the intervening years. Undeveloped, undermanned and in a permanent state of siege, the plantation remained a mere *congeries* of military outposts, apprehensively preparing for the next onslaught of the unsuppressed and reconciled natives.[96]

Sussex's attempt to establish a plantation in Ulster was even less successful. The north-east coastline which had recently been the target of massive Scottish migration was another of the vital problem areas which the viceroy identified for immediate treatment in 1556. His plans for the north, moreover, were of equal ambition with those he laid for Laois–Offaly, for he was concerned not merely to expel the Scots, but to establish a number of self-sufficient colonies along the coastline which would secure the territory permanently for the crown.[97] In the summer of 1556 a rapid march northwards brought Sussex victory against the Scots in his first military engagement in Ireland. The Scots were badly mauled, and Sussex believed that he had permanently ended their challenge. He hastily despatched his plans for colonisation to the Marian council and impatiently awaited its

---

[93] 'Proceedings of the earl of Sussex', July 1557, TCD, MSS, 581; Sussex to privy council, 7 Apr., SP 62/2/32. *AFM sa* 1557.
[94] HMC, *Haliday MSS*, pp. 39–45; *Cal. pat. rolls Hen. VIII–Eliz.*, p. 369.
[95] White, 'Tudor plantations', I, p. 422.
[96] Ibid., II, ch. 10.
[97] Articles sent by Mary and Sussex's opinion, 2 Jan. 1557, SP 62/1/22, enclosures (i) and (ii); 'Articles to be declared to the Queen', 15 Apr. 1557, SP 62/1/31.

approval.[98] But even before the council had time to consider his proposals, the Scots were reported to have returned, apparently in even greater numbers, and to have renewed their alliance with the disaffected son of the earl of Tyrone, Shane O'Neill. The projected colonies would have to await yet another military expedition. In the spring of 1558 Sussex indeed secured the consent of the crown to an ambitious amphibious operation which aimed at stopping the flow of migrant Scots by attacking their home base in the Hebrides. In attempting it Sussex overreached his resources: plagued by mishap from the outset, the expedition was brought to a halt by a combination of bad weather and fever, having executed no more than a few raids upon the outer isles.[99]

Sussex continued to press his plans on Elizabeth, but the treaty of Cateau-Cambrésis removed any immediate threat which the Scots may have posed to England's security, and the incentive to heed the viceroy's urgings was correspondingly lessened. Instead the council favoured the extension of the *de facto* toleration to those Scots who had already settled, and instructed Sussex accordingly.[100] His hopes for military achievement thus ended, Sussex lost interest in the entire problem. Dismissing the possibility of establishing royal colonies through an accommodation with the Scots, he simply left the matter open to private operators.[101] As in the case of Laois–Offaly, Sussex's ends were indistinguishable from the means which he adopted to attain them. And ultimately it was the means which mattered most. For once his original tactics had failed or grown obsolete, Sussex considered the end itself as unobtainable. This insistence on the enforcement of old decisions and strategies long after they had ceased to be relevant is even more striking in an area in which his real failure did not become immediately obvious: in his efforts, that is, to uphold the original agreements concerning reform in the Gaelic lordships.

Sussex, as we have seen, was no opponent to the principle underlying surrender and regrant. His argument with his predecessors was tactical, even psychological. The grace with which the crown had offered security of title to those who had no prior legal rights was worthy of the highest respect: it was not to be besmirched by cowardly concesssions to impudent resistance. Such regard for the honour of the crown was noble and no doubt sincerely felt, but it was also tactically advantageous; for it greatly simplified the earl's position. It gave him a fixed principle on which to make decisions without

[98] Sussex's proceedings, Apr. to Oct. 1556, Jan., Apr. 1557, TCD, MS 581; Philip and Mary to Sussex, 23 May 1557, BL, Cotton MSS, Titus B XI, no. 243.
[99] R. Dunlop, 'Sixteenth-century schemes for the plantation of Ulster', *Scottish Historical Review* 22 (1924–5), pp. 5–60; Sussex to Mary, Sept., Oct. 1558, SP 62/2/69–71, 75, 76.
[100] Sussex, 'Instructions', 16 July 1559, SP 63/1/60.
[101] See ch. 7, below.

delving too deeply into the intricacies of each particular issue, a principle which allowed of the one solution which Sussex knew best how to administer: the imposition of the crown's will by force.

It was moreover the principle which guided Sussex in selecting which of the many cases of surrender and regrant should be reserved for his special attention. Thus for lesser Gaelic clans like the O'Byrnes and the O'Tooles amongst whom the process of surrender had not yet been brought to completion he could spare little effort. These were minor problems which could be handled without much difficulty in time; and so he ignored them, delegating responsibility to captains who were required only to keep the clans under control by whatever means they might. This delegation of political authority to purely military figures was to be of grave consequence.[102] But the short-term results of Sussex's own selection were no less serious.

The first area in which Sussex elected to defend the honour of the crown by upholding the now disputed succession arrangement was Thomond. There, despite the circumspection of St Leger and Crofts and their recognition that the original settlement had grossly misunderstood the real distribution of power among the O'Briens, Sussex came easily to the decision that Conor O'Brien, the third earl, was the rightful heir to the entire O'Brien lordship and all the rights that went with it. Conor's case was strong in law: he was the eldest son of the second earl and had been nominated by his father as heir. It was arguable, therefore, that failure to support him would cast the whole principle of primogeniture into disrepute.[103] Yet Sussex's predecessors had not been overscrupulous on this point. The succession of the first earl had not been determined on grounds of primogeniture, and both St Leger and Crofts had been willing to contemplate further compromises in order to attain real political stability in the lordship.[104] But not Sussex; to him it was not simply primogeniture, but the whole authority of the crown that was at risk; for Thomond's enemies, he believed, were aided and abetted by the opponents of all English authority in Ireland. The government, therefore, had no choice but to support the earl or admit its own impotence. In honour of the crown, then, as well as in defence of Conor O'Brien, Sussex marched into Thomond in June 1558, expelled the rebel Sir Donnell and formally installed Conor as earl.[105]

It was a fine performance, amply reported upon in Sussex's characteristic style. But very soon what was by now becoming the typical response to the viceroy's forays made itself evident: Sir Donnell and his supporters returned

---

[102] Sussex, 'Memorial', Apr. 1562, SP 63/5/101, see ch. 7, below.
[103] Sussex to Boxoll, 26 Apr. 1558, SP 62/2/37.   [104] See ch. 2, above.
[105] 'Proceedings of the earl of Sussex', June–July 1558, TCD, MSS, 581.

almost immediately after Sussex's departure and renewed their war against Thomond. In 1559 they defeated the earl and his ally Clanrickard heavily at Spancel Hill.[106] And though a further intervention by the government in 1560 procured another temporary relief for the earl, Thomond remained engulfed in a bitter internecine war for the rest of Sussex's Irish service. Peace eventually came to the lordship only when Sussex's successors conceded to Sir Donnell O'Brien the independent status which the lieutenant had regarded as unacceptably compromising to the honour of the crown and the viceroy.[107]

Sussex's folly in Thomond was more deeply overshadowed by his inflexible determination to destroy Shane O'Neill. The story of Shane's relations with the Dublin government hardly needs retelling.[108] But the extent to which its course was determined not by the crown nor even by Shane himself, but by the lieutenant's overriding concern to have his own way needs to be emphasised. In constitutional terms the succession dispute in Tyrone left a good deal more room for manoeuvre than had apparently been available in Thomond. It is true that the baron of Dungannon had been recognised as the first earl's eldest son and heir in the agreement of 1543. But sufficient evidence existed to call Dungannon's legitimacy into doubt. Thus it was possible that the original patent might have been invalidated on purely technical grounds without reflecting any discredit on the crown or on the principle of primogeniture. In political terms the weakness of the baron's influence among the O'Neills was undeniable, and after his killing in 1559 it seemed sensible that the government should seek to respond to political realities in the lordship by reaching some accommodation with the undoubted leader of the dynasty, Shane.[109] This was the view formed by Sir Henry Sidney during his brief period as lord justice in 1559.[110] And it was endorsed by the Elizabethan council which, acknowledging that Shane was 'the person legitimate in blood' and that he was also now 'in quiet possession' of all his father's properties, advised that he be allowed to succeed to the title without delay.[111]

---

[106] *AFM*, sub anno.

[107] Fitzwilliam to Cecil, 29 Apr. 1560, SP 63/2/12 and 4 May 1561, SP 63/3/64; Sussex to Cecil, 1 Mar. 1563, SP 63/8/13; *AFM*, sa 1560, 1562.

[108] The only scholarly biography, however, remains unpublished, T. B. Lyons, 'Shane O'Neill: a biography', MS thesis (UCC, 1947); see also, James Hogan, 'Shane O'Neill comes to the court of Elizabeth', in *Feil-Scribhinn Torna*, ed. S. Pender (Cork, 1947), pp. 154–70.

[109] Brian, his eldest son, remained in the area of Armagh where he was supported by the garrison which Sussex established in the city. Young Hugh, it appears, was withdrawn from the region in 1559 by Sidney, and was lodged in Dublin as a ward of the crown, see TCD, MSS, 1087, fos. 15–17.

[110] Sidney's 'Memoirs', *UJA*, III, p. 39; 'Notes of the earl of Sussex', Feb. 1559, SP 63/1/13.

[111] Sussex's 'Instructions', 16 July 1559, SP 63/1/60.

This was not Sussex's view. His government, he declared, had determined in favour of Dungannon from the beginning. The late baron had served the crown loyally until his death, while Shane had indulged in treasonable conspiracies with the Scots in those years. To abandon the baron's sons now simply because Shane had murdered their father and usurped his rightful place in Tyrone was not only dishonourable in itself, but would destroy the confidence of any Irishman who had ever contemplated placing his trust in the crown. Sussex refused to be part of the betrayal and threatened to resign should he be required to pursue a conciliatory approach to Shane.[112]

In the event Sussex did resume office under Elizabeth with instructions to institute negotiations with Shane.[113] He did so, however, without enthusiasm, giving O'Neill no indication of the crown's conciliatory attitude, and maintaining his argument with London that compromise would only lead to further trouble. The council reconsidered; and at the end of 1559 Sussex was summoned home to present his case anew. Armed with his first major treatise on the reformation of Ireland, and sustained by the general conspiracy theory which both he and Fitzwilliam had assiduously cultivated, Sussex posited the problem of Tyrone in the broadest possible context. It was not just a matter of determining a local succession dispute, Shane's resistance to the government had already acquired ramifications which spread throughout the entire realm. He was a shining example to all who wished to throw off their allegiance to the crown; he was the chief encourager of the midlands rebels and of the dissident O'Briens; he was the trump card of the Geraldine conspiracy. Sussex's case was attractively simple, for it seemed to promise an instant solution to all manner of difficulties in Ireland, both general and specific. Both parts of his argument were mutually sustaining: Shane's removal was imperative, if the grand Geraldine conspiracy was to be smashed; but in practical terms, it was also easy. Thus a single and none too costly military expedition seemed to offer the key to destroying all resistance to the crown in Ireland.[114]

Not a profound analysis, to be sure, but it was sufficient to persuade the privy council to give Sussex his head, for the time being at least. He returned to Ireland in the autumn of 1560 with instructions to proceed against O'Neill by force.[115] This was the argument which the lieutenant was to employ with declining plausibility over the next three years. Increasingly, the rooting out of Shane, and that alone, became the one primary problem which Sussex felt called upon to solve. That done, everything else would

---

[112] 'Notes of the earl of Sussex', Feb. 1559; Sussex to Cecil, 25 Mar. 1559, SP 63/1/25.
[113] Sussex's 'Instructions', 16 July 1559, SP 63/1/60.
[114] Sussex's 'Memorial', May 1560, SP 63/2/20; Eliz. to Sussex, 15 Aug. 1560, SP 63/2/30, Sussex's 'Opinion', 11 Sept. 1560, Lambeth MSS, 624, fos. 271–80.
[115] Eliz. to Sussex, 15 and 31 Aug., SP 63/2/30, 31.

simply fall into place; all would be 'settled'. The execution of a single military objective became the sole justification of Sussex's presence in Ireland, the one item on his personal programme. Thus far had the internal logic of his administrative techniques progressed.

Each year between 1560 and 1563 Sussex made war on O'Neill, each year without any success. In 1560 he greatly underestimated the difficulty of the task, and his undermanned and undersupplied army was forced to retire without ever encountering Shane. In 1561 a much larger expeditionary force was attacked in the rear by Shane's kerne and put to flight. Following this disaster the privy council temporarily withdrew its confidence from the lieutenant. Negotiations were reopened with O'Neill, and early in the following year he was summoned to attend at court. During 1562 Sussex could do no more than launch a few unofficial raids on Tyrone in the hope that he might encounter his enemy by chance. But in 1563, following another strenuous campaign to win over the council to his view, he was permitted to fit out the largest expedition ever to go in search of O'Neill. It yielded no better results than the campaign of 1560: having spent the summer months scouring the country in search of O'Neill, Sussex's army was at length forced to retire through lack of supplies. It caught no glimpse of Shane. This was to be Sussex's last operation in Ireland. It exhausted him physically and it ravaged his nerves; but what is more important, it ruined him politically.[116]

(VII)

Sussex's claims to credibility as the crown's chief officer in Ireland were inherently fragile. They depended on his continued ability to convince his superiors that his chosen policies responded to the real needs of the crown and to represent all criticism of his administration as self-interested and malicious. He had enjoyed considerable success on both grounds, but in neither case were his capabilities unlimited. Sooner or later, the burden of his own manifest failures would have brought him down. But even before this extreme had been reached, his individual style of government became vulnerable to attack from an unexpected quarter. Sussex had perfected the technique of insulating himself from Irish-based criticism for a limited but not inconsiderable space of time. What he was unable to insure himself against, however, was a systematic attempt to undermine his reputation at the very source of power itself, the royal court. His lack of preparedness is understandable. Sussex's style of government – in all ways unlike his

---

116 For an account of these campaigns by a military historian, see Cyril Falls, *Elizabeth's Irish wars* (London, 1950), ch. 6.

predecessor's – was designed to be proof against the weaknesses that had brought St Leger down. Thus he was firmly detached, avoiding entangling alliances with local interests and any personal dealings in crown properties. He was not only honest, but appeared to be so as well. Again, Sussex was active, and ready to confront all the major challenges to government without flinching. For these reasons, Sussex could hope to retain the confidence of the crown for far longer than St Leger. Yet Sussex assumed too easily that such precautions had been sufficient to defend his position at court because he failed to anticipate the overriding influence which a royal favourite might exercise in any matter that concerned him.

The emergence of Lord Robert Dudley's interest in Irish affairs can be dated with reasonable accuracy. It appeared in the middle of 1560 as the first debate on the problem of Shane O'Neill was in progress and mounted steadily until Dudley achieved his objective of destroying Sussex and replacing him as governor with one of his own *protégés*.[117] Through Dudley's influence, the earl of Kildare was rehabilitated, and his offers to bring O'Neill to obedience by peaceful means were listened to attentively at court.[118] When, after Sussex's failures, Kildare made good his promise to bring O'Neill to court, it was Dudley who acted as the former rebel's host and escort.[119] Despite his submission, his pledges for future good behaviour and his assurance to Lord Robert that he would act only by his advice, Shane's visit to court proved to be a disappointment. Once back in Ulster he resumed his characteristic attitudes and Sussex was again able to win the privy council to his way. As a means of dislodging Sussex, Shane was as yet a rough-hewn instrument.

Dudley, however, had other options to hand. At the very time when he was ostentatiously entertaining O'Neill, the favourite was busy gaining an audience for a group of law students, Palesmen who had drafted a lengthy statement of grievances for presentation to the privy council.[120] Though more detailed and more narrow in scope, their case was essentially the same as Archbishop Dowdall's.[121] Sussex's military government had oppressed the loyal subjects of the Pale beyond toleration. His troops were a source of untold misery to the ordinary people. He had wasted rather than defended the Pale. The students' allegations were treated with the utmost seriousness

---

[117] H. Radcliffe to Sussex, 12 Dec. 1560, BL, Cotton MSS, Titus B XXII, no. 12.

[118] Cecil to Throckmorton, 10 May 1561, BL, Add. MSS, 35830, no. 33.

[119] Hogan, 'Shane O'Neill comes to the court of Elizabeth', pp. 154–70; Shane to Dudley, 2 Nov., SP 63/7/40.

[120] Sir Oliver Plunkett et al. to Dudley, 27 May 1562, SP 63/6/13. One of the signatories of the students' book, Richard Netterville, was already known to be one of Dudley's retainers, Fitzwilliam to Cecil, 25 Mar. 1561, SP 63/3/41.

[121] Students' book, c. 21 Mar. 1561, SP 63/5/51.

by the privy council who interviewed them on at least three occasions. Though they were finally admonished for their impertinence by a short spell in the Fleet, Sussex was compelled to reply to each of their charges in detail and to give assurances that all genuine grievances would be carefully examined.[122] At the end of the affair many senior councillors, including Secretary Cecil and Lord Keeper Bacon, remained unconvinced by Sussex's insistence that the allegations had been without foundation.[123]

Dudley pressed the advantage. In the following May he presented to the council a letter from the leading gentry of the Pale which at once deplored the insolence of the students and reiterated their complaints.[124] More importantly, he extended his patronage to an older and more influential agent whom the Palesmen now despatched to present their grievances and to seek the appointment of a commission of inquiry, William Bermingham. Bermingham, who had already colluded with the students, repeated their charges.[125] But he developed their case in one significant respect: it was not the Pale alone, he argued, that suffered from the burden of Sussex's adventures, his army had also wasted large sums of the royal treasure through sheer negligence and downright corruption. Bermingham averred that an investigation of the army's finances would save the crown some £30,000, half of which would be made good through the discovery of inaccuracies and discrepancies in the muster rolls.[126] It was, he suggested, this dual opportunity of profiting simultaneously from the crown and the community that undermined any sense of urgency among the soldiers. Their real interest lay in inaction; the completion of their work would only spell an end to their gains. Seen in this light, the grievances of the Pale and Sussex's obvious lack of military success were symptoms of the same malaise which had its roots in Sussex's over-large and idle army. It was an outrageous suggestion; but it was also alarmingly plausible. To find out for itself, the council decided in July 1562 to send a commission to investigate the condition of the army in Ireland.[127]

It was then that Dudley executed his most important coup. The man nominated as the crown's commissioner in Ireland was yet another of his

---

[122] Sussex's 'Interrogatories' and students' 'Answers' *c.* 21 Mar. 1562, SP 63/5/52–56, 58; Sir Oliver Plunkett et al. to Elizabeth, 27 May 1562, SP 63/6/12; 'Examination of matters relating to cess', 26 Nov. 1562, BL, Add. MSS, 40,061, no. 6, fo. 43.

[123] Sussex's replies to students, *c.* 21 Mar. 1562, SP 63/5/55–57; 'Answer made by one Barnewall to Sir Nicholas Bacon', *c.* Easter 1562, BL, Add. MSS, 40,061, no. 5.

[124] Sir Oliver Plunkett et al. to Dudley, 27 May 1562, SP 63/6/13.

[125] Fitzwilliam to Cecil, 13 June 1562, SP 63/6/24; Bermingham's 'Interrogatories', 21 June, SP 63/6/28; Arnold to Cecil, 13 Aug., SP 63/6/67 and enclosure.

[126] 'Instructions to Arnold', 7 July 1562, SP 63/6/49; Bermingham to Northampton, 16 July, SP 63/6/53.

[127] 'Instructions to commissioners', 7 July, SP 63/6/49–50.

protégés, Sir Nicholas Arnold. Arnold's connection with the Dudley interest stretched far beyond Lord Robert's rise to influence under Elizabeth. He had come to prominence in local affairs in his native Gloucestershire under Northumberland and had been forced into exile under Mary for his part in the conspiracy organised around Ambrose Dudley. Under Elizabeth his political career rapidly recovered. He resumed his place among the governing elite in the shire and served with Sir Henry Sidney on the council in Wales. It was in his Irish service, however, that his allegiance to the Dudley interest became most evident.[128]

Arnold at first appeared to be sympathetic to Sussex's difficulties, but as Sussex soon discovered his friendliness was no more than a guise to cloak his true intentions.[129] Throughout the winter of 1562–3 Arnold worked meticulously, seeking out evidence to confirm Bermingham's allegations. He combed the muster-master's accounts, and examined the captains for verification of their length of service. He took counsel with leading spokesmen of the Pale and entertained the grievances of the countrymen against the army.[130] When he finally submitted his report in the summer of 1563, his findings were all that Sussex had feared. Though his researches were still only preliminary, Arnold claimed that he had uncovered sufficient evidence of abuse to justify a far more extensive inquiry into the complaints of the Palesmen. Not only the captains, but the ordinary soldiers and the husbandmen would have to be interviewed before an accurate estimate of the crown's true losses in Ireland could be made. The council accepted his recommendation, and in October Arnold was appointed as a joint commissioner with Sir Thomas Wrothe to resume his investigations.[131]

The new commission's powers were even wider than Arnold had hoped. In addition to examining the army accounts, the commissioners were directed to investigate all allegations of abuse made against the soldiers and to ensure that the soldiers were punished and the citizens compensated in cases where the charges were proven. They were to investigate the Irish revenues, and in particular 'to inquire what commodities and profits have been taken of the counties of Offaly and Leix yearly'. The investigation of Sussex's financial management would prove embarrassing enough, but the commissioners were empowered to inquire into far wider aspects of his

[128] On Arnold, see DNB (supplementary vol.); J. E. Neale, The Elizabethan house of commons (London, 1949; rev. edn, 1963), p. 61; P. Williams, The council in the marches of Wales under Elizabeth I (Cardiff, 1958), pp. 142, 242–3; D. M. Loades, Two Tudor conspiracies (Cambridge, 1965); J. R. S. Phillips, The justices of the peace in Wales and Monmouthshire, 1541–1689 (Cardiff, 1975), pp. 54, 92, 252, 354.
[129] Sussex to Cecil, 23 Aug., 23 Sept. 1562, SP 63/6/69, 7/20.
[130] 'Relation of matters between Sussex and Arnold', c. Nov. 1562, SP 63/7/50 and enclosure.
[131] Arnold's 'Memoranda', Sept. 1563, SP 63/9/12–15.

performance. His claim to have enforced a widespread respect for English law and to have ensured allegiance to the new 'orders of religion' was to be tested. His record in defending the Pale and in punishing those who had attacked it was to be checked. The commissioners were to be free to offer advice to the lieutenant in dealing with Shane O'Neill and were to devote attention to Shane's claim that Sussex had attempted to have him poisoned 'in such sort as Shane O'Neill may in reason perceive how grievously do we take such a horrible attempt'. So broad an investigation not only questioned Sussex's ability as a manager of money; it seemed to render his ability to govern open to doubt. In the hands of a partial commissioner it constituted a deadly challenge to his survival as viceroy.[132]

In the sixteenth century a commission of inquiry was an almost certain way to ruin a man, innocent or guilty. By the autumn of 1563 there appeared to remain only one hope for Sussex's survival as governor. He must secure the defeat of O'Neill or at least convince the queen and her council that an unequivocal victory over the rebel was imperative. But Dudley had anticipated even this last plea. Even as Sussex prepared his last major assault on Ulster the council's resolution to support him was already being eroded.[133] The council's last minute reservations about attacking O'Neill coincided with the return of Sir Thomas Cusacke to high political influence. Following the scandal of St Leger's last years Cusacke had spent some years in disfavour. He had been readmitted to the Irish council in 1558 but it was not until the spring of 1562 that Cusacke had presumed to offer the English council any further advice as to the government of Ireland. Thereafter, however, his fortunes rapidly recovered. In March 1563 his suit to attend at court was granted and he was immediately accorded a place of influence in the privy council's reconsiderations of Irish policy.[134]

Though he dealt not with matters of cess, or any of the other complaints specifically directed against Sussex, Cusacke challenged the lieutenant on the very issues which he himself had designated as the priorities of his administration. He counselled a more flexible approach towards the dispute in Thomond, and a more sympathetic approach towards the earl of Desmond who had been detained in England on Sussex's advice since 1560. But most of all he urged a renewal of the conciliatory overtures which had been made to O'Neill in 1562. On all these issues Cusacke carried his point. The council began to consider offering new terms to Sir Donnell O'Brien.

[132] 'Instructions', to Wrothe and Arnold, 20 Oct. 1564, Jan. 1565, SP 63/9/45, Lambeth MSS, 614/143–52.
[133] Sussex to Cecil, 6, 31 Mar. 1563, SP 63/8/15, 25.
[134] HMC, *Haliday MSS*, pp. 53, 55; Sussex to Cecil, 14 Aug. 1561, SP 63/4/35; Cusacke to Cecil, 17 Feb. 1562, SP 63/5/53; Sussex to Cecil, 11 Apr. 1563, SP 63/8/28; 'Memorial for Sir Thomas Cusacke', *c.* Aug. 1563, SP 63/8/64; Elizabeth to Sussex, 7 Aug., SP 63/8/66.

Desmond was released from confinement and despatched to Munster with a commission of peace whose articles had been drafted by Cusacke. And in August, Cusacke himself was returned with plenipotentiary powers to make peace with O'Neill.[135] The timing of his return was propitious; for by then Sussex's grand campaign was already grinding to a halt through lack of supplies and lack of success. There was little excuse to forestall the peace mission. Cusacke opened negotiations immediately, and in September signed a treaty which assented to almost all of O'Neill's major demands. His claim to the title of O'Neill and to all the rights that went with it was acknowledged. His disputes with the lesser clans of Ulster were to be submitted to arbitration, and his suit to be made earl of Tyrone was to be again submitted for the favourable consideration of the privy council. As a token of good-will, the government undertook to withdraw the garrison which Sussex had installed at Armagh. It was, as the historian Bagwell noted, a treaty in which Shane appeared to gain everything and to yield nothing. Four months later, it was ratified by the queen at Windsor.[136]

Sussex's collapse at the end of his 1563 campaign, the treaty at Drum Cree and the almost simultaneous arrival of a new commission of inquiry effectively ended the earl's Irish service. In the following months he withdrew altogether from the concerns of government and waited only for his recall which came, at last, in April 1564.[137] His place was taken by Commissioner Arnold who was appointed lord justice in the same month. Cusacke was made acting chancellor, apparently through Dudley's influence, for he looked anxiously to his patron to have his patent formally passed.[138] Under Arnold, the earl of Kildare was reappointed to military responsibility in Leix–Offaly and assumed foremost place with Cusacke upon Arnold's council.[139] Lesser men enjoyed rehabilitation. John Parker, who had undergone a second disgrace through suspicion of his participation in the Palesmen's complaints, was returned to favour.[140] Even the broken Andrew Wise returned to service in Ireland as secretary to the new

---

[135] Desmond to Privy Council, 4 Aug. 1563, PRO, SP 63/8/61; 'Articles for Thadhg O'Brien', Nov. 1563, BL, Cotton MSS, Titus B XIII, no. 31; Eliz. to Sussex and council, 7 Aug., SP 63/8/65–6.

[136] 'Peace', 11 Sept. 1563, SP 63/9/9–11; 'Letters patent', 15 Jan. 1564, SP 63/10/5; Bagwell, *Tudors*, II, p. 63.

[137] Eliz. to Sussex, 22 Apr. 1564, SP 63/10/52; HMC, *Haliday MSS*, pp. 134–5.

[138] 'Cusacke's requests', 16 Jan., 22 Mar., 17 Apr., SP 63/10/9, 38, 51; Cusacke to Dudley, 9 June, 1564, SP 63/11/3.

[139] Arnold to Kildare, 5 Aug. 1564, SP 63/11/55; Radcliffe to Cecil, 31 Jan. 1565, SP 63/12/24; Fitzwilliam to Sussex and Cecil, 12, 13 July 1565, BL, Cotton MSS, Titus B XIII, no. 46 (xiii), SP 63/14/14.

[140] Eliz. to Sussex, 9 Nov. 1563, SP 63/9/57.

commissioners.[141] Dudley appeared to have captured Irish government for his own interests.

The favourite's tactics were not remarkable; they were the same as he had employed elsewhere in different areas and upon different issues.[142] But what is worthy of note is the fact that he chose to exercise them with such consistency and with such determination in Ireland. As an extensive area of government involvement and expenditure, it was useful to acquire a substantial following in what might be seen as a kind of extension to the great Dudley interest in the west country and in Wales. But such a moderately useful aim hardly justifies the trouble which Dudley went to in systematically undermining the crown's government there. Since an alliance had already been offered to him, extreme tactics hardly seemed necessary. The most crucial factor in turning Dudley's attention to Ireland was contributed, in fact, by Sussex himself. For it was Sussex who first gave clear articulation to the idea that the government of Ireland was a single, arduous, but essentially simple problem. It was Sussex who isolated a number of key problems upon which alone, he claimed, the entire settlement of Ireland depended and who suggested thereby that Irish service could be short lived, dramatic and even glorious. It was Sussex who transformed the drab processes pursued by St Leger into a brisk and streamlined programme of action. It was Sussex, that is, who elevated the Irish question from a matter of mere local administration to one of national importance. For Dudley, therefore, intervention in Ireland offered not simply the addition of another regional connection to his livery, but another challenge in his struggle for the highest political stakes, another Newhaven adventure, another marriage question. Thus it was that Sussex unwittingly converted the Irish problem into an issue of far greater importance than he himself could control.

(VIII)

Sussex's legacy to Dudley, however, was ambiguous in a number of critically important respects. Despite the succession of the favourite's *protégés* to the highest political offices, the bulk of Sussex's administrative establishment remained untouched. The army in particular constituted a daunting threat to the security of Arnold's new regime. Fitzwilliam, its most senior officer, refused to yield up his accounts, either as vice-treasurer or treasurer-at-war,

---

141 Wrothe and Arnold to privy council, 16 Feb., 16 Mar. 1564, SP 63/10/15, 34; Wrothe to Cecil, 28 July, SP 63/11/39.

142 See, for example, Derek Wilson, *Sweet Robin: a biography of Robert Dudley, earl of Leicester* (London, 1981); Wallace MacCaffrey, *Shaping of the Elizabethan regime: Elizabethan politics, 1558–72* (London, 1969); Peter Clark, *English provincial society from the reformation to the revolution* (Hassocks, 1977), pp. 136–8, 165, 261–3.

and his fellow captains followed his example.[143] Though they had undoubtedly retained private accounts of their service, they refused to deliver any evidence by which the accounts of the clerk of check might be tested. Without these records, no detached assessment of the army's official muster-rolls could be essayed, unless the commission chose to admit the depositions of the rank and file. This was a clumsy, undependable, time consuming and socially distasteful method of auditing accounts. But Arnold was ultimately forced to have recourse to it. The captains complained both collectively and individually: it was outrageous to have their word tested against the evidence of mere foot-soldiers, it was a clear proof of the malice that underlay all of Arnold's dealings with them.[144] Arnold's fellow commissioners, Sir Thomas Wrothe and the auditor William Dix, were disquieted, and the privy council, to whom all the complaints were directed, became concerned that the commission should not waste more money through delays than it might reclaim through the checks. The commissioner's zeal brought no credit to the lord justice.[145]

Arnold himself was convinced that the captains' attempts to cripple his administration went far beyond their obstruction of his commission's proceedings. They had, he believed, sought to discredit his government by deliberately provoking trouble amongst the Gaelic Irish. He alleged specifically that Sir Henry Radcliffe had intrigued with the O'Mores and the O'Connors to provoke renewed rebellion in the midlands.[146] Later investigations revealed that some of Radcliffe's men had indeed spread rumours amongst the clansmen, and it is true that the captains made much play of the renewed disorders in their complaints against Arnold.[147] But the notion that the captains could have so manipulated the Gaelic clans in their own interests is inherently implausible. The susceptibility of Arnold's regime to political disturbance was indeed a legacy bequeathed by Sussex; but it derived from sources more complex than the machinations of a few conspiratorial captains.

Because Sussex himself had so consistently fused ends and means, assaults

---

[143] Arnold and Wrothe to privy council, 7 Apr. 1564, SP 63/10/39; Captains' 'Memorandum', 29 June, SP 63/11/16; Bermingham to privy council, 24 Feb. 1565, SP 63/12/36; Dix to Cecil, 16 July, SP 63/11/33; 22 Nov., SP 63/11/106. Fitzwilliam did not deliver his account for inspection until July 1565, Fitzwilliam to Cecil, 13 July, Dix to Cecil, 14 July, SP 63/14/14, 33.
[144] Captains' 'Memorandum', 29 June, SP 63/10/36; Fitzwilliam to Cecil, 31 Jan. 1565, BL, Cotton MSS, Titus B XIII, nos. 45–6. Radcliffe et al. to Cecil, 30 Jan., Radcliffe to Cecil, 31 Jan., SP 63/12/22–24.
[145] Dix to Cecil, 22 Nov. 1564, 17 Jan., 13 Apr., SP 63/12/14, 13/12.
[146] 'Articles against Arnold' and his 'Answers', Aug. 1566, SP 63/18/82–3.
[147] Sidney to privy council, 30 May 1566, SP 63/17/68. Curiously, the chief deponent here had the same name as Sussex's witness for the Geraldine conspiracy, Robert Adams.

on him had never been limited solely to criticism of his administrative methods. Implicitly, and as the attack developed explicitly, it contained the added charge that the lieutenant's methods had failed because they were directed towards a policy that was in itself unnecessary and nefarious. The argument had been most clearly voiced by Sir Thomas Cusacke, but Arnold himself was compelled to support the view. His assent was never simply a matter of principle, an impartial rejection of Sussex's analysis. For Arnold was dependent for his own survival upon the support of those interests who had been most threatened by the lieutenant's policies. Thus his own attitudes had not only to be different from Sussex's; on the most important issues, they had necessarily to be the exact opposite. This enforced dialectic effectively defined Arnold's brief regime.

Sussex's encounter with the Palesmen entailed, for instance, that Arnold could have no large cesses, no extensive billeting, no substantial army. He was forced to depend more heavily, consequently, upon the general hosting of the Pale. It was a cheaper and more popular expedient; but it was also unwieldy and inefficient. Under Arnold, the government's military prowess was so diminished that it was hard pressed to snuff out the latest revolt of the gravely depleted midland clans. Of more serious consequence was Arnold's necessary alliance with the Geraldine interests. It entailed, admittedly, some real advantages. The earl of Kildare, from having been the most dangerous opponent of the Dublin administration, now became its foremost supporter. He rendered sterling service to Arnold in suppressing the revolt in the midlands.[148] But the friendship rekindled the old Geraldine–Butler feud and set in motion a whole series of disturbances in which one side attempted to improve and the other to defend its position of influence. In Thomond, internecine war erupted once more as the Clanrickard Burkes rushed to the support of Conor O'Brien, the earl, and the earl of Desmond sent forces to aid Sir Donnell, each side hoping to make an end to the matter once and for all.[149] Clanrickard himself was reported to be deeply aggrieved at the aspersions which Arnold was rumoured to have cast upon his legitimacy, and was suspected, for the first time in his career, to be contemplating rebellion.[150]

But it was in Munster that the most serious disturbances took place between the Butlers and the Desmond Geraldines. Tension had mounted between the two families since the return of the earl of Desmond late in 1563. Throughout 1564 Ormond complained about attacks on his lands

---

[148] Fitzwilliam to Cecil, 19 Oct. 1564, SP 63/11/94; privy council to Kildare, 22 June 1565, SP 63/13/8; Oliver Sutton's 'Articles', Dec. 1565, SP 63/15/54.
[149] Arnold to Thomond, 2 July, to Pembroke, 3 July 1564, SP 63/11/20, 21.
[150] 'Articles against Arnold' and his 'Answer', Aug. 1566, SP 63/18/82–3.

and towards the end of the year he hinted that he might be forced to act in his own defence if the lord justice did not intervene. Arnold was unwilling to act, and so Ormond made good his threat. In January 1565 he surrounded Desmond and his large retinue near the hill of Affane on the border between the two earldoms with an even larger force of his own. In the ensuing battle several hundred of Desmond's men were killed, and Desmond himself carried off as Ormond's prisoner.[151]

The outbreak of unrestrained feudal warfare was even more embarrassing to Arnold than the war in the midlands. It is probable that Ormond was chiefly responsible for the battle at Affane, but the Butlers can be credited with manipulating the Geraldines no more than the captains can be presumed to have surreptitiously motivated the clansmen.[152] A more positive impetus was at work in both instances. A general release of aggression from all who had suffered constraint and repression under his government was Sussex's most damning political bequest to Arnold. The knowledge that their own stubborn resistance had contributed to the overthrow of the iron-fisted governor, coupled with the realisation that Arnold was pitifully dependent on their support, induced them to press for more and soon. This reaction is evident in the revitalised aggression of Sir Donnell O'Brien, in the new self-confidence of Desmond and even in the pathetic attempts of the O'Mores and O'Connors to redraw the boundaries in Leix and Offaly. But nowhere is it more obvious than in the case of the man who had done most to secure Sussex's ruin, Shane O'Neill.

It was the queen and her council who gave Shane the opportunity to test the extent of his new power. The letters patent of January 1564 confirming the peace of Drum Cree differed slightly from the original which Cusacke had drafted. One clause which released O'Neill from obligation to attend on the governor until a final agreement had been concluded was omitted. Since Sussex had withdrawn from office and since no governor had ever been able to procure Shane's attendance against his will, the alteration was trifling, made only to save the honour of the crown.[153] But Shane objected both to the change and to the dignified and somewhat condescending tone in which the patent was couched. He demanded to have the new document invalidated and to have the articles which he had signed with Cusacke endorsed *verbatim*. It was, as the councillors knew, an impossible demand and they urged Cusacke to persuade Shane to relent.[154] But throughout 1564 Shane's demands grew more importunate. He not only wanted the original articles

---

[151] See George Butler, 'The battle of Affane', *The Irish Sword*, 8 (1967–8), pp. 43–51.
[152] Ibid.
[153] Cusacke to Cecil, 22 Mar. 1564, SP 63/10/38, to privy council, 8 June, SP 63/11/1, enclosing abstract of points of difference.
[154] Privy council to Cusacke, 2 Apr., SP 63/10/42; Eliz. to Cusacke, 24 June, SP 63/11/15.

ratified, he pressed also for the prompt concession of his two major suits, the grant of his father's title and the grant of an English wife. The unhappy Cusacke did his best to persuade each side of the other's good-will but his diplomatic endeavours were increasingly outpaced by Shane's actions. O'Neill renewed his pressure on the lesser chiefs of the province and began to enforce his claims over the O'Donnells. Then under the guise of doing 'some notable service whereby he might be the better accepted of the queen' he moved against the Scots of Clandeboy.[155] His early efforts were indecisive, but in April 1565 he inflicted a crushing defeat on the MacDonnells at Glenshesk. He claimed, of course, that his action had been undertaken in good faith, yet he refused to give up the Scots he had captured and immediately began colonising Clandeboy with his own people.[156]

Against all this Arnold and Cusacke were powerless to act. Though the evidence mounted increasingly to the contrary, they continued to insist upon Shane's trustworthiness. When Calough O'Donnell came to Dublin to protest at Shane's depredations, Arnold sought to suppress the complaint. But Calough left without licence for court to present his grievances directly to the queen. His lurid account of Shane's conduct coincided with the first news of O'Neill's victory over the Scots. Together they reconverted the council overnight to Sussex's view that Shane could never be dealt with by conciliation.[157]

Almost everything had gone wrong for Arnold. His commission moved slowly and as yet produced no results. The army's resentment mounted daily against him and even his fellow commissioners openly dissented from his actions. He had permitted Gaelic rebellion, feudal warfare and now these alarming developments in Ulster to flourish uncontrolled: in less than a year his administration had been entirely discredited. Arnold's failure demonstrated more effectively than anything else the impact of Sussex's governing style over the course of Irish politics in the previous ten years. After Sussex it was no longer possible to return – as Arnold had attempted – to the politic manipulative ways by which St Leger had built a party for himself within the country. It was no longer possible partly because the administration which Sussex had so carefully constructed would not facilitate it. But more importantly, it was not possible because the essential elements of such a party, the men of powerful connection in the country, lacked both the will and the ability to reconstruct such a fabric. But it was impossible most of all because Sussex's friends and supporters would apply to any who attempted

[155] O'Neill to privy council, 8 Aug. 1564, SP 63/11/76.
[156] For an account, see G. A. Hayes McCoy, *Irish battles* (London, 1969), ch. 6.
[157] *DNB* sv; Calough O'Donnell to Elizabeth, 29 Oct. 1564, SP 63/11/96; Randolf to Cecil, 24 Dec. 1564, 4 Sept. 1565, *Cal. SP (Scotland), 1564–1565*, pp. 110, 203.

it the same techniques of slander and subversion which had been used so effectively against St Leger and Sussex himself.

Thus in the spring of 1565 Dudley, the recently created earl of Leicester, was placed in an awkward position. He needed desperately to change his agents, but to do so without conceding a retrospective victory to Sussex. He needed a man who would at once retain the loyalty of the majority of Leicester's Irish allies and still act decisively against those who went too far. He needed a man whose reputation and experience would be sufficient to command the confidence of the crown in any action he undertook in Ireland, and who would yet remain amenable to his own will. He needed, that is, an alternative Sussex in his camp. He looked to Sir Henry Sidney.

4

Reform on contract: the viceroyalties of Sir Henry Sidney, 1566–1578

(1)

Sir Henry Sidney, it seems, has always been popular. The favourite of the favourite, he was the great hope of countless court dependants who looked to him for the advancement of their political, economic and cultural enterprises. Sidney was popular too in Ireland, with the Palesmen who openly rejoiced on his appointment, with certain Anglo-Irish lords like the earl of Kildare who had schemed to bring it about, and with several Gaelic chieftains who regarded 'big Henry of the Beer' as their special protector.[1] In turn each of these groups was to grow disillusioned with their sometime patron. Yet Sidney has retained his appeal to later generations of historians. In the eyes of sober and cautious Richard Bagwell, Sidney was an energetic and disinterested servant of the crown, while the nationalist-minded E. A. Dalton praised his direct and generally sympathetic dealings with the native Irish. And most recently he has been awarded pride of place in sixteenth-century Irish history as the man responsible for laying the foundations of the Elizabethan conquest of Ireland.[2]

The only difficulty with these remarkably sustained good opinions is that they are not entirely consistent. Sidney was praised by the Palesmen for reasons far different from those which made him popular with the Gaelic Irish, and the sources of his reputation with both groups were utterly distinct from those which attracted so many English careerists to his side. Similarly the credit which Sidney has received from historians has also been quite diverse. The conscientious provincial governor of traditional accounts is not the bold strategic innovator of modern revisions, but the initiator of

---

[1] For Sidney's contemporary reputation see Arthur Collins, *Letters and memorials of state – from the De Lisle and Dudley Papers* (2 vols., London, 1746), pp. 83–92; Hooker's 'Chronicle of Ireland' in Holinshed's *Chronicles* (1586), pp. 151–2; *ALC*, s.a., 1578, 1583; 'The book of Howth', *Cal. Carew Mss*, V, pp. 206–7.

[2] Bagwell, *Ireland under the Tudors*, II, pp. 350–2; E. A. Dalton, *A history of Ireland from the earliest times to the year 1547* (2 vols., Dublin, 1903–6), pp. 73–85; N. P. Canny, *The Elizabethan conquest of Ireland: a pattern established 1565–76*.

colonisation and military conquest in Ireland is equally unlike the man who has been credited by other historians as the author of a major experiment in peaceful tenurial reform known as composition.[3] Such contrasting perceptions of Sidney are not simply the result of repeated misapprehensions on the part of his observers, though doubtless this has often been the case. They have their origin rather in the deeply inconsistent character of Sidney's conduct itself: for Sidney was indeed willing both to defend the interests of native lords and to promote those of English adventurers in Ireland; he was indeed happy to propose coercion and to advocate peaceful reform; and finally, Sidney was ever able to alter each of his attitudes and projects to accord with his own needs as viceroy and with the demands of the monarch he served.

The sources of Sidney's persistent eclecticism were complex. That it was at heart a matter of temperament is probable but untestable. But more overt reasons for his attitude could be found in the circumstances in which Sidney assumed and maintained the Irish viceroyalty in the years between 1565 and 1571 and between 1575 and 1578. Like Sussex, Sidney took office with the aim of solving the Tudors' salient problems in Ireland. Yet the manner in which he held office differed considerably from that of his predecessor. Unlike Sussex, Sidney was not a noble whose right and whose obligation to do service for his sovereign were sanctioned by his station. He had gained access to high office only by a repeated demonstration of a great competence and achievement. His reputation as a crown servant, then, stood in need of constant reaffirmation and defence. Neither was Sidney another St Leger, that extraordinary commoner who had enjoyed special privilege as a personal companion of King Henry. He remained instead at one stage removed from his monarch: a talented outsider whose ideas, recommendations and requests would be mediated through a filtering rank of more favoured men whose attitudes and abilities he could do little to influence.

Finally, he had come to the Irish office under particularly unhappy circumstances. Unlike both Sussex and St Leger he had not taken power amidst the disgrace and ruin of his predecessor. Sussex's real inadequacies had certainly been revealed in the years before; but he had not been wholly discredited. Attempts to link him to the scandal of the army's finances had proved futile, and the dismal failure of Arnold's alternative strategy seemed only to confirm the view that, whatever his personal deficiencies, Sussex's fundamental approach toward the government of Ireland had been sound. By the time Sidney took up office, then, Sussex was back in favour at court, a principal adviser to Elizabeth on Irish matters.

[3] Ciaran Brady, 'The government of Ireland *c.* 1540–1583', PhD, University of Dublin, 1980, ch. 5.

Sussex's recovery was to trouble Sidney in several ways. He was of course a highly informed and deeply hostile critic determined to seek revenge upon the *protégé* of the favourite who had brought him down. He provided a focus for whatever Irish enemies the new governor might acquire, many of whom could be sure to receive a sympathetic hearing from the earl. But the greatest influence which Sussex continued to exercise over the Irish office was at once more positive and more subtle. For in spite of the disappointment of his own efforts, Sussex had fundamentally transformed the way in which the Tudor problem in Ireland was to be perceived. In his rejection of St Leger's processes of political management, and in his division of Irish policy into crucial issues which were to be grappled with at once and those which would be easily resolved thereafter, Sussex had produced a model of government that was immensely attractive in its simplicity, economy and apparent conclusiveness. Moreover, by his isolation of particular issues and his specification of the means with which they were to be treated, Sussex had supplied an agenda for the future reform of Ireland to which all of his successors were compelled to address themselves. In all these ways Sussex had established a standard which Sidney himself was bound to meet if his claims to have superseded the earl were to be justified.[4]

Yet even if he was to aim at these ambitions the new viceroy was of necessity compelled to seek the support of interests whose own aims were by no means consistent with these inherited objectives. For those in Ireland and at court who were likely to offer most succour to Sidney's government were inevitably those who for a variety of reasons had been hostile to Sussex's aims and methods while in power. Thus from the beginning there existed a fundamental tension between the objectives which Sidney was bound to pursue as viceroy, and the means by which he hoped to attain them. Yet because the interests which were attracted to his cause were a heterogeneous group, motivated by considerations of a quite different order, the viceroy was granted limited room for manoeuvre in which he might fashion temporary if fragile coalitions in support of his government. Eclecticism, then, was the means by which Sidney sought to consolidate his

---

[4] Fitzwilliam to Sussex, 1 Apr., 10 Oct. 1565, BL, Cotton MSS, Titus B XIII, nos. 46, 52; Cecil to Fitzwilliam, 6 Sept. 1565, Bodleian, Carte MSS, 58/56; Cecil to Smith, 16 Oct. 1565, BL, Lansdowne MSS, 102, no. 66; De Faix (French ambassador) to Francis I, 16 Oct., BN, MS, 15,971; Sidney to Leicester, 13 Dec. 1565, SP 15/12/87, 'There may be fairer semblances between yours and others but trust not before trial for in such trust is often treason'; on the character of the early Elizabethan court in general see, Wallace MacCaffrey, 'Place and patronage in Elizabethan politics' in S. T. Bindoff et al. (eds.), *Elizabethan government and society* (London, 1961), pp. 95–117, Simon Adams, 'Eliza enthroned? the court and its politics', in Christopher Haigh (ed.), *The reign of Elizabeth I* (London, 1985), pp. 55–78; Pam Wright, 'A change of direction' in David Starkey et al., *The English court from the wars of the roses to the civil war* (London, 1987), pp. 147–72.

viceregal authority in circumstances of acute difficulty; and the remarkable fact of his service is not that he often failed in this endeavour, but that he succeeded for so long in doing so.

(11)

The underlying tension between Sidney's aims and the means at his disposal was made apparent even in the first year of his government. Immediately upon appointment, Sidney set about establishing his executive authority in the same way as Sussex had done ten years before. Within the army he instituted an almost complete turn-over of personnel. Over 90 per cent of his captains were new to Ireland, and most of the remainder were men who had never been close to Sussex. Marshal Stanley was forced from office by Nicholas Bagenal who had spent time with Sidney in the West Country following his earlier dismissal under Mary. Jacques Wingfield, Sussex's 'false apostle' who had allied himself to the Leicester group following his disgrace for a display of cowardice against Shane O'Neill in 1562, returned with Sidney fully rehabilitated as master of ordinance. Of Sussex's senior councillors, only one, Fitzwilliam, retained office; and he was Sidney's brother-in-law. There was a new clerk of check and a new clerk of ordinance. Sidney also sought to execute a purge among the constableships: he replaced Henry Stafford with Ralph Morton at Dungarvan, Hugh Lippiat with Francis Cosby at Philipstown, and Henry Radcliffe with Henry Colley at Maryborough. These changes were not made simply for novelty's sake. Both Cosby and Colley were veterans who had served their time under St Leger; and Sidney showed similar confidence in the old soldier Nicholas Heron who retained his position at Leighlin.[5]

Sidney introduced extensive changes in the civil administration also. But here his reshuffling did not involve the appointment of large numbers of English officers as is often assumed. At the highest level those to whom he looked for advice were not new men but those who had been ousted by Sussex and had served under Arnold. Kildare remained the most senior member of the Irish council and retained the high military responsibilities which Arnold had assigned to him. Likewise Sir Thomas Cusacke was

---

[5] Compare HMC, *De Lisle and Dudley MSS*, I, pp. 389 ff., 404, with army lists in *Fitzwilliam Accounts*, e.g., pp. 54–9; 'A particular instruction by Queen Eliz. to Sidney', 9 July 1565, SP 63/14/6; Sussex to queen, 23 Mar. 1566, SP 63/16/65; queen to Sidney, 11 June 1567, *Sid. SP* (IMC, 1966), no. 41 (26), p. 69; Bagenal was not keen to resume the office and Sidney sought without success to have it granted to Thomas Stukley, Sidney to Cecil, 7 Mar. 1566, SP 63/16/52; privy council to Sidney, 18 Feb. 1566, SP 63/16/28; for Wingfield's desertion of Sussex and the phrase quoted in the text, see Fitzwilliam to Sussex, 12 July 1565, BL, Cotton MSS, Titus B XIII, no. 46; 'Advertisement out of Ireland', 3 Mar. 1566, SP 63/16/43; Sidney and council to privy council, 13, 15 Apr. 1566, SP 63/17/8, 13.

retained in favour. Francis Agard (whose father had been so closely allied to St Leger and Brabazon) became one of Sidney's most trusted advisers. Thomas Jenyson, St Leger's auditor who had been dismissed in the scandal of 1556 was also returned to office.[6] And when Sidney did add a new man to the council, he bore a name laden with connotation, Warham St Leger, the viceroy's son.[7] Of the group on whom Sussex had depended only Fitzwilliam and Robert Dillon continued to enjoy a seat on Sidney's inner council.[8] This appointment policy could not be said therefore to have amounted to a 'colonisation' of the Irish civil administration. Though both English newcomers and Irish outsiders benefited from his deployment of patronage, Sidney was primarily concerned to fashion from these diverse clients a dependable executive group who would at once facilitate the implementation of his chosen policies and defend him against any mischief which Sussex's surviving Irish interest might attempt.

In contrast to his views on office-holding, however, Sidney's attitude towards his predecessor's policies was a good deal more receptive. For in this he not only adopted the lieutenant's administrative technique, he commandeered his programme of reform, lock, stock and barrel. Sidney's formal set of instructions, in the drafting of which he took a major part, was a most impressive document. Lengthy, comprehensive and detailed it is among the most thorough of briefings ever given to a Tudor governor in Ireland. Almost every aspect of government responsibility – law and order, financial reform, the organisation of the garrison, the propagation of religious reform – received detailed attention. It is easy to be deceived by the apparent thoroughness of the instructions and even of late some historians have been persuaded to see them as the foundations of a radical 'new departure' in Tudor Irish policy. Yet, though they are replete with the rhetoric of change they emerge on examination to be nothing more than a recapitulation of the principal reforms deemed by Sussex to be immediately requisite for Ireland. Despite, for instance, the apparent freshness of the decision to institute provincial councils, the actual proposals were identical to those envisaged by Sussex in his large reform treatise of 1562. Admittedly, Sidney at first seemed to think that a more martial presidency

---

6 Sidney to Leicester, 1 Mar. 1566, SP 63/16/35 and to privy council, 13 Apr., ibid., 17/8; *Fiants Eliz.*, nos. 741, 823–4, Sidney to privy council, 12 Dec. 1566, SP 63/19/71. Cusacke to Cecil, 7 Mar. 1566, SP 63/16/48: Sidney to privy council, 15 Apr., SP 63/7/13; to Cecil, 18 Nov., SP 63/19/51. 'Memoranda of private suits', Oct. 1565, SP 63/15/10; Sidney and council to privy council, 15 Apr. 1566, SP 63/17/13; Sidney's 'Opinion', 4 July, SP 63/14/3; for service in Wales, see J. R. S. Phillips, *The justices of peace*, pp. 18–19; 'A particular instruction' from Eliz. to Sidney, 9 July 1565, SP 63/14/8.
7 Sidney's 'Opinion' upon his instructions, 4 July, SP 63/14/3; 'Remembrances for Ireland', July, SP 63/14/10.
8 HMC, *Haliday MSS*, pp. 154 ff.

which Sussex had reserved for Ulster might profitably be extended to Munster also, but his own draft instructions for the new presidents showed that he had accepted Sussex's civil model. His views on the president's powers and responsibilities were identical, his projections of the council's security requirements and even his estimate of its costs were almost the same.[9]

A similar lack of originality was evident in Sidney's views on colonisation. He believed that Sussex's attempt to construct a model community in Laois–Offaly should be continued. He deplored the deterioration of the plantation there into a number of besieged military outposts and pledged himself to its reconstruction through 'the building of houses and towns and the setting up of husbandry'.[10] He also shared Sussex's views about the settling of the north-east coast, believing that 'the surest and soonest way' to deal with the Scots was 'to inhabit between them and the sea whereby . . . all hope of succour may be taken from them' and then to proceed to the expulsion.[11]

What is true of the central planks of the programme applies equally to its other elements. Its financial proposals were derived from those made by Gilbert Gerrard and Sussex in 1561.[12] The doctrinal and liturgical directives were based upon those given to Sussex in 1559.[13] Clauses relating to army reform were based on the recommendations made by Sir Nicholas Arnold at the time of his first commission of inquiry.[14] Finally, on the issue which had dominated Sussex's last years in Ireland and which had destroyed Arnold's credibility, Sidney was emphatically orthodox. Shane O'Neill, he believed, might in the end be brought to obedience, but it was certain that he would only be taught to know his fault by force. Clearly, Sidney's instructions constituted not 'a programme of striking originality', but an excellent summary of the conventional wisdom of the day.[15] In so far as they reflected Sidney's own thinking on Ireland, they demonstrated simply that he had absorbed the experience of others, and that his own understanding of Ireland's problems was well informed and up-to-date.

---

[9] First draft, 2 July 1565, second draft, 5 Oct., SP 63/14/2, 15/4. Sidney's 'Articles for public affairs', 20 May 1565, SP 63/13/46; compare 'Instructions for the government of Munster', 1 Feb. 1566, SP 63/16/22, with Sussex's recommendations in Lambeth MSS, 609.
[10] Sidney's 'Articles', 20 May, SP 63/13/46.
[11] Ibid.
[12] Cf. BL, Add. MSS, 4767, no. 22.
[13] Sussex's 'Instructions', 19 July 1559, SP 63/1/57–9; R. D. Edwards, *Church and state in Tudor Ireland*, pp. 177–86.
[14] Cf. Arnold's 'Memoranda', Sept. 1563, SP 63/9/12–13.
[15] For a different view, see N. P. Canny, *From reformation to restoration: Ireland 1534–1660* (Dublin, 1987), pp. 71–98, and *The Elizabethan conquest of Ireland*, passim, esp. ch. 3, from which the phrase quoted is taken.

That they should have been so is not surprising. At a time when Sussex's reputation as a strategist was again in the ascendant, they were designed to reassure the queen and her councillors that Sidney was sound on Ireland and unlikely to run its government aground, as Arnold had risked doing, through the wrong-headed application of out-moded policies. Thus Elizabeth could expect from Sidney all the gains to be reaped from the reappointment of Sussex without any of the obvious risks which that decision would have entailed.

Sidney, however, promised not only to be more efficient than Sussex, he would also be more economical. With the aid of information he had procured both officially and secretly from sources in Ireland, he drew up a schedule which promised to maintain a less costly military establishment than either Arnold or Sussex. By written agreement he bound himself to maintain a garrison costing not more than £1,288 a month. No increase in men or wages was to be made without permission from Whitehall and permission was to be sought only in the most urgent circumstances. Sidney calculated that his government would cost less than £15,500 p.a., a figure more than £4,600 below Sussex's costs in 1563. He promised to have fulfilled all his undertakings within three years of taking office after which time the costs of running Ireland would be greatly reduced.[16] If there was any originality in Sidney's promises of service, it was surely to be found here. In Sidney, Elizabeth seemed to have found a man who embodied all of Sussex's qualities without any of his defects.

Leicester's strategic *volte-face* in abandoning Arnold and promoting the aggressive Sidney was therefore a shrewd tactical manoeuvre. For in changing his agent he at once acknowledged the force of Sussex's theoretical analysis while continuing to deny the earl's competence as a practical administrator. Yet he had retained this advantage only at the cost of narrowing the issues under debate in Ireland from questions of high policy to crude and even sordid matters of personality. For Sidney this personalisation of the Irish viceroyalty was doubly unfortunate. It rendered him in the first place vulnerable to the most petty of personal criticisms: every minor miscalculation could be inflated into a major blunder, every hazard of fortune attributed to the governor's incompetence, every executive decision made suspect of malice and partiality. Such problems were perhaps only more severe in degree than those which had exasperated all of his predecessors. But for Sidney they were deepened by the way in which

---

16 'Book containing the rate . . . of fees and wages', 5 Oct. 1565, SP 63/15/5. Information was procured covertly for Sidney by Jenyson and Wingfield, see Jenyson's 'Brief declaration', c. Apr. 1565, SP 63/13/16 and Fitzwilliam to Sussex, 12 July 1565, BL, Cotton MSS, Titus B XIII, no. 46; 'State of the army in Feb. 1563', SP 63/14/31; Sidney's proposed garrison, 15 July 1565, SP 63/14/19; Sidney to Cecil, 17 Apr. 1566, SP 63/17/14, 15.

Leicester's promotion of the new governor's practical superiority as an administrator focused attention on the one readily discernible standard of measurement: the war against Shane O'Neill. For although Sidney's programme was indeed a good one, and one that he genuinely hoped to implement as soon as possible, the real reason that he was chosen for office was that he seemed likely to succeed where Sussex had been so signally lacking. Thus whatever its intrinsic merits, the implementation of Sidney's reform programme remained subordinate to and dependent upon this short-term expectation which had finally secured his appointment.[17] And it was, of course, in this area that he could expect to exercise least control.

The fundamental priorities of the queen and her council were revealed in the striking contrast between the all but total support he received in his campaign against O'Neill and the persistent lack of enthusiasm which greeted every effort he made to implement his promises in other areas. Once he had decided that no progress could be made by negotiation with O'Neill, Sidney's advice to proceed by force in Ulster was unanimously endorsed by the privy council. The vice-chamberlain, Sir Francis Knollys, was despatched to confer with him on how best this was to be done, and he supported all of Sidney's recommendations. Though they entailed radical departures from his original estimates, Sidney's demands for more troops, munitions and victuals, and his plan to establish a garrison at O'Neill's rear in the Derry were all accepted with little complaint; and though Sussex sought to argue that these demands were inordinate, the governor was authorised to spend up to £35,000 (st.) in his campaign against O'Neill.[18]

The degree of royal largesse, however, was strictly defined. For even as Sidney received support and encouragement in the war in Ulster, his attempts to launch his chosen policies elsewhere met with coolness, obstruction and rebuff. Even before his arrival in Ireland, Sidney's image as a total surrogate for Sussex had begun to fade. In the second half of 1565 as Elizabeth grew tired of unseemly displays of court rivalries, her attitude toward Leicester cooled and Sussex grew in favour. The effects of this changing atmosphere were directly felt by Sidney. Though his appointment had been decided upon in March, he was not actually confirmed in office until late October. In tardily granting her assent, the queen also gave

---

[17] For a succinct statement of Sidney's personal attitude towards his brief in Ireland, see Sidney to Leicester, 1 Mar. 1566, SP 63/16/35.

[18] Sidney to Cecil, 17 Apr., SP 63/17/15; 'Memorial' for Knollys, SP 63/17/20, Knollys to Cecil, 19 May, SP 63/17/56. Cecil to Sidney, 18 May 1566, SP 63/17/54: Elizabeth to Sidney, 15 June, SP 63/18/17; Cecil to Sidney, 24 June, SP 63/18/27; Elizabeth to Sidney, 8 July, SP 63/18/46; 'Memoranda', July 1566, SP 63/18/36, 38, 39–40; Cecil's 'Memoranda', May 1566, SP 63/17/71.

evidence of her growing disenchantment: in the first draft of his instructions, it was assumed that Sidney would succeed to Sussex's title as lord lieutenant, but when he took office he did so as mere lord deputy.[19]

Once in Ireland Sidney experienced increasing difficulty in establishing his executive authority. His replacements of Sussex's men in Dungarvan and Leighlin were overturned; his decision to appoint Bagenal as marshal was hotly disputed until Stanley voluntarily relinquished service. In the church his recommendations of Terence Danyell for the see of Armagh and Hugh Brady for the see of Dublin were ignored, and in the army even innocuous attempts to fill vacancies were greeted with suspicion and deferred. Sidney showed some sympathy for Arnold's difficulties and he was accused of conspiring against Sussex; he praised Kildare and Cusacke for their efforts on his behalf, and he was rebuked for being 'guided in the government by councillors of Irish birth'. When he attempted to arrange an exchange of lands between Bagenal and Thomas Stucley, he was suspected of fraud.[20]

Sidney was convinced that Sussex lay behind all these frustrations. He was not entirely mistaken; for since his departure from London, Sussex and his ally the duke of Norfolk had been actively campaigning against him at court, accusing him variously of vanity, malice and even cowardice.[21] Sidney was infuriated by these slights and despite Cecil's assurances of the queen's good-will, he demanded to be allowed to return to face his adversaries: he even

[19] Fitzwilliam to Sussex, 1 Apr. 1565, BL, Cotton MSS, Titus B XIII, no. 46, Sidney's 'Memoranda', 20, 25 May, SP 63/13/45–6, 49; memorandum of privy council, 4 June 1565, *Cal. SP Foreign (1564–5)*, p. 386. Cecil to Fitzwilliam, 6 Sept. 1565, Bodl., Carte MSS, 58/56. Fitzwilliam to Sussex, 10 Oct. 1565, BL, Cotton MSS, Titus B XIII, no. 52; French ambassador, de Faix, to king, 16 Oct., BN, MS, 15,971; *APC (1558–70)*, p. 264; 'Instructions for Sir Henry Sidney', 5 Oct. 1565, SP 63/15/4, 6; Cecil to Smith, 16 Oct., BL, Lansdowne MSS, 102, no. 66; compare draft instructions of 4 July, SP 63/14/2 with formal instructions of 5 Oct., SP 63/15/4.

[20] Sidney to Cecil, 9 June 1566, SP 63/18/8; Eliz. to Sidney, 20 Oct., SP 63/19/24; Cecil to Sidney, 10 July 1567, SP 63/21/58; Sidney to Cecil, 4 Mar. 1567, SP 63/20/41; Sidney, 'Memorandum', 12 May, 63/20/87; 'Memorial for Sir Edward Horsey', 20 Oct. 1566, SP 63/19/25, Eliz. to Sidney, 11 June 1567, *Sid. SP*, no. 41 (26); Sidney to Cecil, 24 Nov. 1565, SP 63/15/51 and Eliz. to Sidney, 6 July 1567, *Sid. SP*, no. 42; Sidney to Cecil, 23 Apr. 1566, SP 63/17/31, Brady was known to be a *protégé* of Leicester, Fitzwilliam to Sussex, 31 Jan. 1566, BL, Cotton MSS, Titus, B XIII, no. 46, reporting information conveyed by arch-bishop Loftus; Sidney to Privy council, 13 Apr., 30 May 1566, SP 63/17/8, 68; Sidney to Leicester, 1 Mar. 1566, SP 63/10/35 and 28 June, HMC, *De Lisle and Dudley MSS*, II, pp. 2–3; Cecil to Sidney, 27 Mar., SP 63/16/67, Eliz. to Sidney, 28 Mar., *Sid. SP*, no. 12; Sidney to Cecil, 7 Mar. 1566, SP 63/16/52, 17 Apr., SP 63/17/15, Cecil to Sidney, 27 Mar., SP 63/16/17; Eliz. to Sidney, 31 May, *Sid. SP*, no. 13.

[21] Sidney to council, 15 Apr., 11 July 1566, SP 63/17/13, 18/54; to Cecil, 17 Apr., SP 63/17/14; for an account of the general divisions at court in this period, see Conyers Read, *Mr Secretary Cecil and Queen Elizabeth* (London, 1955), ch. 16; Sidney to Leicester, 28 June; HMC, *De Lisle and Dudley MSS*, II, pp. 2–3.

challenged Sussex to a duel.[22] Sussex was certainly anxious to do the deputy any harm he might, but it would be wrong to assume that Elizabeth was wholly given over to the Norfolk interest. Instead, the queen who had been persuaded to accept Sidney in Ireland as an alternative and superior Sussex was determined that he should remain that and nothing else. Concerned that Leicester might through Sidney extend his clientage networks far into Ireland, the queen moved to curb the deputy's powers of patronage. Her desire to maintain administrative continuity and political balance was on one level perfectly reasonable, yet her persistent interventions in matters of appointment seriously damaged the viceroy's prestige and credit. What was merely a source of irritation in questions of patronage, however, became a matter of extreme gravity when Elizabeth sought to counter the new governor's attitude toward the faction-ridden Anglo-Irish.

Since the great houses of Ormond and Kildare had rapidly become aligned with the rival groups of early Elizabethan politics, with the Butlers supporting Sussex and their rivals the Geraldines seeking the friendship of the earl's English opponents, it was inevitable that Sidney should look to the Geraldines for support and advance their interest as much as he could. Such alterations of alliance between new governors and old factions had been common in Ireland since the 1530s, but Elizabeth was determined on this occasion to prevent it. Even before he left for Ireland she wrote to 'Harry' in a secret and almost intimate manner, urging him to 'make some difference twixt tried just and false friends'. The Butlers, she intimated, had always been loyal servants of the crown; she did not wish to see them alienated through the employment of policies and officers sympathetic to their enemies. And she warned Sidney explicitly that if he proceeded to do so, she would stop him: 'If I had not espied though late *leger de main* used in these cases, I had never played my part. Nor if I did not see the balances held awry, I had never myself come into the weigh-house'.[23]

At first Elizabeth held her hand, waiting to see if Sidney would heed her warning. She grudgingly accepted Warham St Leger as Sidney's man in Munster, but refused to appoint him formally as president there.[24] She sought balance simply through the dispensation of favour to Ormond, renewing his leases, repaying debts owed to him and restoring to him the

[22] Sidney to privy council, 18, 30 May, 11 July 1566, SP 63/17/55, 68, 18/54; to Cecil, 3 June 1566, SP 63/18/1; Cecil to Sidney, 16, 24 June, SP 63/18/1, 19, 27 May; Eliz. to Sidney, 5 July, *Sid. SP*, no. 21.

[23] Eliz. to Sidney, 6 Jan. 1566, Collins, *Letters and memorials of state*, I, p. 7.

[24] St Leger to Cecil, 6 Mar. 1566, SP 63/16/47; St Leger to Sidney, 3 July 1566, SP 63/18/54, enclosure (i). It is clear from Fitzwilliam's account that a presidential council in Munster actually functioned under St Leger between Jan. and Dec. 1566, NRO, Fitzwilliam MSS (Irish), no. 47.

privileges and liberties which Arnold had revoked.[25] Sidney coped with such moderate interferences calmly. He deferred action on several of the queen's directives concerning Ormond, and did his best to conceal Desmond's continuing disorders. He wrote pressingly to Cecil and the council on Desmond's behalf affirming that the earl was well-intentioned but arguing that his financial situation was precarious and that the queen's coldness and favour toward his enemy could well drive him into a rebellion which the government could not contain.[26] Thus playing for time, Sidney hoped that his good service elsewhere might allay the queen's mistrust and allow him a free hand in Munster.

In the autumn of 1566 Sidney did what was expected of him and opened his campaign against O'Neill. But as with Sussex it was Sidney's 'luck not to light upon him'.[27] As his supplies ran low and his costs mounted so dissatisfaction with his performance mounted at court. His troubles deepened when Sir Edmund Randolf, the garrison commander at the Derry was killed in a skirmish and the demoralised outpost was totally destroyed by an explosion of gunpowder. As preoccupation with the war against O'Neill grew, so the gap between the immediate objectives of the crown and the larger ambitions of the deputy widened, and Sidney's competence as a governor came to be judged simply by his ability to deal with Shane. Sidney found his predicament intolerable. 'With what peril shall I follow the fortune of the wars', he complained, 'when every accident though ne'er so well intended, yet following out not so fortunate shall seem a jealous suspicion to the canker conceived'.[28] As the campaign dragged on Sidney's sensitivity to slander at court became obsessive: 'A governor', he declared, 'is no longer to be detained than maintained'. By late 1566 after the disaster at the Derry his demands for recall had become incessant. 'For God's sake', he begged Cecil in January 1567, 'take me out of this world'.[29]

O'Neill's elusiveness thus threatened to consume Sidney as it had destroyed Sussex. But there was worse to come. Disappointed with Sidney, Desmond had returned to a reliance on his own resources. He had gathered

---

[25] Eliz. to Sidney, 31 Mar., 14 May 1566, *Sid. SP*, nos. 13, 15 Aug., ibid., no. 23; Cecil to Sidney, 31 Mar., SP 63/16/71; Eliz. to Sidney, 21 Aug. 1566, SP 63/18/94, *Cal. pat. rolls Henry VIII–Eliz.*, p. 511.

[26] Sidney and council to privy council, 13 Apr., 11 July 1566, SP 63/17/8, 18/54; and to Leicester, 19 Aug., Collins, *Letters and memorials of state*, I, pp. 15–17.

[27] Sidney's 'Memoir', *UJA*, 1st ser., 3, p. 41.

[28] Sidney to privy council, 18 May 1566, SP 63/17/55.

[29] Ibid., or less felicitously 'My counsel is that the governor's continuance here and continuance there be concurrent and correlative', Sidney to Leicester, 28 June, Collins, *Letters and memorials of state*, I, pp. 14–15; Sidney to Cecil, 24 June, SP 63/18/25; to Leicester, 28 June, Collins, I, p. 14; to privy council, 11 July, SP 63/18/54: to Cecil, 18 Nov., SP 63/19/51 and 18 Jan., SP 63/20/13.

a large army, collecting his feudal dues by destraint and resuming bush warfare with the Butlers.[30] Reports of these mischiefs, suitably embellished by Ormond, further weakened Sidney's credit with the queen. 'We think surely since your going from hence you are entered into some great mist or darkness of judgement', she warned him, 'and are like to enter into so great errors for the government of that realm as are not to be suffered in one that is appointed to govern as you are'.[31] Through the winter of 1566–7 Elizabeth's displeasure increased. St Leger was forbidden to deal in Ormond's affairs and in December withdrawn from Munster altogether. By early 1567 Elizabeth's suspicions against Desmond had hardened into certainty. She was convinced that Desmond was wholly responsible for the feud with the Butlers and that matters 'hitherto on the part of the earl made doubtful were very true and manifest and only delayed by him to avoid due punishment here'. By his recent disorders, she reasoned also, Desmond had forfeited his recognisance of £20,000: on 3 April she ordered his arrest.[32]

Long before then, however, Sidney had accepted defeat. As early as August he had warned Leicester that he could not continue to shield the earl indefinitely.[33] Weeks later he told him that he believed a rebellion in Desmond to be inevitable.[34] This was a radical departure from the assumptions on which Sidney and Leicester had originally planned the establishment of a Munster presidency, and Sidney felt required to justify his views by sending a special messenger to Leicester 'in order that you may see the mutability of men and how my opinion is altered for the Desmond and why'.[35] By January 1567 he had cooled down. Setting out on his Munster circuit, he knighted Desmond's brother John and placed him at the head of a commission of peace in the Desmond lordship; but anticipating an imminent directive from Westminster, he arrested the earl himself outside Kilmallock. Sidney's plans for Munster, like his hopes for Ulster and all his other schemes, seemed thus to have ground to a halt.[36]

But suddenly the viceroy's fortunes changed. In early June in the midst of secret negotiations with Alexander MacDonnell, Shane O'Neill was

30 Sidney to Leicester, 18 Aug. 1566, Collins, *Letters and memorials of state*, I, pp. 6–7; Eliz. to Sidney, 13 Aug. 1566 and 24 Mar. 1567, *Sid. SP*, nos. 23, 34; Cecil to Sidney, 20 Oct., SP 63/19/27.

31 Eliz. to Sidney, 13 Aug., SP 63/18/80.

32 Eliz. to Sidney, 14 May 1566, *Sid. SP*, no. 14, Sidney to privy council, 12 Dec., SP 63/19/71; Eliz. to Sidney, 16 Jan. 1567, *Sid. SP*, no. 32; Eliz. to Sidney, 23 Apr., 24 May 1567, *Sid. SP*, nos. 34, 27, the quotation is from no. 37.

33 Sidney to Leicester, 19 Aug. 1566, Collins, *Letters and memorials of state*, I, pp. 15–17.

34 Sidney to Leicester, 5 Sept., HMC, *Pepys MS*, p. 90.

35 Ibid.

36 'Order for the commiting of the earl of Desmond', HMC, *De Lisle and Dudley MSS*, II, p. 5; *Fiants Eliz.*, no. 1777: Sidney to Eliz., 20 Apr. 1567, SP 63/20/66; Sidney, 'Memoir', *UJA*, 1st ser., pp. 43–4.

assassinated and his army put to rout. Though it is probable that Sidney intrigued with the Scots in advance of their meeting with O'Neill through William Piers of Carrickfergus, Sidney could claim no overt credit for this event.[37] Yet he could claim that his own efforts against O'Neill had been indirectly responsible for Shane's last desperate actions. He had served well in the north; but more importantly he had grudgingly allowed his own aims elsewhere and the interests of his allies to be systematically overridden by the royal will, and so he remained her majesty's fully accredited viceroy when this piece of good fortune fell to him. Thus by a combination of luck, hard work and sheer acquiescence in defeat, did Sidney's first term end in sudden and unexpected success.

(III)

It is difficult to exaggerate the importance of the elimination of Shane O'Neill. The English government's failure to subdue him had become a serious international embarrassment, an indication to foreign observers of the essential weakness of the regime.[38] It had become an obsession at court to which all other Irish affairs had been subordinated for almost a decade. O'Neill's death, therefore, presented the government with an unprecedented opportunity. For the first time since the beginning of the reign it had the chance of essaying the general reform of Ireland. A special subcommittee of the privy council was established to review reform proposals. Secretary Cecil was to travel to Ireland to review the situation for himself and Sidney was directed to submit his own recommendations at the earliest possible moment.[39]

Sidney's new proposals were entirely consistent with those which he had advanced two years earlier.[40] He recommended that the Scots be expelled from the north-east through the enterprise of English adventurers, or through the efforts of captains recently discharged from the garrison. The intended colony, however, was to be limited to the area now inhabited by the Scots: the Gaelic lords who had cooperated in the war against O'Neill were to be received by the queen and allowed to resume their lands under English tenure. Sidney wanted the province surveyed and a rental drawn up;

[37] Fitzwilliam to Henry Fitzwilliam, 11 June 1567, NRO, Fitzwilliam MSS (Correspondence), no. 27; for a detailed account see Ciaran Brady, 'The killing of Shane O'Neill: some new evidence', *The Irish Sword* 15 (1982–3), pp. 116–23.

[38] See various ambassadorial reports in *Cal. SP Spain (1558–67)*, pp. 555, 572, 574, 580, 599; *Cal. SP Rome (1558–71)*, p. 168, *Cal. SP Venice (1558–80)*, p. 382; king's council to de Sossy (French ambassador), 26 July, 12 Aug. 1566, BN, Fonds, Français MS, 17832.

[39] Winchester to Sidney, 1 July 1567, SP 63/21/41; Eliz. to Sidney, 11 July, *Sid. SP*, no. 42; Cecil to Sidney, 22 July, SP 63/21/70.

[40] Memoranda of Sidney's propositions, June, July 1567, SP 63/21/20, 48.

a resumption of the crown's rights in the area, he argued, would yield a handsome revenue. At this stage, however, Sidney had no intention of destroying the power of the native lords, or even that of the O'Neills. He recommended that Turlough Luineach O'Neill, the man who had assumed the chieftaincy after Shane, be elevated to the peerage and that he be granted suzerainty over all the inhabitants of Tyrone. Far from being a threat to the government, he believed that Turlough would be an effective means of containment: 'To keep the O'Neills from combination nothing can work a better effect than to give Turlough Luineach a superiority over the rest'.[41] He would welcome and lend support to a president who was to be established at Armagh. The continued toleration of Gaelic captaincies, Sidney admitted, was not ideal, but it was the only realistic way to commence the reduction of the province to English order. 'So as that which is wished for and cannot be perfected may by preparation be made after to succeed'.[42] The echoes of Sussex's gradualism were unmistakable.

Having despatched his proposals, Sidney set about preparing for their execution. He journeyed to Tyrone to assure Turlough of the crown's favour, and hinting strongly that he would be created an earl, he secured the captain's agreement to the establishment of a provincial council. He appointed the dean of Armagh to ensure the maintenance of good relations between Turlough and Dublin and he commissioned the Palesman Thomas Fleming to commence the survey for the proposed rental.[43] Sidney made similar preparations for reform in the south. Though Desmond remained under arrest at Dublin, Sidney confirmed and extended the powers of Sir John of Desmond, and he left Sir Warham St Leger, now settled in his own lands in Desmond, as his unofficial agent in the province, awaiting the time when he would be officially recognised as president.[44]

The character of these proposals was evidence of Sidney's belief that despite the frustrations and disappointments of his first years in government, it was still possible to return to the conventional reform strategy which he had advanced in 1565. Yet the real attraction of Sidney's ideas continued to rest on the basis of his recently revived personal prestige; and as such it was inherently unstable. Even by the time he had arrived at court the euphoria that had greeted first reports of Shane's end had subsided.

[41] Sidney's 'Memorandum', 15 July 1567, SP 63/21/48.
[42] Eliz. to Sidney paraphrasing Sidney's advice as related by Francis Agard, 6 July 1567, *Sid. SP*, no. 42.
[43] Turlough's submission, 18 June, SP 63/21/22; Turlough to Eliz. and Sidney, 15 Dec., SP 63/22/43, 44; Sidney, 'Memoir', *UJA*, 3, pp. 92–3; Danyell to Cecil, 5 Oct., SP 63/22/1; 'Rental of Ulster', 1567, SP 63/22/66; 'Notes for Mr Secretary', July 1568, SP 63/35/14.
[44] St Leger remained on full salary as president, without a council until 15 Aug., NRO, Fitzwilliam MSS (Irish), no. 47.

Sidney found himself coldly received and his achievements denigrated.[45] As the aura of victory palled around him, Sidney began to appear once more as the controversial man of faction whose propositions were to be viewed in that light. Elizabeth was again suspicious, and she began to dismantle the preparations which the viceroy had made for his future reform programme. In Sidney's absence she ordered the lords justices, Sir William Fitzwilliam and Chief Justice Weston, to dismiss Sir John of Desmond from his commission, had him arrested and despatched along with the earl from Dublin to the Tower of London.[46] On her instructions the lords justice similarly reversed Sidney's Ulster policy. They refused Turlough the *de facto* recognition which Sidney had allowed him, censured his use of the title O'Neill and insisted on his resubmission to the government. At the same time, Elizabeth also encouraged Hugh MacNeill More, Turlough's rival and demanded far harsher treatment of Shane's former supporters than Sidney . had advised.[47]

In the midst of these reversals Sidney was struck down by illness.[48] He had suffered grievously from gall-stones during his Irish service, and two months after his return from Ireland his condition worsened. Thus at a crucial time in the debate on Ireland he was forced to withdraw to Penshurst until he passed a stone 'the quantity of a nutmeg'. In his absence the privy council was deluged by a wide variety of schemes. Lord Treasurer Winchester wanted the least change possible. The military establishment was to be reduced and the problem of the north was to be resolved by generous and loose understandings with the indigenous powers. Colonisation was to be attempted only with their cooperation. Winchester wanted Desmond returned to Munster as quickly as possible and like Sidney he believed that Kildare was a man of great potential service who should be encouraged and appointed to oversee the arrangement of affairs in Ulster.[49] Other views were far less sympathetic. Vice-chamberlain Knollys agreed that a colony should be established in the north; but perversely he wanted an agreement made with the Scots to expel the Irish.[50] Even where there was agreement

---

[45] Sidney, 'Memoir', *UJA*, III, p. 94; Collins, *Letters and memorials of state*, I, p. 88.

[46] Eliz. to lords justice, 3 Nov. 1567, SP 63/22/20; lords justice to Eliz., 12 Dec. 1567, SP 63/22/40; 'Writ of arrest', 17 Nov., Bodl., Carte MSS, 58/97; Fitzwilliam to Sidney, 20 Nov., Carte MSS, 58/102.

[47] Fitzwilliam to Cecil, 22 Nov. 1567, SP 63/22/23; lords justice to Eliz., 23 Nov., SP 63/22/23; lords justice to Turlough Luineach, 18 and 14 Nov., Bodl., Carte MSS, 58/195 and 105; Fitzwilliam to Leicester, 9 Dec., Carte MSS, 58/123–4, Fitzwilliam to Eliz., 27 Dec., Carte MSS, 31/9; Eliz. to the lords justice, 10 Dec. 1567, SP 63/22/37.

[48] This paragraph is based on an account by Sidney's physician, *c.* Feb. 1568, SP 15/14/6.

[49] Winchester to Sidney, 24 June 1567, 1 July, SP 63/21/28, 41, Winchester's 'Opinion', June, SP 63/21/33 enclosure (i).

[50] Knollys' 'Opinion', 7 July 1567, SP 63/21/56.

that colonisation should be directed against the Scots, serious differences arose over the extent of the area to be planted and the treatment of the native Irish tenants and freeholders within it. Some sought to have the entire area east of the Bann cleared for a thorough English plantation, others to have portions of the coastline and some islands farmed out as a fief, while others, including Cecil, paid serious attention to the moderate propositions of Rowland White who argued for the integration of native and English settlers in pocketed agricultural colonies.[51] In regard to Munster the council was equally open to suggestion. A plan to farm the fishing of the south and south-east coasts which involved the confiscation of much coastal land in Desmond was entertained and the personal projects of Sir Peter Carew who laid claims to extensive territories in Munster, Leinster and even in the Pale were encouraged.[52] Thus while the debate over policy continued, Sidney's plans to establish a new territorial settlement under the aegis of provincial councils simply became one among many in the richness of choice that now seemed available to the English crown.

It was only the rapid deterioration of the situation in Ireland in Sidney's absence that determined the council's decision to return him in 1568. The removal of Sir John of Desmond had greatly exacerbated existing centrifugal tendencies within the lordship, and Desmond had become a battleground for warring factions. The Butlers took advantage of these disorders by reviving old territorial disputes and increasing their raids on Desmond territory. As the lordship grew in danger of total disintegration a new leader, James Fitzmaurice Fitzgerald, took it upon himself to defend the Geraldine inheritance from all encroachments, feudal and governmental, and commenced open war with the Butlers and their allies.[53] In Ulster, Turlough Luineach, disappointed by the failure to honour Sidney's promises, also took matters into his own hands. He made peace with the Scots, began importing large numbers of mercenaries and formed an alliance with the MacDonnells against a government from whom they feared a mutual threat.

[51] Cecil, 'Memorial', Nov. 1567, SP 63/22/34.101; Thornton to Cecil renewing his suit for Island Magee, 2 July 1568, SP 63/25/19; 'Propositions by an Irishman', c. Jan. 1568, SP 63/23/29; Hatfield House, Cecil MSS, CP, vol. 207 passim: for an account of White's connection with Cecil and a formal presentation of White's mature views, see N. P. Canny (ed.), 'Rowland White's "Discours touching Ireland c. 1569"', *IHS*, 20 (1976–7), pp. 439–63.

[52] 'Device for the plantation of Ireland with Englishmen', Jan. 1568, SP 63/23/26; 'Demands of Sir Warham St Leger et al. for the fishing of the South', c. 1568, SP 63/26/81; for the general background to these colonisation projects, see Canny, *The Elizabethan conquest of Ireland*, ch. 4; also John Hooker, *Life of Sir Peter Carew*, ed. John MacClean (London, 1857).

[53] Lords Justice to Eliz., 23 Jan. 1568, SP 63/23/16 and enclosures, esp. Countess of Desmond to commissioners, 11 Jan., 63/23/16, enclosure (ii). Lords Justice to Eliz., 8 Feb. 1568, SP 63/23/32 and enclosures (vi–ix), Fitzwilliam to Draycott, 8 Feb., Bodl., Carte MSS, 58/263.

They were soon joined by O'Donnell himself embittered by the lack of favour he had received since the killing of Shane O'Neill. Against these ominous developments the lords justices were powerless. Their belated attempts at conciliation only convinced the Ulster lords that something more threatening was at hand.[54]

It was this sudden resurgence of crisis in Ulster and in Munster that occasioned Sidney's resumption of office. Once again the immediate reason for his appointment lay not in the appeal of his ideas which more than ever were buried under a mass of competing propositions, but in the urgent needs of the government. The tension between the long-term aims of the governor and the priorities of his superiors which had vitiated Sidney's first service in Ireland thus remained alive. If anything the situation facing Sidney was worse. The council's failure to endorse a positive programme was accompanied by an increased insistence on economy. The emphasis of the instructions he received in August was almost entirely financial. No grants were to be made without a new survey, rents were to be raised where possible and entry fines were to be increased. A commission on arrears was to see that all debts were followed up and all debtors destrained. With the garrison maintained at 1,500 men, Sidney was to appoint no new captains and all pensioners were to be put in places of employ.[55]

In contrast to the specific nature of these restrictions no guidance was given as to which of the many schemes now crowding the council the deputy should favour and which he should reject. The responsibility of fashioning a coherent plan of government out of these scattered ideas – none of which had been formally endorsed by the council – was formidable and highly intimidating. But the new circumstances seemed at least to offer Sidney an escape from the taint of party which had dogged his first years in office. By appearing to support all of the options which had been proposed to the council, by welcoming the offers of all who had been licensed to adventure in Ireland, by returning to Ireland in a time of crisis and under extremely restricted conditions, Sidney could give no better token that he sought office neither for political nor personal reasons but simply to do good service for the crown. The conditions under which he was to prove his worth were indeed harsh; yet he was confident that he had found a means both to meet all his various commitments and to institute his own chosen policies with authority. The means in which he placed so much confidence was a parliament.

---

[54] Fitzwilliam to Cecil, 17 Jan. 1568, SP 63/23/11 and enclosures (i–iv), and 22 Jan., SP 63/23/15; lords justice and council to Eliz., 23, 26 Jan., 8 Feb., SP 63/23/16, 20 and enclosures, 32 and enclosures; Bagenal to lords justice, 20 Mar., SP 63/23/74, enclosure (viii); lords justice to Cecil, 23 Mar., SP 63/23/75.

[55] Sidney's 'Instructions', final draft, 21 July 1568, SP 63/25/50.

Sidney had first sought to reconvene parliament in 1566, but the meagre revenue it then promised was not thought to be worth the trouble, so, like so much of his first reform programme, the idea was shelved.[56] O'Neill's death in rebellion, however, significantly altered the situation. Plans to pass an act of attainder were immediately laid, and when Sidney's return was again made certain, the Irish council submitted a large collection of draft legislation for the inspection of the viceroy and the privy council.[57]

Several of the bills were of a purely financial nature, concerning the renewal of the subsidy, the regulation of trades and the introduction of a new impost on wines which it was hoped would yield £6,000 pa.[58] But for Sidney the most important measures were those which laid the basis for the extensive reform of land tenure in Ireland. Chief among them was the bill for the attainder of Shane O'Neill. An extraordinary piece of legislation which seemed to aim at the resolution of several different issues at once, the bill was in many ways a symbol of Sidney's revised attitude toward government. By accepting at full value Shane's occasional boast that the O'Neill was lord of all Ulster and by citing a large set of precedents granting the crown full title to the province, the bill seemed to give the government the right to dispose of most of the land in Ulster as it pleased. Yet by means of a severely doctored history several of the provincial lords including O'Donnell, O'Reilly and Maguire were claimed as ancient loyal subjects of the crown and traditional enemies of the O'Neill, and their time-honoured allegiance, the preamble implied, was now to be rewarded by tenurial security. Again, while several other lords were cited as abettors of O'Neill in rebellion, and so deserving of attainder also, the act contained a clause excusing their contribution on grounds of coercion, recording their submission and requests to be reconciled and referring their subsequent fate to the discretion of the viceroy himself. This assertion of viceregal discretion was buttressed by fulsome praise of Sidney himself. It was Sidney who had first determined that Shane should be destroyed and who had brought him down. No mention was made here of Sussex's strenuous efforts to prove that Shane was irreconcilable, nor of the early disasters of Sidney's own campaigns against him, and the dubious intrigues surrounding Shane's assassination were obscured by a lurid tale of drink, sex and murder at the feast. More importantly, Sidney's success against Shane was claimed to have

[56] Sidney to Cecil, 18 Nov. 1566, SP 63/19/51; Eliz. to Sidney, 16 Jan. 1567, SP 63/20/8.
[57] 'Abstract of Bills', SP 63/27/12–15; *Cal. Pat. Rolls Henry VIII–Eliz.*, p. 503; Loftus to Cecil, 2 Apr. 1568, SP 63/24/1; Cecil, 'Memorandum', 24 Apr., SP 63/24/16. I have followed Victor Treadwell's reconstruction in 'The Irish parliament of 1569–71', *Proc. RIA*, 65 (1966–7), sec. C, pp. 55–89.
[58] For an analysis, see Treadwell, 'The Irish parliament of 1569–71'.

been part of his larger achievement in establishing English rule in Ireland, not by force but by the abolition of that bug-bear of reformers, coyne and livery. The complete settlement of all Ireland's ills, the preamble declared, with all of the optimism and urgency of Sussex's propaganda style, was now on the point of fulfilment if only the viceroy was granted the freedom and the support to finish the job.[59]

The attainder of Shane O'Neill thus constituted the mast-head of a series of bills by which Sidney planned to recover the initiative of reform. Alongside it were a series of lesser bills of attainder concerning crown lands in Munster and Leinster. But of greater significance were the bills suppressing coyne and livery, proposing the shiring of all unorganised territories and giving total discretion to the deputy and council in the negotiation of all surrender and regrant agreements with the lords of Ireland.[60]

In his correspondence with London, Sidney was careful to relate this ambitious political programme to the purely fiscal side of his proposed legislation. The rent of the attainted lands in Ulster at the rate of a mere penny an acre would yield £700, but in less conservative estimates Sidney was prepared to guess that the imposition of a small land tax would produce some £5,000 p.a. The extension of the subsidy into new shire grounds would transform that modest income into a handsome £7,500 p.a. Regrants of lands would net an immediate lump sum of £2,000, while the new yields to be acquired thereby could yield an annual £13,500.[61]

In presenting his policy goals in such terms, Sidney paid obeisance to the Tudor insistence on the primacy of economy; yet he exploited this concern to win support for a scheme which both he and Sussex had regarded as essential to reform but had so far been unable to put into operation: the establishment of provincial councils. For shiring, the collection of subsidy and of new rents could be effected only through the extension of the government's executive arm. The crucial importance of presidencies was thus made manifest; they were to realise the gain already inherent in the situation in provincial Ireland. Their establishment could no longer be seen as a costly and uncertain experiment, but merely as the completion of a process already well under way. This presentation of councils as both the instruments of social reform and the coping stones of a new financial structure worked the desired effect at Westminster. By the time he left for Ireland the queen had decided to establish presidents in both Munster

---

[59] Davies' Speaker's address to parliament in 1613, Henry Morley (ed.), *Ireland under Elizabeth and James I* (London, 1897), p. 400.
[60] *Irish Statutes*, I, 11, Eliz. I, *c.* 9, p. 322; 'Abstract of bills', SP 63/27/12, nos. 15, 27, 29.
[61] 'Ulster rented and divided', *c.* 1567, SP 63/22/66; 'Estimate of yearly profits, 1568', SP 63/26/65.

and Connacht and the Munster president's instructions were already drafted.[62]

Sidney's success in securing support for this central instrument of reform government could not entail the abandonment of the other projects which the council had entertained in the months before. The council had already approved the idea of establishing colonies in Munster and Ulster in principle, and it was expected that Sidney would lend support to any authorised expedition. Sidney indeed had little desire to suppress private enterprise; for the more projects he incorporated in his government, the greater the basis of support he acquired and the less vulnerable he became to allegations of favouritism. So just as he bowed to the economic priorities of the crown, Sidney accepted and encouraged the speculative enterprises of others. He recommended proposals from Warham St Leger, Jerome Brett and Jacques Wingfield for settlements in Munster and he firmly supported Sir Peter Carew's efforts in Meath and Idrone.[63] In the north he informed Turlough Luineach that he would not accept his promises of good-will until he had acknowledged the crown's rights in the province.[64] He supported the project of the Chatterton brothers to establish a colony in the Fews and he suggested that further places in the province might be planted by enterprising Englishmen to the profit of the queen and the adventurers alike. But he encouraged such projects without prejudicing the larger rental plan which he was promoting in relation to the provinces as a whole and which he assured the queen would produce a satisfactory revenue even if no planting were undertaken at all.[65]

This ambivalence concerning Ulster was typical of Sidney's revised outlook. In order to maintain his own authority he was prepared to accommodate any course that had received approval at Westminster. Thus while he regarded the winning of rents from the indigenous population as the best available policy, he was not prepared to exclude any other approach in its interests. Alternative enterprises were acceptable as long as they were successful and as long as they did not conflict with his own general aims as governor. The character of Sidney's new government was thus neither predominantly 'tough' nor 'soft': it was essentially eclectic, the product of

---

[62] Cecil's 'Memorandum', 29 Apr., SP 63/24/16; Sidney, 'Memorandum', 27 June, SP 63/25/11. Sidney to Cecil, 8 Aug., Collins, *Letters and memorials of state*, I, pp. 34–6: 'Instructions for Sir John Pollard', Oct. 1568, SP 63/26/9, 10.

[63] Sidney's 'Remembrances', July 1568, SP 63/25/13–15; Sidney to Cecil, 17 Nov., Collins, *Letters and memorials of state*, I, p. 39; Carew to Cecil, 26 Dec., SP 63/26/59; Wingfield to Cecil, 12 Nov., SP 63/26/59.

[64] Sidney to Cecil, 12 Nov., SP 63/26/18 and 30 Nov., Collins, *Letters and memorials of state*, I, pp. 40–1.

[65] Sidney to Cecil, 30 Nov., Collins, *Letters and memorials of state*, I, pp. 40–1.

his determination to repudiate his image of party interest and to secure the greatest freedom possible in the discharge of his office.

This attempt to contain diversity within the framework of a single government programme was, however, an extremely dangerous undertaking. But Sidney made every effort to minimise the risks. He planned to restore order in Desmond by returning Sir John and by reappointing St Leger to a position of authority.[66] He wanted Ormond sent home to curb the unrest of his brothers, and he sought to placate Kildare by having his long-awaited patent of restoration passed for him.[67] The O'Neill attainder expatiated on the common interests that linked the governor to the old colonial community, and contained a provision protecting the rights of Anglo-Irish claimants to land in Ulster.[68] To reduce friction to a minimum Sidney was even prepared to enter a dubious victualling contract to ease the burden of supply on the Pale.[69] At the same time he pressed hard for the rapid establishment of presidents in Munster and Ulster, impressing Cecil, in the manner of Sussex, of the absolute urgency of their despatch.[70]

But despite his pleadings Sidney's friends at court let him down. He left Ireland as the major problems which had dominated the first decade of Elizabethan domestic politics were about to reach their climax: 'the business of the Scottish queen', Cecil wrote apologetically to Sidney, 'secludeth all audience from other causes'.[71] In this atmosphere Sidney's demands for aid in Ireland lost their urgency. Six months after his arrival in Ireland nothing had been done to further his plans for Munster. Ormond remained at court, leaving his family's response to the activities of Sir Peter Carew in the hands of his less responsible brothers.[72] Sir John of Desmond remained in the Tower and his absence was exploited by Fitzmaurice as a sign that Sidney was no longer able to defend the Geraldine and had come only to do Ormond's bidding in the province. This appeal transformed Fitzmaurice from a mere contender for power within the lordship to a leader of a united Geraldine

---

[66] Sidney to Cecil, 8 Nov., Collins, *Letters and memorials of state*, I, p. 37 and 17 Nov., p. 38; 'Memorial of things for Ireland. 12 Nov., SP 63/26/19.

[67] Sidney to Cecil, 12 Nov., SP 63/26/18; Sidney's 'memo', 27 June, SP 63/25/11; Eliz. to Sidney, 30 Aug., SP 63/25/72–3.

[68] *Irish Statutes*, I, 11 Eliz. 2 sess c. 7, p. 322.

[69] 'Agreement between Eliz. and Thomas Might, victualler', 24 May 1568, SP 63/24/36; *Cal. Carew MSS (1515–74)*, pp. 379–83.

[70] Sidney to Leicester, 8 Aug. 1568, to Cecil, 14, 19, 30 Nov., Collins, *Letters and memorials of state*, I, pp. 34–41; Sidney to Cecil, 12 Nov., SP 63/26/18.

[71] Cecil to Sidney, 15 Dec., SP 63/26/57; MacCaffrey, *Shaping of Eliz. regime*, chs. 10–13.

[72] Bertrand de Salignae de la Mothe Fenelon, *Correspondance diplomatique 1568–75* (8 vols., Paris and London, 1838–40), I, pp. 142, 452; Cecil to Sidney, 6 Jan. 1569, SP 63/27/2.

revolt.[73] As this occurred Sidney remained as yet without a president in Munster, for the most misfortunate of reasons. Inadvertently, Cecil had submitted an unrealistically low estimate of the presidency's costs. He attempted to withdraw it; but the queen stuck fast, and the first candidate for office refused to serve. A more willing nominee was found, but by the time Elizabeth was persuaded to approve a more liberal budget he was dead. After this run of luck the privy council began to lose interest, and the matter was not revived until November 1570.[74] By the time a president actually arrived in Ireland, Sidney's recall had already been determined.

The same indecision crippled Sidney's plans for the north. Despite the time spent on their consideration, the council baulked at giving sanction to any of the colonial projects submitted; but refused likewise to give any ruling on Sidney's alternative plan for a provincial rental. Such delay was fatal. Turlough Luineach, unimpressed by Sidney's hardened attitude, continued to import Scots and to extend his power over the lesser lords of the province, forcing Sidney's allies like Maguire and O'Reilly to make their peace with him.[75] Finally in the Pale Sidney's parliament met amidst the tension generated by Carew's claims against the popular and influential Sir Christopher Cheevers, the opposition proved to be far greater than Sidney had expected.[76] The value of his financial proposals was whittled away, and his attempt to get priority for his tenurial legislation was thwarted by the introduction of a host of private and commonwealth bills. Outside parliament there was further trouble. The victualling contract collapsed almost immediately and Sidney was forced to cess his troops on the country.[77] The country resisted, Dublin refused to meet the rate and Sidney arrested the mayor. 'I fear my lord deputy and the people here are altered in disposition of misliking far from that I have known', noted Sir Nicholas White.[78] But there was worse to come. At the end of the first parliamentary session Sir Edmund Butler, whose opposition in the commons had already

---

[73] Lords justice to Eliz., 23 Mar. 1568, SP 63/23/74; Thomas Lord Fitzmaurice to lords justice, 6 July, SP 63/25/45, enclosure (ix); Piers Walshe to lords justice, 11 Sept., SP 63/26/4, enclosure (vii); Desmond to Fitzmaurice and other Geraldines, 18 Nov., SP 63/26/35–42; Fitzwilliam to Cecil, 14 Jan. 1567, SP 63/27/14; Sidney, 'Memoir', *UJA*, 1st ser., 3, pp. 96–7; St Leger to Sidney, 14 Feb. 1569, SP 63/27/23; Skydde, mayor of Corke and Ursula St Leger to Sidney, 17–18 June 1569, SP 63/28/35–7.
[74] Cecil to Sidney, 3 Sept., 5 Nov. 1568, SP 63/25/75, 26/14; Pollard to Cecil, 13 July, SP 63/29/11, see also sketch of Pollard in *DNB*; Sidney to Cecil, 8 Nov. 1570, Samuel Haynes (ed.), *A collection of State Papers . . . 1542 to 1570* (London, 1740), pp. 622–3.
[75] Fitzwilliam to Cecil, 14 Jan. 1569, SP 63/27/4; Turlough Luineach to William Piers, 30 Jan., Bodl., Carte MSS, 131/91.
[76] Weston to Cecil, 17 Feb., SP 63/27/25; Treadwell, 'The Irish parliament of 1569–71', pp. 67–73.
[77] Might to Cecil, 3 June, SP 63/28/20; White to Cecil, 10 Mar., 10 June, SP 63/27/44, 28/24.
[78] White to Cecil, 10 Mar., SP 63/27/44; Sidney to Cecil, 25 Nov. 1569, SP 63/29/81.

brought him into conflict with the deputy, quit Dublin altogether. By June 1569 the Butlers were 'out' in open alliance with the rebel Geraldines.[79] The unprecedented union of these immemorial enemies at last provoked Whitehall to action. Sidney finally received the extra men and munitions he had long requested; but there was yet no decision on presidencies or on colonial enterprises. In the meantime Sidney made do. He himself took responsibility for containing Turlough Luineach in the north and appointed Humphrey Gilbert as colonel in Munster with full authority to suppress the rebellion there.[80] He abandoned all hope of establishing a peaceful territorial reorganisation in the province and recommended that Gilbert and his men be rewarded with extensive grants of rebel lands.[81] But in the midst of this crisis Sidney lacked the influence with the council to gain a favourable response from the privy council for any project, radical or otherwise. The crown was unwilling to consider anything further than the suppression of this dangerous rebellion, while at the same time a powerful attack on Sidney's competence as governor was now being advanced by Sidney's most influential Irish critic, the earl of Ormond. The spread of the rebellion and its duration, Ormond argued, had been due entirely to Sidney. His failure to control the Geraldines coupled with his indiscriminate support for plantation projects and his harsh attitude toward the crown's loyal supporters in Munster had been sufficient to incite reaction. Having provoked the crisis, Sidney then failed to take the conciliatory steps which would have most easily resolved it. Instead, with Gilbert and Carew he had pursued a policy of ruthless exploitation which had unnecessarily prolonged the war and made it more bitter. Ormond's criticisms were not as weighty as they might have been under different circumstances: Elizabeth was angry with the Butlers, and supported Sidney's demands for an unconditional surrender before any recriminations were entertained. The argument that Sidney's government was provocative became decisive only when it became apparent that the costs it involved were too high.[82]

The price of repression was indeed enormous. To meet the rebellion in Munster, the privy council was forced to transport 600 fully equipped men from England, which by the time of their discharge early in 1571, had cost the crown some £7,300. Sidney was also forced to forego his promise of an

---

[79] For a full account, see David Edwards, 'The Butler revolt of 1569', *IHS* 28 (1992–3), pp. 228–55, which differs considerably from J. Hughes, 'Sir Edmund Butler of the Dullough, Knt.', *Journal of Royal Hist. Arch*, 4th ser., 1 (1870–1), pp. 152–92, 211–31; see also Canny, *Elizabethan conquest*, ch. 6.

[80] Gilbert to Cecil, 8 Oct. 1569, SP 63/29/67; Gilbert's 'Instructions', 3 Sept. 1569, NAI, Lodge MSS, Patent rolls Henry VIII to Eliz., fos. 29–31.

[81] Sidney to Cecil, 25 Nov., SP 63/29/81, to privy council, 27 Dec., 63/29/86, to Cecil, 4 Jan., 63/30/2.

[82] Ormond to Cecil, 28 Aug., 5, 27 Oct., SP 63/29/47, 66, 75.

early reduction in garrison strength and to maintain an establishment of over 2,000 men: its annual charge ran to almost £40,000. By March 1571, the crown had spent some £148,000 since Sidney's return to Ireland in 1568 and there were still some £73,000 in debts outstanding. On top of all this, the auditor's report on Fitzwilliam's massive ten-year account, which Sidney had long delayed, came out finally in the summer of 1570. Its disclosures were appalling. For the decade ending June 1569, the costs of administration had amounted to £348,000, almost 90 per cent of which had been met out of the English treasury.[83] Much of this expenditure had occurred during Sidney's period in office and the increase in Irish revenues during that time had been marginal. The conclusion was inescapable: Sidney's practice of government, for all his promises, was intolerably prodigal. And once this understanding had been acquired his recall became almost inevitable. The decision, however, was deferred until the rebellion in Munster had been satisfactorily suppressed. Sidney himself, exhausted by his efforts and disgusted by the lack of support he had received, pressed repeatedly to be recalled, and when at last he returned to court in the spring of 1571, he was icily received. 'Melius merui', he concluded.[84]

(iv)

Sidney's second term in office was a decisive turning-point in his attitude towards service in Ireland. He no longer felt optimistic about the possibility of winning the ordinary people to English ways. Everyone in Ireland, he feigned to believe, was irretrievably estranged from English government and confirmed in a subversive papistry. He could conceive of no policy that would reduce them to order and obedience. Back in England he renounced all interest in dealing further with matters of Ireland, and urged his patron Leicester to leave him free from all future entanglements.[85] Sidney's disillusion is understandable. The attempt to maintain a varied set of policies within the framework of a single, centralised programme of reform had not merely failed, it had proved disastrous. As chief governor he had been let down by all sides. The native lords had made no distinction between his careful proposals for social and tenurial reform and the peripheral private

---

[83] 'Account of Sir Humphrey Gilbert', 31 Mar. 1571, SP 63/31/45; 'The state of the garrisons in Ireland', Mar. 1571, SP 63/31/46; 'Account of debts', Mar. 1571, SP 63/31/47; 'Account of Sir William Fitzwilliam, 1559–69', NRO, Fitzwilliam MSS (Irish), no. 47; 'Brief of the account of Sir William Fitzwilliam', 24 June 1569, SP 63/28/53.

[84] Sidney's 'Memoir', *UJA*, 1st ser., 5, p. 308.

[85] Sidney to Cecil, 25 Nov. 1569, SP 63/29/81, to privy council, 4 May 1570, 63/30/50; La Mothe Fenelon, *Correspondance*, IV, p. 70; Sidney to Leicester, 31 July 1571, BL, Add MSS, 32091, no. 66; Burghley to Fitzwilliam, 9 July 1571, Bodl., Carte MSS, 57/95–6; La Mothe Fenelon, *Correspondance*, V, p. 52, 162; *Cal. SP Spanish 1568–79*, p. 328.

enterprises which he had been prepared to tolerate: and they had reacted against both with equal ferocity. At court his own friends had failed him, neither authorising nor maintaining any of the projects they had forced upon him. One lesson seemed clear: the attempt to implement any general programme of reform from the centre of power which both he and Sussex had variously essayed was, like the attempt at a thorough conquest, simply impracticable.

The chief casualty of this failure of the central government was the traditional conception of the presidency. In the explosion that followed upon Sidney's attempt to impose his patch-work programme, all hope of establishing conventional presidential councils in the provinces evaporated and a new hybrid institution began to emerge. Sidney, like most of those who reflected upon Irish policy, had regarded the common law as the chief medium of social reform within the country and had looked to the presidency as the means by which the law was to be engrafted and maintained in the outlying provinces. From the beginning the presidency was to be an organ of civil administration with the commission of *oyer et determiner* as its principal vehicle of operation. Initially, it was expected that the president himself would be a partial man, but he was to be accompanied by two civilian counsellors and was required to consult with the chief landholders of the area when sitting in judgement. In theory then the president's main responsibility was to be the enforcement of a civil code; in practice, however, it became something quite different.[86]

The first official sent by Sidney into Munster in 1569 was not, as he had hoped, a president, but the colonel of a military expedition, whose task was entirely military and whose instructions bore little relation to the civil responsibilities of the classical presidency. Humphrey Gilbert ruled not by common law and scarcely by law at all, but by ruthless coercion.[87] In Connacht, where late in 1569 Sidney actually succeeded in having a conventional presidency established, the results were bitterly disappointing. The enthusiastic new president, Sir Edward Fitton, held sessions throughout Galway and executed all manner of malefactors and idlemen. He rode roughshod over the local customs, commanded the booking of the entire population and ordered the suppression of unreformed religious practices.[88] At the same time he appointed a deliberately cool attitude towards the earl of Clanrickard and gave open countenance to his enemies. Fitton's impolitic

---

[86] See Pollard's 'Instructions', Oct. 1568, SP 63/26/9; Gilbert to Sidney, 1 and 6 Dec. 1569, SP 63/29/82–3.

[87] T. Churchyard, *A generall rehearsall of the warres*, sig. Q.I–R.1; see also D. B. Quinn (ed.), *The voyages and colonising enterprises of Sir Humphrey Gilbert* (2 vols., London, 1940), I, pp. 16–19.

[88] Rokeby to Cecil, 4 Jan. 1570, SP 63/30/4; Fitton to Cecil, 15 Apr., SP 63/30/43.

proceedings greatly inflamed tempers within Clanrickard, but when he attempted to pursue the same tactics amongst the O'Briens in the far more unstable lordship of Thomond, he encountered insurmountable opposition. Thomond refused either to meet him or to grant him supplies; and Fitton was unable to force him.[89]

This simple act of defiance immediately exposed the president's fundamental impotence, and the discontent which had spread throughout Connacht since his arrival in the province now erupted. Though there were few instances of outright defiance, Fitton was effectively crippled by a general refusal of the countryside to feed his meagre retinue. Forced to rely on the townsmen, he withdrew first to Galway and then to Athlone, and impotently watched his office melt away as his men deserted.[90]

Fitton drew stark lessons from his experience.[91] The conventional presidency, he came to believe, was wholly unsuited to Ireland where English law was neither respected nor understood by the people, and its palpable weakness in the face of resistance had only brought it into further disrepute. Fitton claimed to have levied some £9,000 in fines and recognisances, but had failed to collect any; his efforts to do so had simply aroused derision. English law, he concluded, would never be effective until it had sufficient military support to enforce its authority: 'It is not our mere will that will make them yield . . . power is the thing that must bridle them'.[92] Fitton's chief justice, Ralph Rokeby, echoed his opinion. The natives, Rokeby believed, would never be weaned to English government by 'leniety and gentleness': 'It is not the mace nor the name of a lord president and council that will frame them to obedience. It must be fire and sword, the rod of God's vengeance that must make these stubborn hearts and cankered hearts to yield for fear'.[93] Fitton estimated that a force of at least 300 men would be necessary to serve the president's needs.

There was something of a paradox here. The problem of supply had already crippled Fitton's small presidential retinue. He could reasonably expect no increased support from the central government. So how was this vastly increased force to be maintained? To this conundrum, the president advanced a remarkably simple solution. A larger force, he suggested, would lead to a more equitable distribution of the burden of supply both socially and geographically. It could be disposed throughout the province in such numbers as the president now maintained with him in any one area, but the

---

[89] Fitton to Sidney, 22 Feb. 1571, SP 63/30/15: 'Information against the earl of Thomond', 7 Nov., SP 63/30/91.
[90] Fitton to Cecil, 22 Aug., SP 63/30/86.
[91] Fitton to Cecil, 15 Apr., 27 Aug., SP 63/30/43, 80.
[92] Fitton to Cecil, 15 Apr., SP 63/30/43.
[93] Rokeby to Cecil, 15 Apr., SP 63/30/44.

powerful landholders, who had hitherto resisted all demands with impunity, could now be compelled to assume their share of supply by the threat that the entire presidential force might be brought to bear against them. A big establishment would thus solve its own supply problem while enabling the president to enforce his decisions authoritatively.[94]

While the Connacht president was formulating this argument in rather straitened circumstances at Athlone, something very similar had already been put into practice by Colonel Gilbert in Munster.[95] For Gilbert the problem of billeting a large force upon the countryside had been a necessity from the beginning. Faced with both a problem of supply and the danger of alienating large numbers by his exactions, Gilbert attempted to overcome both problems at once, simply by regarding a willingness to grant provisions as a declaration of loyalty. In doing so, he converted a mere logistic expedient into a policy of government. The yielding of purveyance was held to imply a *de facto* assertion of allegiance to the crown, and Gilbert for all practical purposes, was willing to respond to it as such and to offer his protection in return. He exploited, that is to say, coyne and livery in the most traditional and familiar fashion. Fresh from his successes in Munster, Gilbert pressed the lessons of his own experience upon the council. He described at length the kind of man who would operate most successfully as the agent of the crown in the outlying regions. The new style president was not to be obstructed by legal scruples. He should be severe and ruthless in the enforcement of his own will and yet honest and consistent in his dealings with the native inhabitants: 'for though he once betray his faith they will never afterward trust him'. He must also treat the natives with courtesy and respect: 'for they are naturally the proudest and distainfullest people that live'.[96] But he must be adamant in his decisions. Mercy once refused was never again to be offered. Justice and the form it took was to be exercised at his discretion. Allegiance was to be exacted personally – even spectacularly – and was to be maintained in the most traditional of ways: coyne and livery. In short, the presidents were to transform themselves into a faithful image of the most successful species surviving in their environment: the Anglo-Irish feudal magnates.

It is probable that Sidney was aware of these developments in the

[94] Fitton to Cecil, 8 Feb. 1571, SP 63/31/6; same to same, 27 Aug., including his 'Division of Connaught', SP 63/30/80 and 81.

[95] Gilbert to Sidney, 15 Nov., 1 Dec. 1569, SP 63/29/82–3; J. Hooker, 'Chronicle of Ireland', in Holinshed, *Chronicles* (1808), VI, pp. 378–80; Gilbert, 'Notes for the presidency of Munster: *c.* 1569', Lambeth MSS, 614/73–84.

[96] 'A discourse for the reformation . . . of Munster', Feb. 1574, BL, Add. MSS, 48015, fos. 378 ff., second copy in Add. MSS, 48017, fos. 136 ff.; another 'Discourse', *c.* 1573, BL, Add. MSS, 4763, fos. 343 ff.

provinces; he certainly had access to information from both Fitton and Gilbert. But their individual experiences hardly seemed relevant from his particular perspective. On the contrary, they seemed to point to a further disintegration rather than a consolidation of the central governor's authority. The first real synthesis of the lessons of 1568–71 for both presidents and governor alike was produced instead by an unknown and relatively lowly figure, Edmund Tremayne. Tremayne had been sent to Ireland in July 1569 to report to the council upon the joint Butler–Geraldine rebellion which had just broken out. His account of Sidney's proceedings was highly favourable and he seems to have served for a time as the deputy's private secretary. He returned to England with Sidney in the spring of 1571. But he retained a keen interest in Irish affairs thereafter. He was sent again to Ireland as a special agent in 1573 and between 1571 and 1575, he penned a series of 'advices' upon the reform of Irish government. By the end of 1571, however, Tremayne's fundamental ideas had already been clearly worked out.[97]

His review of recent Irish policy was both critical and constructive. The attempt to employ English law alone, as the singular weapon of reform in Ireland was, he maintained, doomed from the start. Irish modes of government left the magnates 'so absolute in their authority, so licentious and gainful, as whosoever should be suffered to rule after this sort will never rule after the English manner'.[98] In comparison to their current situation, the common law had little to offer the great lords and they would continue to resist its introduction until they were compelled by other means to accept it.

Yet, though the failure of peaceful attempts at anglicisation was obvious, the traditional means of coercion were also clearly inadequate. The history of the Anglo-Normans gave a salutary warning. A renewed conquest no matter how forceful its original impetus, would soon be contaminated by the Gaelic order and would shortly decay, for 'the sweetness and gain of the Irish government hath been such that it hath rather drawn our own nation to become Irish than any way wrought the reformation of the Irish to reduce them to English law'.[99] The recent experiments in colonial enterprise had also proved unworkable. 'None will come from hence but such as have nothing to begin with, and such doing no good at home and getting no thrift at home will never do any good here.'[100] Rumours of such enterprises had only provoked the rebellions of 1569–71; they would have the same effect

---

[97] Tremayne to Cecil, 12 Apr. 1570, SP 63/30/42, and 23 July, 63/30/71 and 20 Feb. 1571, 63/31/15. On Tremayne generally, see sketch in *DNB*; this summary of Tremayne's views is based upon his several memoranda scattered in the state papers and elsewhere: see SP 63/32/64–6, 35/21; BL, Add. MSS, 48015, fos. 274–279; BL, Cotton MSS, Titus B XII, fos. 357–60.

[98] SP 63/32/66.   [99] BL, Add. MSS, 48015, fo. 274.   [100] SP 63/32/66.

in the future. 'Few will inhabit there but we shall demand more men in wages to keep it than we shall pay in rent'.[101] In any case, like the Anglo-Norman settlements, the new colonies would soon decay, 'and within less than a descent become as Irish as the worst'.[102] The only way to reduce Ireland into a peaceful and obedient realm was the way of assimilation. 'The Irish government is never to be reformed till the common law have its course.'[103]

But how, given the experience of 1569–71, was this to be done? Tremayne's answer was simple and ingenious. The key to the magnates' strength lay in their uncontested exercise of coyne and livery. This extensive system of obligations enabled the lords to maintain large private armies which effectively guaranteed their own privileged position by intimidating the countrymen into providing for all their needs. These private armies provided the basis of a deeply rooted system of oppression against which English law alone could offer little resistance. The only way in which the crown might overcome the challenge of the great lords was to beat them at their own game. What the queen needed, that is, was 'an army so great that she may say she will [have] no army but her own, her . . . sword shall stunt all strife and her will shall determine all causes, and therefore all lords and rulers of countries to give over all [their] forces'.[104] The strategy of this grand expeditionary force was simple: it would operate through intimidation, not through overt violence. Divided amongst the governor and three presidents, the army would proceed into the provinces and secure the assent of the great magnates to a number of key conditions. They were to be brought 'to declare the limits of their tenantry and who be their tenants . . . and that known, then might such a composition be made by the good allowance of the same lords that there should certainly be known what they should receive and what the tenants should pay'. These composition arrangements, Tremayne submitted, should be generous and impartial. Care was to be taken that the lords be genuinely compensated for any powers they were to surrender. As much as possible was to be done to ensure their peaceful acquiescence in the scheme.[105]

There was, however, to be one further condition included in the proposals made to the magnates which was designed to guarantee their compliance. The great lords were to yield to the officers of the crown the same services they were accustomed to exact upon their inferiors. They were to give coyne, or purveyance, or cess to the troops of the grand army. Like Fitton and Gilbert, Tremayne argued that the very size of the army would be sufficient to procure its own means of sustenance. But the ends of these

---

[101] SP 63/32/64.   [102] Ibid.   [103] SP 63/32/66.
[104] Ibid.   [105] BL, Add. MSS, 4805, fo. 277.

tactics, he was anxious to point out, were not primarily exploitative. 'This is not to oppress the good subjects, but rather to protect them from evil'.[106] The country which was already sorely burdened with the extortions of the magnates' retainers and galloglass would readily embrace the far lighter demands of the English army. Even then, its use as a tactic was to be limited in time and scope.

The army I mean [is] not so much for holding them in obedience as to wring them thereby so hard, as for their ease they should desire to be loosed by some composition to remove the garrison. And the composition won – partly in money and partly in provision as the country will bear – will grow to such a sufficient revenue as I suppose will find in garrison a sufficient army to keep this realm in continual obedience.[107]

The great lords, that is, were to secure a commutation of coyne and livery from the crown in just the same way as their tenants had received it from them.

This, it might seem, was nothing more than Fitton's ideas writ large. But Tremayne was insistent that his scheme be launched on a national scale and not simply left to the discretion of semi-autonomous local officials. It was imperative that the queen be seen to give her willing approbation to the plan as a new national policy: 'As Her Majesty is the natural liege sovereign of both realms, so should there be made no difference of subjects so far forth as both shall show like obedience to her causes.'[108] It was important also to secure in advance the co-operation of the earls of Ormond and Kildare who were to use their great influence in propagating the scheme amongst their dependants. Finally, a centralised approach was to be preferred for purely tactical reasons. The scheme was to be first introduced in the English Pale where cess was already in operation and where a demand for a financial commutation had already been voiced. The successful conclusion of a composition here would secure an immediate increase in revenue and the crown's initial outlay in fitting out the grand army would already begin to be recouped. More important, the success of the plan in the Pale would act as an example to the other provinces of the benefits to be derived from compliance. A sort of domino reaction would be precipitated, and one by one the provinces would gradually follow suit.[109]

The composition scheme seemed comprehensive in its uses. It appeared to provide a means of implementing permanent social and legal arrangements rapidly and on a general scale. It promised to do so, moreover, with the minimum cost to the crown and with the promise of a handsome return. Most important of all, its very adaptation of the prevailing mode of politics in the

---

[106] SP 63/32/66.   [107] Ibid.
[108] BL, Add. MSS, 48015, fo. 277.   [109] SP 63/35/21.

gaelicised areas seemed to guarantee its continued success. 'Composition for cess' augured well, because it seemed to transform necessity into virtue.

The general idea of 'composition', of course, did not originate with Tremayne. The commutation of feudal dues and the raising of a rent from within the Gaelic lordships had been a recurring suggestion in reform tracts since the 1520s.[110] But the peculiar synthesis of these policies and their special application by the chief governor as devised by Tremayne marked a crucial stage in the evolution of Tudor experience of Ireland. The lesson that English laws and customs would never be introduced peacefully and easily into the country had now been fully absorbed. It was clear that some expense and some concession to local modes of conduct would have to be consented to before any progress would be made. Yet the new plan retained many of the most attractive characteristics of the old optimistic prognostications that had encouraged Sussex and, for a while, Sidney. Here was a strategy whose costs were limited and could be assessed clearly at the outset. It was, moreover, one which divided naturally into two distinct phases: a primary phase in which the most crucial and most dramatic work of enforcement was to take place, and a longer more mundane period in which the recently contracted obligations were to be refined and maintained. It was, as Tremayne echoing Sussex argued, a strategy which demanded only 'a set purpose' on the part of the crown to ensure its success, and promised great glory to the man who would initiate it.[111] Here in form, if not in substance, was the classic programmatic approach, which Sussex had enunciated and which appeared to have collapsed under Sidney, alive again. Thus, when Tremayne actually presented his ideas to Sidney, it is not surprising that the former deputy, notwithstanding several recent refusals to return to Ireland, began again to campaign for reappointment in 1572.[112]

Under different circumstances the attractions of the new strategy might have been sufficient to bring Sidney back to power. But in the early 1570s the standard of competition was more exacting than ever. Elizabeth, too, had been shaken by the crisis of 1569–71, and had drawn her own lessons from the experience. She resolved never again to tolerate a comparable expenditure of royal treasure in Ireland. The country's affairs were henceforth to be administered with the minimum cost and with the least possible recourse to Whitehall. In this forbidding atmosphere, two alternative strategies had emerged both of which paid more respect to the queen's fiscal conservatism than Sidney's novel propositions. One was that of the new lord

---

[110] See, for instance, the anonymous treatise of 1528, BL, Lansdowne MSS, 159, no. 1.
[111] BL, Add. MSS, 48015, fo. 276.
[112] La Mothe Fenelon, *Correspondance*, V, p. 268; Jenyson to Sidney, 2 Jan. 1572, Bodl., Carte MSS, 57/305–6; Fitzwilliam to Mildmay, 26 Mar. 1572, Carte MSS, 57/337–8.

deputy, Fitzwilliam, who attempted to cut public expenditure to the bone while working towards private settlements in Laois–Offaly and Clanrickard and for the victualling of the garrison in the Pale.[113] The second was that of the enterprising earl of Essex who gained acceptance for his colonisation project in Ulster simply by undertaking to absorb most of its costs himself and to begin paying a rent to the crown within two years.[114] Both methods had their own internal weaknesses and tended to come into conflict with one another. But they co-existed with mounting tension throughout the early 1570s and jointly, through their mutual recriminations and self-justifications, clouded Sidney's field of opportunity.

Sidney did his best to clear the way. He used his special influence as an authority on Irish affairs to criticise Fitzwilliam's administration and eventually succeeded in having a set of serious allegations brought against his much aggrieved brother-in-law.[115] He obtained and exposed confidential information about the administration's poor financial performance.[116] He promoted false rumour about his own imminent reappointment in order to undermine the deputy's power of command. The irascible Fitzwilliam, moreover, unwittingly contributed to Sidney's campaign. He quarrelled violently with Fitton and Essex, and he was not above sending pungent and offensive exonerations of his own conduct to the council and on occasion to the queen herself. By the summer of 1574, angered by slanders and frustrated by lack of support in his dealings with Clanrickard and Desmond, Fitzwilliam was more than anxious for his own recall.[117]

The campaign to undermine Essex was less easy. Essex's offer was attractive, and the earl was less vulnerable to criticism than the unfortunate Fitzwilliam. Again, Sidney used his authority to advise against the extensive powers of autonomy Essex sought in Ulster and succeeded in having them curtailed.[118] He seems to have participated in Leicester's furtive efforts to

---

[113] For a general account of Fitzwilliam's first viceroyalty, see Bagwell, *Ireland under the Tudors*, II, chs. 29–32.

[114] For general accounts, see R. G. Morton, 'The enterprise of Ulster', *History Today* 17 (1967), pp. 114–21; W. B. Devereux, *Lives and letters of the Devereux earls of Essex* (2 vols., London, 1853), I, pp. 113 ff., Essex's undertaking is discussed from a different perspective in ch. 7, below.

[115] Fitzwilliam to Mildmay, 26 Mar. 1572, Bodl., Carte MSS, 57/337–8; Essex to Fitzwilliam, 14 Sept. 1573, SP 63/56/189; Burghley to Fitzwilliam, 7 Oct. 1573, SP 63/56/212; Smith to Fitzwilliam, 26 Jan. 1574, SP 63/56/279; Burghley to Fitzwilliam, 5 Feb., 20 June 1574, SP 63/55/130–1, 56/447.

[116] Jenyson to Sidney, 1 Feb. 1574, Bodl., Carte MSS, 56/282; Jenyson to Burghley, 3 Feb. 1575, SP 63/49/53.

[117] See Fitzwilliam's notes on R. Pavy to P. Green, 10 July 1574, SP 63/47/15; 'Articles to be considered', 30 May 1574, SP 63/45/40; Fitzwilliam replies, 7 Jan. 1575, SP 63/49/15; Burghley to Fitzwilliam, 20 July 1574, Bodl., Carte MSS, 56/486; Fitzwilliam to Walsingham, 25 Mar. 1574, SP 63/45/26; Fitzwilliam to Burghley, 2 Jan. 1575, SP 63/49/3.

[118] Sidney's 'Opinion' on Essex's affairs, May 1573, SP 63/40/60.

have the whole enterprise quashed, and Essex was certain that the two were responsible for the queen's decision not to appoint him deputy in place of Fitzwilliam once the latter's recall had been determined.[119] But despite all the doubts cast upon Essex's personal competence, his limited, but concrete offers remained more immediately attractive than the general propositions outlined by Sidney. After two years, Essex promised, the Ulster plantation would begin to yield an annual rental of £5,000 which would soon recoup any outlays the crown was prepared to make in its support. On the face of it, Essex's offer seemed difficult to surpass.[120]

Neither Tremayne nor Sidney had been prepared at the outset to supply a precise estimate of the costs of their intended operation or the time necessary to give it effect. Rumour had it that Sidney would need 10,000 men for his purpose, and Fitzwilliam was certain that the proposed scale of operations was far too grandiose to gain acceptance at Whitehall.[121] Even Sidney's first competitive tender, which projected a minimum force of 2,300 men costing £30,000, had for an unstated period of time, contrasted poorly with Essex's simple offer.[122] The council's attitude in comparing the alternative schemes was summed up by Burghley: 'note by this [Sidney's scheme] no territory is won and by the former both territory and subjects are'.[123] It was the need to supersede Essex's highly competitive offer that forced Sidney to make final amendations to his already dangerously simplified plan. His revised proposal, shorn of the careful qualifications that had characterised Tremayne's presentation, was terse and to the point. Like a victualler bargaining for his contract, Sidney promised Elizabeth to render Ireland totally self-sufficient within three years for a total of just £60,000.[124]

Sidney achieved this reduction of time and costs in his typical way. The number of troops required was cut to a mere 1,100. These were to be divided evenly amongst three presidents, leaving a task force of 350 with the deputy. The men were to be paid in English sterling as the favourable exchange rate would grant them an automatic discount on all goods purchased in Ireland. Payment was to be made monthly so that the cess prices could be met on demand. Mounting indebtedness would thereby be prevented and a stable relationship maintained between the queen's price and the market. The £60,000 required was to be paid over to the deputy

---

119 Essex to Burghley, 12 Apr. 1576, BL, Harl. MSS, 6992, no. 14.
120 'Estimate of the charge of the recovery of Ulster', Oct. 1574, SP 63/48/35–6.
121 *Cal. SP Spanish (1568–79)*, p. 474. See also Burghley to Fitzwilliam, 12 Nov. 1574, Bodl., Carte MSS 57/172.
122 Burghley's 'Notes', c. 1574, SP 63/48/75, 77.
123 Ibid.
124 Sidney's revised offers c. July 1575, SP 63/52/83; Nov. 1575, SP 63/53/67.

in twelve installments of £5,000 each to be sent at regular intervals. Any extraordinary expenses were to be met from these installments alone, and Sidney hinted that even the amount fixed would begin to grow superfluous to his costs after the first year.[125]

This drastic simplification of Tremayne's plan was as dangerous as it was characteristic. It was prompted by no concern to improve the substance of the plan, but only by a desire to enhance his appeal at court. It was a move that was at once essential to the political competition in which he was continually engaged, and totally irrelevant to the demands of the situation in Ireland. As ever, it exposed him to risks which Sidney had always seemed willing to take. It provided his enemies with the easiest possible measure by which to gauge his performance, quarter by quarter; and worse, the terms of his 'contract' made the success of his service more than ever dependent upon the vagaries of court. But the appeal of the new programme both to the man who was to implement it and to the government which was to reap its benefits was undeniable. Sidney's appointment was finalised in July 1575, and in August his instructions drafted in close accord with the terms of his offer were presented to him. Sidney was promised the imminent appointment of two new presidents and the chancellorship, vacant since 1573, was to be filled by one of his own colleagues on the council in Wales, William Gerrard. As a concession, the earl of Essex was to be allowed to remain in Ulster as president under the authority of the deputy.[126]

(v)

Sidney landed at Drogheda on 8 September, and immediately began to put his plan into operation. Representatives of the gentry and merchants of the Pale were summoned and informed of the proportion of cess which the deputy deemed necessary for the supply of the army in the coming year. The government, he told his audience, was no longer able to bear the major portion of the victualling, as it had done in recent years; the community would henceforth be obliged to increase its contribution. The estimated requirement was enormous:[127]

[125] Sidney's offer, Nov. 1575, SP 63/53/67; for the terms of payment, see Sidney's 'Instructions', 2 Aug. 1575; Lambeth MSS, 614/29; Sidney's 'Reckoning', *c.* Aug. 1575, HMC, *De Lisle and Dudley MSS*, II, pp. 22–4.

[126] Sidney's 'Instructions', Lambeth MSS, 614, fos. 29 ff.: Eliz. to Sidney, 28 Sept. 1575, SP 12/45/90; Sidney to privy council, 27 Apr. 1576, SP 63/55/34.

[127] 'Memoranda of cess for the deputy', Sept. 1577, SP 63/59/23; I have added the deputy's household cess to the general cess demanded, SP 63/55/12; for a general account, see 'Notes of Lord Chancellor Gerrard', *Anal. Hib.*, 2, pp. 129 ff.

Wheat	Beer malt	Oat malt	Oats	Beeves
6,200 pks.	4,500 pks.	9,000 pks.	13,300 pks	3,500 hd.

The Palesmen made the expected response and Sidney followed through with his alternative proposal. If the Palesmen would accede to the abolition of all personal exemptions and agree to the conversion of cess into a low monetary tax, he would undertake to abolish the practice of cessing altogether. This was a finely calculated bluff. Tremayne had argued that the burden of the cess had been artificially inflated both by the corruption of the cessors, and by the large number of exemptions, or 'freedoms', given to private persons by governors in the past. Both abuses could now be corrected at once. The 'new freedoms' which had been acquired under a statute of 27 Henry VIII and reaffirmed by the parliament of 1557, allowed that those bound to attend hostings were discharged 'from all coyne and livery and of carting and cartages' which would otherwise be assessed upon their lands.[128] Since service at hostings, however, applied to those with land valued at above £20 p.a., and since only those with considerable wealth and influence could acquire the inquisition and certification necessary to gain exemption, it was clear that these freedoms were the preserve of a privileged elite.[129] The existing resentment of the majority could easily be channelled against this group by Sidney's simple argument: if the burden were more equitably distributed, it would be lighter all round. There was a further inducement: since the cess now demanded amounted to a charge of over £9 on the ploughland, and since other cesses in times of scarcity had been almost as high, Sidney's offer to commute all charges for a fixed cash payment of a mere £2,134 per ploughland seemed generous in the extreme.[130] These attractions were enough to convince Sidney that he could rely upon the support of 'the major and wiser sort', and he set out upon his provincial circuit in full confidence that an agreement could be reached.[131]

But Sidney was unlucky. Bad harvests in two successive years, 1574–5, had been followed by a visitation of plague that crippled economic activity.[132] Only some of the delegates appointed to meet him actually risked

[128] *Irish Statutes*, I, 28 Henry VIII, *c.* 22, pp. 173–4; for an example of an official letter granting a freedom from cess, see NAI, Ferguson MSS, Memoranda Rolls, VI, no. 3.
[129] Tremayne to Sidney, 24 Jan. 1576, SP 63/55/6, Gerrard to Burghley, ? Nov. 1576, Lambeth MSS, 616/112.
[130] Sidney to privy council, 27 Jan. 1577, SP 63/57/5; the figure of £9 is corroborated by the Palesmen, Lambeth MSS, 628/151.
[131] Sidney to Privy Council, 15 Dec. 1575, SP 63/54/17.
[132] Annals of Dudley Loftus, Marsh's Library, MSS, Z3.2.7, *sa*; Sidney to privy council, 28 Sept. 1575, BL, Cotton MSS, Titus B X, fo. 5.

the journey to Drogheda, and the unrepresentative nature of the meeting augured ill for the success of Sidney's plan. In the absence of a formal agreement, the country simply refused the proposed cess, and Sidney, now genuinely anxious to secure a winter's supply, cut his demands in half. This concession, however, only underlined the artificiality of the earlier assessment and lent further support to the popular suspicion that the cess had been inflated only to coerce the Palesmen into making an agreement against their better interests.[133]

Since his appointment, doubts had been expressed in Ireland about the assumptions underlying Sidney's government. Nicholas White was uncertain about 'this rule by composition', and he warned Burghley that if Sidney had, as it was rumoured, undertaken the government of Ireland on the basis of a private contract, he could expect little support from the community.[134] Now the crudity of Sidney's attempt at blackmail tended to confirm the Palesmen in their fears and they reacted sharply against him. Within weeks the potential support Sidney believed to exist had evaporated and a solid front of opposition began to form against him. It became impossible to collect even the moderate cess he had settled for. Tension between the ordinary soldiers and the countrymen increased. Those with freedoms simply ignored the proclamation abolishing them and the leading gentry circulated a petition seeking the right to present their grievances to the crown.[135]

Crisis was reached in the late autumn of 1577, when the Palesmen refused either to yield another cess or to consider an offer of composition, but demanded to be allowed to send agents to present their case at court.[136] As winter approached, however, the Palesmen dug in: in a number of meetings held with the governor they remained fixed in their determination to resist a financial commutation which they declared could possibly become a greater burden on later generations. Sidney they alleged had no legal justification for the action he sought to undertake and they would not be compelled by mere force to yield to an unconstitutional innovation. They offered, however, to find an alternative means of easing the government's supply difficulties.[137]

For Sidney, of course, any alternative to his own composition scheme was totally unacceptable, but Chancellor Gerrard was perturbed by the

---

[133] 'Memoranda on cess', SP 63/55/12.
[134] White to Burghley, 9 Oct. 1575, 31 Jan. 1576, SP 63/53/42, 55/11.
[135] Sidney to Burghley, 13 Mar. 1576, SP 63/55/27 and enclosures.
[136] 'Petition . . . of the Pale', Lambeth MSS, 628/121. Gerrard to Burghley, 1 Nov., Lambeth MSS, 616/112.
[137] Charles MacNeill (ed.), 'Lord Chancellor Gerrard's notes in his Report in Ireland', *Anal. Hib.* 2 (1931), pp. 93–291.

Palesmen's argument. Though he continued to affirm the governor's rights as the representative of the sovereign, he was anxious to reach a practical compromise. In return for an agreement to yield the current cess, he promised to persuade the deputy to agree 'that hereafter no cess should be imposed but by parliament or grand council or by direction from Her Highness', and assured the Palesmen that he would further any truly workable plan which they offered as an alternative.[138] Already, therefore, a serious difference existed between the compromising chancellor and the deputy for whom the enforcement of the original scheme was an essential prerequisite to the success of his national programme of composition. For the moment, however, the cleavage remained obscure. The Palesmen rejected Gerrard's overtures and their agents, Barnaby Scurlocke, Richard Netterville and Henry Burnell, left for England without licence in February 1577.[139]

To travel without licence to court on a mission that challenged the official interpretation of the queen's prerogative and, worse, her claim to her subjects' wealth was a perilous undertaking at any time. But the agents' audacity is an indication of their confidence in the strength of their case. The climate at court was unusually favourable. The Palesmen could count on the support of the earls of Ormond and Kildare now resident there. They could count too on the unnerving effect which trouble in the English Pale always produced upon the privy council. Burghley, advised by the unsympathetic Sir Nicholas White, remained cool towards Sidney's proceedings, and even Walsingham, from whom Sidney expected full support, advised caution.[140] But these were minor advantages to the Palesmen: the greatest blow to Sidney's credibility in the eyes of his superiors was dealt in Ireland even before the agents set sail.

Sidney had set about the reorganisation of the provinces with great optimism and energy. This time there were no initial frustrations. The presidents had arrived on schedule, and the death of Essex in September 1576 allowed Sidney to assume personal responsibility for the most delicate operation in Ulster. On the surface, progress was rapid. Sidney negotiated his composition arrangements with the greater and lesser lords of each province and obtained assurances that they would obey the newly established presidents. By the autumn of 1576, he had toured the entire

---

138 Gerrard to privy council, 8 Feb. 1577, Lambeth MSS, 628/145; 'Proceedings in the cess', ibid., pp. 141–4.

139 'Proceedings in the cess', pp. 141–4, Baltinglass et al. to Eliz., 10–11 Jan. 1577, SP 63/57/1–4.

140 White to Burghley, 10 Feb. 1577, SP 63/57/25; Burghley to White, 15 July, BL, Lansdowne MSS, 102, no. 90; Walsingham to Sidney, 11, 30 June, Collins, *Letters and memorials of state*, I, pp. 195–5, 199–200.

country and could boast that even the most lawless areas of Connaught would bear their own charges within two years.[141] Almost immediately, however, the deputy was confounded by an outburst of resistance that spread rapidly throughout the provinces. In his haste towards success, Sidney had fatally damaged the delicate mechanism upon which the plan of general composition was planned to function.

The success of composition, according to Tremayne, depended upon the careful use of persuasion backed up by force. A sufficient desire for change, he believed, existed within the lordships to allow a peaceful adaptation to presidential rule if the matter was handled carefully. Though the threat of force was to be used at the outset to gain a hearing from the new proposals, it was imperative that any suspicion of long-term exploitation be assuaged.[142] Tremayne's concern that the crown be seen to be impartial and benign was founded upon the experience of 1569–71. Sidney shared the experience, but he had not absorbed all of its lessons. Whatever the intrinsic merit of the new plan of reform he adopted, Sidney was primarily concerned that it should appear to be effective. His programme should be seen to be in operation; the terms of his contract should appear to be honoured. Accordingly, Sidney approached the composition plan with an eye for those characteristics which would give the earliest indication that his work was actually yielding a return on investment. Thus the financial arrangements took paramount place in all the negotiations he undertook, and the immediate yielding of tribute was understood to be an essential condition to any further agreement. Besides demanding the annual rents which the original plan envisaged, Sidney made it clear that he would hold the freeholders liable for arrears on any religious properties occupied by them, and to make the point, he commissioned the first general survey of monastic sites in Munster and Connacht.[143]

Thus, the exploitative image which Tremayne had sought to avoid by concentrating responsibility for the plan in the hands of a central governor rather than in semi-autonomous presidents, reappeared, now made all the more sinister by its apparent authority. In these circumstances, a breach in understanding arose between Sidney and those with whom he attempted to negotiate. Throughout the country a rumour became current: Sidney, it said,

[141] Sidney to privy council, 27 Apr., 15 June 1576, SP 63/55/34, 58.
[142] See in particular his treatise in BL, Add. MSS, 48015 fos. 274–9 and SP 63/32/66.
[143] Sidney to privy council, 28 Sept. 1575, BL, Cotton MSS, Titus B X, no. 1, fo. 5; Sidney to privy council, 27 Apr., SP 63/55/34; to Walsingham, 27 Apr., SP 63/55/37 enclosing Alford's survey; 'Book of arrearages in Connaught', misdated July 1576, HMC, *De Lisle and Dudley MSS*, II, pp. 42–4.

had come to take the land to farm.[144] This general distrust imposed a mounting strain on the delicate chain of compositions which Sidney had forged. Thus, when the earl of Clanrickard's sons burst out in rebellion, Sidney found himself confronted with the imminent collapse of his entire scheme.

Significantly, Clanrickard's attempt to justify his sons' actions was based entirely on economic grounds. Sidney, he claimed, had rejected the equitable fine which Fitzwilliam had placed upon his country for the spoil of Athenry and imposed an enormous demand of £6,000 in cash. He had charged the earl and his immediate family with arrears on monastic lands totalling £10,000 and had threatened them with more. He had overridden Clanrickard's claims to immunity and imposed cess upon his demesne lands. The earl himself had been forced to sell his plate in order to meet the deputy's charges. Sidney's exactions were so great, he pleaded, that they had given rise to the fear that the deputy was minded to bring the entire lordship into ruin. His sons had risen out in desperation to salvage their inheritance.[145]

No less significant than the attempt of the Galway Burkes to generalise their case as a struggle against exploitation was the response they elicited from their neighbours. Sidney's financial squeeze threatened every lord in the province to a greater or lesser extent, so the charge that the composition plan was but another form of English rapacity provided a ready platform for a general call to resistance. The Galway freeholders rallied to the Mac an Iarlas, but more important, their rebellion lent further encouragement to growing discontent with Sidney's overhasty proceedings in Munster. The landholders of Cork and Kerry banded together to refuse President Drury either a cess or a composition. Desmond, who acted as their spokesman, wrote to Burghley, Leicester and the privy council complaining of the evils suffered by his people at the hands of Drury's soldiers. 'The intolerable burden that the subjects bear here', he warned Burghley, 'do so alienate and discourage their heads that I fear great inconvenience thereby to ensue', and hinting at the general resentment aroused by Sidney's personal motivation, he concluded, 'private gain will bring nothing to perfection in this realm, but rather an overplus of charges'.[146]

These disturbances seriously threatened Sidney's tenure of office.

---

[144] MacNeill, 'Lord Chancellor Gerrard's notes', *Anal. Hib.* 2, p. 117; for similar views, see White to Burghley, 9 Oct. 1575, 31 Jan. 1576, SP 63/53/42, 55/11.

[145] Clanrickard to Elizabeth and council, 25 May 1576, SP 63/55/48–9 and enclosure 49 (i); Clanrickard to Fitzwilliam, and to Ormond, 25 May, 28 June, SP 63/55/54, 70.

[146] Sidney to privy council, 27 Jan. 1577, SP 63/57/5; Ormond to Burghley, 8 July 1576, SP 63/56/5. 'Combination against cess', 18 Oct. 1576, SP 63/56/38, Desmond to Burghley and to Leicester, 20 Mar. 1577, SP 63/57/43–4.

Elizabeth's enthusiasm for his plan had cooled almost immediately after his departure, and her disenchantment had been deepened by Sidney's early admission that his initial costs would be rather larger than he had originally expected. Walsingham had much trouble in extracting even the earliest instalments of treasure from the royal purse, and in the second year the queen began to default. Now, the recurrence of general resistance was painfully reminiscent of 1569. The queen drew the parallel, and she blamed Sidney for it.[147] So when the agents of the Pale arrived in London, they were after some initial bluster treated with unexpected mildness. To Sidney, on the other hand, Elizabeth wrote sharply: 'The bruit is now that you have taken the whole land to farm and finding the same not to bear the ordinary charge of the garrison and other necessary payments, you have imposed this large cess . . . You gave us hope to diminish our charges and increase our revenue, but we find the former still to be great and the latter . . . is much decayed'.[148] To have caused such a stir throughout the country at a time when a Spanish attempt upon the coast was believed to be imminent was, Elizabeth implied, grossly irresponsible. It was rumoured she had a mind to revoke him.[149]

The leverage upon which Tremayne had counted had indeed materialised, but it had worked in reverse. The Palesmen now appeared as the major obstacle to the whole scheme of composition and its fate seemed to hinge on Sidney's ability to discredit their agents. Thus he dispatched his most trusted agent and private secretary, Edward Waterhouse, to court to vindicate his actions; his son Philip was drafted into the cause, and in July 1577, Lord Chancellor Gerrard was sent, armed with accounts, records and testimonials, to give a full dress presentation of the government's case.[150]

Sidney himself emphasised the exemplary importance of his work in the Pale. The success of his efforts in the rest of the country, he asserted,

147 Sidney to Walsingham, 15 Nov. 1575; 5 Mar. 1577, BL, Cotton MSS, Titus B X, no. 1, f. 9; to privy council, 27 Jan. 1577, SP 63/57/5; Walsingham to Burghley, 8 Dec. 1575, BL, Harl. Mss, 6992, no. 16, to Sidney, 28 Jan. 1576, Collins, *Letters and memorials of state*, I, pp. 85–6; Sidney to privy council, 9 July 1576, SP 63/56/6. 'Note of expenses and receipts', c. June 1578, SP 63/61/21; 'Memorial for Sidney', Nov. 1576, SP 63/56/48.

148 Eliz. to Sidney, 17 July 1577, Lambeth MSS, 628/275.

149 Sidney to Eliz., 20 May 1577, SP 63/58/29; 'Instructions to Waterhouse', HMC, *De Lisle and Dudley MSS*, II, pp. 55–6.

150 Sidney to Walshingham, 4 Feb. 1577, SP 63/57/4; same to Privy Council, 7 Mar., SP 63/57/39; to Eliz., 20 May, SP 63/58/29; to Walsingham, 15 May, BL, Cotton MSS, Titus B X, no. 1, f. 61; 'Instructions to Waterhouse', HMC, *De Lisle and Dudley MSS*, II, pp. 55–6; 'Instructions to Gerrard', Collins, *Letters and memorials of state*, I, pp. 222–5; Philip Sidney, 'Discourse on Ireland', c. June 1577, BL, Cotton MSS, Titus B XII, fos. 557–9; the constitutional implications of the controversy are discussed in ch. 6, below.

depended upon it. If his actions there were not upheld, then his ability to govern the rest of the country would be greatly endangered. The struggle in the Pale was not simply a matter of principle, 'but one of the exchequer and the treasury in the Tower . . . not to be so lightly sacrificed'.[151] The composition money in the Pale was therefore a useful source of revenue in itself. But it was far more important; it was 'the foundation that I have chiefly to build on'.[152] Concessions to the Palesmen now would risk the destruction of a plan that was already beginning to bear fruit. 'As confidently as I can conceive of anything', Sidney told Walsingham, 'I am persuaded that if Netterville had not been sent, I had before this time assured Her Majesty of above 10,000 marks of increase in revenue yearly . . . for I held a straighter hand in the matter of cess rather to bring them to a certain rent'.[153] Walsingham transmitted the message to the queen: 'Your subjects dwelling outside the English Pale and now grown to composition with your deputy for such lands as they hold by usurpation would brake off', he warned, if Elizabeth withdrew her support from Sidney; the loss to the crown would be immense.[154]

This counter-attack brought some relief. The agents were re-examined by the privy council and placed under arrest. Sidney was formally exonerated, and he was authorised by the queen to take all necessary steps to bring the Palesmen to submit. Representatives of the Pale were summoned to Dublin, informed of the queen's displeasure and imprisoned in the Castle, pending an acknowledgement of their fault and an allowance of the composition. At this, the opposition faltered, and though he was unable to gain a full submission, Sidney did win their consent to a year's composition on the terms originally proposed.[155]

The Palesmen had clearly gone too far in upholding their privileges so boldly upon an issue which touched the royal prerogative, and Sidney had benefited from Elizabeth's characteristic reaction. Yet Sidney could not make matters appear as unequivocal as he would have them. The agents in the Tower soon withdrew from their exposed position, conceded the viceroy's right to impose cess, and reconstructed their case by emphasising the practical abuses from which they had suffered. The cess had been unprecedentedly high, and Sidney had demanded it at a time of genuine scarcity when the difference between the queen's price and the market had

[151] Sidney to Walsingham, 15 May 1577, BL, Cotton MSS, Titus B X, no. i, f. 9.
[152] 'Instructions to Waterhouse', HMC, *De Lisle and Dudley MSS*, II, p. 56.
[153] Sidney to Eliz., 20 May 1571, SP 63/58/29.
[154] Walsingham to Eliz., 15 Apr. 1577, SP 63/58/3.
[155] Eliz. to Sidney, 14 May 1577, SP 63/58/20; privy council to Sidney, 14 May, SP 63/58/21; Sidney to Eliz. and to Walsingham, 20 June 1577, SP 63/58/50, 51; 'Certain examinations', 1 July, Lambeth MSS, 628/353.

been at its greatest ever known. The annual loss to the country they estimated to be over £6,500. On top of this, came the informal extortions of the soldiers themselves whose cost to the country was incalculable. The deputy had not raised a finger to curb these abuses and he had not even attempted to ease the country's burden by making full use of the corn-leases incident to his office. His proposal of composition, on the other hand, was by no means as generous as he made it out to be. The new subsidy would work out at around 9d per acre, but the current lease value of an acre within the Pale, was only 12d. Thus, 'the landlord by these means shall become not only a base freeholder on his own land, but also should be left only 3d rent out of an acre by the year'. Again, since cash was chronically scarce, 'it is likely that in time corn and cattle, the principal things that the country breedeth and bringeth forth to bear charges withal, would grow so cheap as is [sic] would become little worth and so would the payment of 5 marks be as chargable as their present burdens are'.[156]

To prove that their complaint lay only with Sidney's abuses, the agents presented an alternative scheme of feeding the army without significantly increasing the costs of either the queen or the country. They offered to supplement the pay of 1,000 soldiers by 1d (st.) a day, thus making it easier for each to buy supplies at reasonable prices. At the same time, they renewed an offer first made to Fitzwilliam to undertake a victualling contract themselves. The new penny subsidy, they argued slyly, would be largely recouped by the profits to be made from the victualling.[157]

These proposals made room for the compromise which the queen and her council were anxious to reach. But, more importantly, they reinforced a doubt ever present during Sidney's viceroyalties that the evils of governing Ireland were not inherent in the situation, but were derived directly from the methods of this man whose appointments to office had always been won amidst an atmosphere of personal rivalry, competition and private enterprise. Thus with the prospect of local political and financial settlements already on offer, one question became obvious: was Sidney's forceful and provocative conduct as chief governor really necessary. The suggestion that Sidney had, in fact, become superfluous was for the first time made explicit neither by the Palesmen nor by his enemies at court, but by his own chancellor, William Gerrard.

---

[156] 'Submission of Scurlocke et al.', Lambeth MSS, 629/119; 'Questions to be resolved',and 'Answers', *c.* July 1577, Lambeth MSS 628/150–2; 'Notes touching the victualling', BL, Cotton MSS, Titus B XII, fos. 336–7; 'Note on grievances of the English Pale and remedies thereto', *c.* July 1577, SP 63/58/74–9.

[157] Burnell's 'Device', *c.* Nov. 1577, Lambeth MSS, 628/147. 'Resolution of privy council', 11 Nov., SP 63/59/45.

Though Gerrard had been a colleague of Sidney's on the council in Wales, he had never been an unquestioning supporter.[158] It was, indeed, while he was at court presenting a long discourse on the defects of the Welsh council, that the decision to send him to Ireland was made.[159] Gerrard's initial views about Ireland had much in common with Sidney's. He supported the deputy's use of the prerogative, his attitude towards the Clanrickard rebellion was severe and he had little affection for 'the filthy people' in general.[160] But his views were at once more extreme and more moderate than the deputy's. The problems facing the government in Ireland, he believed, were a good deal more profound than any previous governor, including Sidney, had seemed to appreciate. Lawlessness was endemic not merely in the gaelicised areas, but even in the English Pale itself, where the oppression of coyne persisted. There the Anglo-Irish lords and the newly settled English captains raided each other and oppressed the ordinary people with impunity. The number of retainers held by some of the gentlemen was as large as any outside the Pale, and none would easily be brought to dispense with them. Until the English Pale itself, he argued, had first been reclaimed and reformed, 'the policy to wade further to gain territories is as it were, to suffer the parts at home to burn and to seek to quench a fire far off'.[161]

Recent governors had failed to grasp this point. In their haste towards a final solution they had built their ambitious schemes upon the shakiest foundations and each had in turn suffered collapse. The attempt to establish English law in the provinces by peaceful means had been a failure from the outset, but more forceful methods had been more expensive and more dangerous. The maintenance of the English army had of late become so burdensome that the lawful rule of government had grown indistinguishable from the oppression of the over-lords. Expediency and military necessity had obscured the bed-rock of common law upon which alone good government was founded. The overemployment of martial law had brought the entire English legal system into disrepute. Attempts to impose English rule immediately and conclusively by force or by intimidation had prevented the pure virtues of the common law from being made manifest to the ordinary

---

158 *DNB* sv; P. Williams, *The council in the marches of Wales* (Cardiff, 1958), pp. 124, 251–4; Gerrard's 'Discourses on Wales', ed. D. L. Thomas, *Y. Cymmrodor* 13 (1899), pp. 134–63.
159 'Petition of Sir William Gerrard', 23 Apr. 1576, SP 63/55/33; Walsingham to Sidney, 28 Jan. 1576, Collins, *Letters and memorials of state*, I, pp. 85–6.
160 Gerrard to Walsingham, 29 June 1576, SP 63/55/72.
161 The following account is based upon several expressions of Gerrard's opinions in *Anal. Hib.* 2 (1931), pp. 93–8, 183–7; 'Observations on the government of Ireland', SP 63/60/20; 'Remembrances for Ireland', SP 63/60/33; 'Treatise on the reformation of Ireland', BL, Cotton MSS, Titus B XII, fos. 229–30; the quotation is from *Anal. Hib.*, 2 (1931), p. 96.

people. Haste had secured superficial gains only; impatience had been the ruin of policy.[162]

To this rather pessimistic statement of the problem, however, Gerrard proposed a surprisingly moderate solution. Since past governors had over-reached themselves and failed, it was now imperative to withdraw from the unrealistic aims they had set themselves. Plans for large-scale expansion were to be abandoned. The Pale was first to be regenerated, and this done the government's main vehicle of expansion was to be neither military nor diplomatic, but judicial. The inherent attraction of English law was to be used 'by little and little to stretch the Pale further' until at last the entire country had been encompassed.[163] Gerrard rejected the argument that the law would be powerless against the degenerate Anglo-Normans and that 'the sword must go before to subdue these'.

For can the sword teach them to speak English, to use English apparel, to restrain them from Irish exactions and extortions and to shun all the manners and the orders of the Irish. No, it is the rod of justice that must scour out these blots. For the sword once went before to settle their ancestors and in them yet resteth this English nature to fear justice. So as justice without the sword may suffice to call them to her presence.[164]

Gerrard's attitude towards the Gaelic Irish was more ambivalent. While the reconstruction of the old colony was under way, he believed that a policy of containment was best pursued; he was even willing to recommend the use of force against them when necessary. But he nevertheless believed that good example and persuasion would in time 'win the Irish to love and embrace English government'.[165]

On this basis, Gerrard advanced major practical recommendations for administrative reform. A new decentralised structure based on the division of the country into judicial circuits was to be established. Three circuit judges were to act under the general supervision of a lord justice, but upon most issues each was to be autonomous in his own sphere. Leinster, the most important area of government attention, would be the joint responsibility of the lord justice and the lord chancellor; the circuits of the other judges were to be limited to those areas now thought most amenable to the introduction of English law. The garrison was to be reduced to the amount of troops necessary to protect and maintain the prestige of the circuit judges. Gerrard was confident that any extraordinary requirements would be met with the

---

[162] See in particular, his 'Observations', SP 63/60/20.
[163] Gerrard to Walsingham, 8 Feb. 1577, SP 63/57/18.
[164] Gerrard's 'Notes', *Anal. Hib.* 2 (1931), p. 96.
[165] 'Observations', SP 63/60/20.

cooperation of the local sheriffs and senechals and, when necessary, by the earls of Ormond and Kildare.[166]

However practicable Gerrard's proposed scheme was in the long term, its immediate implications for Sidney were grave. If the militarist approach was to be abandoned in favour of more limited juridical aims, the lord deputy, as the director of a centrally organised programme of reform was clearly redundant. Gerrard himself was the first to make these implications concrete in the matter of the composition. Unlike Sidney he had always maintained a distinction between the real grievances of the Palesmen and the manner in which they presented their case. Even before he left Ireland to defend his governor, the chancellor's independent opinion was well known to the Palesmen. He had publicly condemned the abuses of government officials; he had even approved of a jury's indictment of cessors, 'the worst officers in all the land'.[167] Not without reason was he 'suspected over much to favour [the Palesmen's] cause'.[168] For Gerrard the conflict with the Palesmen had nothing to do with Sidney's grand plan of composition. Thus, when their agents dropped their challenge to the prerogative, he ceased to oppose them, and going far beyond the letter of his instructions, formally accepted their alternative offer.[169]

If this in itself were not fatal to Sidney's chances, the chancellor had recourse to one further argument certain to lead to the deputy's disgrace: he talked of costs. Past methods of government had been woefully extravagant, not merely because they had been futile, but because they had been pursued to the neglect of far more immediate sources of gain. While the governors pursued their lofty ambitions, negligence and corruption on the bench, in the exchequer and throughout the entire civil administration had allowed secure revenues to fall away. Despite the queen's commands, slovenly record-keeping, half-hearted enforcement and downright embezzlement continued in every department. The costly pursuit of new sources of revenue elsewhere was quite pointless when the government could not even exploit those nearest to hand. Gerrard, of course, did not lay the blame for all these faults upon his immediate superior; he wrote of methods of administration rather than of personalities. But at one point he made his meaning absolutely clear: 'If Her Majesty be minded to continue the deputy', he warned, 'then expence and surpluage must be thought on'.[170]

By the time he made these insinuations, their relevance was fully

---

[166] 'Notes', *Anal. Hib.* 2 (1931), pp. 183–7; 'Treatise', BL, Cotton MSS, Titus B XII, fo. 330.
[167] Gerrard to Walsingham, 8 Feb. 1577, SP 63/57/16.
[168] Gerrard to Walsingham, 8 Feb., SP 63/57/18.
[169] 'Resolution of privy council', 11 Nov. 1577, SP 63/59/45; Eliz. to Sidney, 22 Mar. 1578, SP 63/60/23.
[170] 'Observations', SP 63/60/20; 'Notes', pp. 183–7; 'Remembrances', SP 63/60/33.

appreciated at court. The general resistance provoked by Sidney's measures had imposed a heavy strain on his strictly limited resources. The original estimates which had been insufficient from the start, now proved to be wholly inadequate to the demands he was forced to meet. By Michaelmas 1577, Sidney had exceeded his original costing by over £14,000 and was almost £9,000 in debt.[171] Gerrard's arguments, then, simply confirmed a view that was already taking shape in Whitehall. By the beginning of 1578, even Sidney's closest supporters had lost confidence in him. The normally sympathetic Secretary Wilson wrote sharply: 'It is told me that grievous exactions are used under your government after a very strange manner . . . And great pity it were that Her Highness's prerogative, which is sacred and very honorable being well used, should be a colour or pretence to some private gain without public profit'.[172] Waterhouse was despondent, and Walsingham urged that he accept defeat gracefully by reaching an amicable agreement with the Palesmen. By May, Sidney's revocation was determined; and instructions, drafted in accordance with Gerrard's recommendations, were being prepared for a new lord justice.[173]

[171] 'Notes of expenses and receipts', SP 63/61/21.
[172] Wilson to Sidney, 23 Mar. 1578, Collins, *Letters and memorials of state*, I, p. 245.
[173] Walsingham to Sidney, 27 Feb., 23 Mar., Collins, *Letters and memorials of state*, I, pp. 240, 244, Waterhouse to Sidney, 4 July, p. 265; 'Instructions' for Lord Justice Drury, 29 May 1578, Lambeth MSS, 611, Fos. 351–60.

INTERLUDE: GOVERNMENT IN
IRELAND, 1536–1579

'It is a strange desire to seek power and to lose liberty; or to seek power over others and to lose power over a man's self'. (Francis Bacon)

(I)

In the autumn of 1578 a watershed in the course of Tudor attempts to govern Ireland appeared to have been reached. The new government established in August constituted a direct repudiation of Sidney's methods. Thenceforth power was to be divided between the lord justice, the lord chancellor, the circuit judges advocated by Sir William Gerrard, and an autonomous president in Connacht. All of these were men of limited expectations. Priority was again given to the reform of the financial administration. Gilbert Gerrard's proposed reforms of the early 1560s were to be revived, and the new lord justice's instructions were based on those given to Sir William Skeffington almost fifty years before. Costs were to be curtailed and existing sources of revenue were to be better exploited, but no substantial increase in income was anticipated. In general, the instructions were loosely conceived. Wide discretionary powers were granted to the chief officers but no programme was underwritten. The new establishment was clearly an attempt to sever the administration of Irish affairs from the machinations of English domestic politics and to allow the appropriate processes of management to emerge from within. It was a major change of direction.

Sidney's departure, then, might well appear to mark the end of an era. A figure of extraordinary energy, his experience in Ireland had transcended a mere personal history, and had come to embody the systematic development of a general administrative practice. Under Sidney's contract government the 'programmatic style' had attained its most succinct and terse statement; and all its paradoxes were made fully explicit.

159

(11)

In 1556 a unique and fully developed strategy of governing Ireland came to an end. Over the previous twenty years, Lord Leonard Grey and Sir Anthony St Leger had developed an administrative technique that had transformed the chief governor from being merely the representative of the English crown in Ireland into the role of the leading spokesman of a uniform Irish interest. Grey's initiative had undoubtedly been the most rudimentary. Confronted with the host of problems consequent upon the Kildare rebellion, and with the refusal of his superiors at court to support an independent administration, he had struggled to reconstruct a platform of political stability which would enable an English governor to operate as effectively as any Anglo-Irish lord. Grey's methods were makeshift, though it is remarkable how close he came, given his unpromising circumstances, to making them work.

St Leger's approach was more subtle. Through diplomacy, patronage and not least through his connivance in the massive expropriation of crown revenues, St Leger had gradually extended his personal influence over the whole country. In the power vacuum created first by the fall of the Geraldines and later by the eclipse of the Butlers, he had constructed for himself a basis of support amongst the native inhabitants which enabled him to exert an influence over developments in the country neither by force nor by simple conciliation, but by the sheer reflexes of interest. But St Leger had presented himself as more than a surrogate Kildare. By promoting the idea of a notional Irish king – for whom he was but a mere representative – he sought to transcend the old oppositions of Geraldines and Butlers and to create instead an alternative king's party whose leader could enjoy most of the power and little of the weaknesses of traditional factional politics. St Leger's success was considerable: gradually he succeeded in eroding the indigenous sources of opposition to his rule; and even the dangers of his active participation in the unauthorised exploitation of crown lands, upon which so much of his influence counted, were successfully neutralised.

But St Leger's diplomatic initiative depended upon the existence of a king. And, after 1547, such a solid embodiment of his myth could never be vouchsafed. The mid-Tudor period imposed a variety of demands upon St Leger and those who followed his policy. Unexpected, extraneous pressures forced an alteration in the Dublin government's priorities; but, most damagingly, they made plain the fundamental fragility of the whole Tudor dynasty. St Leger's efforts to cope with these changes derailed his long-term strategies and profoundly weakened his status both in Ireland and at court.

Yet when the fatal challenge to his regime was made, it came neither from the Irish lordships nor from the crown, but from a clique of ambitious young adventurers who had unexpectedly acquired a positive interest in capturing the government of Ireland for themselves. This unusual desire to be sent to Ireland arose, in part, from their superficial and short-sighted examination of how St Leger operated as governor there. On looking towards Ireland in the mid-1550s, they defined a set of salient political and military problems with which St Leger's administration had seemed incapable of dealing. On looking again, they saw that the administration's political and financial practices were both highly compromising and legally dubious. And on the strength of these two observations they concluded that the problems of Irish governance were capable of subdivision into two distinct categories. There existed a number of primary difficulties which needed to be resolved before any further progress could be made. Then an impersonal and efficient administrative structure needed to be imposed upon the country to consolidate and develop the authority which the ruthless removal of the most outstanding challenges to the will of the crown had already gained. With the defeat of the most dangerous threats to English rule and the installation of the reformed and extended administrative framework throughout the country, the natural tendency towards peace and order, which had sustained St Leger's corrupt and negligent regime for so long, would then take its course. Ireland would be reduced to English ways by the same exertion of central authority and the same administrative implements which had brought the most outlying parts of the realm of England into conformity.

The attraction of this analysis, however, was greatly enhanced by the private advantages which it seemed to bring to those who would give it effect. It allowed an ambitious young politician to formulate and implement an aggressive reform policy while avoiding the dual dangers of isolation in Ireland or unwanted interventions from London. The new strategy could be easily conceived and expounded. The primary problems to be resolved were quite palpable and, for the second phase, the instruments of administrative reform were close to hand. The entire operation was capable of being organised into a simple and clearly articulated programme of action. The time needed to remove the old obstacles and construct the new order could be readily estimated and an assessment of the costs of the work of clearance and reconstruction could easily be made. And by way of conclusion to every set of proposals submitted for inspection, the same promise could be confidently advanced: this done and the governance of Ireland would cease to exist as a problem of policy and become a matter of routine administration. Such an approach not only promised glory to its undertakers when the task had been completed, it seemed also to grant them the greatest possible political autonomy within the bare framework of time and costs during the period when the work was under way.

In theory, this government through redesigned reform programmes constituted the most complete delegation of authority that the crown could grant to its public servants. It represented Tudor rule at its most flexible. Under its terms any prospective candidate for service could present his own analysis of the Irish problem and offer his own solution. General conciliation and downright force, colonisation and composition through both diplomacy and intimidation – the whole range of the 'tough–soft' spectrum espied by historians – were equally acceptable in principle. A governor might pursue mutually contradictory policies at once; he might eschew past opinions, turn on his old friends and befriend his old enemies without demur from Westminster, once the terms of his programme had been sanctioned. But the appearance of autonomy was deceptive. The ignorance and indifference of the crown which had permitted the submission of reform programmes in the first place pertained only to means and techniques; the fundamental conservative imperatives to preserve political stability and administrative economy remained unalterable. Thus whatever theoretical attraction a programme might have, it would nevertheless be judged in practice by the degree to which it honoured or offended against these basic principles. A judgement in terms of the amount of trouble aroused or of treasure spent was easy enough for the most neglectful sovereign to make; it was never long in forthcoming. Though ostensibly heuristic in spirit, the farming out of the government of Ireland was in fact the very opposite. By removing their moment of interference from the level of concrete policy-making to the more manageable plane of guiding principle, the sovereigns consolidated, rather than diluted their control over affairs in Ireland.

Their concern with the preservation of these basic principles, moreover, was progressive. As the treasury's disbursements mounted, the crown began to look not merely for greater savings, but for a positive increase in revenues to recoup past losses. Initially, this increasing financial concern was a major inducement to the formulation and acceptance of programmes: it was a final blow to St Leger. But as the programmes themselves faltered, it became the major impediment to their recovery. The outlay of capital and confidence which the new plans normally required placed their authors in a peculiar relationship with the crown. The notion that a personal obligation was placed upon the governor by his appointment was inherent in the process from the beginning, but it became increasingly more apparent during Sidney's viceroyalties and was made bluntly explicit in the simple contract arrangement of his last Irish service. Then, the strict interpretation of the contract and Sidney's failure to honour its terms overrode all other considerations. Though Sidney could point to a definite financial improvement in his last years, though he could promise real profits in the future and argue that earlier gains had been forestalled only by accident, Sidney had clearly defaulted on his promise. His net return was a loss, and for that there was no forgiveness.

The concern with the maintenance of political stability was expressed in a less fluid and almost dialectical fashion. Though the royal government might be willing to contemplate a revolution in policy, it was determined not to abandon those subjects whose loyalty had long been proven or to embrace too readily those whose past records had been dubious. Thus the sanctioning of many programmes of action might not always entail the authorisation of their most practical implications. A governor might find his whole operation suddenly proscribed because its implementation tended to change the traditional relationship of the government towards particular interests. Sussex had experienced something of this frustration under Mary when the highly respected Archbishop Dowdall brought his administration under critical examination. But again, it was the latecomer, Sidney, who suffered most from these constraints. No matter how impartial his concern, he could expect to be supported in no policy that conflicted with the interests of the trusted Butlers or did much to improve the standing of the Geraldines. For all their apparent originality and autonomy, the programmatic governors were no less free of the basic concerns of the crown than any other royal servant.

Inevitably the strain of their paradoxical position began to influence the content of the governors' programmes. Gradually, short-term effectiveness and superficial achievement took precedence over the objective needs of the situation. Sussex more than once succumbed to the temptation to exchange the genuine attainment of his ends for a shabby and sometimes sordid conclusion. His government finally collapsed through his obsessive attempts to destroy Shane O'Neill. But it was under Sidney that the process reached its ultimate stage. Increasingly, his programmes were designed around the simple end of showing political and financial results of an immediately tangible nature, and the methods he adopted to achieve those ends became fundamentally militaristic and coercive in form. As a result, Sidney's projections gradually became devoid of political, ideological or even factional consistency. They oscillated freely from open conciliation to outright confrontation. Often they were so confused and so interchanged as to preclude differentiation; sometimes, as in the cases of Carew and Essex, they were but willing concessions to circumstance; on occasion, as in his sudden compulsions to destroy Desmond and Clanrickard, sheer opportunism intervened and there were no projections at all.

During Sidney's last years in office, the persistent neglect that had in the first place encouraged the development of the programmatic style rebounded upon the crown with a vengeance. The delegation of authority within narrow, but implicit limits led progressively towards the explicit acceptance of those constraints and to their transformation into the principal ends of policy. But this progression did not complete a circle; it launched a spiral. Consistent and direct policy-making at court on the basis of the determining principles of economy and stability might have laid the foundations of a stable, if imperfect, Irish policy. But in the hands of independent adventurers for whom service in Ireland was a private enterprise, such implicit guidelines appeared not as the mandates of conservatism, but as the only criteria of success to whose end any means whatever might be employed. Thus did an administrative theory, founded on simple and irreducible premises, produce a volatile and highly opportunistic executive practice.

There remained a further paradox. Being poorly informed and preoccupied with other affairs, the queen and council were ill-equipped to make a rational choice between competing programmes, each offering to bring about the same conclusive result. To simplify matters, they made their choice in terms of personnel. There was some logic in the practice. The personalisation of policy greatly facilitated the channelling of information to and fro, and the allocation of responsibility. It gave an area of manoeuvre to the crown which a more centrally directed policy would have precluded: when a policy went badly wrong, it could be abandoned simply by replacing the governor. But the effect of this administrative short-cut was to convert the Irish office into one more target for the competition of court rivals, and thus to compromise the possibility of an independent and objectively based Irish policy. At court, the quality of each governor's service tended to be assessed not by any objective standard of competence, nor by the nature of the problem he confronted, but by the current political status of the interest group to which he belonged. This constant exposure to irrelevant and often slanderous criticism greatly distracted the governors. It rendered them extremely vulnerable to the machinations of opposition groups in Ireland who readily supplied their enemies at court with damaging information about the state of affairs in the country. The combination of accusations at court and opposition in Ireland was fatal: neither Sussex nor Sidney could overcome it. The sum effect of these influences was to place every policy, whatever its promise, under the constant threat of random discontinuity and sudden death.

This evil was by no means the fault of the crown nor of the system at court alone; for the governors themselves knowingly undertook the risks of the system and adapted themselves to the challenge. Sussex and Sidney both constructed in Ireland a microcosm of the competitive world of connection from which they had come. Both took care to magnify the importance of their achievements and to see that their endeavours were well publicised at home. Each openly criticised the defects of his predecessor and his successor. Both formed a working alliance with one of the two great Anglo-Irish factions, and both constructed a minor clique of their own within the Irish administration. Most important, both realised that the allowance of their service at court took precedence over all considerations within Ireland and framed their actions accordingly. Each took pains to ensure that their actions were interpreted in the most favourable light at court. Each tended to minimise the importance of the obstacles they confronted and to exaggerate their ability to cope with them. To give concrete demonstration to their overarching claims, each displayed a marked tendency to abandon a cautious procedure in favour of the spectacular coup. In sum, the governors themselves came to regard Ireland with grave ambiguity, perceiving it both as a specific problem in itself and as a dangerously incalculable factor in the politics of court; and their own programmes, founded upon this shaky dualism, became increasingly less relevant to the situation in which they were meant to apply.

Again, it was Sidney who brought such tendencies to their fruition. Sir Henry was never able to exert the influence which the noble earl had enjoyed both in England and in Ireland. The very circumstances of his first appointment eliminated the possibility of his universal acceptability and a reputation for ruthless ambition and controversy dogged him throughout his career. If he could never command total respect at court, his influence with the Anglo-Norman factions was also far less secure than Sussex's had been. The alliance with the Geraldines which had helped undermine his predecessor and had given him his initial popularity was based more on promise than performance. Under the strain imposed by Sidney's concessions to the crown's political conservatism, it soon deteriorated. It was, in any case, incapable of offering him the kind of support which Ormond had lent Sussex on both sides of the Irish Sea. In his relative isolation, Sidney was driven to rely on his own resources. He attempted to compensate for the weaknesses on his flanks by making vastly inflated promises which temporarily brought him the support of the crown. But the exclusiveness of his promises only intensified his isolation, and by 1577 his power bases in England and in Ireland had grown too narrow to bear the increased pressures he sought to place upon them. His failure in that year represented the essential weaknesses of the programmatic approach writ large. In 1562–3 Sussex had run aground when it was claimed that he had perverted the general good-will of the sovereign for her subjects; in 1577, Sidney faced universal resistance because it was believed that he had taken the whole land to farm. That an administrative method which imposed the most fundamental constraints and impediments on its executors should have provoked the alarming impression that the government of Ireland was left prey to the most dangerous of free-booters, is, perhaps, the highest irony of the period. But that Sidney should have fallen through a combination of the same forces and over substantially the same issues that had brought his rival Sussex to ruin was not ironic; in so far as he had brought to maturity the assumptions and techniques enunciated by Sussex in 1556, it was inevitable.

(III)

The turning point of 1578, however, was never attained. A quarter of a century of rule by programme had left a deep imprint upon the country. It had prevented the government from formulating a stable policy towards each group in Irish society, and it had generated among the Gaelic lords, feudal magnates and Palesmen alike a profound uncertainty about their relationship with Her Majesty's government. It had exploded the controls moderating the traditional rivalry of the great feudal houses, leaving all of them unsettled, and some of them desperate. It had oppressed the community of the Pale to such an extent that the most loyal subjects of the crown in Ireland grew seriously estranged from their own governors. And it had belied the promise of 1541, flooding Gaelic Ireland with a host of settlers and lawless adventurers of a type with whom the clansmen were already familiar. In short, under Sussex and Sidney, the credibility of the Dublin administration as the impartial dispenser of justice in the realm had been deeply mortgaged in the eyes of every group in the island, and despite Gerrard's late attempts at salvage, the loss of confidence was already irredeemable. Within a year of its establishment, the new decentralised government was destroyed by the eruption in rebellion of one of the groups who had suffered most from the inconsistency and incompetence of English rule in Ireland in the previous two decades.

Part 2

THE IMPACT OF REFORM GOVERNMENT, 1556–1583

5

Reform government and the feudal magnates

(1)

'Reformation' rather than 'damnation', it has been said, was the fundamental aim of Henrician policy toward the great Irish magnates in the early 1530s.[1] By the promise of patronage and the threat of royal disapproval it had been hoped that the feudal lords could be persuaded to join in the government's campaign to reassert English rule in Ireland by encouraging their allies and their clients to see the advantages of political change. The rebellion of the Kildare Geraldines, as we have seen, profoundly disrupted such hopes. But despite this unexpected setback and its highly disturbing reverberations, the rehabilitation of the Anglo-Irish magnates and their co-option into the work of political reform remained a central objective of successive Tudor governments.

The re-establishment of the house of Kildare and the return of Gerald the eleventh earl to Ireland in 1554 in the company of the tenth earl of Ormond whose minority had also been spent in exile from Ireland gave eloquent testimony to the Tudor concern to restore the magnates to their accustomed place of influence. Both were immediately appointed to the Irish council to serve with the ageing but powerful earl of Desmond and in 1558 they were joined by the second earl of Clanrickard and by the fourteenth earl of Desmond just then elevated to the peerage upon his father's decease. Neither Clanrickard nor the young Desmond appeared frequently at the council board, but like Ormond and Kildare each was appointed at the beginning of Elizabeth's reign to important commissions within their own region and each received personal assurance from the queen of her sincere goodwill.[2]

In practice, moreover, Elizabeth maintained a surprisingly tolerant attitude toward these overmighty subjects. She showed a willingness to

---

[1] Bradshaw, 'Cromwellian reform', p. 80.
[2] Register of the Irish council, HMC, *Haliday MSS*, passim; Memoranda of royal letters to the Irish nobility from Mary and Elizabeth, SP 62/2/2–7, 63/1/65.

overlook their occasional misdemeanours and even to pardon their more serious breaches of the peace. Each of the great houses was permitted at least one overt denial of the Dublin government's authority and most got away with a good deal more. Even Desmond whose conduct in the 1560s seemed forever to have forfeited the confidence of the queen was fully rehabilitated in the early 1570s and patiently reassured of Elizabeth's forgiveness. Elizabeth, like her predecessors, was concerned to impose a greater restraint upon her powerful subjects, but she was by no means desirous to destroy them.[3]

The queen's ministers, for the most part, shared her outlook. All were agreed that bastard feudalism should be abolished, but most were uncertain as to when and how abolition was to be accomplished. Sidney was the most uncompromising in principle; but despite his fulminations against the system he displayed a practical willingness to tolerate its use by friends and enemies alike.[4] Sussex, as we have seen, was much more moderate and gradualist in his views and accordingly more tolerant in his practice.[5] Secretary Cecil was concerned that the government should not overreact to the occasional 'peccadilloes' of the great lords and his more aggressive successor, Walsingham, recognised the necessity of discounting their unruly habits.[6] As late as 1578 an extended debate among the privy councillors revealed that their views on the question of the timing of reform were still quite undecided.[7]

The clearest indication of the crown's genuine concern to reach a peaceful accommodation with the great lords is provided by the chief instrument which it adopted as a means of regaining control over the outlying regions of Munster and Connacht, the provincial council. In contrast to plans for Gaelic Ulster, the original councils devised for the other provinces were not conceived as self-sufficient, essentially military agencies. On the contrary, their very effectiveness was understood to be heavily dependent on the co-operation of the lords themselves. The magnates were given seats on the council, their legal advisers were permitted to attend with them and a number of figures known to be partial toward them were selected as councillors. Unlike his counterparts in Wales, the president in provincial Ireland was authorised to use martial law, but the occasions on which he

---

[3] For a fuller discussion see, Ciaran Brady, 'Faction and the origins of the Desmond rebellion of 1579', *IHS* 22 (1981), pp. 289–312.

[4] 'Discourse on coyne and livery', *c.* 1578, Lambeth MSS, 607, fo. 136.

[5] Ch. 3 above.

[6] Cecil to Challoner, 8 June 1562, *Cal. SP Foreign (1562)*, p. 83; Walsingham to Burghley, 26–7 July 1574, BL, Harl. MSS, 6991, nos. 47–8; Walsingham to Drury, 14 June 1579, SP 63/67/4.

[7] Collection of several submissions in Beale papers, BL, Add. MSS, 48015, fos. 291–306.

might do so were severely restricted: at no time was it to be applied against persons holding property or goods valued at 40 shillings or more.

Finally, the president's total retinue of fifty men, several of whom were non-serving officers, was minute in comparison to the standing forces and feudal hosts of the magnates. Far from acting as an instrument of force, the president's troop was intended to serve merely as a body-guard to protect the president from ambush or casual assault. In times of crisis it was expected that the lords themselves would raise the forces necessary to serve as the council's military arm. Clearly, then, provincial councils were designed to make substantial inroads on the local autonomy of the magnates, but they could not be said to have threatened their influence, still less to have posed a fatal challenge to their existence.[8]

This original model, of course, was given little chance to operate in the provinces, and was replaced by a far more martial and coercive instrument of government. But even the composition presidencies introduced in the late 1570s were originally intended not to destroy the lords but to stabilise their position within the realm. Under composition arrangements the lords were to be compensated for their surrender of their informal exactions and they were thereafter to be supported by the president in collecting their legally recognised dues. Composition entailed some loss of freedom and of potential income, but given the chronic uncertainty of their informal revenues and the exceedingly high cost of their collection, the new stability would seem to have offered a sufficient compensation. In Desmond's case, at any rate, composition promised to double his average real earnings.[9]

Yet for all of that, the government's sustained efforts to deal with the feudal magnates by means of accommodation, consultation and gradual reform came to naught, and indeed resulted in a veritable deterioration in relations in the latter half of the century. Between 1560 and 1580, each of the four great earls either openly rebelled or were guilty of serious collusion with actual rebels. Ormond was best behaved; but even he was not without blemish. In his dealings with the earl of Desmond in the 1560s and with Sir Barnaby Fitzpatrick in the 1570s he showed a marked propensity to settle disputes by force and without recourse to law. His loyalty was even more seriously in doubt during the early months of his brothers' rebellion in 1569,

[8] The instructions given to St Leger, Pollard and Perrot in 1566, 1568 and 1571 respectively, showed little substantive difference, SP 63/16/22, 26/9, Collins, *Letters and memorials of state*, I, pp. 48–59. A comparison between the Munster presidency and the council in Wales is essayed in P. Williams, 'The Munster council in the later sixteenth century', *Irish Comm. Hist. Sciences Bull.* 94 (1961).

[9] The fixed annual revenue of £2,000 which Desmond accepted in 1579 was about twice the figure estimated to be his optimum annual income in 1568, 'Extent of Desmond's revenues', *c.* 1568, SP 63/22/74; Gerrard to Burghley, 3 Jan. 1579, SP 63/65/3.

when first his inaction and later his special pleading did much to encourage the rebels in Munster.

Kildare's misconduct was more overt. On three occasions between 1561 and 1582 he was summoned to court, each time to undergo examination upon allegations of treason, each time with greater justification. Clanrickard was believed to have connived at, and even to have provoked, the two major rebellions of his sons in the 1570s. In 1579 he confessed himself guilty of treason and escaped a traitor's death only by a royal pardon. The stormy career of the last earl of Desmond from his first clash with Ormond in 1560 to his final rebellion in 1579 is well known. This bare factual record would appear to make one simple and commonplace conclusion seem incontrovertible. The crown's proposals of reform were, in whatever guise, intolerable to the great lords, to such an extent, indeed, that conflict between the reforming state and the old feudal elite was altogether unavoidable.[10]

This neat, but rather determinist conclusion is not, however, entirely satisfactory. In matters of timing alone, it is somewhat out of sequence; for while the introduction of reform through provincial councils is conventionally assumed to have marked the flashpoint of confrontation, the causal connection between the two events appears on closer inspection to be far from clear. Desmond co-existed happily with Warham St Leger, the first English officer to exercise the powers of a president in his lordship for almost a year.[11] Though he was resolutely opposed to St Leger's appointment, Ormond welcomed his successor as president, Sir John Perrot, and sought to have his term of office renewed.[12] Even Clanrickard's initial response to the appointment of Fitton was sufficient to convince the president's chief justice of his genuine good-will.[13] Conversely, not every outbreak of rebellion can be readily accounted for by the appearance of a president. Though Ormond felt threatened by Sidney's choice of St Leger, he

[10] The disorders of the magnates are most conveniently traced in Bagwell, *Ireland under the Tudors*, II, passim; on Ormond, Desmond and Clanrickard respectively, see also Edwards, 'The Butler revolt of 1569'; Ciaran Brady, 'Thomas Butler, tenth earl of Ormond (1531–1614) and reform in Tudor Ireland', in Brady (ed.), *Worsted in the game: losers in Irish history* (Dublin, 1989), pp. 49–60; Brady, 'Faction and the origins of the Desmond rebellion'; Bernadette Cunningham, 'The composition of Connacht in the lordships of Clanrickard and Thomond, 1577–1641', *IHS* 24 (1984), pp. 1–14.

[11] Fitzwilliam's account, 1559–69, shows that St Leger served with the entertainment and retinue of a president throughout 1566, despite his failure to obtain a formal patent, NRO, Fitzwilliam MSS (Irish), no. 47; see also St Leger to Leicester, 6 Mar. 1566, to Sidney, 3 July, SP 63/16/47, 18/54 (ii).

[12] Ormond to Cecil, 5 Mar. 1571, SP 63/30/27; Ormond to Heneage, 4 Feb. 1571, NLI, MS, 2301, fos. 37–8; Ormond to Burghley enclosing his 'Opinion on Ireland', 8 Dec. 1574, SP 63/48/70, 70 (i).

[13] Rokeby to Cecil, 4 Jan. 1570, SP 63/30/4.

did not resort to violence; when his brothers did rebel, it was in reaction to a very different threat from Sir Peter Carew. James Fitzmaurice, the Butlers' erstwhile Geraldine ally, rose out only after St Leger had been withdrawn from Munster and before any successor had been chosen to replace him. Desmond's own rebellion in 1579 occurred long after he had established a friendly relationship with President Drury and when the presidency itself was in abeyance.[14] Finally, Kildare, the most consistently mistrusted of all the Irish earls, never had a president to contend with at all.

Such inconsistencies do little more perhaps than pose a puzzle. Yet they cast doubt upon the prevailing assumption that the great lords were so imprisoned within their own anachronistic world of feudal, and bastard feudal practices that they regarded all change as an immediate and deadly threat. The magnates of sixteenth-century Ireland were indeed attached to the system of patronage and protection, rivalry and intimidation by which they maintained and extended their political and social influence. And the greater their attachment, the more difficult it was for them to respond positively to the reform proposals being proffered to them. There is an indisputable geographical fact that the two western earls, who were most deeply steeped in the ways of coyne and livery, were the most turbulent and unstable, and ultimately the least successful in their attempt to adapt to the new conditions. Yet such indications notwithstanding, the easy equation of a commitment to feudalism with an inevitable tendency towards rebellion is deceptive in its simplicity.

Not all of the magnates it should be recalled were heavily dependent upon coyne, and none of those who were profited greatly from it. Kildare had surrendered all his feudal powers upon his return from exile. He continued to have recourse to physical intimidation in order to sustain his influence within his locality, and employed a number of retainers, usually with the foreknowledge and consent of the government, for this purpose. But large portions of the Kildare revenues had for long been realised as fixed cash payments, and the earl's rental had been further regularised through the crown's leasing of large tracts of his demesne land to Palesmen in the years after 1534.[15] The commutation of the Butlers' feudal services for a fixed payment was already sufficiently advanced for the earl of Ormond to surrender his feudal powers voluntarily in 1564.[16] Commutations of service

[14] Brady, 'Faction and the origins of the Desmond rebellion'.
[15] 'Rental book of the earls of Kildare', ed. from BL, Harl. MSS, 3756, Gearóid MacNiocaill (ed.), *Crown Surveys of Lands*, 1540–1 (IMC, 1992), pp. 232–57.
[16] C. A. Empey, 'The Butler lordship to 1509' (Ph.D., University of Dublin, 1970) Ormond's proclamation 'for the taking away of . . . coyne and livery', 1 July 1564, SP 63/11/39, enclosure (ii). Edwards, 'The Butler revolt of 1569', pp. 237–42.

were common in Desmond and there is evidence that it was also in operation in Clanrickard.[17]

The reasons for the decline of coyne and livery are not hard to find. As a system of estate management it was highly uneconomic.[18] The maintenance of large groups of professional military retainers was wasteful both of men and material. It created no surplus wealth and depended for its success upon the most thorough exploitation of the resources available to it from year to year. The finances of those magnates who depended most heavily upon it were in a permanently precarious condition. These economic deficiencies in the system were exacerbated by its political weaknesses. Desmond and Clanrickard encountered regular opposition in their attempts to exact their claims. The inevitable disorders which accompanied their efforts aroused the unfavourable attention of the Dublin administration, and government intervention almost invariably supported those upon whom they had made their demands. The western earls were thus placed in an exceedingly difficult predicament. The more they attempted to preserve their local status, the more their credit with the government declined; the more they worked to earn the good-will of the crown, the less they could afford to maintain their old ways at home. Though both tried, neither managed to extricate himself successfully from this dilemma, and their failure is reflected both in their declining reputations at court and in their deteriorating economic and political status at home. As his conflicts with the government increased in the 1570s, Clanrickard claimed that the chief cause of his lordship's instability was its poverty.[19] Desmond made similar claims to indigence, and even as early as 1566 Sidney was afraid that the earl's desperate financial position would drive him to rebellion. Desmond's circumstances were indeed unhealthy; in 1568 it was estimated that he normally realised less than one-eighth of his potential annual revenue.[20]

Seen from this perspective, Kildare's quiet acceptance of the demise of

[17] Desmond survey of 1572, Lambeth MSS, 611, fos. 205 ff.; Note on Clanrickard's rental, 31 July 1579, SP 63/67/73, enclosure (i); 'Note on Clanrickard's manor-houses', 31 Mar. 1580, SP 63/72/26.

[18] On the English experience of the costs of 'bastard feudalism', see Lawrence Stone, *The crisis of the aristocracy* (Oxford, 1965), ch. 5, J. M. W. Bean, *The estates of the Percy family, 1416–1537* (London, 1958) and *The decline of English feudalism 1215–1540* (Manchester, 1968); G. A. Holmes, *The estates of the higher nobility in fourteenth-century England* (Cambridge, 1957); J. R. Lander, *The crown and the nobility 1450–1509* (London, 1976), esp. pp. 30–3, and on Wales, T. B. Pugh, *The marcher lordships of South Wales 1415–1536* (Cardiff, 1963), pp. 160, 175 ff.

[19] 'Clanrickard's articles', 16 May 1571, SP 63/32/35, 'Declaration of services', 8 Mar. 1579, SP 63/33/4.

[20] Sidney to privy council, 11 July 1566, SP 63/18/54; 'Extract of such yearly rents as the earl of Desmond ought to have', *c.* 1568, SP 63/22/74.

coyne and livery, Ormond's voluntary commutation of his dues and the two western earls' declarations of their willingness to surrender the old ways in favour of an alternative means of maintaining their status appear to be something more than disingenuous. Some adequate form of commutation made good sense: the problem was to find a means of undertaking such a change without jeopardising those vital interests which coyne and livery for all its evils had preserved. The magnates' attachment to the system in other words was essentially defensive and therefore conditional. Their large private armies may have been wasteful, yet they were regarded as necessary weapons of deterrence, without which the magnates would be left defenceless against the assaults of their factional enemies and powerless over their insubordinate inferiors. Where any great lord continued to have resort to retainers, all must needs have them or suffer eclipse. No one could afford to surrender them unilaterally. This argument from fear was the one most commonly advanced by the magnates in defence of their persistent use of coyne and livery: Desmond and Ormond both excused their maintenance of private armies in terms of their mutual distrust; neither was willing to concede a military superiority to the other.[21] Clanrickard argued that it was necessary for the preservation of order in the west until a more formal policing system could be established.[22] Its sudden removal, he claimed, would only stimulate the ambitions of men of lesser power and lighter allegiance whom the earls now kept under control. When Desmond was at length persuaded to assent to the abolition of coyne in 1574, he gave voice to what was but a commonly shared anxiety: 'I do hope that my agreement and easy consent to reduce those parts to English government should not extend so far as to my destruction, so that Her Majesty will think it reasonable either to suspend the execution of that part . . . or else make it general to all others to lay away weapons at me.'[23] The magnates would be willing to disarm if they could be assured that their political and social standing would not be endangered.

The economic inefficiency of coyne and livery, and its high political risks were enough to make the lords quite conditional in their attachment to the system, and open to suggestions for change. Yet coyne and livery was not, as many Elizabethans like to suggest, simply an evil in itself, a set of bad habits which the lords might be persuaded to renounce. It was rather the central mechanism of a larger political system which extended throughout the whole island and it could not therefore be isolated and defused until the

---

21 Ormond to Cecil, 22 Nov. 1564, SP 63/11/108; Ormond's 'Opinion', *c.* 1574, SP 63/48/70, enclosure (i); Sidney to Privy Council, 11 July 1566, 63/18/54; Desmond to Sidney, 6 July, 63/18/54, enclosure (ii).
22 Clanrickard's 'Articles', SP 63/32/35.
23 Desmond's 'Articles of submission', 7 July 1574, SP 12/45/84.

larger system itself had been confronted and dissolved. The great earls were not to be treated as isolated anachronisms, indulging in an outmoded politics that had long since lost its relevance. They were the leaders of one of the great political networks which extended throughout Ireland, transcending regional and ethnic distinctions and influencing the outcome of almost every political issue and every dynastic dispute. The position of the magnates within these connections greatly enhanced their power, allowing them to exert an influence over people and territories over which they possessed no legal claims. But such influence was not easily deployed. The factions themselves were not disciplined or coherent units, answerable at all times to the will of their leaders. They were deeply unstable structures, constituted by elements whose interests were not always compatible and whose allegiance to their patrons was highly conditional. The manipulation of such highly heterogeneous followings made up of dynastic relations, personal retainers, dependent clients, and erstwhile political allies whose loyalty could never be easily assumed was an extremely delicate operation, demanding a ceaseless round of political adventure and intrigue. A leader was required to assess the complex circumstances carefully, to balance and contain conflicting pressures within his own following and above all to demonstrate his authority continually through the reward of loyalty and the punishment of betrayal.

It was this complex and delicate calculus of faction rather than any abstract consideration that conditioned the responses of the great lords to all of the initiatives of Tudor reform and to the establishment of presidents. Thus, Desmond at first accepted the presidency because he already knew and had confidence in the presidential nominee and the man who had appointed him, while Ormond and Clanrickard reacted with hostility to presidencies because of their mutual distrust of the man who introduced them, Sir Henry Sidney. To them the presidencies' threat lay not in the nature of the office, but in the character and allegiance of the man who was to discharge its responsibilities. They doubted, that is to say, the official claim that each president would be 'a special person by birth indifferent and free from all partiality towards the people of the country'.[24] The magnates' response to presidents, in other words, simply reflected their degree of confidence in the good-will of the chief governor. Their attitude sprang from no outdated attachment to an outmoded and wasteful system, but from a recognition that the governors of Ireland were not indifferent arbiters of power but were themselves locked into the same political system within which the lords had been accustomed to operate.

The pervasive atmosphere of faction thus made for much frenetic

---

[24] The prescription was included in all presidential instructions, see note 16 above.

and apparently erratic politicing among the great lords. But it was not fundamentally anarchic. In the midst of their great rivalries the faction leaders had for long accepted implicit limitations on the extent of their competition. There was no attempt at mutual annihilation, no prolonged war and no pursuit of revenge above all other considerations. They had agreed also on the central objects of their pursuit: power over men, control over the judicial and administrative offices of government and the pursuit of positions of favour at the royal court itself. The Geraldine débâcle of the 1530s had seriously disturbed the equilibrium inherent in this system. Yet it had not overturned it. The loss of Geraldine control over the viceroyalty had merely concentrated efforts on the pursuit of influence over the new English appointees to the office.

The politics of Irish factions presented a difficult but by no means insurmountable problem to the agents of the Tudor reform policy. As formidably empowered officials and as influential courtiers in their own right, the new English viceroys could hope to exploit their unique positions as links in a chain of connection binding Irish interests to highly placed figures in the court itself. The exploitation of the viceregal office in this way was quite congenial to the personal ambitions of certain viceroys, most notably Grey and St Leger. But it was also highly conducive to the advance of political stability in Ireland as a whole. The sustained manipulation and cultivation of factional interests over a long period could allow the viceroy to reshape alignments in the way that most suited him. This is what Grey had attempted to do by his patronage of the Geraldines, and it was what St Leger had more boldly essayed in his construction of a new political following. Neither of these attempts, as we have seen, succeeded. But their individual failure was not in itself disastrous. For both had been based on a broad understanding of the place of coyne and livery within the national political system which, had it been maintained by their successors, might have allowed for the continuing restatement of the traditional conventions of competition from viceroyalty to viceroyalty and thus confirmed a rough and ready equilibrium. Either St Leger's success, therefore, or the adoption of his methods by those who displaced him would have offered the possibility of progress or at least guaranteed stability. But after 1556 neither alternative was possible.

After 1556 the English governors were not just well connected courtiers, they were, in addition, administrators committed to the execution of specific programmes whose objectives were ultimately though not intentionally indifferent to the interests of any Irish factional alliance. As the commitments of the governors increased, so the demands of their dual role became increasingly difficult to meet. Their ability to tailor the actions of the government to the requirements of their Irish allies deteriorated seriously.

Moreover, even when they sought to help their friends, the intrinsic weaknesses and vulnerabilities of their position left these governors unable to project an image of permanence and stability sufficient to encourage their Irish allies and discourage their enemies. This increasing unwillingness and increasing inability of the governors either to reward their friends or suppress their foes was the key element in determining the course of relations between the crown and the Irish magnates in the years after 1556. Its ill-effects had already begun to become apparent under Sussex, but as with so much else, they came to fruition under Sidney.

(ii)

In one sense, the replacement of the corrupt and generally pro-Geraldine St Leger by an energetic young reformer who was known to be favourable to the Butlers seemed to herald the reversal of fortunes for which the Butlers had been striving for almost two decades. At first, the new governor did his best to confirm the Butlers' confidence. While he did his utmost to exclude the earl of Kildare from influence, Sussex took pains to increase Ormond's participation in government. Ormond was appointed to commissioners of peace for Munster and Leinster. He was authorised to use martial law within the counties of his own lordship, and he was twice made a commissioner for ecclesiastical causes. The earl came to prominence as a councillor: his attendance at council meetings increased, and in 1559 he was appointed lord treasurer and thereby allowed to take precedence at the board over Kildare as the highest peer in the realm.[25] With service came reward. First and most important, Ormond secured in 1557 the confirmation of his palatine liberty in Tipperary and regained the prize wines of Youghal and Kinsale which his father had enjoyed. New grants of large monastic properties were granted to him; several of his existing leases were renewed on the most generous terms.[26] But more important was the less tangible political influence which Ormond won under Sussex. The lieutenant concluded a long-standing dispute with the Fitzpatricks of Upper Ossory in the earl's favour, and sided unhesitantly with him in his territorial and jurisdictional disputes with the earl of Desmond. In 1560, when special commissioners actually determined a boundary dispute in Desmond's favour, Sussex had the case referred to London in order to have the judge-

---

[25] *Fiants Eliz.*, nos. 181, 183, 214, 263, 469, 542, 666; appointment to the lord treasureship, no. 133.

[26] *Cal. Pat. Rolls Henry VIII–Eliz.*, pp. 384–5, 387, 391, 394; *Fiants Eliz.*, nos. 497, 504, 563. In 1561, Ormond obtained a waiver of all outstanding arrears on crown leases, no. 303.

ment reversed. As the Ormond–Desmond feud intensified in the early 1560s, Sussex remained steadfast in his support for Ormond.[27]

The benefits won through the Sussex connection were not however limited to the interests of the earl himself. Ormond's brothers and his uncle, the Viscount Mountgarret, were encouraged to attach themselves to the government and were appointed to positions of executive responsibility and received the customary favours in return.[28] But the connection's most important linkage went far beyond the Butler family. The historical association of the Butlers with the Burkes of Clanrickard had only recently been revived first by the elevation of Ulick Burke, a grandson of the seventh earl of Ormond, to the peerage as earl of Clanrickard, and later by the Butlers' unwavering support to Ulick's heir, Richard, in his attempts to assert his authority in Clanrickard after his father's death in 1544.[29] By 1556 Richard's position was secure, and the alliance between the Burkes of Clanrickard and the Butlers of Ormond was fixed. Thus, when the new governor chose to patronise the Butlers, he also acquired natural allies west of the Shannon at the same time. Sussex took the earl's son, Ulick, into his own household service.[30] He praised Clanrickard's services in Connaught, and recommended him frequently for reward. Under Sussex's patronage, Clanrickard's disputed succession to the earldom was confirmed by letters patent, a large number of crown lands were leased to him, and his most ambitious suit was consented to: he was appointed captain of all Connaught.[31] Not surprisingly, Clanrickard was a loyal supporter of the crown throughout Sussex's period in office, ready to supply troops and victuals whenever they were requested and to offer his services on any occasion in the support of the Dublin government. In the same way, Clanrickard's chief Gaelic ally, Conor O'Brien, the highly insecure earl of Thomond, experienced similar benefits from a viceroy determined to preserve him from the attacks of his own kinsmen, and responded with

---

[27] Irish council book, HMC, *Haliday MSS*, pp. 4–5; Sussex's 'Memorial', May 1560, SP 63/2/20; Sussex's 'Relation of the state of Ireland', 1562, SP 63/5/101; Philip and Mary to Ormond, 13 May 1557, HMC, *Ormond MSS*, vol. I, p. 4.

[28] 'Award for the earl of Desmond', 23 Aug. 1560, SP 63/3/32; Eliz. to Sussex, 15 Dec., SP 63/2/50; Sussex to Eliz., 23 Oct. 1561, SP 63/4/62; *Fiants Eliz.*, nos. 54, 56, 64, 142, 'Memorial of suits granted', July 1559, SP 63/1/63.

[29] GEC, *Peerage* (rev. edn), III, pp. 228–9, Clanrickard's 'Note of services', 8 Mar. 1579, SP 63/66/4, Clanrickard to privy council, 31 Jan. 1551, SP 61/3/5. On troubles in Clanrickard generally, see K. W. Nicholls, *Gaelic and Gaelicised Ireland in the middle ages* (Dublin, 1972), pp. 148–51.

[30] 'Book of . . . lord lieutenants household', 10 July 1564, SP 63/11/23.

[31] Sussex to Eliz., 24 Aug. 1562, SP 63/4/43, to privy council, 28 Dec. 1562 and 5 Feb. 1563, SP 63/7/58, 8/8; 'Memorial of suits granted', July 1559, SP 63/1/63; *Cal. pat. rolls (England) (1558–60)*, II, p. 95.

equal demonstrations of loyalty.[32] Under Sussex, the commitment of the Butlers, the Galway Burkes and the O'Brien followers of the earl of Thomond to English rule in Ireland, was as unshakeable as their good fortune.

Sussex had few qualms about his blatant alliance with the self-interested Butler group. He was fully aware of the faction-ridden environment in which he worked and was confident of his ability to exploit its ramifications in his own interests. Under his tutelage, the Butler faction was to form the nucleus of the loyal subjects of the crown in Ireland; their Geraldine opponents he believed would gradually be reduced to impotence and despair through political malnutrition. The lesser members of the group would transfer their allegiance either to the Butlers or to the government itself. Its leaders, deprived of their power base, would be forced either to acquiesce in the government's will or to engage in a futile display of resistance. A timely offer to Kildare of lands in England, 'of like value or better', than his Irish holdings would, Sussex believed, pre-empt even this last possibility. The danger to the state would be defused, and factions would reign no more.[33]

Yet Sussex greatly overstated his ability to use faction to serve his own ends, and underrated his own vulnerability to factional intrigue in England itself. His overconfidence led him to oversimplify the options available to the Geraldines in face of his assault. The stark alternatives of rebellion or acquiescence were not the only ones open to them: there remained subversion. By co-operating with Sussex's enemies at court in the general campaign to undermine his government, the Geraldines succeeded not only in forestalling his attacks, but in securing his total defeat. The combined campaign of disobedience and slander which the Geraldine–Dudley alliance mounted against him proved far more powerful than his understanding with the Butlers. Sussex was not only a manipulator of faction; entrapped by his own overreaching commitments, he was also its victim.

Inevitably, the coming of Sidney irrevocably changed the fortunes of the Butlers. Yet to begin with, the group seemed to adapt to the unfavourable conditions with ease. Ormond remained at court, and used his growing personal influence with the queen to limit Sidney's encroachments upon his interests. His success in securing Sir Warham St Leger's dismissal from office in Munster left an indelible mark upon Sidney. Thereafter, the deputy treated Ormond with a pained and formal respect, though Sidney's own memoirs clearly reveal the extent to which his initial defeat rankled

---

[32] John O'Donoghue, *Historical memoirs of the O'Briens* (Dublin, 1860), chs. 11–12, Sussex's 'Relation of service', July 1562, SP 63/5/101; Sussex to Eliz., 24 Aug. 1561, SP 63/4/43; to privy council, 28 Dec. 1562, SP 63/7/58.

[33] See his analysis of faction in his 'Opinion', 1560, Lambeth MSS, 614/271 ff., the quotation is on fo. 274.

throughout his career.[34] But there were clear limits to Ormond's influence at court. The failure and dissolution of the Norfolk–Sussex group with whom he was most closely associated between 1567 and 1569 restricted him to the exercise of a purely negative and self-protective role in the determination of events.[35] He was unable to make any positive contribution to the formulation of policy. More important, he was unable to prevent the return of Sidney and his adherents once the deputy had won reappointment through the presentation of a new programme for the reform of Ireland. Most important of all, he was unable to secure the exclusion of an integral part of that programme: the enterprise of Sir Peter Carew.

The Butler response to Sidney's new programme of 1568–9 was at first well orchestrated. While the earl remained in his accustomed position at court, Butler resistance in the Irish parliament was led by Mountgarret in the Lords and in the Commons by Ormond's brother, Sir Edward, and his attorney, Sir Christopher Barnewall, who had been canvassed as the 'popular' candidate for the speakership.[36] But the plan soon went badly awry. The Butler group failed to halt the progress of Sidney's legislation, and at the end of the first session, Sir Edward withdrew from the parliament and together with his brothers, Edmund and Piers, threatened to make common cause with the rebel Geraldine, James Fitzmaurice.[37] Confronted with the disastrous news of a Butler rebellion against the rightful representative of the crown, Ormond hesitated. It is possible that he hoped that the scandal of provocation would in itself be sufficient to ruin Sidney. But if this was his strategy, he miscalculated. The extent of the rebellion and the fear of foreign intervention were enough to commit the crown unequivocally to a policy of suppression. For the moment, all criticism of Sidney was laid aside, and those who were laggard in their support of his efforts became suspect. Ormond's inaction, in particular, became the target of critical comment at court. He was soon commanded to look to his responsibilities.[38]

Ormond's misjudgement of the political climate was a disappointing indication of his limited influence at court. But the consequences of his

[34] Contrast Sidney to Ormond, 4 May 1570, SP 63/30/50, enclosure (iii) and 22 Sept. 1576, Collins, *Letters and memorials of state*, I, p. 390 with his private attitude toward the earl at these times as expressed in his 'Memoir'.

[35] Wallace MacCaffrey, *The shaping of the Elizabethan regime* (London, 1969), chs. 7–13; Neville Williams, *Thomas Howard, 4th duke of Norfolk* (London, 1964), chs. 8–10.

[36] V. Treadwell, 'The Irish parliament of 1569–71', *Proc. RIA* 65 (1966–7), sect. c, pp. 55–89; Edwards, 'The Butler revolt of 1569', esp. pp. 246–55; Hughes, 'Sir Edmund Butler of the Dullough', pp. 153–92: pt. 2 (1871), pp. 211–32. On Barnewall's connection with the house of Ormond, see Edmund Curtis (ed.), *Ormond Deeds iv, 1547–85*, pp. 42, 81, 89–93, 292.

[37] The most recent account of the Butler participation in the rebellion is Edwards, 'The Butler revolt of 1569'.

[38] La Mothe Fenelon, *Correspondance*, II, pp. 142, 201 and 240.

overconfidence were much more damaging in Ireland. There, his continuing absence and the apparently free hand given to Sidney and Carew seriously alarmed his dependants. The rumour spread that the earl had been put to death and that Sidney had been ordered to undertake the reconquest of all Ireland.[39] Fear of their common extinction temporarily closed old wounds between the Butlers and the Desmond Fitzgeralds, and by the end of 1569, the alliance between Fitzmaurice and Ormond's brothers was bound fast. Sir Edmund's decision to join in confederacy with Fitzmaurice not only served to bring out the majority of the Butlers in rebellion, it also carried major implications for Butler allies west of the Shannon. Sidney's purpose to appoint a president in Connacht in 1569 aroused anxieties similar to those he had stirred up in Munster in 1566. But the Butler rebellion and the apparent impotence of the earl of Ormond greatly exacerbated fears of Clanrickard and Thomond. Thus, by the time Sidney's president, Sir Edward Fitton, actually arrived in Connaught, the province was already fraught with an explosive tension towards which the inexperienced president was quite insensitive.[40]

Ormond too, when he returned to Ireland in the autumn of 1569, was dangerously unaware of the ramifications which the Butler resistance to Sidney had acquired. He read the situation merely as an expression of animosity towards Sidney that had grown strangely out of hand. Sidney had for once got the better of the Butler family and so they had overreacted. His task, it seemed, was simply to bring about the rapid pacification of his brethren through his own personal assurances, and to lay the blame for the whole unnecessary disturbance upon the overreaching lord deputy. At first Ormond's strategy seemed to succeed. He secured an early meeting with his kin, soothed their fears and persuaded them to submit. He reported his success to the queen in a highly indignant tone. Nothing, he argued, had prevented the Butlers from making an earlier submission other than their deep and well-founded suspicions of the deputy whose harsh dealings had eventually goaded loyal subjects beyond endurance.[41] The earl's allegations were supplemented by the protestations of the newly reconciled Sir Edmund Butler whose formal supplication for pardon was little less than an indictment of the greedy and malicious conduct of Sidney and Carew.[42]

This diplomatic offensive was sufficient to alarm Carew, but Sidney

[39] Edward Langham to Sidney, 22 June 1569, SP 63/28/48.
[40] Canny, *Elizabethan conquest*, ch. 7.
[41] Ormond to Cecil, 28 Aug. 1569, 7 Sept., 10, 27 Oct., SP 63/29/47, 60, 66, 75.
[42] Edmund Butler to Ormond, 24 Aug., SP 63/29/47 (i) to Cecil, 6 Sept., SP 63/29/59, Ormond's 'Report' of Sir Edmund's conduct, 7 Sept., SP 63/29/60 (i); 'Supplication of Sir Edmund', SP 63/29/60, enclosure (iii).

remained unmoved. He received Sir Edmund's submission coldly, publicly rebuking him for the outrages committed by his followers. He had the indictment of the earl's brothers for high treason proclaimed, abrogated Ormond's safe-conduct and ordered their immediate arrest.[43] Against all this, Ormond could do nothing. Sidney's treatment of Sir Edmund greatly alarmed his brother Edward who had not yet honoured his pledge to come in, and it confirmed many of the Butlers in the wisdom of their initial response. Ormond's moderate tactics seemed futile; the only way to deal with their old enemy was by open rebellion. Now in command of all the Butler rebels, Edward threatened to wreak his revenge on any Englishman who came his way and reopened the alliance with Fitzmaurice. The loss of his brother's confidence was a serious blow to Ormond's hopes, but his apparent failure in his own country provoked even more damaging reactions in the west.

The earl of Thomond took the Butler protestations of malice at their face value and interpreted Ormond's frustration as the intended result of a concerted attack upon the Butlers and their adherents. He adopted, consequently, a highly suspicious attitude towards President Fitton, refusing to meet with him and denying his men vital supplies of food. In January 1570 he openly defied the president's authority in his lordship.[44] Clanrickard, at first, held aloof from such hasty action, but his son John lent support to Thomond's insurrection and Fitton was convinced that he did so with the connivance of his father. In the spring of 1570 almost the entire Butler interest seemed to be in a state of rebellion. The fundamental disposition of the group had never before been so much in question.[45]

Ormond acted as quickly as possible to salvage the situation. He undertook the hunt for his outlawed brothers personally, and having captured them, handed them over to Sidney unconditionally. This time the Butlers were unambiguously contrite. They acknowledged all guilt for the rebellion 'which neither we mean nor indeed can justify or defend by any colour'. They pleaded humbly for mercy.[46] Ormond was prepared to offer Sidney this diplomatic victory. He was even willing to openly proclaim his friendship with the deputy and to withdraw the aspersions he had earlier cast upon him. For by now the earl was determined to attain a far more pressing objective: on the day after the formal submission of his brothers the earl was

[43] George Wyse to Cecil, 29 Oct., SP 63/29/77: Ormond to Cecil, 27 Oct., SP 63/29/75; Sidney to Cecil, 25 Nov.; to Privy Council, 27 Dec., SP 63/29/81, 86.
[44] Gilbert to Sidney, 13 Nov. 1569, SP 63/29/82. Rokeby to Cecil, 4 Jan. 1570, SP 63/30/4; White to Cecil, 9 Feb., SP 63/30/12; Fitton to Cecil, 22 Feb., SP 63/30/15.
[45] Fitton to Cecil, 22 Feb., SP 63/30/15; Rokeby to Cecil, 15 Apr., SP 63/30/44.
[46] 'Submission of Edmund and Piers Butler', 28 Feb., SP 63/30/23, no. 19: Wyse to Cecil, 4 Mar.; Ormond to Cecil, 5 Mar., SP 63/30/25, 27.

granted an open commission to lead an expedition into Thomond against the rebels.[47] Sidney made the appointment grudgingly, but under the circumstances he had little choice. Thomond's rebellion was a further embarrassment to an already harassed deputy, and with his own meagre resources already overstretched by the disturbances in Munster, he could hardly afford to ignore Ormond's offer to suppress the rebellion rapidly at his own cost. Ormond made the most of his opportunity, and within weeks he had brought the troubled earl of Thomond to submission. His success in salvaging the fortunes of his family and in gaining the government's commission in Thomond strengthened the resolve of the wavering Clanrickard. By early 1571 he too had patched up his differences with Fitton and joined with the president in suppressing his own sons' disorders.[48] By then Sidney, under heavy criticism for his mismanagement of the crown's finances, had made up his mind to leave Ireland, and Sir William Fitzwilliam, a client of Sussex's and a good friend to the earl of Ormond, had been selected as chief governor in his stead. The Butler group seemed to have met its crisis, and to have survived it.

Their success, however, was defective in a number of respects. Though they had escaped the worst consequences of their actions, the experiences of direct confrontation with the government had left them and their adherents with serious internal scars. At best, they were distrustful: despite repeated efforts to have his brothers' proclamation as rebels annulled, Sir Edmund and Sir Edward remained technically outlawed, their right of succession to the childless earl indefinitely suspended.[49] At worst, it encouraged their contempt for the process of English government of whose beneficence they were no longer confident. Ormond was unable to suppress his brothers' persistent exaction of coyne and livery, or their private feuds with the O'Mores, the O'Carrolls and the Fitzpatricks. Their excesses remained a continuing embarrassment to him at court.[50]

Ormond could exercise even less restraint over his allies in the west. Thomond remained unreconciled, and within weeks after his submission to Ormond, he fled to France, hoping rather naïvely to organise an invasion.

[47] 'Commission and instructions', 1 Mar., SP 63/30/23.
[48] Ormond to Cecil, 3 July 1570, SP 63/30/47, to Heneage, 4 July, SP 63/30/68; to Cecil, 7 Dec., SP 63/30/96; Fitton to Burghley, 20 May 1571, SP 63/32/39; to Irish council, 9 Mar. 1571, SP 63/31/33 (ii).
[49] Though pardoned in 1573, *Cal. Pat. Rolls Eliz.*, p. 640, Ormond's brothers remained unrestored, and when the earl died (1614) leaving no living male heir, the title descended upon his nephew, Sir Walter Butler of Kilcash, GEC, *Complete Peerage*, X, pp. 146–8; see also W. Roberts, 'Genealogical history of the Butlers', TCD, MSS 842.
[50] Fitzwilliam to Burghley, 30 June 1573, SP 63/41/61: Ormond to Fitzwilliam, 28 Oct., Bodl., Carte MSS, 56/216–17; Eliz. to Fitzwilliam, 17 Nov., SP 63/42/81: same to same, 15 May 1574, Carte MSS, 56/594; Heneage to Fitzwilliam, 27 May, SP 63/56/398–9.

His cool reception at the French court persuaded him of the error of his ways, and before long he was at the door of the English ambassador in Paris offering submission on any terms. Thomond posed no real threat, and the privy council – still determined to reform rather than destroy the magnates – was willing to allow of his reinstatement under terms. But the entire affair did little to bolster confidence in the large claims which Ormond had made for the contribution of the Butlers to the reform of Gaelic Ireland.[51]

Far more damaging was the persistence of disorder in Galway. Despite Clanrickard's co-operation with Fitton, relations between the earl and the president remained cool. Fitton continued to suspect Clanrickard of complicity in his sons' actions, and began gathering evidence to show that the earl's ostensible support for the government had been undertaken only with the consent of the rebels. Clanrickard naturally resented these investigations, and Fitton's selection of a notorious opponent of the earl to be sheriff in Galway only fuelled his discontent.[52] But, besides this deliberate harassment, Fitton inadvertently provoked much animosity through the billeting of his troops upon the country. Early in 1572, when Clanrickard refused to support the reinforcements which Fitton had imported to quash the rebels, the country followed his example, and the troops were forced to withdraw. Fitton directly challenged the earl. In less than a year he had Clanrickard twice arraigned before the Dublin council charged with responsibility for the outrages of his sons, and on the second occasion, the president insisted upon the earl's arrest.[53] But he went too far: his temerity provoked a short dispute with the partisan Fitzwilliam and resulted in the temporary suspension of his authority in Connacht in the autumn of 1572. For the time being, Clanrickard and his sons were to be left to themselves.[54]

A further weakness in the Butler phalanx remained. Their success against Sidney was due less to their own independent power than to the fact that the deputy himself had been willing to accept Ormond's conciliatory overtures and had been prepared for reasons of his own to leave the government of Ireland in the hands of a Butler partisan. The Butlers had not defeated Sidney: they had merely survived him. Thus their ability to exert a positive

---

[51] Norris to Cecil, 22 July 1570, *Cal. SP Foreign (1569–71)*, p. 296; same to same, 23 July, p. 297; Norris to Eliz., 9 Aug., p. 310; to Leicester, 22 Oct., p. 395; HMC, *Haliday MSS*, pp. 210–17: Thomond to Eliz., 28 May 1572, SP 63/36/25; Eliz. to Fitzwilliam, 1 Mar. 1574, SP 63/45/1.

[52] Fitzwilliam and council to Eliz., 22 May 1571, SP 63/32/41 and enclosure (i): Fitton to Burghley, 20 May 1571, SP 63/32/39.

[53] Fitzwilliam to Burghley, 21 Apr. 1571, SP 63/32/13; Fitzwilliam and council to Eliz., 22 May, 63/32/41 and enclosures; Fitzwilliam to Eliz., 15 Apr. 1572, SP 63/36/2; 'Order committing Clanrickard', 22 July, SP 63/37/12; Eliz. to Fitzwilliam, 5 Aug., SP 63/37/23; Privy Council to Fitzwilliam, 22 Aug., Bodl., Carte MSS, 57/403.

[54] Fitton to Burghley, 6, 9 Sept. 1572, SP 63/57/52; Weston to Burghley, 20 Oct. SP 63/38/16.

influence over Irish policy remained as limited as it had been when Sidney first took office. They were unable to stifle Sidney's critical voice as an adviser on Ireland, or to forestall the return of Fitton as commissioner in Connacht in 1573. Finally, they were unable to prevent Sidney's resumption of office for the third time once he had set his mind to it.

Sidney's return late in 1575 convinced the Butler group of the need for conciliation. Ormond was dutifully welcoming, and his deeply disappointed brethren preserved at least an outward show of humility.[55] Even the Clanrickards showed a willingness to make peace with the deputy. Despite the recurrence of disputes with Fitton, they came to Sidney on his tour of Connacht early in 1576 and submitted.[56] Sidney, however, was not to be assuaged by gesture. The Burkes, he believed, had enjoyed too much liberty in his absence. Their treatment of Fitton and of Sidney's Irish friends in Galway and Athenry was not to be so lightly forgiven. Thus the deputy's response to their overture was angry: he stormed at them, rebuked them for the spoil of Athenry, and substantially increased the fines which the more sympathetic Fitzwilliam had set on them. Ignoring their pleas of safe conduct, Sidney treated the Mac an Iarlas now as he had treated the Butler brothers six years before: he placed them under arrest and brought them back with him to Dublin. All this was too much. Here was the old antagonist of the Butlers come again to wreak his malice upon their weakest members. Their natural reaction was to behave as Ormond's brothers had acted when they had felt themselves helpless in face of Sidney's power. They escaped from Dublin, and on making their way across the Shannon, proclaimed their rebellion against Sidney with a dramatic gesture of defiance. Once again, an important segment of the Butler group had gone beyond the control of the earl of Ormond and was in open opposition to the government of the realm.[57]

Sidney responded to their challenge with ruthless determination.[58] He returned to Clanrickard in July 1576 and summarily arrested the earl on the capital charge of treason. His action made demonstrable what the Burkes had long maintained: that Sidney was intent not merely on the reduction of the province to civility, but upon the complete destruction of the house of Clanrickard. They were not, by this time, entirely wrong. Sidney wanted the ruin of Clanrickard to be accomplished in the most ostentatious manner. Clanrickard was to be tried on a lengthy list of charges before the Irish

[55] Sidney to privy council, 15 Dec. 1575, SP 63/54/17.
[56] Sidney to privy council, 27 Apr. 1576, SP 63/55/34.
[57] Sidney to privy council, 27 Apr. 1576, SP 63/55/34; 'The arrearages of Connaught', *c.* Apr. 1576, HMC, *De Lisle and Dudley MSS*, II, pp. 42–4; White to Burghley, 27 June 1576, SP 63/45/68; Clanrickard's 'Petition', 25 May, SP 63/55/49 (i).
[58] Sidney to privy council, 9 July, 20 Sept. 1576, SP 63/56/6, 31.

council, or, if necessary, by 'a common jury of persons'. Sidney, Lord Chancellor Gerrard and the new president in Connacht, Nicholas Malby, pressed the London government repeatedly for permission to procede against the earl in Dublin. Sidney wrote to Walsingham to have the government's case examined by the highest legal opinion in England, seeking to close any loop-holes through which the earl might escape. He urged the secretary to use all the influence at his disposal to maintain the queen in a resolution to bring Clanrickard to justice.[59]

Though it was not entirely uninfluenced by plain malice, Sidney's desire for Clanrickard's blood was motivated by other considerations. His aim remained as it had been in 1565: to attain a mastery over the great lords whose particular factional alignment had left them disposed to assume a hostile attitude towards his government. Originally, Sidney seemed to believe, like Sussex, that his end might be achieved without resort to violence, but experience had led him gradually towards an opposite opinion. His encounter with Ormond, on the one hand, had clearly revealed the limits of his power over his antagonists as long as they remained within the confines of the law. Yet on the other hand, he had learned that many of the Butlers and their adherents in Connacht were strongly susceptible to provocation and could easily be induced into illegal and violent actions which their prudent and subtle leader found increasingly difficult to justify. Now this latest rebellion of the Burkes offered a unique opportunity to Sidney to demonstrate conclusively that the Butler group, the protestations of the earl of Ormond notwithstanding, were a profoundly undependable element in the Irish polity. In the face of incontrovertible evidence of the treason of the Mac an Iarlas and the complicity of their father, it would be impossible for Ormond to rally to their defence as he had done for them and for others in the past. And his failure to preserve his most important allies in the west would be a blow not only to the earl's prestige, but to the actual power-base of the Butler group as a whole. Whether Clanrickard was technically guilty of the charge of treason was not of primary importance: Sidney's chief concern was that one whose continuing disregard of the viceroy's authority had been sheltered by the great Butler influence should be rigorously punished for his insolence. The deadly assault on Clanrickard, thus, was not an administrative necessity, but a political challenge to the Butler group as a whole, a reversal of Sussex's original strategy against the Geraldines in a much more ruthless and violent form.

His very haste, however, to secure an exemplary judgement against

[59] Sidney to privy council, 22 Jan. 1577, SP 63/57/5; same to Walsingham, 4 Feb., SP 63/57/13; to privy council, 17 Mar., SP 63/57/39 and enclosures; to Leicester, 19 May, Lambeth MSS, 607/26.

Clanrickard weakened Sidney's case. His repeated requests to have the earl tried at Dublin were ignored, and in the end, the privy council decided to have the hearing transferred to London. It was not until early 1579 that the crown's law officers were ordered to commence the preparation of charges against Clanrickard, and at the same time the earl was invited to prepare his own defence and to present a full account of his good services to the crown in times past.[60] Clanrickard readily confessed the rashness and ingratitude of his conduct and he was bound by recognisance to remain in London. But the charge of treason which had menaced him for over two years was abandoned. By this time too, Sidney's hour had passed, his hopes of subordinating the Butler interest to his own will lost in the collapse of his general plan for the reform of all Ireland.[61]

The results of Sidney's Irish service were, therefore, highly inconclusive. In spite of his three periods in office, the deputy had failed to undermine the power of his Butler opponents either by a gradual erosion of their credibility, or by an open attack upon them. On each occasion the opportunity of dealing decisively with the Butlers had come within his grasp, yet on each occasion it was forfeited by extrinsic demands and the intrinsic weaknesses of his own self-imposed programme. The Butlers, then, had survived, not by their own strength, but through Sidney's political deficiency; and they had not emerged from the ordeal unscathed. The group from whom Sussex had expected so much at the beginning of Elizabeth's reign had become seriously estranged from the government by 1579. The experience of the intervening period had left Ormond and his brothers deeply disenchanted with the reformist promises of English government in Ireland, and though they had been spared the worst consequences of subjection to an unfavourable governor, they remained unable to secure the permanent presence of more friendly figures in high office. They had been no more able to maintain Sussex and Fitzwilliam in power than they had been able to prevent Sidney's reappointments. Their confidence, therefore, in the fickle and treacherous office of chief governor deteriorated seriously throughout the period. They tended increasingly to seek their security in the negative, inhibiting, but protective personal influence of the courtier earl, and in the consolidation of their power within the locality. In either case, the reformist policy programmes of the Dublin governor were irrelevant and unwelcome to the Butlers.

The alienation of Ormond's western allies from the Dublin administration

---

[60] Privy council to Sidney, 29 May 1578, *Cal. Carew MSS (1575–88)*, p. 130; *APC (1578–9)*, pp. 56, 87, 160.

[61] Clanrickard's 'Notes of service' and 'Petition', 8 Mar. 1579, SP 63/66/4–5; 'Submission', 24 June, SP 63/67/6 enclosure (i).

was manifested more overtly by rebellion. Since 1570 the resort to force of arms had become the typical response of the Clanrickard Burkes to Sidney's attempts to govern them. But increasingly, they displayed an alarming tendency to remain in rebellion after the immediate threat from Sidney had passed. Neither Fitzwilliam nor Clanrickard was able to curtail the activities of Clanrickard's sons during Sidney's and Fitton's absence, and after Sidney's withdrawal in 1578, when Drury succeeded in mollifying much of the resentment against the general composition plan elsewhere, the Burkes remained locked in a vicious war with President Malby.[62] Sussex's early hopes that the house of Clanrickard would be the medium through which the benefits of English government would be reintroduced into Connacht seems to have been entirely lost by his successor's failure either to conciliate his old opponents or to carry out his chosen programme regardless of their opposition. But the damage done by Sidney's methods of government went further than the alienation of the powerful and hitherto loyal Butler group. The same determination to place the considerations of his chosen programme above all others, and the same radical instability which his programmatic commitment entailed produced even more fateful consequences for the viceroy's erstwhile Irish allies, the Geraldines.

(III)

On the surface, the Geraldines seemed to inherit under Sidney the same position of influence which the Butlers had enjoyed under Sussex. Lord Justice Arnold had greatly rewarded the earl of Kildare for his services in the Dudley interest. The earl became one of Arnold's closest political counsellors and was granted extensive responsibility for the government of Leinster and the midland plantations.[63] Sidney retained Kildare in the position of confidence he had come to enjoy under Arnold, and he also proffered more tangible rewards, granting Kildare the extensive manor of Geashill in Offaly along with several other lesser leases.[64] No clear sign of discontent was expressed by either side during Sidney's first tour of duty, and when Sidney departed for England in July 1567, Kildare accompanied him to court. The two men also returned to Ireland in August 1568, and a bill granting Kildare's long desired suit for the restoration in blood of his

---

[62] Malby to Walsingham, 12 Apr. 1578, SP 63/60/37; 3 May, SP 63/60/55; to Burghley, 23 July, 63/61/41, enclosing 'Note of his services'.
[63] Commission to Kildare, 4 Aug. 1564, SP 63/11/55; George Stanley to Cecil, 13 July 1565, SP 63/14/17: *Fiants Eliz.*, nos. 543, 721, 823.
[64] Sidney to Leicester, 6 Mar. 1566, SP 63/16/35, to Eliz. and privy council, 22 Nov., SP 63/19/55; to Eliz., 12 Dec., SP 63/19/71; to Eliz., 20 Apr. 1567, SP 63/20/66; *Fiants Eliz.*, nos. 626, 1100, 1240, 1275.

house was included in the deputy's parliamentary programme. The bill, which became an act in 1569, guaranteed the descent of the earldom to the nearest eligible Geraldine heir, regardless of the conduct of the current incumbent and his immediate family. It was an act of faith in the future loyalty of the house of Kildare, and as if to confirm its confidence, Kildare rendered Sidney valuable service in the Munster rebellion of 1569–71.[65]

But from the beginning the Geraldine alliance with Sidney was seriously defective. Sidney's own struggle for office had made his character references dubious. His recommendation of Kildare's suits never carried the same confidence which Sussex's prestige had brought to Ormond's. Thus his requests to have the earl raised to the order of the Garter were refused. Kildare's land suits were closely examined and considerably qualified and in spite of Sidney's praise, damaging allegations about the earl's abuse of his powers were received at court.[66] Even the act of 1569 was soured by reservations. It was not after all, a complete restoration of the *status quo ante* 1537. The act of attainder remained unrepealed; it had simply been superseded by a further act of parliament which could be reversed in the normal way.[67] By the close of Sidney's second period in Ireland, then, it is not surprising that a strain in relations between the deputy and the earl was beginning to become apparent.[68]

There were, however, deeper reasons for the loosening of ties between Sidney and Kildare. The principal attraction of a Geraldine alliance for Sidney, as for St Leger and Grey before him, was the Irish group's capacity to support the implementation of ambitious reform policies in the country. But this the eleventh earl of Kildare had signally failed to do. Though his services in undermining Sussex had been invaluable, his own efforts at promoting an alternative policy in regard to Ulster had been little short of disastrous. Shane O'Neill's refusal to accept any check on his ambitions deeply compromised all who had dealt with him, but Kildare above all. Regarded by his enemies as proof of Kildare's treacherous disposition and by his friends as evidence of his limited political influence in Ireland, the attempt to conciliate and the failure to contain O'Neill irrevocably damaged Kildare's reputation in government. Thus, while Sidney was happy to accept Kildare's support, he was determined also to distance himself from the

[65] *Irish Statutes*, 11th Eliz. cap. 14.
[66] Countess of Kildare's answer to privy council's orders, *c.* 1566, SP 63/19/93; and BL, Cotton MSS, Titus B XI, fo. 247; Cecil to Sidney, 10 July 1567, SP 63/21/58, Eliz. to Sidney, 30 Aug. 1568, 17 May 1570, *Sid. SP*, nos. 55, 75; allegations of Oliver Sutton were heard in 1565 and 1568, SP 63/15/54, 56, 57, 63/23/85 and 63/24/6.
[67] See J. H. Round, 'The earldom of Kildare', *The Genealogist*, new ser., 9 (1892–3), pp. 202 ff.
[68] Kildare's 'Memorandum', 20 Mar. 1570, Morrison MSS, HMC, *Rep. 9*, app. 2, p. 418.

policy to which the earl had so committed himself early on. Kildare's continuing favour with the viceroy thus depended upon his overt acknowledgement of the error of his previous advice, and by implication, on the acceptance of the validity of his old adversary's strategy which Sidney himself had now embraced.

Kildare's subordination to other men's objectives and techniques deepened considerably on Sidney's return to Ireland in 1568. Sidney's second heterogeneous programme of government did not pose such an immediate danger to Kildare as it did to Ormond, but its long-term implications were alarming none the less. The deputy's willingness to give prior consideration to the claims of a number of adventurers who came to Ireland to seek their fortune was a departure from the patronage methods of Grey and St Leger and constituted a serious challenge to Geraldine influence with the governor. His aggressive justification of claims such as Carew's on strictly legal grounds, implied a willingness to expose his friends as well as his foes to similar dangers in the future. But most immediately alarming to Sidney's Irish friends was the ease with which he was prepared to abandon them altogether once he had decided that his programme was a failure. Though he made a strenuous effort on the point of his departure to assure his friends that he would continue to use his influence on their behalf when he had returned to England, nothing was so indicative to the Geraldines of Sidney's fundamental indifference to their cause than his willingness to surrender the government into the hands of the Butler partisan, Sir William Fitzwilliam.[69]

Sidney's assent to his replacement by a viceroy from whom Kildare could expect little favour convinced the earl of the futility of the factional game which had hitherto consumed so much of his energy. Disillusioned, Kildare determined in the early 1570s 'to make my own way'.[70] He grew introvert, devoting his time to more covert and more dubious means of consolidating his power within his locality. His new strategy was launched with an ominous sign. Some time in 1571 he removed from his comfortable residence at Maynooth to occupy more spartan quarters in his castles at Rathangan and Kilkea. He undertook extensive renovations at Kilkea. In the main hall of the castle he built a large and imposing fireplace and on it had inscribed the old feudal war-cry of the Geraldines, 'Cromaboo'.[71]

Kildare was intent upon more than defiant gestures. Though deprived of the right to enjoy coyne and livery in his own lordship, he converted a group

---

[69] Sidney's valedictory speech to parliament in 1571, Campion's *Histories* (ed. Vossen), pp. 147–50.
[70] Phrase attributed to Kildare by his servant, James Keating, SP 63/51/42 (i).
[71] Walter Fitzgerald, 'Kilkea Castle', *Jn. Kildare Arch. Soc.* 2 (1896–9), pp. 3–32.

of landless mercenaries drawn from the gaelicised Keatings whom he had been given authority over for government service into a small private army of his own. The earl also used his official dealings with the O'Byrnes, the O'Mores and the O'Connors to strengthen his personal ties with their respective chieftains. Hugh MacShane O'Byrne and Rory Og O'More, the chief scourges of the Pale, paid frequent visits to Kildare, and tailored their activities to his interests. Kildare used these means to strengthen his authority in Leinster through sheer intimidation. Clansmen who refused the earl's good-lordship were punished by raids perpetrated by his outlaw bands, those who accepted it were left unharmed. Similar tactics were employed against the earl's tenants in Co. Kildare, many of whom were Palesmen who had settled in the region during the Geraldine exile. Since his return they had lived in constant tension with Kildare, and it was they who supplied the most damaging material to the earl's detractors, during the struggles of the 1560s. The earl was anxious to guard against the recurrence of such subversion, and he used his kerne to intimidate his tenants into silence.[72]

It was one of these Pale settlers, John Alen, a nephew of the late lord chancellor, who had come to inherit his manor at St Wolstan's, who drew the attention of the Dublin administration to the earl's proceedings early in 1574.[73] Alen's charges were serious. The earl, he asserted, was intent on nothing less than the subversion of the commonwealth. He was surrounded by a group of papist traitors who assured him of foreign aid should he rise out against the queen, and his clansmen awaited impatiently the rebellion in which Kildare 'would kill all the English churls or drive them to the sea'.[74]

The evidence produced through extensive inquiry did little to support such claims. Kildare, they revealed, had been engaged in some highly dubious and quite illegal practices, aimed at strengthening his position in Leinster and the midlands: but they were hardly directed at the overthrow of the Dublin government. Rather he was intent on defending by private means the position of provincial influence which was being denied to him in

---

[72] 'Allegations against Kildare', 1574, SP 63/41/59–63; 'Book of matters against Kildare', 15 May 1575, SP 63/512/26 enclosure (i); Kildare's 'Answers', Dec. 1575, SP 63/54/9, 10, 15 and the evidence of his servants, Dec. 1575, SP 63/54/1–4 and 14.

[73] H. L. Lytner, 'The family of Alen of St. Wolstons', *Jn. Kildare Arch. Soc.* 4 (1903–5), pp. 95–110.

[74] See charges of Alen and Richard Fitzgerald, 10 Feb. 1575; SP 63/49/59, 61; Robert Keating, 25 May 1575, SP 63/51/42 enclosure (iii), and Hubert Mc Thomas, 6 July 1575, SP 63/52/48 enclosure (xii) from which the phrase is quoted. For an account of a genuine, if highly unrealistic, foreign plot within Kildare's household with which the earl himself had no connection, see Colm Lennon, *Richard Stanihurst: the Dubliner, 1547–1618* (Dublin, 1981), pp. 111–14.

public service. Yet with Fitzwilliam as governor, and a number of overtly hostile figures on the Irish council, Alen's charges were vigorously promoted by the Dublin government until Elizabeth was persuaded to order Kildare's arrest and transmission to London for further examination. Between September 1575 and December 1576, Kildare and the several witnesses named in Alen's case were questioned about a lengthy list of formal charges made against the earl. A number of witnesses, including Kildare's chief steward and his attorney, were held under arrest, and for a time the earl's position looked grave. Nothing was revealed, however, either by Kildare or by the numerous witnesses, to substantiate Alen's most serious allegations, and so the council at length decided to let the inquiry drop. Some influential friends at court, moreover, seem to have intervened on his behalf, for in September 1575 he attended court in the company of Leicester's close associate Sir Nicholas Bacon, and was graciously received. He returned to Ireland in 1578.[75]

Kildare survived, like Ormond, largely through the crown's continuing tolerance of the moderate illegalities of its nobility. Yet the fact that the leading peer of the realm could readily be brought so near to destruction was a telling commentary on the weakness of the Geraldine group and the futility of Kildare's policy of local retrenchment. The entire affair left the earl in a distressing position. He was, on the one hand, without sufficient favour or credit at court which would allow him to exert a significant political influence in Ireland in an official and peaceful fashion. But on the other hand it was now clear that it was impossible for him to establish such an influence in any informal or extra-legal way. Deserted by former friends who no longer had an interest in the factional rivalries which had brought him to favour before, surrounded by enemies who would make the most of any indiscretions, Kildare was destined for political impotence. This was a sorry position for an earl whose political ambitions at his return to Ireland had been so grand; yet for his more unstable cousin in Desmond, the consequences of Sidney's betrayal were a good deal worse.

For the Desmond Geraldines, even more than for Kildare, the realisation of Sidney's limited commitment to their welfare came early and suddenly. The collapse of Sidney's attempt to install a sympathetic president in Munster, his forced arrest of Desmond himself and his failure to maintain Desmond's brother, John, in a position of official authority in the lordship were damning admissions of the deputy's inability and unwillingness to help his

---

75 Burghley et al. to Fitzwilliam, 9 Apr. 1575, SP 63/50/52; for the examination, see note 76 above; Walsingham to Burghley, 9 Sept. 1575, BL, Harleian MSS, 6992, no. 11; Bacon was a close associate of Leicester, see A. Hassell Smith, *County and court* (Oxford, 1974), passim.

friends when they needed him most.[76] They were a clear sign that the alliance with Dudley in which they had invested so much was ultimately worthless. The Desmond Geraldines were now allyless, defenceless against the attacks which might be made upon them by their numerous local enemies and by the Butlers in particular. The effect of this reversal upon Desmond himself was devastating. His apparent betrayal and his subsequent seven years' imprisonment rendered the already psychologically unstable earl deeply mistrustful of the crown's intentions. It led him to exaggerate the nature of the challenge which the government presented, to see hidden threats even when none existed. It left him incapable of reacting coolly in his own interests as a peer of the realm.[77]

But the impact of Sidney's desertion extended beyond its effect upon the personality of the earl. The exposure of the Geraldines' friendlessness gave wonderful encouragement to their subordinates and to their independent enemies to improve their own standing within the province at the expense of the house of Desmond. Sir Maurice Fitzgerald of the Decies, Sir Cormac MacCarthy of Muskerry and the Lords Barry and Roche successfully renounced all obligations to the Desmond lordship and their autonomy was recognised by the government.[78] Lesser tenants of the earl manifested their independence in a less demonstrative but hardly less effective way: during his years of imprisonment, Desmond's revenues plummetted.[79] More serious, however, than Desmond's loss of mastery over his underlings and enemies was his loss of authority over his own adherents. In his absence and in the absence of his brother, the mantle of leadership within the lordship devolved upon the chief professional military retainer of the Geraldines, James Fitzmaurice Fitzgerald. Fitzmaurice asserted his undisputed authority over the stricken Geraldines by the simple evocation of *la patrie en danger*. The fate of the earl, he claimed, was the inevitable result of Desmond's weakness and his naïve acquiescence in the aggressive encroachments of the English government. The only way in which the Geraldines could now preserve their country was through an all out attack upon the English and

[76] See ch. 4 above.

[77] Desmond's personal instability was widely recognised; Fitzwilliam to Lady Sussex, 12 Dec. 1567, Bodl., Carte MSS, 57/118; Perrot to Burghley, 13 July 1573, SP 63/41/76: Desmond to Eliz., 12 Sept. 1574, SP 63/47/56; Sidney to privy council, 20 Feb. 1578, SP 63/60/14; for an account of Desmond's history, stressing psychological factors, see Richard Berleth, *The twilight lords* (London, 1978).

[78] 'Matters to be ordered with Desmond', 20 May 1562, SP 63/3/11; Grant to Lord Barry, 12 Mar. 1568, SP 63/23/69; grant to Sir Maurice Fitzgerald, 16 July 1568, SP 63/25/39; Lord Fitzmaurice to lords justice, 6 July 1568, SP 63/25/45 enclosure (ix); Carew to Sidney, 12 July 1569, SP 63/29/10; Sidney to privy council, 26 Oct., SP 63/29/70.

[79] Countess of Desmond to commissioners, 11 Jan. 1568, SP 63/23/16 enclosure (ii); Fitzwilliam to Cecil, 22 Jan. 1568, Bodl., Carte MSS, 58/225–6; Desmond to Cecil, 26 Sept. 1568, SP 63/25/89; same to several Geraldines, 18 Nov., SP 63/26/35–45.

their supporters in Munster. With this appeal Fitzmaurice marshalled sufficient support against the Geraldines to plunge Munster into a rebellion that was at first spectacularly successful and even to the end continued to enjoy the sympathy of the non-combatant population. Moreover, despite the ruthlessness of the government's campaign, Fitzmaurice not only survived, but actually enhanced his prestige within the province. President Perrot, who had great confidence in Fitzmaurice's future, pronounced him to be 'a second St Paul', and believed he would be a great influence in establishing the authority of English law and order in the province.[80]

But Fitzmaurice was not to be reconciled. He had established his immense personal authority only by leading the Geraldines to the point of the most radical opposition to English government in general. By attacking Sir Warham St Leger's farm at Kerricurrihy and the farms of neighbouring Englishmen, he renounced any further intention of courting English allies. His religious demonstrations outside Youghal, his public appeals for foreign intervention and his ostentatious resumption of old feudal and Gaelic practices were all eloquent declarations of his intent to have no further truck with the gradualist processes of integration which the Geraldines had been subjected to under the rule of the last two earls.[81]

Thus, when Desmond was at last returned to Ireland in 1574, he found himself in a position of acute difficulty. Though he was genuinely anxious to reach a permanent accommodation with the crown which would save him from a recurrence of the events of 1566, it was no less imperative for him to re-establish his authority over the discontented elements of his sprawling lordship. Yet since Fitzmaurice had in the intervening years reaffirmed the traditional modes of Geraldine authority, the earl had little choice but to upstage his cousin in spectacular displays of feudal independence. Desmond's dilemma became apparent immediately on his return home. On being presented by Fitzwilliam with a set of conditions designed to guarantee his future conformity, the earl turned stubborn. He refused to commit himself to anything further than the promises of good behaviour which he had made in England, and when Fitzwilliam attempted to coerce him, he escaped from Dublin and renounced all obedience to the deputy. His defiance of Fitzwilliam was accompanied by all the trappings of a traditional Anglo-Irish revolt. He and his countess donned Gaelic costume.

[80] Fitzwilliam to Draycott, 8 Feb. 1568, Bodl., Carte MSS, 58/263; same to Leicester, 5 July 1568, Carte MSS, 58/618; Countess Desmond to Desmond, 23 Nov. 1569, SP 63/29/79; Sidney, 'Memoir', *UJA*, 1st ser., 5, pp. 96–7; Perrot to Burghley, 12 Apr; 1573, SP 63/40/11; for a military account of the rebellion, see Cyril Falls, *Elizabeth's Irish Wars* (London, 1950), ch. 11.
[81] On religious aspects of the rebellion, see M. V. Ronan, *The reformation in Ireland under Elizabeth 1558–80* (London, 1930), pp. 253–5, 285–7.

Government-occupied castles were retaken, and Englishmen captured within them were paraded around the lordship.[82] But there was, as government officials noted, a marked contrast between Desmond's public braggadocio and the appeasing and often obsequious tone of his communications to the council in Dublin. For all his bluster Desmond had killed not a single Englishman, nor had he engaged in any actions that might reasonably be construed as treasonable. Bereft of any dependable English allies, compelled to rely on violent and radical supporters as the only means of re-establishing his power in Munster, he was trying, not very successfully, to play both sides against the middle.

In the event, Desmond was rescued from his difficulties by no clever stratagem of his own, but by the liberal toleration of the crown. Though Desmond had defied Fitzwilliam and violated his obligations to the queen herself, Elizabeth and her councillors were anxious to ensure that Desmond was not forced into desperate action through other men's malice. Suspicious of Fitzwilliam's well-known animosity and Perrot's newly expressed jealousy towards the returned earl, Elizabeth moved now to correct the balance in Desmond's favour as she had once altered it greatly to his detriment in 1566. Thus the Geraldine allegation that Desmond had been unfairly treated by Fitzwilliam was received with a sympathy similar to that with which Ormond's charges against Sidney had been heard. Fitzwilliam was restrained from acting against the earl, and, consecutively, Sir Edward Fitzgerald, Kildare's brother and an influential courtier in his own right, the earl of Essex and Kildare himself were sent to convince Desmond of the crown's sincere intentions towards him. In the end they persuaded him to submit to Fitzwilliam.[83]

Desmond's salvation at the point of his destruction served at least to show that, as in the case of Kildare, the crown was not bent upon his ruin and was indeed willing to allow him room for manoeuvre. But Elizabeth's concern for Geraldine welfare was predicated on nothing more positive than a conservative impulse to maintain a balance between traditional factional rivals, and extended to nothing beyond a preventive, moderating

[82] Perrot to Burghley, 30 Apr., 21 May 1573, SP 63/40/19, 50; 'Order for Desmond's release', 8 May 1573, Bodl., Carte MSS, 56/63–4; Desmond to Privy Council enclosing further conditions, 18 May 1573, SP 63/40/39; Fitzwilliam and council to Eliz., 25 May 1573, SP 63/40/52; Walshe to Burghley, 30 Nov., 3 Dec. 1573, SP 63/42/88, 43/5; Fitzwilliam to Burghley, 5 Dec., SP 63/43/7 and enclosures; Walshe to Fitzwilliam, 21 Dec., SP 63/44/3 enclosure (i).

[83] Leicester to Desmond, 18 June 1573, SP 63/41/42; Fitzwilliam et al. to privy council, 31 Jan. 1574, SP 63/44/20 and enclosures; Essex to Desmond, 5, 10 June, SP 63/46/52, 57; Fitzwilliam to Burghley, 18 July, SP 63/47/23; Fitzwilliam to Eliz., 3, 12 Sept. 1574, SP 63/47/54; Desmond to Fitzwilliam, 1 Aug., SP 63/47/39; Burghley to Fitzwilliam, 23 Sept., Bodl., Carte MSS, 56/514.

intervention when a crisis seemed to have arisen. It did not imply that a policy generally favourable to the Geraldine interest would henceforth be adopted by the government, nor that a governor would be specially chosen because of his friendship for them. In matters of policy the old priorities of economy and efficiency continued to prevail. Thus when Sidney returned to Ireland in 1575, he came not as a friend of the Geraldines, but as a man with a general programme which promised to meet all the requirements of the crown.

Sidney, in fact, was willing enough to be personally sympathetic to Desmond and on his tour of Munster early in 1576, declared himself to be fully satisfied with the earl's demeanour.[84] He also took some practical precautions to bolster Desmond's local position, including him in the new presidential council, while his old opponent, the earl of Clancar who had occupied a position under Perrot, was removed. The bishops of Waterford, Cork and Limerick were also dropped while the only ecclesiastic to be retained, the archbishop of Cashel, was known to be sympathetic to the earl. Three of the six other councillors nominated had some personal connection with Desmond.[85] But Sidney's new programme left little room for personal favouritism. He was determined to extract a satisfactory composition from the province, and he was not about to allow Desmond's fragile loyalty to prevent him from doing so with all speed. He was, moreover, no longer concerned about the selection of a suitable candidate for the office of president. The choice was left with Walsingham, and the man sent, Sir William Drury, had no previous experience of Ireland, no connection with the Geraldines, and was certainly no friend of the earl of Leicester.[86] But Sidney accepted him gladly none the less.

Though it entailed genuine advantages for Desmond both financially and politically, the plan of composition in the short term tended only to recreate the critical circumstances which Desmond had barely survived in 1574. The presence of a new and unfriendly president who was attempting to extract an entirely new and arbitrary tax from the province by means of intimidation posed a serious challenge to the earl's shaky local prestige. Drury's forceful proceedings inevitably provoked a fierce opposition, and Desmond was compelled to place himself at its head.

Within months of Drury's arrival relations between the president and the earl had become seriously strained. Desmond joined in the general refusal to yield Drury his supplies, and he wrote to the privy council representing the

---

[84] Sidney to privy council, 27 Feb. 1576, SP
[85] Drury's 'Instructions', 20 June 1576, BL, Cotton MSS, Titus B XII, no. 85; the three favourable councillors were Andrew Skydde, James Miagh and Henry Davells.
[86] *DNB*, sv; Drury was once imprisoned at Leicester's request, MacCaffrey, *Shaping of Eliz. regime*, p. 74.

province's grievances against the president. Tension between the two powers continued to mount, and when Drury held sessions within the earl's palatine liberty at Tralee in July 1577, Desmond was within an ace of coming into open conflict with the president.[87] Gradually, however, Drury's appreciation of the gravity of the situation and Desmond's of the personal benefits that would accrue to him under Sidney's scheme began to exercise a moderating influence. In January 1578, under Sidney's auspices, the earl and the president were formally reconciled, and thereafter, relations between the two improved greatly.[88] By the time Drury succeeded Sidney as governor, he was on terms of genuine friendship with the earl. From Drury, Desmond received more praise and more recommendations for reward than he had ever enjoyed from Sidney, and the earl responded to such encouragement enthusiastically: by the end of the year he had assented to the commutation of all his rents and services into a fixed cash rental of £2,000 p.a.[89]

But the composition scheme which seemed to reunite Desmond to the crown under the good offices of his new-found ally in government did little to heal deeper scars inflicted by the Geraldines' factional defeat. Instead, Desmond's personal salvation through the plan of composition tended only to make things worse. The new plan brought no comfort to Desmond's old opponents who had benefited so much from his years in eclipse. To some, who were now compelled to pay a commuted rent which they had renounced, it amounted to little less than a betrayal on the part of the government of their long-expressed aspirations for autonomy. To those who were forced to pay a novel rent to the crown, it was a substantial material burden. To all who were confronted with the prospect of a gloomy future under the shadow of the newly rehabilitated and stabilised house of Desmond, it constituted a disastrous political reversal. But to Desmond's former friends, to old feudal retainers like Fitzmaurice, whose position within the lordship had been greatly strengthened by Desmond's estrangement from the crown, the new reconciliation spelled an immediate loss

---

[87] Drury to Walsingham, 24 Nov. 1576, 24 Feb. 1577, SP 63/56/51, 57/27; Drury to Leicester, 8 July 1577, *Cal. Carew MSS (1574–88)*, p. 104; Drury's challenge to Desmond's palatine authority was not as great as has been assumed, for he exercised his right only to try the four pleas (arson, rape, counterfeit and treasure-trove) traditionally reserved to the crown, and he issued notice of a similar intent to hold sessions within Ormond's liberty of Tipperary; see D. M. Kennedy, 'The presidency of Munster', unpub. MA thesis (UCC, 1973).

[88] Sidney to privy council, 20 Feb. 1578, SP 63/60/14.

[89] Sidney to privy council, 1 July 1578, SP 63/61/29; Drury to privy council, 24 Mar., 14 June, 1 July, SP 63/60/25, 61/1, 30: same to Walsingham, 25 Aug., SP 63/60/61; to Leicester, 26 Aug., *Cal. Carew MSS (1575–88)*, p. 137; Gerrard to Burghley, 3 Jan. 1579, SP 63/65/3; Drury to Privy Council, 20, 28 May 1578, *Cal. Carew MSS (1575–88)*, pp. 140–2, SP 63/63/29; same to Burghley, 6 Jan., SP 63/65/5.

of status. Fitzmaurice read the signs early. Disillusioned by Desmond's unwillingness to continue in radical opposition to the crown, he and his lieutenants took sail for France early in 1576, there to seek aid for the renewal of his holy war. For the majority of the swordsmen who remained, however, there was no choice but to turn their hands to the plough, or to run the risk of being cut down as mere vagrants by the president or even by the earl himself. They looked sullenly for Fitzmaurice's return.[90]

The disenchantment both of Desmond's enemies and his friends with the new settlement was uniquely experienced by the earl's own brother, Sir John. Even as they abandoned Desmond under intense pressure from the crown, Sidney and the Leicester group had continued to hold out much hope for Sir John. Sir John was more intelligent, more stable, more adaptable than his elder brother. In the light of Desmond's sheer incorrigibility, it seemed obvious that the future of the Geraldines lay in the hands of Sir John. Thus it was Sir John whom Sidney wished to leave as commissioner in Munster after his arrest of Desmond; Sir John, who was to lead St Leger in his colonisation project in Munster; Sir John who was to be returned to Munster in place of the earl in the early 1570s.[91] Sidney at all times spoke well of Sir John. He made light of his reckless conduct and even secured an early release for Sir John from jail when his treasonable dealings with the Mac an Iarlas had landed him there in 1576. Even in 1583, Sidney regarded the government's failure to co-opt Sir John as a servant of the crown as one of the greatest blunders of the reign.[92]

But for all their good-will, Sidney and his associates achieved little of substance for Sir John. The pretensions, plots and ambitions they had stirred in him came all in the end to nothing, and in the mid-1570s John was confronted by the growing realisation that the great promise which his early career had shown would never be fulfilled. His half-idiot elder brother seemed actually to have muddled through. And as Desmond's male heir grew steadily into a healthy boyhood, it seemed increasingly unlikely that Sir John would ever again be permitted a significant role in the governance of the lordship. But Desmond's success meant more than the failure of his brother's future hopes, the record of his past infidelities to the earl's cause

---

[90] Fitzmaurice to Ormond, 28 Feb. 1575, SP 63/50/21 enclosure (i); Munster commissioners to Fitzwilliam, 20 July 1575, SP 63/52/66 and enclosures; privy council to Desmond, 19 Aug. 1575, SP 63/53/15; Sidney to privy council, 17 Mar. 1577, SP 63/57/39.

[91] John of Desmond to privy council, 11 June 1569, SP 63/28/26; same to Leicester, 7 Feb. 1571, SP 63/31/5; same to Burghley, 1 Aug. 1571, SP 63/33/23; Perrot to Fitzwilliam, 22 Aug., 4 Dec. 1571, SP 63/34/4 enclosure (iii), 63/34/33 enclosure (i); Desmond to privy council, 20 Aug. 1571, SP 63/33/36.

[92] Sidney bestowed a knighthood on Sir John in 1567, 'Creation of knights', Lambeth MSS, 621/12; for his emphasis on the dangerous consequences of the alienation of Sir John, see his 'Memoir', *UJA*, 1st ser., 3–4, passim.

returned immediately to plague him. Sir John found himself excluded from the councils and the favour of the earl; he was even lucky to be allowed the small piece of property which Elizabeth herself had secured for him within the lordship.[93] It was at this time, therefore, that, like that other botched career of Sidney's administration, Thomas Stuckley, Sir John changed sides. He began to intrigue with the Burkes in Clanrickard and to communicate with Fitzmaurice in France. He made serious efforts to detach his younger brother, Sir James, from the earl and to arouse hostility to the earl amongst the Geraldines.[94] But the progress of *détente* between Desmond and Drury made such a radical reaction seem increasingly futile. By the end of 1578 Sir John could do little more than wait, like the old swordsmen, for Fitzmaurice to return.

(IV)

In 1579 the forces that had been gathering about him exploded under Desmond's thinly laid crust of stability and engulfed his house. In July Fitzmaurice returned with a small expeditionary force proclaiming holy war. The swordsmen of the lordship rallied to him, and almost immediately Desmond was left militarily powerless. By September he could count on little more than his own household staff.[95] In the meantime, his old enemies did nothing. Some, like Clancar and Lord Barry, secretly encouraged the rebels; others, like Mac Carthy of Muskerry, merely allowed them safe passage through their territories.[96] None lifted a finger to support Desmond against them. In early August Sir John murdered Henry Davells, the English official who had been sent to liaise with Desmond. His act at once committed him irrevocably to rebellion and cut short the policy of ambiguous inaction by which Desmond hoped that, as in 1574, he might yet regain control of the situation. Jubilant rebels and outraged government officials now demanded that the earl act decisively, and as Desmond's room for manoeuvre narrowed precipitately, one further factor intervened to close the trap. In September fatal illness forced Drury, who had long extended a patient tolerance to the earl's indecision, to resign responsibility for the

---

[93] Fitzwilliam to Eliz., 25 Nov. 1574, SP 63/48/59.
[94] Sidney to privy council, 17 Mar. 1577, SP 63/57/39; Drury to same, 24 Apr., SP 63/58/4 and to Walsingham, 24 Apr., SP 63/58/5; 'Collection of matters against Desmond', 5 Nov. 1579, SP 63/70/5, 6.
[95] Malby to Walsingham, 10 Sept. 1579, SP 63/69/17; Waterhouse to Walsingham, 3 Aug., SP 63/68/2.
[96] Drury to Walsingham, 23 Aug. 1579, SP 63/68/52; St Leger to Burghley, 15 Nov., SP 63/70/20; Wallop to Sussex, 28 Nov., SP 63/70/36; St Leger to Burghley, 29 May 1580, SP 63/73/33; Myagh to Walsingham, 1 June, SP 63/73/41; 'Matters against Lord Barry', July 1580, SP 63/73/31; White to Burghley, 22 July, SP 63/73/56.

crisis in Munster to Sir Nicholas Malby. Malby did not share Drury's sympathetic disposition. He wrote to the earl, demanding that he immediately join with the government forces for joint action against the rebels. He invaded the lordship billeting his troops upon Desmond's tenants and treating the inhabitants as potential rebels. Desmond reacted sharply against this coercion. He refused to join Malby or even to talk with him. Malby's last messenger was greeted by a musket shot from Desmond's chief house at Askeaton.[97]

The crisis of the Desmond rebellion irrevocably altered the political disposition of the remaining Anglo-Irish houses; almost at once it changed decisively both the way in which they related to the central government and the way in which they related to one another. It was in almost every case a change for the worse. Ironically, only for the weakest of their number did it bring some benefit. For the Clanrickard Burkes, the insurrection of the Geraldines brought a sudden and unexpected relief. Hard pressed by the ruthless Malby during the winter of 1578–9, the Burkes, who had for long teetered on the edge of total extinction, found themselves the objects of much more conciliatory overtures from their governor once Desmond had been proclaimed a rebel. The fear that contagion from Munster would rapidly undermine the position of influence he had only recently created for himself in the province forced Malby to abandon his uncompromising attitude. He began to play fast and loose with the earl's sons, exploiting their mutual suspicions and their common desire to be pardoned for their rebellion. His anxiety to shore up his own position led him to recommend that both be received to mercy on generous terms and eventually to request that the old earl himself be released from his enforced exile so that he might re-establish order within his lordship.[98] When Clanrickard finally returned to Connacht in 1582, Malby extended him a cautious welcome, and when the earl died in April 1583, Malby hastened to recognise his eldest son, Ulick, as the earl's legitimate successor. Under Ulick Burke, the Clanrickards were brought at last to peace.[99]

But the impact of the Munster conflagration upon the Burkes was somewhat more complex. Their cessation from rebellion did not entail the revival of their old relationship with the crown, or with the administration in Dublin. Still less did it imply the independent reconstruction of their factional alliance with the Butlers. Reconfirmed by a man anxious to preserve his own position as a quasi-autonomous provincial governor, their new legitimacy

---

[97] Malby to Walsingham, 12 Oct. 1579, SP 63/69/52 and enclosures.
[98] Malby to Walsingham, 8, 10, 12 Dec. 1579, SP 63/70/46, 51, 55; same to same, 25 Apr., 11 June 1580, SP 63/72/68, 73/52; Malby's request for pardon, SP 63/87/74; Malby to Walsingham, 21 June, 1 Sept. 1582, SP 63/93/37, 95/5.
[99] Malby to Walsingham, 10, 14 Sept. 1582, SP 63/95/26, 27, 44.

was founded not on their willingness to serve the general interests of the crown, but upon their responsiveness to the will of Sir Nicholas Malby. In peace as in war, then, the province of Connacht remained in the early 1580s as independent of the control of the central administration as it had been thirty years before. Sussex's hopes that the house of Clanrickard would provide the basis of stable and loyal government in the province had never materialised. Instead, through his own inability to sustain them and through Sidney's equal inability either to subdue or to destroy them, the Clanrickards had survived within a new hybrid regime over which the central government had little control.

Desmond's rebellion saved the Burkes, at least, and allowed them to regain a significant provincial influence which had well-nigh been lost. But it brought no similar consolation to the other great houses. For Ormond, the proclamation of his traditional factional rival and his own appointment as military governor in Munster in December 1579 may appear to have fulfilled a long nurtured ambition. But the circumstances of his apparent triumph were very different from those of his old feudal conflicts with the Geraldines in times past. Ormond's own vulnerabilities had been exposed in the previous decade. He had not destroyed Sidney in 1578 any more than he had ruined him in 1571. In both cases, Sidney's failure had been an intrinsic one brought on by the overarching claims of his own programme rather than by the strength of his enemies. Despite his lack of positive achievement he had at least shown that a governor's independence of, or opposition to, the Butlers was not necessarily fatal. Thus the men who succeeded the deputy after 1578 did not hasten to make their peace with Ormond. Some, like Lord Justice Drury, explored the possibility of greater co-operation with the Geraldines, but others, like Malby, attempted to carve out for themselves a special place within the Irish political structure and still others, like the newly appointed officials, Sir Henry Wallop, Geoffrey Fenlon and the influential privy councillor, Sir Edward Waterhouse, attempted to establish a position independent of and inimical to all factions. None of these tendencies was pleasing to Ormond, and the latter two were greatly accelerated by the crisis provoked by Desmond's rebellion.

Ormond, therefore, took little joy in Desmond's misfortunes. He attempted at first to rescue the earl from the brink and when Desmond was irretrievable, he sought again as he had done in the early 1570s, to bring the rebellion to an early and relatively bloodless close. But now Ormond's position was immeasurably more difficult. His strategy was deeply suspected by the new viceroy, Lord Grey de Wilton and by Wallop, Fenton and Waterhouse. As the rebellion persisted, their hostility towards the earl mounted. By the middle of 1580 they had set about breaking his general political influence in Ireland by bombarding his friends with hostile criticism and restoring his known enemies, like Sir Barnaby Fitzpatrick, to favour.[100] They encouraged his military subordinates to behave contumaciously: when Thomas Masterson, the seneschal of Wexford, ambushed and killed a group of the Kavanaghs who had been received under Ormond's protection, he was protected by the council against the earl's demands for retribution.[101] They charged him with inaction and alleged that he had prolonged the campaign unnecessarily by showing too much clemency to those in rebellion.[102] The campaign of vilification continued until, in the late spring of 1581, Ormond was at last removed from his post.[103] The earl, however, fought back. He accepted his dismissal gracefully, answered the most serious of the allegations made against him, and refused to enter into recriminations. His reputation recovered steadily as his successors in Munster failed to produce any better results, and in January 1583 he was reappointed governor in time to preside over the end of Geraldine resistance.[104]

Ormond's recovery, however, was far from total. The group who had sought his disgrace had certainly been worsted at court, but they remained as a formidable opposition to the earl in Ireland, with their ability to influence the routine decisions of the Dublin government against him largely undamaged. More immediately important than these ominous forebodings, however, was the more general lesson which the Butlers had derived from the recent past. Having been persuaded since the 1530s to identify their interests with those of the reforming government, they had been repeatedly forced to acquiesce in the appointment of governors who were either overtly or tacitly inimical to them. A gap had thus appeared between their loyalist principles and the practical effects of obedience to the crown's representative which had produced serious tensions at the top of the group and an even more dangerous instability in its lower branches. The events of the 1560s and 1570s in sum, tended to cast doubt upon the Butlers' assumption that they were the natural allies of the English administration in Dublin. And with the power of their old factional rivals, whose very enmity had lent credence to the claims to a superior loyalty, broken, they now confronted in the 1580s a new Dublin-centred opposition, with sources of influence far more challenging than any presented by the Geraldines. That their interests

---

[100] Wallop to Walsingham, 19 May 1580, SP 63/73/19; Waterhouse to Walsingham, 13 Aug., SP 63/75/37; Wallop to Walsingham, 14 Jan. 1581, SP 63/80/5.
[101] Waterhouse to Walsingham, 24 Apr. 1580, SP 63/72/65; Ormond to Walsingham, 21 July, SP 63/74/54.
[102] Wallop to Walsingham, 29 Feb., 19 May 1580, SP 63/71/63, 73/19; Fenton to Burghley, 8 Sept. 1580, SP 63/76/19; Grey to Leicester, 20 Mar. 1581, SP 63/81/36; same to Walsingham, 12 May, SP 63/83/6.
[103] Wallop to Walsingham, 6 Apr. 1581, SP 63/82/9.
[104] Ormond to Burghley, 15 Apr., 1 Oct. 1581, SP 63/84/19, 86/3; *Fiants Eliz.*, no. 4102.

would continue to be represented at Whitehall by the highly influential courtier earl was a matter of no small consolation. But the effect of this understanding was to confirm the Butlers and their allies in their determination to withdraw all practical support from the Dublin government and to work instead to undermine its authority by a direct appeal to the crown.

Kildare's experience during the crisis of 1579–83 was more critical. Like Desmond, Kildare had also enjoyed a brief return to power and influence under Drury. He had smoothed Drury's difficulties with the community of the Pale, and after that became a close counsellor of the governor. When Fitzmaurice landed, Kildare travelled to Munster with Drury and made a good impression, making no 'show to pity name or kindred in the cause'. Drury appointed him to guard the Pale with a force of over 600 men.[105] But Drury's death precipitated a serious decline in Kildare's credit; as the same group who had attacked Ormond now began to apply the very same tactics in their attempt to discredit him. He was treated coldly by the Irish council. His opposition to the appointment of Robert Dillon, a member of a family traditionally hostile to the Kildares, as chief justice of the common pleas was ignored.[106] His military subordinate, Henry Harrington, seized one of his retainers in one of his own houses and hanged him summarily as a felon without reproof.[107] More seriously, a subtle campaign of detraction was mounted against the earl's capabilities as a military commander. Treasurer Wallop and Secretary Fenton complained frequently of Kildare's inaction. Wallop charged him with profiteering and with deliberate idleness, and even Gerrard echoed his allegations.[108] Kildare was clearly unnerved by the slanders. 'I find such impediments here to bring my device to fruition', he complained to Walsingham, 'maintained by some who disdain my charge and cannot broach to have anything prosper . . . wherein I have to deal.' 'All you Englishmen are joined in one', he was reported to have exclaimed in anger, 'and an Irishman can have no right or justice at your hands.' It was under these pressures that Kildare looked to the Baltinglas conspiracy as a means of upstaging his opponents within the administration.[109]

The Baltinglas conspiracy was not the first sign of a grand Geraldine alliance to come to the aid of the Desmonds. It was almost wholly the

[105] Drury to privy council, 6 Jan. 1579, SP 63/65/4: *APC (1579–80)*, p. 677; Drury to privy council, 31 May, 3 Aug. 1579, SP 63/66/63, 68/6; Waterhouse to Walsingham, 22 Aug., 16 Oct., SP 63/68/48, 69/63.
[106] Kildare to Walsingham, 5 July 1579, SP 63/67/23; Waterhouse to Walsingham, 20 Apr. 1580, SP 63/72/55; Ball, *The judges in Ireland*, I, pp. 158–9, 206.
[107] Kildare to Walsingham and to Eliz., 3, 4 May 1580, SP 63/73/1, 2: Harrington to Burghley and to Walsingham, 7 May, SP 63/73/3, 4.
[108] Wallop to Walsingham, 10, 18 Sept. 1580, SP 63/76/22, 45; Gerrard to Burghley, 28 Sept., SP 63/76/65; Wallop and Waterhouse to Walsingham, 4 Nov., SP 63/78/6.
[109] Kildare to Walsingham, 3 May 1580, SP 63/73/1.

initiative of the Viscount Baltinglas himself, and of a few of his friends amongst the Nugents of Westmeath.[110] Their motives were almost entirely religious: Baltinglas, who had had the benefit of a continental education, had already been in trouble with the government due to an extravagant display of religious dissent, and his closest followers were themselves committed to the re-establishment of the old religion.[111] But the plot inevitably acquired some secular ramifications. The O'Byrnes took the opportunity of this latest stir to resume their favourite occupation of harassing the borders of the Pale. William Nugent, brother of Baron Delvin, joined in the hope of persuading his brother to assume a more aggressive attitude towards the demands of the government, and several of the bastard Geraldines attached themselves to Baltinglas to exert a similar influence upon Kildare.[112] These were not inconsiderable pressures and there is no doubt that the earl felt it necessary to respond to them, but there was never any real chance that Kildare would join Baltinglas in rebellion. Subsequent investigation failed to unearth any evidence of collusion on the earl's part, and it is probable that his characterisation of Baltinglas as 'a simple man without wisdom, judgement or any other qualification meet to embrace such an enterprise' expressed his true opinion. Even the Dublin government came to accept that Kildare had never any intention of aiding Baltinglas; Wallop finally concluded that he had encouraged the viscount simply for the opportunity of acquiring his lands. Wallop, perhaps, was over-cynical, but it is clear that Baltinglas' enterprise offered Kildare a unique opportunity to overcome his increasing difficulties.[113]

Since the outbreak of the Desmond rebellion, rumours of a major rising in the Pale had become rife in Dublin. Wallop and Secretary Fenton were convinced of its imminence and even experienced observers like Malby and Viscount Gormanston, thought it probable. 'Religion will carry men very far', wrote the latter, 'and how men are that way determined is not unknown.'[114] In July 1580, as the atmosphere within the administration came close to panic, Kildare moved to exploit his foreknowledge of the plans

---

[110] The religious character of the rising is emphasised by David Mathew, *The Celtic peoples and renaissance Europe* (London, 1933), ch. 10; for a recent account which revised Mathew, see Helen Coburn Walshe, 'The rebellion of William Nugent, 1581', in R. V. Comerford et al. (eds.), *Religion, conflict and coexistence in Ireland* (Dublin, 1990), pp. 26–52.

[111] Loftus to Walsingham, 11 Sept. 1580, SP 63/76/26 and enclosures.

[112] Baltinglas to Kildare, 22 July 1580, SP 63/74/64, enclosure (i); 'Principal matters against Kildare', 23 Dec. 1580, SP 63/79/27.

[113] Wallop and Waterhouse to Walsingham, 4 Nov. 1580, SP 63/78/6; Gerrard to Walsingham, 27 Nov., SP 63/78/60; Loftus' report of Kildare's speeches, 23 Dec., SP 63/79/26 enclosure (i).

[114] Gormanston to Gerrard, 28 July 1580, SP 63/75/12 enclosure (ii).

of Baltinglas and his small band of desperadoes. On the evening of the 4th, while on a routine patrol of the border of the Pale, he approached his fellow commissioner, Archbishop Loftus, in a melodramatic manner: 'My lord I can tell you news. The Viscount Baltinglas with many other papists here are conspired together and intend presently to rebel. The first exploit they will do is to kill you and me, you for the evil they bear to your religion and me for that I being taken away then . . . here is no one that can make head against them.' Kildare then counselled the archbishop to remain silent until he himself had fully investigated the affair and reported once more.[115] It may seem strange that Kildare should first have disclosed such terrifying news and then sought to dissuade Loftus from taking any immediate action upon it, but Kildare's true motivation is clear enough. He merely wished to rehearse the political role of protector of the Pale and moderator of the Palesmen which he had repeatedly sought to play and which the administrators were now attempting to deny him. That the actual conspiracy was by no means as substantial as Kildare sought to portray it was only a further reason why he should have attempted to delay the government's responses: he needed time to allow the conspiracy to gather momentum and to allow the full impact of his revelations to take effect at Dublin. The earl would thereby have retained the initiative, and either by suppressing or defusing the rebellion could be in a position to claim the entire credit for himself. His critics would be silenced, and he would win the position of high political influence he had long craved and had almost attained under Drury.

In the upshot the whole plan misfired. Loftus was suspicious of such an extraordinary overture, and his suspicions deepened when he learned soon after that the earl and the viscount had been in secret communication some time before Kildare's revelation. Thus Kildare's carefully contrived melodrama degenerated into farce. The government began to collect substantial evidence concerning the earl's awareness of the conspirators' preparations, and in little more than a month after his words with Loftus, he was relieved of his duties, arrested and sent to England to await trial in the Tower. He remained there until released through clemency in 1585, the year of his death.[116]

Kildare's was a strangely misconceived and clumsily executed plan. Yet his willingness to go to such lengths is a measure of the desperate position which he believed himself to occupy. Like Sir John of Desmond, he too, after years of co-operation and collusion with one governmental group, had found himself without any secure access to power. Sidney, who had used him, had proved incapable of rewarding him. Thus deprived of the chief

---

[115] Loftus' report of Kildare's speeches, 23 Dec. SP 63/79/26 enclosure (i).
[116] Grey and council to Eliz., 23 Dec., SP 63/79/26.

means by which he hoped to establish the political influence of his house, Kildare had drifted from a sullen and dangerous introversion to a promiscuous dependence upon whoever would patronise him until finally he was reduced to this ultimate claim to attention. He was yet another of the casualties of the Elizabethan reform governors, exploited and finally alienated because they lacked the capacity either to treat him impartially or to reward him for the special services they had once expected of him.

(v)

By the end of the Desmond rebellion each of the great Anglo-Irish houses had been fatally alienated from the government of their sovereign liege. There had been no winners in this factional competition, only losers to a greater or lesser degree. The Geraldines had come off worst. The house of Desmond was destroyed, the house of Kildare was in disgrace. The Butler connection with its initial advantages suffered less. But the Butlers themselves had had their confidence in the royal government deeply shaken and were now openly hostile towards those who held permanent positions within the Dublin administration, while the Burkes, under the tutelage of their provincial governor, were now entirely indifferent to the concerns of Dublin. The effect of all these individual experiences was to reshape radically the forces which had traditionally governed relations between the great houses. The national networks were sharply divided among themselves between those in exile or at home whose defeat had been so total that they looked for nothing less than the renewal of total war whenever the opportunity arose, and those who had found alternative means of accommodation and survival. Among the survivors, the Butlers and Geraldines, ties of family, clientage and faction continued to exert influence; but since the possibility of winning a dominant influence over the instruments of government was no longer available to either side, the incentive of their traditional rivalry was greatly abated; and as they faced a mutual threat from an impervious Dublin administration, both sides were given strong negative reasons for assuming a common sense of identity. The objectives and strategies of the radical and moderate elements of the old connections were to diverge sharply in the years after 1580; but on one issue they were fully agreed. Neither group had any interest in offering support or regaining the confidence of the English administration in Dublin.

This gradual reshaping of the Anglo-Irish elite was a unique, if inadvertent, product of the policies of Sussex and Sidney. By failing in their attempts either to exploit or to suppress factionalism and by abandoning their attempts mid-way, they had destroyed what functional stability the factional system had possessed leaving the great houses agitated and insecure, a prey to internal division and overt rebellion. The administrators in Dublin in the early 1580s, however, preferred to see the chronic rebelliousness, secret stratagems and sullen hostility with which they were confronted not as the results of recent and extraneous pressures. For them, these were the natural characteristics of the old feudal groups which had been obscured only by deception and naïvety. The conduct of Sussex and Sidney, therefore, had not precipitated a crisis: it had merely forced into the open the inherent disloyalty of the feudal lords. The magnates, it could now be plainly seen, were so addicted to the use of coyne and livery that they would betray their sovereign rather than abandon it.[117] Such an interpretation greatly simplified the task of explaining what had gone wrong in the years after 1556 and provided the new administrators with an easy guideline to follow in all future relations with the magnates: undifferentiated mistrust. But for all its desirability it could never have been realistically sustained were it not apparently confirmed by events far closer to the immediate experience of the administrators within the Pale itself. There, the apparently least degenerate segment of the Anglo-Irish community had, despite repeated professions of its genuine loyalty, consistently opposed and undermined the representatives of the crown sent to govern them. Time and again they had defied the viceroy's instructions, slandered him and appealed to have him dismissed; and some, in the midst of the Desmond crisis, had even conspired at rebellion. When even the most English of the Anglo-Irish could act so treacherously, who in Ireland might be trusted?

---

[117] For early representative expressions of this viewpoint, see Wallop to Walsingham, 9 Sept. 1580, SP 63/76/2; St Leger to Burghley, 24 Sept., SP 63/76/56; Stanley to Walsingham, 26 Apr. 1581, SP 63/82/57. Andrew Trollope to Walsingham, 12 Sept. 1581, SP 63/89/39; for a more general discussion see Nicholas Canny, 'Edmund Spenser and the development of an Anglo-Irish identity', *The yearbook of English studies*, 13 (1983), pp. 1–19, and 'Identity formation in Ireland: the emergence of the Anglo-Irish', in N. Canny and A. Pagden (eds.), *Colonial identity in the Atlantic world* (Princeton, 1987), pp. 159–212.

6

Reform government and the community of the Pale

(I)

The estrangement of the community of the Pale from the Dublin administration in the latter part of the sixteenth century has never been satisfactorily explained. Yet the main outlines of this gradual process are clear enough. The Palesmen who had willingly embraced the Henrician Reformation, who had rejoiced in the constitutional changes of 1541 and whose most articulate spokesmen had repeatedly urged the planting of more Englishmen in the island, began to show serious dissatisfaction almost as soon as the effects of increased governmental activity began to be felt. The earliest signs of dissent appeared in the mid-1550s when Sussex and his associates began to complain of the Palesmen's recalcitrance. But resentment became much more overt a decade later when widespread opposition within the Pale was a source of severe embarrassment to the lieutenant and played a major role in the eventual collapse of his administration. Sidney encountered resistance in the late 1560s and most importantly in the late 1570s when the Palesmen's refusal to accept his composition scheme was a major factor in his downfall. In the early 1580s the conduct of Lord Grey's administration was a source of major discontent within the Pale, and at this time also, a number of Palesmen, led by the young Viscount Baltinglas carried opposition to the government to the point of plotting treason and rebellion.

This last event – Baltinglas's rising and the associated conspiracy of several young men gathered around William Nugent, the baron of Delvin's brother – has traditionally occupied a place of signal importance in historical interpretation. It has been customary to read history backwards from this point, to espy the roots of this rebellion in the events of the previous two decades and to attribute to the Palesmen as a whole, the motivations of the rebels of 1580.[1] The impulse behind Baltinglas and most of those who

---

[1] A traditional account of the rising is to be found in Mathew, *The Celtic peoples and renaissance Europe*, ch. 10; for similar views see the brief discussions in Edwards,

209

followed Nugent was clear: they deeply resented the official religion of the state and were determined to reassert a new and militant catholicism in opposition to it. Here was a definite anticipation of the aggressive counter-reformation which was soon to make its appearance in Ireland. Yet the extent to which the rebels' aims were widely shared among the Palesmen must remain in doubt. Baltinglas and his fellow conspirators constituted only a tiny minority whose fame or notoriety was due to the radical, rather than the representative, character of their actions. They were, for the most part, the younger sons of lower gentry or merchant families who had studied at the universities or at the inns of court. Their conspiracies were hatched in England and until very late aimed at nothing more ambitious than securing the release from the Tower of the Catholic archbishop of Armagh, Richard Creagh.[2] Baltinglas's action was precipitated by unrealistic hopes of the Desmond rebellion. It was made possible in the first place only because certain Gaelic clans in Wicklow and the Geraldine group wished to exploit it for their own interests. But it was unplanned and wholly under-equipped: it was easily and ruthlessly repressed by the government. In its wake, the government executed over twenty young Palesmen, some of whom were only most loosely associated with the conspiracy. But to begin with the young men's cause aroused little sympathy amongst their elders. Even those who were vigorous in their complaints about other aspects of Lord Deputy Grey's conduct disassociated themselves entirely from the conspirators' action.[3]

Until they experienced the ferocity of Lord Grey's repression, Baltinglas' reaction to the government's religious policy must have appeared to most Palesmen to have been altogether too extreme. For up to 1580, at any rate, the enforcement of the reformation within the Pale had been extremely lax. Though the foundations of the Elizabethan religious settlement were formally laid down in the parliament of 1560 and though the machinery of its enforcement had been established soon afterwards, very little was done to bring the changes into effect.[4] Sussex and Sidney were both too

---

Church and state in Tudor Ireland, pp. 256–60, and P. J. Corish, *The origins of catholic nationalism* (Dublin and Sydney, 1968), pp. 12–13.

[2] For the activities of the group in the mid-1570s, see HMC, *Cecil MSS*, II, pp. 94–5.

[3] Fenton to Burghley, 20 Nov. 1581, and to Walsingham, 23 Nov., enclosing names and property of traitors, SP 63/86/72, 80. Recent treatments of the Baltinglas–Nugent affair which offer slightly different perspectives are Ciaran Brady, 'Conservative subversives: the community of the Pale and the Dublin administration, 1556–1586' in P. J. Corish (ed.), *Radicals, rebels and establishments, Historical Studies XV* (Belfast, 1985), esp. pp. 26, 28, and Helen Coburn Walshe, 'The rebellion of William Nugent, 1581', in R. V. Comerford et al. (eds.), *Religion, conflict and coexistence in Ireland* (Dublin, 1990), pp. 26–52.

[4] For general discussions of the course of the reformation and the counter-reformation in Ireland, see Steven Ellis, 'Economic problems of the church: why the reformation failed

preoccupied with the more secular aspects of their programmes to bother over-much with religion, and when they did give some attention to the problem, they appeared to believe that the country could be induced to accept the new regulations gradually, through sheer familiarity. The fact that, as late as 1569, Edmund Campion, a dangerous intellectual dissident, could be lodged consecutively in the houses of the speaker and the leader of the opposition of the Irish commons under the protective eye of the viceroy, is a curious indication of the lack of urgency with which the reformation was pursued by the government.[5] Even after Elizabeth's excommunication in 1570 the level of tension remained low. Known recusants continued to occupy high places within the administration or to enjoy the patronage of government officials. As late as 1578, James Eustace, the future Viscount Baltinglas, was excused for his ostentatious refusal to attend at public worship with no more than a rebuke from the deputy.[6] There were, to be sure, some tense and difficult moments for both governors and subjects during this period, but the issue was not pressed sufficiently by either side to constitute a real source of antagonism.

It is possible, of course, that the rebellion was an early symptom of deeper and hitherto unexpressed currents within the Pale. It has been suggested by some recent historians that by the 1580s the Palesmen had become alienated from the English government for reasons that were fundamentally ideological. By retaining an outmoded confidence in the efficacy of the conciliatory and gradualist policies of the early 1540s the Palesmen, it is suggested, had become angered by the coercive approaches which had since become conventional. Under Elizabeth they found themselves confronted with a set of governors who had little confidence in their conciliatory prescriptions and who were convinced that the forceful uprooting of the island's institutions and inhabitants was the necessary prerequisite to the construction of the ideal society. To the Palesmen such an outlook was anathema, but the governors simply read their failure to accept this analysis as an indication of the Palesmen's own degeneracy. They began to note several unsatisfactory features within the Pale itself, and to apply their own

in Ireland', *JEH* 41 (1990), pp. 239–65; Colm Lennon, 'The counter-reformation in Ireland 1542–1641' in Ciaran Brady and Raymond Gillespie (eds.), *Natives and newcomers* (Dublin, 1986), pp. 75–92; John Bossy, 'The counter-reformation and the people of catholic Ireland, 1596–1641', in Williams (ed.), *Historical Studies VIII*, pp. 155–69; and F. X. Martin, *Friar Nugent, agent of the counter-reformation* (Rome and London, 1962).

5 Edmund Campion, *Opuscula Omnia, nunc primum e M.S. edito* (ed. R. Turner, Milan, 1625), pp. 207–9; for an account of the episode, see Colm Lennon, 'Recusancy and the Dublin Stanihursts', *Arch. Hib.* 33 (1975), 101–10 and on the general context of religion and politics in Dublin, Lennon, *The lords of Dublin in the age of reformation*.

6 Archbishop Loftus to Burghley, 11 Sept. 1580, SP 63/76/26 and enclosures (i)–(iii).

radical solutions to them. The Palesmen responded by reaffirming their uniqueness in a more extreme form than ever. They began to see themselves as culturally distinct from the English and to look with greater sympathy towards the other native inhabitants, the Gaelic Irish, with whom they had been joined in hopeful union in 1541. Thus a new Anglo-Irish nationalism could be seen to emerge, expressed first in the continental writings of Richard Stanihurst and in the exile poetry of William Nugent and even, if in a more subtle manner, in the speech of the Palesman, Sir Nicholas Walsh, in the parliament of 1586.[7]

Such an argument goes some way towards providing a broader context for Baltinglas' revolt. But as a general explanation of political attitudes in the Pale it is beset with difficulty. The governors of the early Elizabethan period, as we have seen, were by no means as radical in their intentions as the argument assumes; conversely, not every articulate Palesman was as committed to the conciliatory recommendations of the Henrician reformers as is supposed. Moreover, it is unlikely that many Palesmen were possessed of such acute intellectual sensitivity to their environment. Finally, the plant of separatism whose roots are deemed to have been discovered in this period was certainly a long time growing, for a curious interpretative gap appears to have emerged between the Anglo-Irish nationalism espied by some historians in the later sixteenth century, and 'the narrow sectarianism' which has been discerned by others as typical of old English political objectives in the early seventeenth century.[8]

Few of the characteristics, indeed, of old English political agitation are to be found in the conduct of Baltinglas' group or in the intellectual currents which accompanied it. The old English were Catholics, to be sure. Yet they insisted that their religious disposition was politically innocent and that it exerted no influence over their loyalty. Their assertions of loyalty were, of course, emphatic. But in practice also, the strategy to which they most commonly had recourse in defence of their interests was conservative. They favoured not violent resistance, but a direct appeal to their sovereign. Their modes of representation were also conventional: they raised petitions, delegated agents to present their case at court and submitted their grievances

---

[7] Bradshaw, *The Irish constitutional revolution*, ch. 9 and 'The beginnings of modern Ireland', in Brian Farrell (ed.), *The Irish parliamentary tradition* (Dublin, 1973), pp. 68–76, N. P. Canny, *The formation of the Old English elite in Ireland* (O'Donnell Lecture, Dublin, 1975) and 'Dominant minorities: English settlers in Ireland and Virginia 1550–1650', in A. C. Hepburn (ed.), *Minorities in history* (London, 1978), pp. 51–69. Though he insists upon the importance of this ideological estrangement, Canny, unlike Bradshaw, does not suggest that it automatically produced a new sense of nationalism.

[8] Aidan Clarke, 'Colonial identity in early seventeenth-century Ireland', in T. W. Moody (ed.), *Nationality and the pursuit of national independence, Historical Studies XI* (Belfast, 1978), pp. 57–71.

in a humble and most specific manner as loyal but privileged subjects of their monarch. In almost every respect, therefore, the political disposition of the old English closely resembled the thoroughly conservative attitude that has been associated with the 'country' opposition of early seventeenth-century England. In every respect, that is, but their religion, which, on the basis of rigorous deduction, could show them to be the most dangerous of subversives. The old English were severely embarrassed by such an analysis. They attempted to evade and to deny it, and their campaigning was in large part designed to preempt it. It is significant, however, that in their efforts to do so they resorted consistently to intellectual justifications and practical strategies that were genuinely conservative in character. They showed both in word and deed a clear awareness of their status as loyal subjects of the crown who were possessed of the right to seek redress for their grievances in the conventional manner long before the painful issue of their recusancy was forced upon them. Politically, at least, they were countrymen before they were Catholic.[9]

The roots of this country-style opposition cannot, therefore, be traced to anterior religious dissent, nor to some disappointment with the reformist aspirations of the mid-sixteenth century; but neither can it be satisfactorily accounted for by a number of more practical issues which have sometimes been suggested as alternative sources of the Palesmen's resentment. The importance of the Palesmen's displacement from government office, for instance, can easily be overstated. After 1556, it is true, no Palesman ever again served as lord justice, lord chancellor or vice-treasurer. Their representation on the council decreased and their hold on the higher offices in the exchequer and the law courts was diminished. But the process of erosion was extremely gradual: in 1541, Palesmen held just under 75 per cent of the offices in the civil establishment; by 1556 their hold had been reduced to 66 per cent, but by 1580 they still held on to over 50 per cent.[10] Moreover, while their general participation in the administration fell, the political influence of individual Palesmen remained strong. Sir Thomas Cusacke just failed to be appointed chancellor for a second time in 1565, and he remained one of the most influential counsellors of state until his death in 1571. Chief Justice Sir John Plunket and Solicitor James Dowdall rose to prominence under Sussex and retained their authority after his departure.[11] Nicholas White rose rapidly to high office under Cecil's patronage in the late

---

[9] Clarke, 'Colonial identity', and *The Old English in Ireland, 1625–42* (London, 1966).

[10] Calculated from Lascelles, Rowley (ed.), *Lib. Mun.*, I, pt. 11; I have expressed the figures as percentages because the number of offices in the establishment varied in this period from thirty to thirty-eight and some offices were left vacant for a period of time.

[11] Ball, *The judges in Ireland*, I, pp. 140–2, 208–9, 157–9; Charles McNeill and A. J. Otway Ruthven (eds.), *Dowdall Deeds* (IMC, 1960) passim.

1560s and remained an extremely important figure within the administration until the 1590s.[12] Luke Dillon became attorney general under Sidney
and rose to be chief baron through the viceroy's influence in 1570. His
influence in the council continued to grow throughout the 1570s and, in
1581, for his service in uncovering the Nugent conspiracy, he was proposed
consecutively for the posts of chancellor and lord chief justice. Dillon
demurred on both occasions, but he used his influence to further the careers
of his family. His cousin, Robert, was appointed chief justice of the common
pleas. Another cousin, Thomas, was made chief justice in Connacht, and a
third, Nathaniel, became the first Palesman to be appointed clerk of the Irish
council.[13] The Dillons' experience was exceptional, but it was by no means
unique: other Pale families like the Fitzsimons and the Barnewalls continued
to enjoy access to office throughout the century. But even had the displacement been more acute, the number of Palesmen involved would not have
been significant. On the far more important level of local government, new
English influence was hardly felt at all. Of the seventy men known to have
been sheriffs in the five shires of the Pale between 1557 and 1580, only seven
were English.[14] Palesmen continued to predominate on local commissions of
peace and martial law. Even the hated purveyors and subsidy collectors were
native born.[15]

Similarly, English acquisition of private property within the Pale was not
a general source of grievance. Englishmen received a greater share than the
Palesmen of lands redistributed by the crown after the dissolution of
the monasteries, but the disproportion was not significant and there is no
evidence that it was the cause of annoyance within the local community.[16]
On the contrary, some of the greatest speculators in monastic properties,
men like Walter Peppard, John Parker and Francis Agard, were often
defenders of and spokesmen for the interests of the Pale at large. The one
partial exception to this generally amicable picture was Sir Peter Carew's
claim to the title of lands held by Sir Christopher Cheevers in Meath in
1568. But even this dispute was resolved by Sir Thomas Cusacke to the
satisfaction of both sides: Carew waived the claim, Cheevers kept the lands
and the issue was never again raised.[17]

---

[12] *DNB*, s.v.; see also ch. 2 above.
[13] *DNB* (supplement) sv Dillon, Luke; Ball, *The judges in Ireland*, pp. 139–59,
211–13, 218–19; J. L. J. Hughes (ed.), *Patentee officers in Ireland* (IMC, Dublin, 1960),
p. 41.
[14] 'List of sheriffs of several counties to c. 1770', GO, MS 287.
[15] 'Memorandum by William Bermingham', July 1564, SP 63/11/25.
[16] Bradshaw, *The dissolution of the religious orders in Ireland*, app. 1, pp. 231–47.
[17] Carew to Cecil, 26 Dec. 1568, SP 63/26/59; J. Hooker, *Life of Sir Peter Carew*, ed. John
MacClean (London, 1857), pp. 78–93.

The grievance which stirred the Palesmen to such general and such frequent displays of discontent with the government as the century wore on was much more pervasive, much more oppressive and much less remediable than any considered so far: increasingly, the Palesmen became estranged from the government they had once welcomed because of the sheer material burden which the maintenance of that government imposed upon them. More than beliefs or ideas, more than competition for land or for office, it was this practical and fundamentally economic resentment which inspired every agitation against the government organised within the Pale until 1580. When the Palesmen complained against Sussex in the 1550s and 1560s, it was not because they opposed his policy towards Shane O'Neill, but because they deeply disliked the demands which he made upon them in order to carry it out. When they rejected Sidney's composition plan, it was not because they wished to destroy his government, but because they were opposed to the idea of allowing the government a permanent and non-parliamentary tax over themselves and their posterity. When they defied Lord Deputy Grey, it was not because they supported Fitzmaurice and the Pope, but because they abhorred his attempt to make them bear the brunt of the costs of the war.

The Palesmen's complaint with the cost of sustaining an enlarged administrative establishment was not only the chief source of their opposition to the government, it was also the key factor in their own interpretation of recent history and a formative element of their ideology. Thus when Palesmen came to assess the significance of the viceroyalty of the earl of Surrey, it was not his contribution towards the formulation of an official Irish policy that they chose to emphasise, but his lenience: 'He . . . rendered to all men whom he charged or bought anything of, rather above the market than equal or under it . . . He would say often that he would eat grasses and drink water rather than be at a banquet with the heavy heart and curse of the poor'.[18] In the same way, St Leger was remembered not as the architect of surrender and regrant, but as a man 'very well liked, were it not that in his time he began to assess the Pale with certain new impositions, not so profitable (as it was thought) to the governor as it was noysome to the subjects'.[19] A comparative nonentity like Sir Francis Bryan, on the other hand, was, according to Campion's account, 'praised over all his predecessors and successors within memory' because he was 'very zealous and careful in tendering the wealth of Ireland'.[20] Sir Edward Bellingham was beloved in the Pale as 'a true payer of all men [who] never took anything but

18 'Book of Howth', *Cal. Carew MSS*, V, pp. 191–2.
19 Stanihurst, 'Chronicle' in Holinshed, *Chronicles*, p. 320.
20 Campion, *Histories* (ed. Vossen), p. 135.

what he paid for'.[21] But the equally energetic Sussex 'was so evil beloved with those of the realm [because] he so used them without pay, for there was such cesses . . . with other great charges, impositions which sore charged the country'.[22] Sir Nicholas Arnold was held to have resided 'too short a while' as lord justice because of 'his upright and reasonable provision of his household cates'.[23] But Sir Henry Sidney, who was once immensely popular with the Palesmen, aroused their increasing antagonism 'because he was not behind in cesses and did not . . . relieve the poor commons' charge, but as his predecessor did . . . so did he continue . . . which made waste of a great part of the English Pale'.[24]

Though it has often been noted by historians this chronic grievance over what the Palesmen termed collectively as 'the cess' has not been systematically examined. Yet it is of central importance in explaining the Palesmen's true disposition towards the government to know just how burdensome the cess actually was, whether it could be directly related to the administrative strategies of certain governors and whether it was sufficiently oppressive to provoke the powerful defiance with which the Palesmen as a whole confronted a government to whose sovereign, laws and values they yet claimed to be unshakably loyal.

Asked to explain cess by his queen, Sidney defined purveyance. 'Cess', he wrote, 'is nothing else but a prerogative of the prince and an agreement and consent of the nobility and council to impose upon the country a certain proportion of victuals of all kinds to be delivered at a reasonable rate as is commonly termed the queen's price'.[25] Yet the term 'purveyance' was rarely employed by contemporaries to account for their complaint, for the burden of supply actually imposed upon the country was the product of a much more general series of demands than the single prerogative tax. Since the thirteenth century, the collection of purveyance in England had been subjected to a number of statutory restrictions on the supply of the royal household. The amount to be taken up, the time of year when supplies were to be collected and the mode in which they were to be collected were each at some time made subject to parliamentary supervision. Similarly, the restriction of purveyance to the royal household only was made explicit: the royal army and the warders of crown castles were expected to make their own arrangements for supply. In practice, however, royal purveyors continued to evade these proscriptions on occasion right up to the reign of

[21] 'Book of Howth', *Cal. Carew MSS*, V, p. 195.
[22] Ibid., pp. 200–1.
[23] Campion, *Histories*, p. 137.
[24] 'Book of Howth', *Cal. Carew MSS*, V, p. 207.
[25] Sidney to privy council, 27 Jan. 1577, SP 63/57/5; his definition was followed by Hooker in Holinshed, *Chronicles* (1808 edn), p. 389.

Queen Elizabeth. But excesses were almost always vigorously opposed by the crown's subjects and were quite clearly on the decline.[26]

In Ireland, however, the process seemed to occur in reverse as the English presence increased. Under Sussex and Sidney, the prerogative right of the crown was given the widest possible definition. It was extended to cover not only the supply of the household of the sovereign's surrogate, the viceroy, a legally problematic issue in itself. It was also used to impose upon the country the obligation of victualling and billeting the entire military establishment in Ireland the whole year round. This was so liberal an extension of the crown's right to take up supplies that even the administration hesitated to call it simply purveyance. But for the countrymen the issue was entirely clear. To them the burden was no mere extension of the prerogative, but a novel and wholly illegitimate imposition extorted from them without consent by the sheer force of the government, and so they accorded to it the same term normally used to denote any levy laid by a great lord upon his subordinates. They called it 'the cess'.[27]

A second confusion – an historical one – is also suggestive: no one knew exactly when cessing began. For some Palesmen their grievance originated with Sussex only, others believed it had begun with Bellingham and the majority tended to trace the roots of the trouble to St Leger. The government, on the other hand, insisted that the essential elements of cess had been practised by the crown's representative since time immemorial. In the late 1570s Lord Chancellor Gerrard extracted a series of precedents from ancient chancery records which, he claimed, demonstrated that each of Sussex's and Sidney's practices had been anticipated some time in the past without any signs of opposition within the Pale.[28] His arguments were quite arcane even then and can hardly be tested now. But the Palesmen's uncertainty of the origin of their grievance indicates that the government's extension of its demands was a gradual and almost imperceptible process and that the Palesmen only began to react against the cess when the burden of maintaining the supply began to pinch. In retrospect, that is to say, there seemed to the Palesmen to have been a point earlier in the century when quantitative change became qualitative, when an occasional expedient

---

26 Allegra Woodworth, 'Purveyance for the royal household in the reign of Queen Elizabeth', *Trans. Am. Phil. Soc.*, new ser. 35 (1945); Michael Prestwich, *War, politics and finance under Edward I* (London, 1972), ch. 5 passim.

27 *OED*, s.v.; though apparently unusual in England, the term was in common enough use in its more general sense in Ireland, e.g. 'a cess of labourers' in the earl of Kildare's rental (BL, Harl. MSS 3756); the ingenious suggestion by H. F. Hore that the word had a peculiarly Irish origin in the Gaelic *cios* (a tax) seems superfluous.

28 'Lord Chancellor Gerrard's notes upon Ireland', *Anal. Hib.* 2 (1931), pp. 93–291; Gerrard to Walsingham, 22 Mar. 1577, SP 63/57/49 and enclosures (i)–(iii).

which they accepted as necessary and inevitable was converted into a major threat to their liberties.

On one point, Gerrard and the government were quite correct. The presence of an English governor in Ireland always entailed some obligation on the part of the country to supply his needs. But the obligation was never clearly understood to be that of purveyance. In theory, at least, the payment of soldiers from England obviated the need to exert the prerogative. A certain proportion of the soldier's wage was allocated for food and the soldier was expected to pay his way without unduly troubling the country through which he passed. The problem of actually finding provisions was to be met in one of three ways. The supply of the viceroy's household and retinue was the responsibility of 'cators', independent operators who took the job on contract and made profits by bargaining for prices in the market place. A similar role was to be discharged by the warders of the crown forts for the bands under their command. But by far the most common means of ensuring supply was through billeting. Though it was rarely employed in England, the absence of sufficient garrison wards on the borders of the Pale made billeting logistically necessary in Ireland. The practice had been formalised by Sir Edward Poynings in the parliament of 1495, and daily boarding charges were fixed at the same time. Each soldier was to pay 1½d for himself, 1d for his servant and 1d for every horse he had with him. Poynings' rates remained unchanged down to the mid-1550s. Together these three methods were believed to be adequate to meet the soldiers' needs in normal times; in emergencies, it was understood that the principle underlying each could be extended without incurring serious difficulty.[29]

The system, of course, was inherently unstable, and trouble arose periodically. Surrey who assumed office in a time of scarcity soon became aware of rising tension between the soldiers and the countrymen and sought to have the army's wages increased.[30] Lord Leonard Grey also provoked some grievance in the Pale.[31] Despite the appearance of occasional complaints, however, several factors tended to mitigate the severity of the problem. The standing garrison in the early days of English intervention was generally small: it rarely exceeded 500 and was often less. Extended periods of high military activity were exceptional and for the most part the army was concerned with the defence of the Pale. Though short-term price fluctuations occurred, serious inflationary influences had not yet attacked the market. There were, moreover, some positive compensations for the

---

[29] Prestwich, *War, politics and finance*, ch. 5; 'Device of how the soldiers may be found without cess', *c.* Feb. 1577, SP 63/57/18 enclosure (iii); *Ir. Statutes* 10 Hen. VII c. 30.
[30] Surrey to Wolsey, 3 Nov. 1520, *SP Hen. VIII*, II, pp. 57–8.
[31] 'Articles of accusations against Grey', *c.* Dec. 1540, *SP Hen. VIII*, III, pp. 248–63.

burden. The presence of a professional army reduced the responsibilities of the local militia. As attendance on hostings declined, the assessment of scutage disappeared altogether: it was last levied in 1531. As long as the garrison remained moderate in size and relatively inactive, therefore, the obligation to supply it was at worst only mildly burdensome.[32]

It was not until mid-century that the first significant changes occurred. In the later 1540s St Leger began to take up provisions for his household at prices fixed independently of the market. The alteration seems to have aroused little contemporary comment, but general satisfaction with the deputy's mild way of government was probably sufficient to hold any displeasure in check. But St Leger was also responsible for a further innovation which, although it appeared innocuous enough at the outset, was to have serious implications for the future. From the mid-1540s he began to convert the obligation to attend on general hostings into a cash payment.[33] His action was not entirely unprecedented. But, under St Leger, conversion became regular and systematic. To begin with the change aroused little antagonism. The government, arguably, was making the best use of the obligations due to it and many Palesmen were more than ready to enter into the exchange. But the implications of conversion were grave. The general hosting, it seemed to indicate, was no longer simply a feudal obligation of circumstance: it was a direct tax upon the country whose form and extent could be altered in accordance with the needs of the government.

Such an understanding was first expressed by Sir Edward Bellingham. On his arrival in the summer of 1547, Bellingham summoned a general hosting and immediately had some of it converted into money. In the following year he took the carriages due for a hosting from the counties of Dublin and Louth and sent them separately to help in the construction of the forts in Laois and Offaly and at the same time he ordered provisions for the forts to be cessed upon the baronies of those counties in lieu of the service due upon a hosting.[34] From cash to supplies: it seemed a simple progression. But the innovation did not go unnoticed. The mayors of Dublin and Drogheda resisted, and Bellingham had much difficulty in raising supplies from the country at large.[35] He defended his actions stoutly by reference to the royal prerogative: 'The king's majesty hath an aid absolute', he told the

---

32 Ellis, 'Taxation and defence in late Medieval Ireland', pp. 5–28.
33 'Extracts from the council books of St. Leger and Croft', BL, Add. MSS, 4763, no. 6, fos. 229 ff.' 'Device how the soldiers may be paid without cess', SP 63/57/18 (iii), 'Estimate of St Leger's receipts and expenditures', c. 1547, SP 60/12/54.
34 'Extracts from council book', BL, Add. MSS, 4763, fos. 229 ff.
35 Mayor of Drogheda to Sir John Alen, 8 Aug. 1548, SP 61/1/55; Bellingham to mayor of Drogheda, Aug., SP 61/1/57; Bellingham to mayor of Dublin, Aug. 1548, SP 61/1/67.

recalcitrant mayors, 'which is committed in part to me his deputy'.[36] But it was highly uncertain that the obligation to supply the king's household could be extended to apply to a full military establishment. What made such an argument plausible in the Irish context, however, was the malleability which the community's military obligations had already been shown to have. If the government had the right to levy money in lieu of military service, could it not also take up supplies provided it was willing to pay for them? By these means the acknowledged obligations of the community and the prerogative rights of the crown became fused in a significant though dubious increase in the government's power over its subjects.

Bellingham had his way, and the practice was emulated by Crofts in 1551.[37] Their actions certainly offered precedents for the future, but in both cases the impact of their innovation was neither serious nor continuous enough to be perceived as ominous. Bellingham had called a cess in pursuit of a short-term aim that was almost universally popular: the defence of the midlands plantation. Crofts had used it to furnish a vital punitive raid against the Gaelic borderers of the north. Bellingham, moreover, was meticulous in matters of payment. His prices were close to those of the market, and he was willing to adjust them when the occasion demanded. He paid the country punctually and he took personal responsibility for the debts incurred.[38] Nothing in his behaviour indicated that he regarded the cess as anything more than an extraordinary expedient. Most importantly, he conceded that the country had the right of consultation in the matter.

After 1551, under Crofts and St Leger, the country enjoyed a breathing space. No further general assessments were raised, and the level of military operations remained low. Precedents for the expansion of government power and their theoretical justification had indeed been clearly established, but the need for their revival and extension only became evident when a new style of administration, committed to the execution of explicit programmes through energetic and forceful enterprise succeeded St Leger after 1556.

The causes of the new administrations' dependence on the cess were multiple. First, the sheer size of the military establishment increased substantially under their charge. Under Sussex the average strength of the standing army was quadrupled to 2,000 men. Sidney increased the garrison to 3,000 during his first campaign against Shane O'Neill, and employed an equal number to suppress the rebellions of 1569–71. In the later 1570s he believed he was cheese-paring when he promised to make do with a force of

---

[36] Bellingham to mayor of Dublin, Aug. 1548, SP 61/1/57.
[37] 'Device for the cess', c. Feb. 1577, SP 63/57/18 enclosure (iii).
[38] 'Accounts of Bellingham's debts', c. 1549, E 101/520/1.

Table 6.1. *General cesses, 1556–76*

Year	Wheat	Beer malt (pecks)	Oat malt	Beeves	Oats
1556	4,000	1,334	2,666	1,000	
1557	2,400	633	1,266	240	
1558	3,280	1,678	3,360	1,240	
1559	3,280	1,678	3,360	1,240	
1560	3,219	1,678	3,360	1,240	
1561	1,868	1,244	2,480	1,340	
1562	1,868	1,244	2,480	1,340	
1563	1,300	1,300	1,300	—	
1566	3,000	1,500	3,000	154	7,500
1569	824	504	176	1,502	2,300
1575	3,000	2,000	2,000	2,000	1,300
1576	3,000	2,000	2,000	2,000	1,300

1,800.[39] By comparison with contemporary continental armies the Irish establishment may appear small. But these figures are deceptive. Inevitably, the garrison had its share of parasites with whom the soldiers' supplies were shared. The maintenance of women and boys as sources of diversion among the soldiery was prohibited, but the rule was impossible to enforce and was winked at by the highest authorities.[40] Horsemen, who normally accounted for more than a third of the establishment, were allowed supplies for one servant and two horses each.[41] Any official figure then needs to be increased by at least a factor of three before a realistic impression of the number of mouths to be fed by the county can be ascertained.

The demands of the new governments were not only higher, they were also more frequent. Bellingham cessed only once and Crofts once: both had done so to meet extraordinary needs. Sussex's and Sidney's demands, however, were continuous and unrelieved. Table 6.1 gives some indication of the burden which both men imposed on the country in pursuit of their ambitions.[42] These figures, it is important to emphasise, represent only the

---

[39] 'Memoranda by Burghley . . . on the garrison in Ireland', Jan. 1575, SP 63/49/49.
[40] Henry Wise and John Morton to Bellingham, 6 Jan. 1549, SP 61/2/4; 'Book on the state of the army', 15 Mar. 1566, SP 63/16/57; 'Schedule of incompetent persons . . . in the band', Mar. 1566, SP 63/16/61.
[41] 'Irish council book', HMC, *Haliday Mss*, p. 5.
[42] Figures for 1556–62 and 1566 extracted from Secretary Chaloner's 'Collection of matters relating to the cess', NAI, MS, 2753, 'Extracts from the council books of St Leger and Crofts', BL, Add. MSS, 4763, no. 6, fos. 229–62; 'Irish council book', passim; reduced figures for 1563 derived from Sussex to privy council, 19 Feb. 1563, SP 63/8/11; for 1569, Bodl., Carte MSS, 58/134, for 1575–6, HMC, *De Lisle and Dudley MSS*, pp. 425–35.

general cesses extracted from the country to furnish particular campaigns. They are exclusive of the routine charge incurred when the army was stationed in the forts or billeted upon the country. Even then they are incomplete. Fitzwilliam, we know from other sources, imposed a general levy, for which no figures survive.[43] There is no entry of the cess of 1569 in the privy council's register though the resentment it provoked in the country is adequately documented.[44]

A third element introduced into the situation by the governors was the high degree of enforcement applied to secure the collection and transportation of supplies. Since they were bound to the crown by a schedule and budget of their own making, delay in the provisioning of the army was more than a mere nuisance and could well be politically fatal. They were, consequently, highly sensitive to opposition. Where Bellingham merely rebuked uncooperative mayors, Sidney arrested them.[45] A lawyer who challenged Sussex's interpretation of the prerogative was promptly put behind bars.[46] A government official who leaked information on the cesses was dismissed.[47] Commissions of distraint were issued to the cessors and goods confiscated for non-payment were sold in the open market.[48] When the law students of 1562 presented their complaints against Sussex at court, the lieutenant began proceedings against their promoters in the Pale with a view to exacting crippling fines.[49] Sidney threatened the whole landowning community with fines in 1577, and in several cases he actually carried out the threat.[50]

But despite this coercion and despite their genuine charge, the general cesses were never the chief source of discontent amongst the countrymen. The Palesmen frequently expressed their willingness to tolerate such occasional demands if they might be relieved of a more grievous and more chronic aspect of the cess: billeting. Sussex, it is true, raised the rates which soldiers were required to pay their hosts and laid down detailed terms of boarding which conveyed the impression of scrupulous fairness. The soldiers were to be placed on the country at the rate of two to every ploughland. For lodging and for one daily meal, each would pay 2s per week, and

[43] Fitzwilliam's commissions for the cess, Feb. 1572, Bodl., Carte MSS, 57/107.
[44] See footnote 42 above; see also White to Cecil, 10 June 1569, SP 63/38/24 and Sidney's speech to parliament in Campion's *Histories* (ed. Vossen), pp. 147–50.
[45] White to Cecil, 10 June 1569, SP 63/28/24.
[46] Sussex to Philip and Mary, 4 Apr. 1557, SP 62/1/29.
[47] Sidney to Sussex, 10 Jan. 1559, BL, Cotton MSS, Titus B XIII, no. 12. This was Barnaby Scurlock, the attorney-general.
[48] 'Students' reply to Sussex's interrogatories', 21 Mar. 1562, SP 63/5/54.
[49] 'Palesmen's petition to Arnold', 20 Dec. 1562, BL, Add. MSS, 40,061, no. 6, fos. 35–40.
[50] 'Lord Chancellor Gerrard's notes', *Anal. Hib.* 2 (1931), p. 134; HMC, *Egmont MSS*, I, pt. i, pp. 7–8.

Table 6.2. *Monthly victualling and billeting rates (per soldier)*

	Amount per month	Cess prices	Market prices	Billeting prices (rates per month)
Wheat	1 peck	6/8	12s	8s
Beer malt	1 peck	6/8	10s	
Oat malt	1 peck	4s	8s	
Beeves	1/3 beef	3s	7s	
		20s 4d	37s	8s

if he were a horseman, 7d for his servant and 7d for each horse.[51] These rates, however, merely reflected the price rise of half a century which had already been acknowledged in the soldiers' wages. In real terms, they were grossly inadequate. A horse that was allowed 12 sheaves of oats a day would consume a whole peck in eight days. A mere 8d, therefore, was paid by the soldier for supplies that would cost him 16d on the general cess and might fetch up 10s in the market.[52] In the same way, the soldiers' daily upkeep cost far more than the sum officially allowed for it. Everywhere in the sixteenth century, soldiers' diets seem to have been far superior to the normal daily intake of civilians of similar social status.[53] But in Ireland in the 1570s, the rates set by the army were unusually high. Each day the soldier was entitled to receive 2½ lbs of beef, 24 ozs of wheat bread and 4½ pints of beer. The allocation of 'achates', i.e. milk, butter and eggs, was left unestimated, but it was clearly intended that the soldier should have these according to his needs.[54] Discounting the additional extortion which inevitably occurred, these rates of themselves amounted to a significant drain on the country's food supply. By correlating the allowed rates of consumption with prevailing market prices, we can arrive at some minimum estimate of the real cost of billeting to the community (Table 6.2).

Every soldier, then, was subsidised by the country by a sum of not less than 29s a month. The figures, moreover, are accurate only in so far as market prices remained normal, and the soldiers were content to take no more than their due. But as Sidney conceded, 'soldiers be no angels'.[55]

[51] 'Irish Council book', HMC, *Haliday MSS*, p. 6.
[52] These estimates are derived from the evidence of the law students' book in March 1562, they were not contested by Sussex in his rejoinders, SP 63/5/51, 57.
[53] Cf. W. G. Hoskins, *The age of plunder* (London, 1976), pp. 113–16; C. S. L. Davies, 'Provisions for armies, 1509–1550: a study in the effectiveness of Tudor government', *EHR*, 2nd ser., 17 (1964), pp. 234–48.
[54] 'Daily diet notes agreed by victuallers, F. Lany and W. Green', 1578, SP 63/64/13.
[55] Sidney to Walsingham, 4 Feb. 1577, SP 63/57/13.

Allegations of abuse and extortion were made with such frequency and such vehemence that no governor felt able to deny them out of hand. Detailed evidence of the relations between ordinary troops and ordinary civilians naturally is rare. But conflict, it seems clear, was common. In 1558 Archbishop Dowdall condemned the unruly behaviour of the soldiers, and in reply Sidney admitted that serious clashes had actually taken place.[56] The students of 1561 produced evidence of one case of murder and theft as a representative sample of many more which they promised to document on demand.[57] An anonymous book of complaints, attributed to the former government official, John Parker, recounted further instances of violence.[58] Several government officers admitted the truth of such charges. Commissioners Wrothe and Arnold openly accepted their validity, and even Sussex himself, though denying all responsibility, conceded that misdemeanours had occurred.[59] But Sidney was more explicit than any. 'The soldiers', he said, 'are so beggarly as it would abhor a general to look upon them, and yet many so insolent as they be intolerable to the people and be so rooted in insolence and rudeness as there is no hope of any to amend them'.[60]

Despite such expressions of regret, however, the possibility of extortion was an essential element of the supply system. In time of scarcity and of high prices, the soldier-lodger would continue to demand his normal allowance. The hard pressed government could not increase his wage, so he would concentrate his pressure on the point of least resistance, the husbandman. The government thus avoided the shock of abnormal conditions, and the country absorbed it whole. In this predicament the poorer countrymen were left with only two alternatives. The worst off simply deserted their holdings. Some migrated beyond the Pale, and some took to the road as beggars. It is impossible to estimate the numbers forced to this extremity, but there is evidence that a significant area of land within the Pale was let go waste at this time as a result of desertion.[61] Less desperate farmers attempted to save their holdings by buying the soldiers off. The going rate for such 'compositions' in the 1560s was around 16d a day or 40s a month – a

---

[56] Sussex to privy council, 7 Apr. 1558 enclosing Sidney to Sussex, 20 Mar., SP 62/2/32 enclosure (i).
[57] Students' reply to Sussex, 21 Mar. 1562, SP 63/5/54.
[58] 'A slanderous book addressed to the queen against . . . Sussex', June 1562, SP 63/6/37.
[59] Wrothe and Arnold to privy council, 16 Mar. 1563, SP 63/10/34; Sussex to Eliz., 24 Apr. 1562, 63/8/35.
[60] Sidney to Leicester, 1 Mar. 1566, SP 63/16/35.
[61] 'Students book', 21 Mar. 1562, SP 63/5/51; Sidney to Leicester, 1 Mar. 1566, SP 63/16/35 and to privy council, 15 Apr., SP 63/17/8; for a later instance, see Jenyson to Burghley, 20 Feb. 1582, SP 63/89/38, see also N. P. Canny, 'Hugh O'Neill, earl of Tyrone and the changing face of Gaelic Ulster', *Studia Hib.* 10 (1970), pp. 7–35.

figure which tends to confirm the estimate of the real cost of billeting given above.[62] Even then, of course, it was unlikely that the soldier could be bought off altogether. The government's attitude towards such deals was nice in the extreme. The soldiers were strictly forbidden to take money from their hosts, but when the offers were seen to be freely made by the countrymen themselves the government saw little to prevent the soldiers from accepting them. The belief that such a distinction could be sustained in times of dearth was at best a comforting fantasy.[63]

The most overt and therefore most recorded cases of intimidation took place when the soldiers were on the move. The temporary nature of their stay and their virtual anonymity gave the troopers ample opportunity for extortion. Sometimes they essayed a quite elaborate fraud. Countrymen were informed unofficially of the commanding officer's intention to billet his force in their townland overnight. Compositions would be hastily collected from the frightened community, and then, before dusk, the soldiers would march off to be bedded down elsewhere.[64] Usually, however, the expropriation was more direct. Once settled in an area the soldiers simply took what they wanted without regard to the scrupulous rates which their captain would conscientiously dole out on the morning of their departure. Not surprisingly, it was on these occasions that the most serious riots occurred. Some idea of the spoils taken in this manner may be gleaned from the charges brought by the elder Viscount Baltinglas against Marshal Bagenal who lodged at his seat of residence one night in 1578. Baltinglas accused the troops of spoiling his tenants of goods to the value of £200 and of taking away enough cattle to keep the band supplied with beef for over two months.[65] Even accounting for exaggeration – and Baltinglas provided a detailed affidavit – the takings of one night's stay were certainly enormous. The Dublin administration denied the charges and the record survives only because the elder Baltinglas retained sufficient influence to have his claims considered by the English privy council.

The Irish administration's unresponsive attitude to this and to other complaints is understandable, since the viceroy himself was amongst the most oppressive of military predators. He toured the Pale regularly, staying in the chief houses of each shire and billeting his troops on the surrounding

---

[62] 'Students book', 21 Mar. 1561, SP 63/5/51.
[63] 'Sussex's reply to the students', 21 Mar. 1561, SP 63/5/57, but see Edmund Spenser's lengthy comment in *A view of the present state of Ireland in 1596,* ed. W. L. Renwick (London, 1934; repr. Oxford, 1970), pp. 79–81.
[64] 'A particular note of the heavy burdens . . . on her majesty's subjects', c. Feb. 1577, SP 63/57/18 enclosure (ii).
[65] Irish Council to privy council, 24 Aug. 1578, including depositions of Baltinglas et al., SP 63/61/57 and enclosures (i–ii), Bagenal to privy council, 24 Aug., SP 63/61/55.

countryside. The visitations, arguably, were part of his official duties. But strong economic motives were also at work, for the perambulation allowed him to keep for other uses the supplies which were taken up for his household at Kilmainham.[66]

The practice of supplying the viceroys' household through cess appears to have fallen into desuetude in the latter days of St Leger, but Sussex revived the custom with a vengeance.[67] In one year alone he cessed almost 35,000 pecks of grain, 700 beeves and 200 muttons for his own use.[68] Sidney took over 740 pecks of grain and 3,000 animals in the first months of 1567 alone.[69] Between September 1568 and March 1569 his butcher slaughtered over 10,000 animals for his household's use.[70] In the later 1570s Sidney made little attempt to curtail his demands: each year he took up over 2,200 pecks of grain and 7,500 beasts.[71] It is possible to compute the costs of the viceroy's demands on the country by a comparison with market prices similar to that attempted above. But even this figure would be an underestimation. The viceroy's cess was collected by special purveyors or 'cators' who made their own profits on the country by extortion, under-pricing and over-levying. The cators were notorious and even the governors shared in the general opinion: 'Albeit I found some of them honester than others', Sidney once conceded, 'yet amongst them all never a perfect honest man'.[72]

The castles and wards which dotted the perimeter of the Pale also offered rich opportunities for illicit gain to those who assumed responsibility for their supply. Again a scrupulous administrative system had been worked out in theory. A monthly estimate of the needs of the fort which took into account probable losses and wastage in this period was calculated, and the commander authorised to cess this amount on the surrounding country at government prices.[73] In appearance this system was less open to abuse than individual billeting, but the potential for profiteering remained great. Here, however, it was the captains rather than the ordinary soldiers who stood to gain most. They cheated their own men, thinning their bread and watering their beer. But they made even greater profits at the expense of the country. The number of men in service in any particular fort was declared to be a

[66] Sir John Alen's advice to Fitzwalter, *c.* Dec. 1556, BL, Lansdowne MSS, 159, no. 3.
[67] 'Sussex's reply to the students', 32 March, SP 63/5/57.
[68] 'Account of the harvest cess for 1561', BL, Add. MSS, 4767, fos. 143–50.
[69] HMC, *De Lisle and Dudley MSS*, I, p. 407.
[70] Ibid., p. 422.
[71] Ibid., pp. 434–8.
[72] Sidney to Grey, 17 Sept. 1580, Collins, *Letters and memorials of state*, I, pp. 279–83.
[73] Radcliffe's account of the victualling of Maryborough, 1561–4, E.101/532/2; 'Victuallers notes', *c.* Dec. 1578, SP 63/64/13; Fitzwilliam's account for Athlone, 1563–4, NRO, Fitzwilliam MSS (Irish), nos. 1, 2.

military secret, a necessary precaution against raiders. But it also provided an excellent opportunity for fraud. Though the garrisons were invariably under strength, the captains assessed supplies for a full complement, and conscientiously calculated the wastage allowances on these terms too.[74] This was the single most profitable abuse: in 1565, Henry Radcliffe was checked over £5,600 and Nicholas Heron over £1,000 on its count alone.[75] But several other perquisites remained available to the soldier-victuallers. The beeves cessed were taken up live and no rebate was given for offal.[76] Since the hides alone were worth twice the price paid for each beast, every transaction resulted in a handsome profit for the captain. Further gains might be made by using the carriages and horses which had transported the cess for private purposes, by using cessed labour in the same way and by taking up non-enumerated goods under the guise of genuine scarcity. But the most commonly practised abuse was simply the captains' refusal to pay up. In part, this was due to a real shortage of funds. But their hold over the community enabled the captains to convert this apparent weakness into a means of driving harder bargains with the husbandmen who were prepared to accept lower prices in return for immediate payment. Such extortion was, moreover, self-protecting, since the plethora of informal agreements made impossible any attempt to estimate the true extent of the debt due to the country.[77]

When the multiple aspects of the cess are considered in this fashion, the severe strain it placed upon the community as a whole becomes evident. The Palesmen at all times insisted that the burden under which they laboured was a cumulative one and that reductions in one area only resulted in increases in others. It is exceedingly difficult to quantify the precise cost of the cess to the country in any one year. Conflicting estimates abound, based upon strikingly different and irreconcilable sets of statistics presented by the government and the community in the course of the debate.[78] For the particularly critical year of 1561, however, sufficient independent evidence exists to allow some effort at an impartial assessment. Such an estimate can make no pretence to total accuracy. No body of evidence is entirely reliable

---

[74] 'Students' book', 21 Mar. 1562, SP 63/5/51.
[75] Radcliffe's Checks', *c.* Jan. 1565, SP 63/12/23 enclosure (i); Heron's 'Checks', 17 Jan. 1565, SP 63/12/12.
[76] 'Students' book', 21 Mar. 1562, SP 63/5/51; the students' claim on this matter was repeated in the later 1570s, 'A particular note on the heavy burden of the cess', SP 63/57/18 enclosure (ii).
[77] Wrothe and Arnold to privy council, 7 Apr. 1564, SP 63/10/46; Arnold to Cecil, 1 Jan. 1566, SP 63/16/1; Bermingham's 'Questions on pay', 23 Sept. 1572, SP 63/9/21; Bermingham to privy council, 24 Feb. 1565, SP 63/12/35; Jenyson's 'Note on losses sustained in the victualling', 20 Apr. 1565, SP 63/13/16.
[78] 'Students' book' and Sussex's 'Reply', 21 Mar. 1562, SP 63/5/51, 57.

Table 6.3. *The cost of the cess, 1561*

	Wheat and beer malt	Oat malt	Beeves
General cess from Pale + annual household cess	5,288 (pecks)	3,846 (pecks)	2,040
Market prices	£1.00 per peck	12/6	22s
Prices paid by cessors	4s per peck	2/8	8s

$$\text{Cost to the country } \pounds \frac{(5288 \times 16)}{20} + \frac{(3846 \times 118)}{12 \times 20} + \frac{(2040 \times 14)}{20} =$$

$$\pounds 4230.4 + \pounds 1,890.95 + \pounds 1,428 = \pounds 7,549.35$$

and it will inevitably neglect a number of variables. But since it must entirely discount the massive amount of informal extortion that took place, it can confidently be said to be conservative.

In 1561, in order to further his campaign against O'Neill, Sussex substantially increased the size of the garrison: for the six-month campaigning season of the year, it stood at 2,500 men.[79] To maintain his grand army on the march, Sussex was forced to exact a heavy general cess from the Pale together with the annual cess which he took up for the supply of his own household.[80] This was a year of unusual dearth in the Pale and prices in the market were unusually high.[81] Table 6.3 also shows the prices paid to the country by the cessors[82] and the estimated cost to the country. The campaign season lasted for six months only. Almost 1,000 soldiers were discharged and left to forage for themselves.[83] Of the remaining 1,500, 300 were kerne who were not normally billeted on the country and 100 were men of the viceroy's band whose supplies had been collected in his household cess. There were, therefore, some 1,000 men who had to be maintained by the country for all or part of the year, 324 men were lodged in the forts of Maryborough, Philipstown, Athlone, Carlow and Monasterevan all year round.[84] Each was allowed, according to Sussex, ½ peck of wheat and 1 peck malt per month for their supply and was expected to pay 5s per month (2d

---

[79] *Fitzwilliam accounts*, ed. A. K. Longfield (IMC, 1960), pp. 40–4, 48–54, 54–9.
[80] See notes 42 and 68 above.
[81] Prices given in the 'Students' book', SP 63/5/51 and confirmed in the separate petitions from the Pale to Sir Nicholas Arnold, BL, Add. MSS, 40,061, no. 6, fos. 35–40. Sussex did not contest these estimates in any of his replies but argued merely that they were unusual.
[82] 'Students' book' and Sussex's replies, 21 Mar. 1562; there was no disagreement over the official figures.
[83] *Fitzwilliam accounts*, pp. 40–4, 48–54.
[84] Estimated from *Fitzwilliam accounts*, and Sussex's 'Replies' to the students, 21 Mar., SP 63/5/55, 57.

per day) to the country.[85] Their charge upon the country amounted there-fore, to:

$$£ \frac{(324 \times 1 \times 1 \times 12)}{2} + \frac{(324 \times 5 \times 12)}{8} - \frac{(324 \times 5 \times 12)}{20} = £3,402$$

The remaining 776 troops may be assumed to have been billeted on the country only for the six months outside of the campaigning season. They paid 8s per month for their keep and if they may be assumed to have eaten no less than their fellows in the forts, their cost may be calculated thus:[86]

$$£ \frac{776 \times 3 \times 1}{1} + \frac{776 \times 6 \times 5}{8} - \frac{776 \times 8 \times 6}{20} = £3,376$$

Fully 260 of these 776 were horsemen, equipped with two horses each and entitled to ⅙ peck per day for each horse in return for 1d per day. In 1561, the market price for oats was 10s per peck.[87] So the upkeep of 520 horses for six months may be estimated:

$$£ \frac{520 \times 1 \times 30 \times 6}{8 \times 2} - \frac{520 \times 1 \times 30 \times 6}{12 \times 20} = £5,460$$

Finally, each of the horsemen had one horseboy who, since he paid half of the soldier's rate for his upkeep, may be taken to have consumed at least half the amount:

$$£ \frac{260 \times 1 \times 1 \times 1 \times 6}{4} + \frac{260 \times 1 \times 5 \times 6}{8} - \frac{260 \times 1 \times 30 \times 6}{20 \times 12}$$
$$= £1,170$$

The additonal charge of the forts and of billeting amounts to £13,408. The total sum of the charge of the cess is, therefore, £20,957. This total is exclusive both of the inevitable extortions of the soldiery and of the innumerable other charges on the country for the provision of 'acates' (i.e. poultry, eggs. etc.).

[85] Sussex's 'Replies', SP 63/5/55. 57; Irish council book, HMC, *Haliday MSS*, p. 6.
[86] Sussex's 'Replies', SP 63/5/55, 57.   [87] 'Students' book', 21 Mar. 1562, SP 63/5/51.

The year 1561, everybody agreed, was an unusually bad year. Market prices were not normally so high and the demands of the government were often less severe. Yet this minimum estimate gives at least some impression of how onerous the upkeep of the army could be in times of dearth.

The oppressiveness of this burden is increased, moreover, when the limited fertility of the farm lands of the Pale is considered. The region was generally agreed to contain no more than 86,400 arable acres at this time in which the average yield was at most 7 pecks per acre and may have been much less.[88] That the cess imposed a major strain on the country's food supplies is made evident by the emergency measures which the government was frequently compelled to enforce in order to maintain its supply. In 1557, Sussex was forced to prohibit the export of grain from the Pale into Gaelic areas and abroad. The ban was reimposed in 1561 and remained in force throughout the decade.[89] Sidney attempted to reintroduce it during his last deputyship and complained of the recklessness of evasion. The danger of scarcity was ever-present within the Pale.[90]

The genuine incapacity of the country was implicitly acknowledged by the viceroys themselves, in the several efforts which they made to alleviate the burden of the cess through reforms or to find some alternative means of supply. From 1556 onward every governor made some gesture in either direction. Sussex issued a public warning to soldiers against extortion and ordered the captains to increase their vigilance.[91] In response to the Palesmen's allegations, he established a commission of inquiry and authorised the plaintiffs to collect evidence in support of their charges.[92] He also made some positive attempts at reform. He had weights and measures standardised to prevent evasion and peculation on the part of the cessors. He resumed dormant corn clauses on crown leases and gained some 900 pecks for the household thereby.[93] He proposed to extend the scheme to all crown properties if the countrymen would give their consent to a general resumption. But the Palesmen showed no enthusiasm and the plan fell

---

[88] The Irish acre, however, was somewhat larger than the statute acre; figures extracted from Palesmen's petition to Arnold, *c.* Dec. 1562, BL, Add. MSS 40,061, no. 6 and Sussex's 'replies' to the students, 21 Mar., SP 63/5/57, which gives the average yield per acre; a far lower average yield, however, of 4 pecks per acre, is suggested in Canny, *The formation of the old English elite*, p. 35.

[89] HMC, *Haliday MSS*, pp. 20, 108; instances of evasion throughout the 1560s occur in NAI, Ferguson MSS, memoranda rolls, I, passim.

[90] Sidney to Burghley, 31 Jan. 1577, SP 63/57/9; same to privy council, 27 Mar., SP 63/57/39.

[91] HMC, *Haliday MSS*, pp. 33, 94; Sussex's 'Orders for the victuallers', 25 Jan. 1561, SP 63/3/6.

[92] Sussex's 'Replies' to the students, 21 Mar. 1562, SP 63/5/55, 57.

[93] Gilbert Gerrard's 'Report', 11 Sept. 1560, BL, Cotton MSS, Titus B XIII, no. 7; 'Book of lands leased', Oct. 1565, SP 63/15/2.

through.[94] Sidney continued and improved upon Sussex's exploitation of the corn leases. Between 1568 and 1570, he took more than 4,000 pecks by this means and he collected similar amounts in his last period of service.[95] But the ameliorative value of this reform was not generally felt. The deputies tended to regard the surplus as an essential source of revenue. So instead of distributing it amongst the bands, they chose to resell it on the open market. Sussex denied that he had made any significant gains by these sales. But Sidney, we know, certainly enjoyed the profits. Of 1,900 pecks raised in this manner in 1575, he put a mere 200 to his own use and had the remainder converted into cash.[96] The resumption of the corn leases undoubtedly reduced the burden of the household cess – in 1576, it accounted for over 51 per cent of the entire intake – but owing to the governors' unwillingness to forego the perquisites of their office, it had little effect on the general charge of the whole garrison.[97]

On this larger question, Sussex made no progress. But Sidney had more enterprising ideas. In 1566 he had the foot soldiers removed from the country and garrisoned in the border towns. There they continued to be supplied by cess, but Sidney hoped that such concentration would reduce the opportunities for extortion. He also planned to remove the horsemen from the ordinary householders and place them on the larger manors of the Pale. Again, the whole country was to be contributory to their upkeep, but the level of abuse was expected to fall. The plan, however, was unpopular with the larger landholders and was never put into operation.[98]

Sidney made two separate efforts to obviate the need for cess altogether. In 1566 he proposed that the currency exchange rate between England and Ireland (£1 (ir.) = £1 6s 8d (st.)) was sufficiently favourable to compensate any losses that might be incurred if the government itself assumed the responsibility of provisioning the Irish garrison. The idea was simple: supplies bought at judicious prices in England could be transported and retailed to the soldiers for Irish money without loss to either party. The soldiers would rest content with the purchasing power of the relatively inferior Irish coin, while the 33 per cent discount allowed to the English treasury by paying them in this money would be sufficient to defray the costs and losses of transportation.[99] Sidney convinced the English privy council of the efficacy of this plan and his campaign against O'Neill was almost

---

94 Sussex and council to Eliz., 20 Aug. 1562, SP 63/3/68; Sussex's replies to students, 21 Mar. 1562, SP 63/5/55, 57.
95 HMC, *De Lisle and Dudley MSS*, I, pp. 418–25, 430–4.
96 Ibid., p. 430.   97 Ibid.
98 Sidney and council to privy council, 13 Apr. 1566, SP 63/17/8: 'Irish council book', HMC, *Haliday MSS*, p. 159.
99 Sidney to privy council, 18 May 1566, SP 63/17/55.

entirely provisioned by supplies from England. But the scheme developed insurmountable problems. Supplies were constantly late in arriving, entire shipments were lost and deficiencies in quality and quantity were frequent. The system revolved around Secretary Cecil, and its administrative requirements placed an intolerable strain upon him. The amount of his time and energy which it consumed was sufficient to ensure its early demise, but Sidney, in any case, had badly underestimated the costs involved and the exchange rate was insufficient to compensate for the losses. By the middle of 1567, the government had spent £22,800 without a rebate.[100] The plan had plunged the treasury and Sidney into debt; it had stretched the Tudor administrative machine beyond its capabilities.

On his return to Ireland in 1568, Sidney made a second attempt to overcome his difficulties with supply by resurrecting an older and somewhat discredited means of provisioning, the victualling contract. Thomas Might, the man who was awarded the contract, had conducted some minor victualling enterprises in Ireland on his own account. But he had never undertaken so ambitious a charge as the supply of a whole army. From Michaelmas 1568 he was entrusted with the provisioning of a minimum of 1,000 men for a year.[101] The government drove a hard bargain, imposing elaborate conditions and offering a rate that left little margin for error. The careful clauses in his contract, however, were entirely irrelevant to the realities of the situation in which Might soon found himself. Having purchased his first supplies with his own cash, the contractor was left short on the very first instalment due to him by the crown and very soon ran into debt. He was unlucky too with market prices, and by the time further credit reached him, he was provisioning the army at a heavy loss.[102] Within a year, Might was forced to surrender his contract to Thomas Sackford, another former servant of Sidney, but Sackford did no better. Prices fell, but not far enough, and it was generally accepted that Sackford was not competent enough to take advantage of the improvement. By the end of 1569, the soldiers were critically short of supplies. Sidney was forced to recommence cessing and Sackford was steeped in debts from which he would never recover.[103]

Sidney's successor, Fitzwilliam, made a further effort to alleviate the

[100] 'Note of money to be defrayed in England', 30 Sept. 1567, SP 63/21/97.
[101] 'Articles of agreement', 24 May 1568, *Cal. Carew MSS (1515–1574)*, pp. 379–83; on the government's difficulties with victualling contractors elsewhere, see C. G. Cruickshank, *Elizabeth's army* (1946, 2nd edn, 1966), pp. 80–2, 85.
[102] Might to Cecil, 21 Feb. 1569, SP 63/27/30; Jenyson to same, 23 Feb. 1569, SP 63/37/34; Might's petition, 5 Mar., SP 63/39/42.
[103] 'Articles of agreement with Sackford', Mar. 1569, SP 63/27/58; Sackford to Cecil, 15 July 1570, SP 63/30/70.

country's burden without increasing the costs of government. Early in 1573, he proposed to the Palesmen that he would withdraw the garrison to the forts on the borders and assume the responsibility of victualling the soldiers himself if they would waive forever the large debt already due to them by the crown for the supply of provisions.[104] The offer was accepted in principle by the nobility of the Pale who undertook to estimate and to negotiate the remission of the debt. Fitzwilliam's superiors also gave their approval and promised to supply him with the necessary treasure to manage independently of the country for a period of three years. But serious difficulties very soon began to make themselves apparent. The strain of being both chief governor and chief victualler began to tell early on the deputy. He found it increasingly difficult to maintain a steady flow of supplies to the soldiers or to prevent their depredations when shortages arose. Prices, too, turned against him, rising steadily throughout 1573 and 1574. And there was one further problem. From the outset, Fitzwilliam realised that the success of his scheme depended upon the maintenance of an adequate and regular flow of treasure from England. But though he requested merely £5,000 pa, payments soon began to fall behind,[105] and by early 1574 he was £6,000 in debt.[106] Fitzwilliam begged for treasure, but it came only slowly, and when it did it was tied up by the vice-treasurer, Fitton, who claimed that he had no authority to disburse it for the deputy's needs. Tempers began to rise in the Pale. By the end of the year the countrymen were refusing to supply the deputy with any provisions and had begun to make manifest their dissatisfaction with the deal that had been made on their behalf.[107] Without supplies, treasure or promise of success, he turned desperately to a victualler who promptly defaulted on his contract, leaving the deputy 'at his wit's end'.[108] Only an emergency injection of treasure early in 1575 saved Fitzwilliam's administration from complete collapse.

These attempts to ameliorate the burden of the cess – government victualling, private victualling, even the efforts to reform and discipline the soldiers – were each dependent for their success on regular and consistent subvention from England; and each of them failed through the central administration's chronic propensity to default. The demands they made upon the secretariat and its administrative machine were simply too great

---

104 Elizabeth to Fitzwilliam, June 1571, Bodl., Carte MSS, 56/128, Fitzwilliam to Burghley, 19 Aug., SP 63/33/35; 'Agreement with the country', 18 Feb. 1572, *Cal. Carew MSS (1515–1574)*, p. 419.
105 Enos to Burghley, ? Sept. 1573, SP 63/42/36.
106 Fitzwilliam to Burghley, 2, 25 Mar. 1574, SP 63/45/3, 25 enclosure (i).
107 Jenyson to Burghley, 14 July, 17 Aug. 1574, SP 63/47/14, 44.
108 Jenyson to Burghley, 3 Feb., 2 Apr., SP 63/49/33, 50/38; Essex to Burghley, 10 Apr. 1575, SP 63/50/55; Fitzwilliam to privy council, 25 May, SP 63/51/41.

and too continuous to be sustained. More importantly, the costs which they incurred were prohibitive. The extra spending which they involved was not to be expected from a government which did not even honour the minimal obligations of the cess. Despite the extremely low prices which the government paid for provisions in Ireland through the cess, large proportions of the acknowledged debt remained unpaid. In the seven baronies of Meath alone, the amount due for billeting between 1564 and 1571 amounted to over £6,300.[109] If the burden was equally apportioned throughout the Pale, as it was supposed to be, then the entire debt due by the government must have been in the region of £19,000. Government officers recognised that the crown's unwillingness to pay up at all was amongst the chief sources of the persistent tension between the army and the community. 'If the country were well paid', wrote Auditor Jenyson, 'they would willingly pay all they do, yea even more'.[110]

The viceroys' inability to find an effective means of diminishing or dispensing with the cess highlights the underlying weaknesses of their situation. Their failure can be attributed to no lack of concern or effort on their part, rather its source lay beyond their grasp in the governmental structures of Westminster and it arose, ironically, from the very attitude that had promoted their style of administration in the first place. A government, that is to say, which was unwilling or unable to formulate and administer a consistent line of policy directly from England, and was equally incapable of catering to the vital logistical needs of the semi-autonomous agents it had chosen to execute the policy for it. Moreover, this very delegation of responsibility tended to reduce, even further, the deputies' chances of maintaining adequate sources of supply. Deprived of ready and continuous access to influence, they were compelled to rely on the advocacy of secretaries and friendly councillors whose concern with Irish affairs was necessarily haphazard and half-hearted. Thus, the problem of supplying Ireland drifted inevitably to the lower end of the council's list of priorities. The reformist efforts of the viceroys were wasted, victuallers ruined and the country driven to desperation by the oppressions of a beggared soldiery.

But the viceroys were neither ignorant nor innocent of the sufferings of the countryside. Political careerists, they had willingly accepted, indeed hoped to take advantage of, the limitations of the Westminster government. It was the central government's weakness which gave them the apparent freedom to make glorious careers for themselves in Ireland and important political gains for their friends at court. They were, therefore, content to accept the

---

[109] 'Account of the cessors books, 1564–71', SP 65/10, fos. 33–4.
[110] Jenyson to Burghley, 14 July 1574, SP 63/47/14; 'Note of Kildare's evil dealing', *c.* Dec. 1561, SP 63/4/87.

less fortunate by-products of administrative laxity and hoped to find some *ad hoc* methods of coping with them as they arose. When all else failed, the cess remained supreme amongst expedients. They turned towards it compulsively as the best means of solving their logistical difficulties because it was cheap, relatively efficient and, most of all, because it was of fixed and estimable cost. Cess prices made stable and predictable the most uncertain of variables, the food supply. They seemed to underpin the entire programme of action which the governors set for themselves. Thus, when all alternatives proved unworkable, they had little choice but to return to it. Their continued exploitation of so valuable an asset, however, depended upon the governors' ability to honour the terms of their own enforced agreements by paying their bills regularly, by keeping the soldiers waged and well governed and by responding to the genuine needs of the country in times of difficulty. Yet it was at this crucial point that they lost control over the whole system. They could not guarantee the soldiers' wages; they could not prevent their extortion. They could not pay their own debts and ultimately they could not respond to the country's legitimate grievances even when they wished to. Ironically, therefore, the governments which were most dependent upon the supply of the country were the least equipped to ensure its efficient and equitable administration. It was this deeply paradoxical relationship that determined the character of the Palesmen's opposition to the cess.

Particular expressions of opposition from within the Pale have been considered earlier. But here discussion will be concerned with its more general characteristics, with its form of organisation, its tactics, its aims and its sense of direction. Each was determined by the nature of the grievance itself. The cess was a general levy, collected systematically throughout the country. The opposition, too, became general and countrywide, easily transcending geographical and factional barriers. Meath, the most fertile and the most heavily cessed of all counties was usually the centre of resistance. The earliest leaders of opposition, Sir Christopher Cheevers, Barnaby Scurlocke and William Bermingham, were Meathmen. But resistance to the cess occurred in every shire, each with its own local organisers. Similarly, the opposition transcended traditional lines of faction. The governors, daunted by such a general display of defiance, liked to argue that it was the work of one of their great noble adversaries, Ormond or Kildare. The earls, it is true, attempted to exploit the governors' difficulties with the country in their own interests and used their influence in support of the countrymen.[111] But neither was capable of controlling the issue or of

---

[111] Sussex's reply to the students, 21 Mar. 1561, SP 63/5/57; Ormond to his agent, Dec. 1577, Bodl., Carte MSS, 1/22–4.

adapting it to their needs. Ormond was unable to silence the country's complaints against his friend Sussex: Kildare could do little to help Sidney. The cess was politically useful to them only so long as they joined with the country in opposing it. Amongst the Palesmen themselves, all traditional rivals, the Prestons and the Eustaces, the Dillons and the Nugents, were united in complaining against a common grievance.[112]

The Palesmen vehemently denied any allegations of an ulterior motivation behind their actions. William Bermingham, the most radical of Sussex's critics, denied any association with Kildare's larger political ambitions, and it is clear that he had no wish to see English deputies withdrawn from Ireland.[113] The students of 1561 declared their intent 'to live no longer in Ireland than an English governor whose government shall depart from the laws of England shall govern there – God is our judge', and they were careful to include a round denunciation of Kildare's doings amongst their general petition for redress.[114] Their normally more reticent elders were equally emphatic:

We protest before God [they declared], we would choose no Irishman, for our choice must lie between the earls of Kildare and Ormond whom neither (though they both be noblemen and ready to serve) . . . should seem fit to us to have government in this realm, and if they were as wise as Solomon were and yet should burden the Pale with kerne and galloglass, we could not bear their government so far is our nature from the nature of the mere Irish and such mutual hate . . . is there between us.[115]

John Alen, nephew of the former lord chancellor and heir to St Wolstan's, was consecutively a leader of the opposition to the cess in this shire and the government's chief witness for a number of serious allegations made against Kildare.[116]

Agitation against the cess was not the product of factional intrigue; but neither was it the result of social tensions within the community of the Pale itself. The chief spokesmen of the country did not belong to the very highest ranks of Pale society, but they were by no means insignificant. Sir Christopher Cheevers and Richard Netterville were both substantial land-holders.[117] Netterville, Scurlocke and Burnell were well accredited and highly respected lawyers. Scurlocke, a former attorney general, was occasionally

---

[112] See for example the names appended to the petition of 27 May 1561, SP 63/6/12–13.
[113] Bermingham's 'Advices', 24 Sept. 1563, SP 63/9/27.
[114] Student's rejoinder to Sussex, 21 Mar. 1561, SP 63/5/54.
[115] Petition to Sir Nicholas Arnold, Dec. 1562, BL, Add. MSS, 40,061, no. 6, fos. 35–40.
[116] Sir Thomas Barnewall et al. to Elizabeth, 21 Oct. 1562, SP 63/7/31; 'Petition . . . to be rid of cess', Oct. 1572, SP 63/48/52 enclosure (i); Alen's information against Kildare, before Feb. 1575, SP 63/49/55; Alen to Burghley, 10 Aug. 1578, SP 63/61/46.
[117] For their respective wills see NAI, Chancery Inquisitions (Wexford) R.C. 5/13, pp. 164–81 and Exchequer Inquisitions (Dublin and Carlow), I, pp. 353–69.

employed by the government as a circuit court judge.[118] Burnell's abilities were widely recognised. He was attorney to the earl of Kildare and later, despite his recusancy, became a justice of the common pleas.[119] William Bermingham who lead the opposition to Sussex in 1562–3 was certainly no Jack Cade. He was thought by the privy council itself to be sufficiently responsible to act as an auditor of the army's accounts and to offer advice on the highest affairs of state. Later in the 1560s he was proposed to be chief sergeant of his own county.[120] His son, Patrick, who assumed his father's role in the early 1580s was also a prominent figure in the community. He served as a commissioner for musters in 1579 and was deemed able to pay a fine of £40 for his part in the agitation against Sidney in the previous year.[121] The nobility of the Pale were generally more discreet in their displays of resistance. But the success of the entire movement, as the government fully realised, was dependent upon their whole-hearted support. When pressed, as in 1561 or again in 1577, they came out to a man in favour of the agitators.[122] Both in terms of its universality, therefore, and in terms of its conservative leadership and loyalist assertions, the agitation against the cess may indeed be labelled, as contemporaries themselves referred to it, as 'the country cause'.[123]

Widespread discontent with the cess, however, was made practically effective in face of severe government repression only through the sophisticated organisation of the opposition's leadership. The cess was systematic; so too were the tactics employed to oppose it. The chief instrument used by the countrymen in each major clash with the government was civil disobedience. With little advance notice, the administration was confronted with an almost complete refusal on the part of the country to yield up the supplies that had been demanded of it. Cesses for the governor's house and for the forts were left unanswered, general levies were inadequately met and clashes between the billeted soldiers and the civilians multiplied. The

---

118 *Cal. pat rolls Henry VIII–Eliz. I*, p. 43, *Fiants Eliz.*, nos. 260, 682, 703–4, 1486, 2117, 2345, 2444, 3350, 3512, 3672, 4149, 4461; Fitzwilliam to Burghley, 15 Apr. 1572, SP 63/36/3; Eliz. to Fitzwilliam, 8 Mar. 1575, SP 63/50/3.

119 Ball, *Judges in Ireland*, I, p. 223, *Fiants Eliz.*, nos. 2990, 2906, 5467, 5582.

120 Bermingham's 'Device', 23 Sept. 1562, SP 63/9/19; 'Advice for the government of Ireland', 14 Sept., SP 63/9/27; 'Notes on superfluous charges', ? Jan. 1565, SP 63/12/1; 'Book . . . on Fitzwilliam's account', Apr. 1566, SP 63/17/44; Sidney to privy council, 24 June 1570, SP 63/30/56.

121 Commission against Turlough Luineach, 21 Aug. 1579, Lambeth MSS, 628/399; HMC, *Egmont MSS*, I, pt. 1, p. 8.

122 'Petitions of . . . the Pale', 27 May 1562, 21 Oct., SP 63/6/12–13, 7/31; Petition to Sir Nicholas Arnold, Dec. 1562, BL, Add. MSS, 40,061, no. 6; 'Names of the lords imprisoned and fined', 1577, HMC, *Egmont MSS*, I, pt. 1, pp. 7–8.

123 The phrase first appears in the state records in Wallop to Walsingham, 15 Jan. 1583, SP 63/99/25, but it is evident from its usage there that it was already widely current in the Pale.

effectiveness of the strike was startling. It ruined Sussex in 1563 and reduced Fitzwilliam and Sidney to desperate straits in turn. Once in action, the strike was justified and publicised by means of a country-wide petition. The Palesmen's petitions followed a pattern.[124] They were usually short: a brief and general statement in justification of the action being taken was followed by a florid protestation of loyalty to the crown. The most impressive feature of the petitions, however, was not their substance, but the list of signatures attached to them. The lists were quite long, containing on average the names of over twenty substantial landholders. More important, they were representative. The names of the leading families in each shire were carefully laid out and grouped together in order to display the unity of the opposition. The names of newly settled English families, such as the Draycots and the Alens were especially pointed up: and in 1562, the presentation of an individual book of complaints by an Englishman who claimed to have had twenty years' experience of service in Ireland was a particularly powerful weapon to the Palesmen who were registering their complaints against Sussex at this time.[125] Printed matter may also have been disseminated to broadcast and sustain the resistance. We know of at least one piece of doggerel against the cess, 'Tom Troth', because of the annoyance which its popularity caused to Sidney during the parliament of 1569–71.[126]

The orchestration of strikes and the circulation of petitions and pamphlets was clearly the work of some organisational core whose very efficiency has left their mode of operation obscure. But some indication of their work may be glimpsed from time to time within the records. Crucial preliminary meetings were sometimes held at the baron of Delvin's residence, or Viscount Gormanston's house in Meath or in Dublin during law-term time. From there, delegates were chosen to traverse the country, collecting information, securing allegiance and gathering signatures for the petition. The agents were carefully selected, sometimes in terms of class: Fitzwilliam noted in 1561,

There be three gentlemen chiefly appointed for the following and setting forth of such complaints as are sent over, and have assigned to them who they shall work within getting constent of hands. For the nobility and the best sort of the gentry is one Sir Christopher Cheevers, for the second sort and chief husbandmen is Barnewall of Stackallen, for the cities and good towns a lawyer called Barnaby Scurlock. All three are of good credit amongst their own countrymen, God would they were as void of malice.[127]

124 See various petitions: 6 July 1561, 27 May 1562, 21 Oct. 1562, Dec. 1562, 10 Jan. 1577, 1 Feb. 1578, 23 Mar. 1582, SP 63/4/17, 6/12, 7/13, BL, Add. MSS, 40,061, fos. 35–43, SP 63/57/1, 60/7, 92/20.
125 'A slanderous book', June 1562, SP 63/6/37.
126 Campion, *Histories*, p. 147.
127 Fitzwilliam to Cecil, 29 Apr. 1562, SP 63/5/98.

Sometimes, only one organiser was chosen, as was William Bermingham in 1562, or his son Patrick in 1581. But most commonly three men were selected to do the country's work.

These 'commonwealth men',[128] as they were referred to, were responsible not only for the organisation and propagation of resistance within the Pale, they were charged also with the execution of the country's most important opposition strategy, the presentation of its grievances at court. The practice of appealing over the governors' heads to the court and the privy council emerged as early as the first resistance to the cess. Archbishop Dowdall, the most prestigious Anglo-Irishman of his day, had gone to London as the unofficial spokesman of his country against Sussex in 1558, and in 1563 the law students used what they believed to be their special position to appeal directly to the queen without first registering their complaints with the viceroy. Thus far, however, the practice was uncoordinated. When Dowdall died, the opposition collapsed and the students were silenced by their arrest.

Systematic organisation began with the country's response to the students' fate, with the mobilisation of petitions in their support and with the preparation of William Bermingham's single-handed mission to court. Before presenting his case in London, Bermingham toured the Pale gaining support and gathering evidence and raising a subsidy from the countrymen to sustain him in his attendance at Whitehall.[129] Bermingham was the first fully accredited country agent. A similar tactic was employed by the country in the early 1570s. In their resistance to Fitzwilliam, the nobility and gentry of Meath circulated a petition around the Pale, seeking financial support for the despatch of three delegates to England. Using the very territorial divisions on which the cess itself was rated, these unofficial commissioners levied a small fixed charge on the countrymen as part of their allegiance to the cause. The great success of the collection seriously alarmed the government. 'Our late reformers of the commonweal', one official noted, 'are making their provision by a general cess amongst themselves which by report cometh to £1,000 and upwards.'[130] The very strength of the movement made the governors see covert opposition everywhere, even on the council itself. 'Secret conventicles are common and preaching in open pulpits by the appointed preachers for the commonweal who under colour of correction spare not to inveigh against the state itself'.[131] The crisis subsided temporarily, but this was the quality of the opposition which

---

128 The label is recorded in Sidney's 'Memoir', *UJA* 8, p. 83, but Sidney indicates that it was conventionally applied by contemporaries. Similar usages are to be found in Symcott to Burghley, 3 Dec. 1574, 10 Mar. 1575, SP 63/48/67, 50/7; see also Canny, *The formation of the Old English elite*, pp. 24–6.
129 Fitzwilliam to Cecil, 28 May 1562, SP 63/6/14.
130 Symcott to Burghley, 3 Dec. 1574, SP 63/48/67.   131 Ibid.

Sidney faced when he attempted to impose his plan for composition upon the country.

The speed and effectiveness with which resistance to the scheme was organised in 1575 took the newly appointed deputy completely by surprise. He was taken aback by the steadfastness of the Palesmen's collective action, their refusal to accept a compromise and their determination to carry the case to the arena towards which they had for some time looked for redress. Though he recovered his nerve and succeeded in coercing the Pale into obedience for a time, he was ultimately defeated by those shrewd and experienced agents who displayed a remarkable ability to conduct the case in unfavourable conditions and to present convincing alternative arguments to the viceroy's claims.[132]

Sidney's defeat at court consolidated the position of Netterville and Burnell as the chief representatives of the country. They were granted plenipotentiary powers by their countrymen in negotiating with Sidney's successor and remained decisive in determining the country's attitude towards subsequent government proposals. In 1581 Treasurer Wallop explicitly conceded their power when he argued that no settlement favourable to the government would be wrung from the country until the two lawyers had been removed from the scene.[133] During the resurgence of agitation against the cess in the early 1580s, however, they remained in the background allowing new men to make the running. This time Patrick Bermingham was delegated to co-ordinate resistance within the Pale and the task of presenting the country's grievance at court was left to his cousin, Gerald Aylmer, a young lawyer who was already in place there as a retainer of the earl of Sussex.[134] Throughout the 1580s Netterville and Burnell, Bermingham and Aylmer acted in unison as the organising core of the country opposition.

Of itself, therefore, and independent of any other influence, the cess did much to determine the political development of the Pale in the first twenty-five years of Elizabeth's reign. Its charge was sufficiently onerous and sufficiently widespread to provide the community with a unifying grievance which transcended all factional and territorial distinctions. Furthermore, the recognition that the Dublin administration was powerless to prevent its own worst abuse in the matter of cess, that it was, indeed, ultimately dependent upon them, transformed dissatisfaction with a single aspect of executive

---

[132] See ch. 4 above.
[133] Wallop to Walsingham, 10 Dec. 1581, SP 63/87/34.
[134] Patrick Bermingham to Richard Plunkett, enclosing commission to collect subsidy, 31 Mar. 1583, SP 63/100/61 and enclosure (i); Bermingham to Aylmer, 9 Sept. 1582, SP 63/95/1; on Aylmer, see Sir Fenton Aylmer, 'Sir Gerald Aylmer, knight and baronet', *Jn. Kildare Arch. Soc.* 11 (1930–3), pp. 367–85.

action into a profound disillusion with the character of the Dublin government, in general. Gradually, therefore, a new awareness of the Pale as a unique political entity with particular problems of its own began to dawn. Older perceptions of the Pale as the last outpost of English civility or as the platform for a revival of English government in Ireland began to fade, and a new understanding of the region as a distinct zone, threatened on the one hand by the incursions of the lawless Irish, and on the other hand by the oppression of an irresponsible government, began to take root.

Finally, the appreciation that the source of their troubles lay not ultimately with the viceroys, but with the government in London which sent them hither, provided the Palesmen with a new strategy to match their new sense of identity. They counted less and less upon the expression of their grievances to the viceroys and more upon a direct presentation of their plight to their sovereign in England. The students of 1561 made their complaints without any prior application to Dublin. William Bermingham did the same. In 1574, agents prepared to go to London without even opening talks with Fitzwilliam; in 1577, they actually did so.[135] Each time they did, moreover, they returned with some sense of achievement. Though initially imprisoned, the students were soon released and the inquiry for which they pleaded was established. William Bermingham's proposals became official government policy for a time, and those of Burnell in 1577 formed the basis of the government's offer on the cess. In 1585 the Palesmen negotiated a final agreement on the cess in England having rejected out of hand Lord Deputy Perrot's proposals on the matter.[136]

The Palesmen's success at court was in large part due to the orthodox and conservative terms in which they defended their position. They insisted at all times that by attacking their governors' authority in this indirect fashion, they were implicitly acknowledging their genuine loyalty to their sovereign. By complaining directly to the queen and by sending agents to court they were, they claimed, simply underlining their true constitutional relationship with their monarch, not abusing it. This argument was emphasised by the students in 1562, and by their elders who petitioned on their behalf; and it was reiterated by Netterville and Burnell in 1577.[137] But it was, perhaps,

---

[135] Symcott to Burghley, 3 Dec. 1574, 10 Mar. 1575, SP 63/48/67, 50/7.

[136] For a full account of Perrot's parliament, see Victor Treadwell, 'Sir John Perrot and the Irish parliament of 1584–6', *Proc. RIA* 85 (1985), sect. c, pp. 259–308; see also T. W. Moody, 'The Irish parliament under Elizabeth and James I', *Proc. RIA* 45, sect. 6 (1939), pp. 41–81; 'Journal of House of Lords in Sir John Perrot's parliament', ed. F. J. Routledge, *EHR* 29 (1914), pp. 104–17.

[137] Students' reply to Sussex, 21 mar. 1562, SP 63/5/54. Gormanston et al. to Eliz., 6 July 1561, SP 63/4/17, Plunket et al. to Eliz., 27 May 1562, SP 63/6/12, 'Submission of the gentlemen of the Pale', June 1577, Lambeth MSS, 628/128; Submission of Netterville and Burnell, June 1577, SP 63/58/42.

most pithily expressed by Sir Nicholas White, the Palesmen's closest sympathiser on the Irish council. Writing to Burghley in 1577, he urged the treasurer to make

some difference between complaining and disobedience. The lords and gentlemen who feel themselves aggrieved with the greatness of the cess contrary to the laws imagined that to complain was the very gate of obedience through which they must enter with humble petition of redress to their sovereign and prince under whose only will and sentence . . . the one [the people] and the other [the viceroy] stand.[138]

This line of defence was nicely calculated to appeal to the sensibilities of Elizabeth and her councillors. Though she was quite sensitive to any threats to the prerogative, Elizabeth was equally concerned to avoid appearing oppressive to natural subjects. By the late 1570s the misbehaviour of the soldiers in Ireland had become something of a scandal in England. Even that brassy chauvinist, Thomas Churchyard, publicly compared 'the misery of Ireland' with the sufferings of the oppressed in Spanish Flanders: the parallel was far from flattering to the English government.[139] But the issue was more than a source of embarrassment. Well attested allegations of abuses in Ireland posed a serious challenge to the conservative assumptions of good lordship on which Tudor sovereignty rested. The queen and her councillors freely acknowledged their responsibility to inquire into such charges and the loyalist protestation of the Palesmen persuaded them on each occasion of the need to take action.[140] On another level, however, the grievances of palpably loyal subjects provided the central government with one of the most dependable checks on the semi-autonomous administrations which they had allowed to operate in Ireland. Thus the crown's occasional interventions on behalf of the Palesmen were also prompted by a quite practical desire to ensure that it was getting good value for money.

The cess, the Pale's struggle against it and the overall success of appeals to the crown were, therefore, of fundamental importance in determining the future political identity of the Palesmen. They were the crown's true subjects in Ireland: steadfast in their loyalty to their sovereign, but unafraid to complain directly of abuses committed in his name. English and loyal, they none the less began to withdraw from the interaction and collaboration with their own administration in Ireland and to define themselves both politically and culturally against the new English administrators who came to serve in Ireland. And in this early stage their withdrawal was encouraged

---

[138] White to Burghley, 13 June 1577. Hatfield House, Cecil MSS, CP, 60/130–2.

[139] Thomas Churchyard, *The misery of Flanders, the unquietness of France* . . . (London, 1579); see also Burghley's comments in a similar vein, quoted in C. Read, *Lord Burghley and Queen Elizabeth* (London, 1960), pp. 9–10.

[140] Report on protest against the cess, 1578, BL, Cotton MSS, Vespasian F IX, 22.

and reinforced by the central government which aided and abetted their resistance to unpopular officials which it continued to despatch to rule over them.

The stability of the Palesmen's new political identity was underwritten by the support of the crown, but that support itself was highly conditional. Elizabeth always reacted strongly to allegations that the Palesmen would impugn her prerogative, but her anger with the Palesmen on these occasions was soon revealed to be the result of misunderstanding and misrepresentation. It subsided when it was made clear that the Palesmen were not opposed to the prerogative in principle, but to its practical abuse in Ireland. This assurance was normally sufficient to satisfy Elizabeth. The viceroys, however, frustrated by their repeated worstings at the hands of the Palesmen, came to enunciate a much broader interpretation of the prerogative than was current in either Ireland or England. They began, that is, to conceive of the prerogative, not merely as the sum of specific or extraordinary powers traditionally enjoyed by the crown, but as something abstract, amorphous and unlimited.

The assertion of this attitude was neither sudden nor unequivocal. Bellingham had employed the prerogative to justify a wide range of demands in times of necessity, but he had conceded that consultation might occur with representatives of the country to determine if such necessity actually existed. Sussex took the case further by insisting that the question of necessity was a strategic issue which could be determined only by a military governor. But he himself shied away from basing his demands on the prerogative alone. Characteristically, the clearest expression of this new view came from Sidney. For long, he too had remained cautious. His defence of the cess of the parliament of 1569–71 had been conceded in the conventional language of good lordship.[141] The garrison, he pleaded, was there to protect the community. The price paid in the cess was well worth the gains of peace and prosperity brought by the military presence. In the later 1570s, however, Sidney abandoned these moderate positions. The prerogative, he told the English privy council, was more than a personal attribute of the monarch. It was an administrative tool which could and should be exploited and expanded to improve the revenues and increase the power of the government.[142] Sir Philip, who presented his father's case at court, put the point quite bluntly. The lawyers' quibbles over the constitutional legitimacy of the cess or its enforced composition, he declared, were

141 Campion, *Histories* (ed. A. Vossen), pp. 147–8).
142 Sidney to Walsingham, 15 May 1577, BL, Cotton MSS, Titus B X, fo. 61; 'Instructions to Waterhouse', HMC, *De Lisle and Dudley MSS*, 1, pp. 55–6; Sidney to Elizabeth, 20 May 1577, SP 63/58/29.

irrelevant. The levy, or its money value, was clearly needed by the English governor in Ireland and therefore he must have it: 'id maxime justum quod maxime convenit reipublicae'.[143] These sentiments were expressed in secret to the council, but Sidney was not averse to making his views plain to the countrymen themselves. To the recalcitrant citizens of Waterford he delivered a scathing rebuke:

Do not you whom God had delivered on several occasions, think that your doing and committing wickedness shall escape his judgement ... beware and humble yourselves in all dutifulness and obedience to his prince. Examine not his authority, neither decipher his power. Compare not your principles with his authority, neither dispute your liberties with his prerogative. For notwithstanding these principles, grants and liberties be great, yet they cannot abate or impugn the least part of your princes prerogative which is so great as nothing can be greater.[144]

These were assertions of a markedly radical character, too radical indeed for the queen and most of her council. As long as the particular issue dividing the governor and the community remained, in the eyes of the crown, a relatively moderate one, such an extreme response seemed unwarranted. Sidney's declamations, for the time being, went unheeded. But the argument he enunciated would soon prove to be a powerful instrument in persuading the crown towards more coercive and oppressive courses of action when the issue alienating the Palesmen from government policy was far more politically explosive than the cess, their recusancy. In the meantime, however, the new viewpoint had immediate relevance for every English official in Ireland who, like Sidney, found himself confronted by an indifferent, sometimes hostile and always formidable community. It provided these embattled administrators with the basis of a new *esprit de corps*. It gave them a new justification for treating the Palesmen with disdain and their more powerful Anglo-Irish relations with outright distrust. Most importantly of all, it provided at least some explanation for an otherwise inexplicable phenomenon: the failure of government to make any progress whatsoever amongst the Gaelic Irish.

---

[143] Philip Sidney, 'Discourse on Irish affairs', *c.* Sept. 1577, BL, Cotton MSS, Titus B XII, fos. 564–5, printed in *Miscellaneous prose of Sir Philip Sidney*, ed. K. Duncan Jones and J. Von Dorster (Oxford, 1973).
[144] 'Annals of Dudley Loftus', *s.a.* 1575, Marsh's Library, MS Z3.2.7.

7

Reform government and Gaelic Ireland

Much to the frustration of modern historians, the Tudors were, for the most part, remarkably incurious about Gaelic Ireland. Though they had for decades struggled to come to terms with that society, extended commentaries on the nature of Gaelic culture, its socio-political structures and its customs began to appear only in the last quarter of the century. And even then the earliest attempts were, like Stanihurst's, highly derivative of older Anglo-Norman descriptions, while the later ones, like Spenser's, were designed with a radically polemical purpose in mind. It was not until early in the following century, in the writings of men like Fynes Moryson and Sir John Davies that sustained analyses and comparative descriptions of that apparently exotic culture were to be essayed. But for the bulk of the Tudor period those most actively engaged with the Gaelic lordships preferred to eschew such high generalisations, and chose instead to confine themselves to close examinations of the balance of power in particular regions, measured assessments of the dispositions of individuals, and detailed elaborations of the policy to be applied in specific cases.[1]

Such an apparent lack of interest in the distinguishing features of Gaelic Ireland was the result neither of ignorance nor of intellectual limitation. It arose instead from a quite deliberate decision to minimise the distinctiveness of Gaelic culture as an entity in itself and to treat of the challenge which it posed to the reassertion of English rule as no more than the most difficult form of the problem which the government faced in the island as a whole.

This approach to the Gaelic lordships had been conditioned from the outset by the analysis of 'the Irish problem' which had emanated from the Pale in the early decades of the century. That analysis, it will be recalled, though urgent and even terrifying in substance, was simple and quite optimistic in the prescriptions it offered. Despite their ancient ethnic differences, the Gaelic and Anglo-Irish lords had, so the counsellors of the

---

[1] Lennon, *Richard Stanihurst: the Dubliner*; Canny, 'Edmund Spenser and the development of Anglo-Irish identity', pp. 1–19.

245

Pale argued, succumbed to the same common evil which rendered many of them indistinguishable from one another and threatened imminently to consume the entire island. This evil that pervaded Ireland was lawlessness: the complete disregard for any system of rules other than those enforced by the terrors of coyne and livery, the protection and intimidation rackets which now dominated the country. This degeneration of law throughout Ireland, though appalling, allowed nevertheless of a response that was in theory at least eminently feasible. It allowed in the first place that Ireland should be treated as a whole, as a single diseased political entity whose ills were to be treated by the same cure. And it suggested secondly what that cure should be. Since almost everywhere in Ireland was now without law or potentially so, nothing other than the gradual, piece-meal reintroduction of English law first among the Anglo-Irish and then among the Gaelic lords would bring the island to order.

The means by which law might be re-established in Ireland were, of course, several. It might be applied by inducement or by force: by gradual diplomatic assimilation, by coercion, or by exclusive colonisation; or by a combination of all three. But the decision on the approach to be adopted in furthering the advance of law was founded on no abstract theories concerning the nature of the people or their cultural dispositions, for such matters were quite irrelevant to the original analysis. It was rather to be determined by strategic and pragmatic considerations as to which was the most feasible and most reliable option in any given circumstance. From the beginning, therefore, the reforming governors' attitude towards the Gaelic lordships was characterised by a judicious blend of conciliation and coercion. Long-term policies of acclimatising the Irish to the ways of English law were occasionally punctuated by quite determined punitive wars; limited colonising projects were launched amidst the general campaign to persuade the Gaelic lords of the benefits of voluntarily introducing English law into their territories.

By the mid-1580s, however, pragmatism and flexibility notwithstanding, the failure of such an optimistic policy was painfully becoming obvious. Far from being made more civil, the Gaelic lords appeared to be more rebellious and more resistant to law than ever. By then a radical but gratifying explanation for this disheartening phenomenon had become available for those willing to use it. Since the Pale had shown itself to be so undependable in times of crisis, it was clear that little trust should be placed in political advice that had issued from thence. Such a repudiation of traditional Tudor thinking was a radical move, and the denial of the ready applicability of English law in Ireland which it entailed was an implication which few even then were prepared to accept. It became current only in the wake of the failure of Sir John Perrot's last great push for reform and of the upheavals

in Ulster which followed from it. But before the appearance of those great
simplifying agencies, the most common response to the failure of English
law to make progress in Gaelic Ireland either by coercion or by persuasion
was one of utter bewilderment: 'there lies some mystery in this universal
rebellious disposition' exclaimed Sir William Fitzwilliam with characteristic
exasperation, 'which God for mercy sake grant not only to be revealed, but
to be provided for'.[2] Simple confusion was indeed the most natural of initial
reactions, for the failure of policy yielded no distinctive explanatory insight
nor any crucial point of change which might have permitted objective
analysis. Instead both colonisation and social reform, the two alternative
modes employed to bring about the assimilation of the Gaelic lordships, not
only failed, but displayed the same features of entropy and decay. Everywhere, that is, among newly established English colonies and recently
reformed Irish lordships, under English captains and under Gaelic chieftains, the campaign to establish law succumbed gradually but inexorably to
the pervasive and apparently ineradicable disease of lawlessness.

COLONISATION

Sixteenth-century schemes for colonisation in Ireland have always seemed to
be distinctly at odds with the claims of government policy. It has always
appeared difficult, that is to say, to reconcile Tudor monarchs' repeated
declarations of their desire to treat all of Ireland's inhabitants as free and
common subjects with their readiness to promote a whole range of diverse
projects aimed at the dispossession of the native landholders and the
establishment of English settlements in the appropriated territories. For
the most part historians have chosen to evade this inconsistency by positing
a neat chronological division between one period, when peaceful reform was
in the ascendant, and another when such aspirations were displaced by an
unapologetic determination to exploit the natives' weakness in order to gain
possession of their territories.

Such an interpretative strategy has considerable merit. It is clear that
proposals for colonial enterprise multiplied in the years after 1560, and it is
clear also that after 1580 demands for the wholesale appropriation of native
lands began to be more frequently voiced and more overtly defended. Yet
this useful simplification has been purchased at some cost. The chronological distinction ignores the many colonial projects which were actively
promoted and the few which were actually implemented in the first half of

---

[2] Fitzwilliam to Burghley, 21 Oct. 1572, SP 63/38/29; see, in general, Ciaran Brady, 'The
road to the *View*: on the decline of reform thought in Tudor Ireland', in Patricia Coughlan
(ed.), *Spenser and Ireland* (Cork, 1989), pp. 25–45.

the century. It discounts also the extent to which earlier schemes acted as models for projects advanced later on. But most importantly, it continues to evade the troublesome fact that, for a crucial period between the 1540s and the 1580s, colonisation schemes were supported and put into operation by the same administrations which continued to affirm as their central objective the long-term transformation of the Gaelic lordships through peaceful internal reform. For much of the sixteenth century, that is, the apparent inconsistency remained, and some attempt must be made to confront it.

One avenue of approach to the problem is suggested by a particular feature of several colonial schemes which has hitherto been little remarked on by historians: that is, their surprisingly conservative and imitative character. The source from which colonising proposals emanated and the area of operations selected changed over the decades. The form in which the proposals were presented and the arguments advanced in their support were clearly not always the same. Yet on a number of key issues those who wrote in favour of colonising enterprise between the early sixteenth century and the mid-1570s showed a surprising degree of consistency.

Almost everyone was agreed, for instance, that any plantation enterprise would be strictly limited in extent. The typical colony would be formed around the nucleus of a single fortified site. The establishment of an interlocking chain of such nuclear colonies was sometimes envisaged, but the success or failure of a plantation continued to be judged in terms of the survival of its individual units. Only rarely in this period was the wholesale confiscation of large tracts of native land under a centrally planned and administered system considered. But this strategy which was to acquire increasing authority in the late sixteenth and early seventeenth centuries remained for the most part an unexplored option in the years before 1579.[3]

The classic exposition of this defensive view was to be found in Patrick Finglas' widely distributed and highly influential 'Breviate of the getting of Ireland' which was produced in its definitive form in the early 1530s.[4] Finglas argued that the fortifications established during the previous attempt at conquest and which now lay derelict throughout the country should be renovated and restored to their original purpose. He estimated that there were some 500 such sites which could still be made to form the

---

[3] Several colonising schemes or plots are discussed and given plausible attributions in White, 'The Tudor plantations in Ireland to 1571'. I am greatly indebted to White's work in the following discussion.

[4] I have consulted the extended copy submitted to the privy council in the early 1530s, SP 60/2/7; several extant copies of the 'Breviate' exist among the papers of leading statesmen which testify to its influence.

basis of the new settlements. The strategy was to be put into operation first in south-east Leinster in the mountainous regions occupied by the O'Byrnes, O'Tooles and the Kavanaghs. The castles there were to be granted away by the king by knight's service only but the grantees were to be required in return to spend 300 marks a year on their holdings until the settlement had been fully established. The grants were to be made to experienced military men and to 'such as have no great possessions in England so that they shall not have an eye to return to England, for such like have been the great decay of this land'.[5]

Finglas was not the first to promote the nuclear garrison. The author of an anonymous treatise of 1515 also recommended the planting of Englishmen in small settlements in Leinster and along the north-east coastline.[6] The Palesman, Thomas Bathe, writing in 1528, had similar ideas.[7] But it was Finglas who made explicit the assumptions on which earlier proposals had been made. In his elaborate historical preface he asserted that the precedent which he regarded as the model for a new colonising enterprise was the original Anglo-Norman conquest.

In the decade after they had been presented at court, Finglas' views, sometimes modified, sometimes made more elaborate, influenced almost every other policy memorandum prepared on the subject. A plan 'for the winning of Leinster' presented to the king by the Irish council in 1537 offered only an extended treatment of the ideas discussed in the Breviate, while independent projects devised by Robert and Walter Cowley in the same period showed a close acquaintance with Finglas' work.[8] Even St Leger, while commissioner in Ireland in 1537–8, echoed Finglas' views.[9] In the 1540s the colonisers' attention shifted gradually from Leinster towards the midland territories occupied by the rebellious O'Mores and O'Connors. Walter Cowley was among the first to make this change of focus as counsellor to Sir Edward Bellingham. But Cowley's midland proposals were essentially the same as those which he had urged for Leinster.[10] He listed the major fortifications in the area and recommended that experienced soldiers

[5] Ibid., fo. 3.
[6] 'State of Ireland and plan for its reformation', *c.* 1515, *SP Hen. VIII,* II, pp. 1–31; White attributes the treatise to Archbishop Rokeby of Dublin.
[7] 'A discourse of the cause of the evil state of Ireland', BL, Lansdowne MSS, 159, no. 1; I have accepted White's plausible attribution of this unsigned tract to Thomas Bathe.
[8] 'Memorial for the winning of Leinster', *SP Hen. VIII,* II, pp. 409–18; R. Cowley to Cromwell, *c.* June 1536, July 1537, *SP Hen. VIII,* II, pp. 323–30, 445–52; Walter Cowley to Cromwell, 19 June, ibid., pp. 332–3: R. Cowley to Cromwell, 9 Sept. 1539, *SP Hen. VIII,* III, pp. 145–9.
[9] St Lever et al. to Cromwell, 2 Jan. 1538, *SP Hen. VIII,* II, pp. 534–9.
[10] Cowley to Bellingham, 24 Mar. 1549, enclosing his 'Device' for Ireland, SP 61/2/25 and enclosure (i).

be appointed to each on the usual generous terms. The one novel element in his scheme, a proposal that individual grants should be relatively large, did not pass without criticism from other strategists, most notably Edward Walshe, and the early failure of initial attempts based on his plans seemed to prove his critics right.[11] Renewed propositions to plant in the midlands in the 1550s showed little divergence from the classical pattern. Despite his strictures on Cowley, Edward Walshe also supported the nuclear garrison plan, as did the more immediately influential Sir John Alen who was Sussex's mentor in 1556. Like Walshe, Alen also dissented from Cowley's ambitious schemes. It was better, he advised, to attempt only what could be held. Beyond this, however, Cowley and Alen were at one in their acceptance of the garrison model. Alen recommended the establishment of a 'few towns well placed, moderately inhabited, industriously occupied . . . justly by laws governed . . . and to every town a head gentleman to hold of the queen and the others to hold of him'.[12] Alen selected twelve sites for such towns which were to form an interlocking defence line to protect the plantation from attack. The chief settlers were to be military men, preferably but not exclusively English, the terms of their leases were to be generous and their grants were to be quickly confirmed by act of parliament. With little modification, Alen's plan was to serve as a blueprint for the plantation which Sussex attempted to establish in the midlands.

Sussex's lack of success in Laois–Offaly did not, however, seriously call into question the assumptions of the classical theory. Indeed even the earliest critics of the midlands failure produced alternative proposals which remained quite compatible with the original model. William Piers in his project of 1565 envisaged the construction of a series of fortified towns along the north-east coast in a manner reminiscent of the 1515 report.[13] Jerome Brett and his associates who sued in 1568 for 'the fishing of the south and south-east coasts and land around the town of Baltimore' were pioneering into new territories but their proposed form of organisation was unoriginal. Humphrey Gilbert's plans for the same region were more ambitious and more elaborate, but even he accepted the convention that a plantation was to be organised around a series of fortified nuclear settlements.[14] Similarly, Sir Thomas Smith's ill-fated attempt to launch a colony in the Ards was, despite the novel ways in which it was publicised and justified, conventional in its structure; for notwithstanding the extensive

[11] D. B. Quinn (ed.), 'Edward Walshe's "Conjectures" concerning the state of Ireland c. 1552', *IHS* 5 (1946–7), pp. 303–33.
[12] Alen's 'Replies to several questions', *c.* 1556, BL, Lansdowne MSS, 159, no. 3.
[13] Piers' 'Plot', SP 63/9/83. I have followed White in assuming a date later than that attributed by the editor of the *Calendar of State Papers*.
[14] 'Note of the demands of Sir W. St. Leger et al.', *c.* 1568, SP 63/26/81.

territory to which his grant entitled him, this too was planned as a series of fortified outposts in hostile territory.[15]

Conventional colonising strategy reached its climax in the earl of Essex's ambitious enterprise in Clandeboy in the early 1570s. After expelling the Scots from the region, Essex planned to erect the traditional fortifications along the coast to ensure that they would never return. Adventurers who had attached themselves to the earl would be placed in command of the new forts and would receive their reward in large tracts of land which were to be annexed to each fort. Essex himself was granted unusually extensive civil and military powers. As 'principal governor and captain general in the northparts of Ireland', he was given authority of all legal and administrative offices, was granted a general commission of 'oyer et determiner' and allowed to make war and apply martial law at his discretion. In Essex's enterprise the model that inspired colonising projects over the past fifty years attained its closest approximation to reality. The earl, that is, had come to Ireland in the most traditional guise of the great feudal overlord come to establish order by force and exact his due reward in return.[16]

The persistence of this defensive model was due to more than a simple lack of imagination among the colonial boosters. The traditional design retained its relevance because some of the essential conditions within which it was devised continued to operate throughout the sixteenth century. The subjection of extensive stretches of Irish land to plantation was from the beginning rendered impracticable by the government's unwillingness to countenance it in any meaningful way. Thus despite the broad terms in which colonial grants were commonly framed, the actual projects necessarily assumed a restricted and defensive character because of the crown's refusal to support the wholesale clearance of the native population which a more ambitious undertaking would have required.

In the same way a common understanding of the insurmountable limitations within which they worked produced a general agreement among the colonial strategists in relation to the treatment of the indigenous population in the areas selected for planting. Because they accepted from the beginning that no exclusively immigrant population would be feasible, or would indeed be permitted by the government, they recognised that natives would have to be admitted into the settlements in one guise or another. Fearing that it might be dangerous 'to depeople the land of England',

---

15 D. B. Quinn, 'Sir Thomas Smith (1513–77) and the beginnings of English colonial policy', *Proc. Am. Phil. Soc.* 89 (1945), pp. 543–60; 'Orders of Sir Thomas Smith, 1 Dec. 1573', Essex Record Office, MS D/Dsh, 01/2.

16 Morton. 'The enterprise of Ulster', pp. 114–21; Devereux, *Lives and letters of the Devereux earls of Essex*, I, passim, esp. pp. 31–6, 59; Essex's 'Offers' concerning Ulster, 26 May 1573, SP 63/40/59, 61 and 65; *Cal. pat. rolls (England) Elizabeth I (1572–5)*, p. 12.

Finglas argued that a new settlement 'may be well inhabited with Irish inhabitants as it was at the conquest for they be not better labourers nor earth tillers than the poor commons of Ireland . . . and they soon will be brought to good frame if they be kept under a law'.[17] This ambiguous reformative/exploitative attitude towards the native population was shared by almost every writer who came after Finglas. Walter Cowley believed that after the natives had been defeated by Bellingham, they might then be induced 'to inhabit and fall to husbandry' in the new colonies.[18] Captain Piers also recognised that the success of a colony depended on the availability of a native work-force and the co-operation of powerful local chieftains who would supply it; only the Scots were to be excluded from his enterprise. Ironically, in view of his subsequent conduct Essex declared upon his arrival in Ireland that his intentions towards the natives were benevolent and conciliatory. Elizabeth had assented to his enterprise on the understanding that he should extend clemency to those who had become 'her disobedient subjects rather because they had not been defended from the force of the Scots than from any other cause'. His mission, Essex claimed, was 'grounded upon Her Majesty's commiseration with the natural born subjects of this province over whom the Scots did tyrannise'.[19]

This element of paradox in the writings of those who at once sought to use the native Irish as hewers of wood and drawers of water and yet promised to reform and improve them is to some extent resolved in the writings of Sir Thomas Smith and of the Irishman to whom he was greatly indebted for his ideas on colonisation, Rowland White.[20] For Smith, and particularly for White, the purpose of new colonies was to be exemplary. They were to stand as model environments whose internal prosperity and contentment would induce the Gaelic leaders outside to emulate their methods. Explicitly rejecting the idea that his enterprise was part of a military conquest, Smith declared that his son was going to Ireland not as 'an invader' but as 'a defender': 'a maintainer of ploughs and tillage . . . a peopler of houses not a desolater . . . come to enrich the country whereof they [the native population] shall also reap more benefit . . . not to impoverish it'.[21]

By definition, of course, this great work had to be performed with little

---

[17] 'Breviate'.
[18] Cowley to Bellingham, 24 Mar. 1549, SP 61/2/25.
[19] Essex to Burghley, 10 Sept. 1573, *Lives of Devereux earls*, I, pp. 34–6, see also same to same, 20 July, BL, Harleian MSS, 6991, fo. 23.
[20] 'Rowland White's "Discors touching the reformation of Ireland", c. 1571', ed. N. P. Canny, *IHS* 20 (1976–7), pp. 439–63, but see also White's earlier treatises, 'A book of the cause of the disobedience . . . of the Irish' after 1559, SP 63/1/72–3 and several drafts left among Cecil's manuscripts at Hatfield House, Cecil MSS, CP, 207, nos. 16–19.
[21] Smith to Fitzwilliam, 18 May 1572, *Cal. SP Foreign (1583 and Addenda)*, pp. 489–90.

dependence upon the surrounding countryside. Englishmen therefore were to predominate in the colony and only those Irish who were willing to co-operate unreservedly in the building of the new community were to be admitted within it. White and Smith were realistic enough to perceive that only those who suffered most from the exactions of the Gaelic system would give such a pledge and it was from the lowest ranks of Gaelic society that they expected to make their recruits. Naturally, such churls would not receive any immediate social elevation by virtue of their inclusion in the colony, but they would now be enabled to carry out the proper functions of their station free from the violence and extortions that had brought such wretchedness upon them. 'The husbandman', wrote Smith, 'shall have his land to occupy upon such easy conditions as shall be thought meet and shall not be oppressed by coyne and livery . . . but contrarywise defended to the uttermost that he may be as rich as he will.'[22] 'It is neither sought to expel nor destroy the Irish race', he concluded, 'but to keep them in order, in virtuous labour and in justice, and to teach them English laws and civility.'[23] White and Smith both believed that the local lords would soon recognise the advantages of the colonists' way of life and looked towards the establishment of friendly relations with the chieftains once the colonies' self-sufficiency had been assured.

There was no doubt special pleading in all of this: a desire to cloak personal interest in the guise of the greater good. Yet the disingenuousness of such statements should not be too readily assumed. White, whose fertile mind was the source of a vast range of civilising and improving projects, clearly believed that the appropriation of small quantities of Gaelic Ireland's greatly underexploited land in order to demonstrate its true potential would be of advantage both to natives and planters alike; while Smith, as the author of the *Discourse of the Commonweal*, was no stranger to the notion that individual economic enterprise could be conducive to the public good.[24] But whether they were sincerely meant or not, these apologias in defence of the exemplary value of colonies were in themselves an acknowledgement of the requirement that colonial promoters must integrate their projects within the larger objectives of orthodox Tudor reform policy.

Seen in this way most of the colonial schemes advanced in the first three-quarters of the century marked no radical deviation from the conventional policy of reform through persuasion. On the contrary, these limited,

---

22 Smith to Fitzwilliam, 8 Nov. 1572, Bodl., Carte MSS, 57/435, see also Smith to his son, 18 May 1572, *Cal. SP Foreign (1583 and addenda)*, p. 490.
23 'Petitions . . . by certain gentlemen who offer to suppress the rebels', c. Apr. 1569, SP 63/28/2; P. J. Piveronus, 'Sir Warham St Leger and the first Munster plantation, 1568–9', *Eire–Ireland* 14: 2 (1979), pp. 16–36.
24 'Petitions', SP 63/28/2.

strategically located settlements with their demonstratively improving pretensions were expected to complement the overall aims of reform government by punishing the rebellious, by restraining the uncommitted and by encouraging all of the rest to share in the great social and economic benefits heralded by the introduction of the laws and customs of English culture.

Amidst this consensus, that the ends of reform would be furthered by colonies which would be exemplary in both the punitive and educative senses, some individual deviations could, however, be discerned. There were, to be sure, the occasional outbursts of frustrated Englishmen who claimed they would have been pleased to see the entire native population extirpated root and branch; but in the years before 1580 such declarations rarely received sufficient elaboration nor did they arise with sufficient frequency to be read as more than expressions of frustration and bad temper. Far more serious were the projects advanced by Sir Warham St Leger and his associates for Munster in 1569.[25] Writing at the time when most of the province was in arms against the crown, the adventurers petitioned to be granted the lands of Clancar, O'Callaghan, the two O'Sullivans and MacDonagh. All of these had been proclaimed rebels, yet the petitioners sought not merely to obtain their lands, but those 'of all their followers and confederates within the province'.[26] Such inclusiveness would have given them ownership of much of west Cork and south Kerry. The petitioners were prepared, moreover, to meet the attendant labour problem head on. They proposed to expel the entire native population from the area and to plant some 3,000 English immigrants in their place.

This was a proposal which clearly anticipated the later attempts at extensive plantation which would be launched in Munster after the Desmond rebellion. Even so it was not without its conservative elements. The plantation was not intended to be exclusive to English adventurers alone, for the petitioners sought that grants be made also 'to such of Ireland birth as are descended from the English nation'.[27] Significantly, Desmond, the region from which rebellion had issued in the first place was to be exempted from the confiscation, and the earl's brother, Sir John, was to be given a leading role in launching the plantation. Thus even here the idea of reviving the old Anglo-Norman conquest remained alive.[28] In the event, however, the very ambition of the scheme proved too much for Elizabeth's

---

[25] 'Memorials of things to be considered upon the articles', *c.* Apr. 1569, SP 63/28/4 and 9. Piveronus, 'Sir Warham St. Leger'.
[26] Elizabeth to Sidney, 7 Aug. 1569, *Sid. SP*, no. 71.
[27] 'Petitions', SP 63/28/2.
[28] Sir John of Desmond to privy council, 11 June 1569, SP 63/28/26; Desmond to privy council, 20 Aug. 1571, SP 63/33/36.

cautious privy councillors who declared that the project contained 'so many difficulties' as to render it impracticable.[29] It was shelved, and Clancar and his followers were pardoned in 1571.[30]

Though it never proceeded beyond the drawing board the 1569 scheme cannot, however, be lightly dismissed. For its appearance at that time was a symptom not merely of an idea that would be more fully developed twenty years on, but of an equally significant though rather more subtle process already well under way. Innovations had certainly taken place in the process of colonisation between the 1540s and the early 1570. But the changes that occurred concerned not the theory of colonisation nor its ultimate objective, but the way in which attempts were made to establish them. The phases through which colonising practice passed were closely determined by the general character of the administration under which individual colonial projects were undertaken. Thus St Leger and Crofts both attempted to incorporate colonising activity within their general policy of collaborating with the gentry of the Pale by promoting an independent project for the midlands advanced by a group of Palesmen and by granting generous leases to Palesmen once the plantation had commenced.[31] Similarly, Sussex's attempt to establish a tightly organised military plantation in Laois–Offaly was intimately related to his highly centralised, exclusive style of government.[32] Sidney too emulated Sussex's example by placing his own military subordinates in positions of strategic importance in the midlands. But as his own control over the viceroyalty loosened, and as he found himself compelled to compete for office on the basis of political promises, so he showed himself to be increasingly disposed to favour smaller individual enterprises in colonisation. The period when Sidney himself was forced to tender for office coincided with a spate of colonising experiments which were farmed out to independent adventurers among whom were to be counted not only the radical proponents of 1569, but the lesser known Ulster schemes of Christopher Chatterton and Nicholas Malby.[33]

Each of these different approaches to the practical problem of introducing a plantation arose from the distinctive administrative styles of the regimes under which they were authorised. But they shared one common fate: they were all failures. The passivity which was essential to St Leger's general style took its toll on the Palesmen's midlands adventure. Once challenged by the

[29] White's 'Discourse',ed. Canny; see also Piers and Malby to lords justice, 18 Nov. 1567, SP 63/22/28, enclosure (i).
[30] 'Offers of Gerald Aylmer et al.', *c.* 1550, SP 63/2/69; White, 'Tudor plantations', chs. 5–6.
[31] See ch. 3 above.
[32] See ch. 4 above.
[33] White, 'Tudor plantations', ch. 8; R. Dunlop, 'The plantations of Leix and Offaly, pp. 61–96.

clansmen, the deputy was unable to give the necessary military support to the planters, and the Palesmen's fragile effort was soon overwhelmed. St Leger's failure was total, yet its implications were not greatly significant. Since his commitment to plantation was strictly limited, defeat did not fatally damage the image of his administration in Ireland. The loss of a colony, like the collapse of an early surrender and regrant arrangement, could be absorbed by his patient mode of government. Because their attitude to government at large, however, was so different, the failures of St Leger's successors in the area of colonisation were far more grave.

In the first place they attempted much more, not because they gave a particular priority to colonisation, but because they sought to be as active as possible in all fields of policy. And because their range of experiment was so wide, much could – and much did – go badly wrong for them. The failure of Sussex's grand enterprise in the midlands was much more inglorious and expensive for his own administration than St Leger's modest investment. The losses of Sidney's period were less spectacular but more frequent, as the cases of Smith, Essex and the Chattertons witness, and more total. When things did go wrong, moreover, neither Sussex nor Sidney could move as did St Leger to gradual disengagement. Their commitment to programmatic pledges made it imperative for them to attempt to salvage something from the loss at no matter what cost. They were under pressure, that is, to defend whatever remained as a genuine achievement of their original intent. Yet because the fabric of their government was seriously weakened by failures on any front, the greater the loss they suffered, the less they were capable of containing it or adapting to its consequences.

Failure, then, was the common experience of successive colonisation schemes in the high sixteenth century: yet its incidence varied considerably both in character and degree, and its political ramifications differed accordingly. In some areas, such as the Ards and Fews, where failure was complete, the consequences were grave but readily apprehended. There the use of the act of attainder against Shane O'Neill to challenge the claims of native landholders greatly increased fears that English law, far from being a medium of reform, could actually function as an engine of aggression. Yet rather than allaying such fears the practical failure to build upon these legal claims allowed anxieties to fester in the belief that the general reformist aspirations currently advanced in the government's official declarations were mere expedients cloaking the truly expropriative intentions of the crown in a period of temporary weakness. Failed colonial projects thus seriously handicapped the efforts of reforming administrators to persuade the Gaelic chieftains of the sincerity of their intentions and of their practical ability to see them through. Mistrust and disrespect of all Tudor schemes were therefore the natural consequence of such total disasters. But elsewhere, where failure was more gradual, or less easily perceptible, a more subtle yet no less damaging process was under way. In Ulster and in the midlands from amidst the ruins of failed plantation projects a series of hybrid settlements was beginning to take shape whose character and effect was wholly different to that for which colonies were originally intended. Sir Nicholas Bagenal's settlement at Newry was one such hybrid.[34]

Bagenal had originally been granted the extensive possessions of the monastery or 'college' at Newry on extremely generous terms in 1550.[35] The intentions of the grant were conventional: Bagenal was to establish a fortified military colony which was to serve 'for the reduction of those rude and savage quarters to better rule and obedience to the King'.[36] To begin with, Bagenal showed little enthusiasm either for the military or the exemplary aspects of his charge and when Sussex's disfavour resulted in his dismissal as marshal, he sought to be rid of the property altogether. Upon his reappointment to office under Sidney, however, Bagenal returned to Newry with renewed enthusiasm. He defended himself there with increasing success against the incursions of Turlough Luineach O'Neill and his allies, and before long was able to mount retaliatory raids of his own. He formed a close alliance with Hugh O'Neill, the baron of Dungannon, and intrigued to detach the O'Neill vassal clans from Turlough by diplomatic means. But Bagenal had grasped the necessity of reaching a permanent settlement with Turlough for the establishment of political stability in Ulster, and in the late 1570s he made strenuous efforts to persuade the English Privy council to accept his views.[37] By 1586, as lord governor of Ulster, he could recommend no better strategy for the province than the continuation of the policy of containment which he had pursued since his return to Ulster in the mid 1560s.[38]

Not surprisingly, therefore, Bagenal was no favourer of thoroughgoing colonising schemes. He was cool towards Smith, and towards Essex he was positively hostile. In the meantime, his own undertaking at Newly prospered. By 1575, the property which he had acquired for the meagre annual rent of £30 11s 8d was estimated to be worth some £1,640 p.a. and

---

[34] On Bagenal generally, see P. H. Bagenal, 'Sir Nicholas Bagenal, knight marshall', *Jn. RSAI*, 6th ser., 5 (1915), pp. 5–26.

[35] *Cal. pat. rolls Henry VIII–Eliz.*, p. 228.

[36] Bagenal to Fitzwilliam, 16 June 1572, SP 63/36/48 enclosure (i); Bagenal to Walsingham, 15 Sept. 1577, SP 63/59/13; same to same, 28 Nov. 1579, SP 63/70/37; same to same, 8 Nov. 1580, SP 63/78/2.

[37] Bagenal's 'Report on the state of Ulster', *c.* 1586, reprinted in *UJA*, 1st ser., 2 (1854), pp. 137–60.

[38] 'Brief of Mr Bagenal's patents', *c.* 1610, BL, Harl. MSS, 2090.

was believed to enjoy an even greater potential.[39] But the colony was hardly the shining outpost of English civility which the Edwardian privy council had expected. His property was leased out in large lots and his greatest tenants were Gaelic Irishmen. The large tenancies were undoubtedly sub-let in turn, but Bagenal made no conditions as to the way in which they were to be leased. Within the castle and town of Newry, native Irish and new English rubbed shoulders on equal terms as soldiers, and laboured together as tenants.[40] Clearly, Bagenal had no personal interest in fulfilling the costly and unrewarding reformative obligations which the government had imposed upon him. But successive Dublin governors, unable to replace him by someone better, were more than willing to claim his personal survival in Ulster as some sort of achievement for their government. Bagenal ended his career as he had begun it. From his early service as a mercenary to Conn O'Neill until his death as the crown's titular 'lord governor' in the province, he remained a self-interested, but extremely useful, go-between, occupying a twilight zone between Gaelic and English polities, concerned primarily with the defence and extension of his own interests and displaying a cold indifference to the success or failure of classical colonising theory.

Throughout his career in Ireland, Bagenal hardly changed, but his close neighbour in Clandeboy, William Piers, did. Once amongst the strongest advocates of extensive English settlement in the north-east, Piers began to change his mind in the late 1560s and to exploit the immediate possibilities of his situation. He used his solid fortification at Carrickfergus as a base from which to impose his demands upon the surrounding countryside. He did not discriminate in his extortions. The Scots and some of the O'Neills of Clandeboy were his chief prey, but he was the bane of Rowland White's life and eventually put an end to White's little colony at the Dufferin. On the other hand Piers entered a close alliance with the most powerful Irish chieftain of the region, Sir Brian Mac Phelim O'Neill. Sir Brian tolerated Piers' extortionate operations from Carrickfergus while Piers in return left Sir Brian unmolested and used what influence he had to secure his recognition as legitimate ruler of the families of Clandeboy in the eyes of the government. Piers continued to report O'Neill's good service and to recommend him for reward into the early 1570s until he found himself at odds with official government policy.[41] Lord Deputy Fitzwilliam, who

---

[39] 'A rental of lands granted to Sir Henry Bagenal', c. 1575; Bodl., University College MS, no. 103.
[40] Ibid., fos. 121–3.
[41] Lords justice to Eliz., 27 Nov. 1567, enclosing several letters of Piers and Malby, SP 63/22/28 and enclosures (i)–(v); White's 'Memoranda', c. 1568, Hatfield House, Cecil MSS, vol. 201, no. 16; Piers to Weston, 5 Aug. 1569, SP 63/29/30; Piers to Eliz. and to Burghley, 6 July 1571, SP 63/33/172; Piers to Fitzwilliam, 1 Jan. 1572, SP 63/35/2.

believed that Piers had once planned to murder him, was highly disapproving of the captain's dealing with the clansmen. But it was the earl of Essex who almost ruined Piers' career. Convinced that Piers had given Sir Brian vital information about his objectives and vulnerabilities the earl arrested and threatened to execute him.[42] With Sidney's return in 1575, however, Piers' career recovered. Under Sidney's auspices, Piers renewed his old tactics forming a new alliance with the remaining strongman of Clandeboy, Brian Mac Fertagh O'Neill. Like Bagenal, with whom he retained close links, Piers also became aware of the desirability of a genuine reconciliation with Turlough Luineach, and he himself drafted a generous settlement which gave O'Neill control over several vassal clans. The extent to which he had absorbed his experience in Ulster may be measured by the difference between the original colonising 'project' of 1565 and the final 'plat' drafted by this land promoter sometime in 1580.[43] Piers was still intent upon the expulsion of the Scots. But now, although a small group of Englishmen were to play an important supervisory role, Turlough Luineach and the Clandeboy Irish under Brian Mac Fertagh were expected to take the major part in the enterprise. This was to be a joint adventure in conquest: no internal social arrangements were proposed, no reformative intentions were expressed. Thus far had Piers' colonising theory advanced.

It would have been of little consolation to Piers, who had suffered politically and financially from his conflict with Essex, that the earl soon came to accept the underlying logic of his mode of operation. As Essex's own enterprise of Clandeboy became bogged down, as his expenses mounted and his allies deserted, the earl began to seek out other less ambitious ways of establishing himself in Ulster. Increasingly, he became less concerned with the expulsion of the Scots or even with the institution of any plantation in the area, and sued instead for a large portion of Farney where he planned to construct a private place of residence for himself amongst the clansmen.[44] His change of direction was heralded by a marked change of tactics. The reformist claims of his earlier proclamations were forgotten; now sudden and spectacular violence became his principal strategy and it proved effective. The murder of Sir Brian Mac Phelim along with the majority of his followers startled Clandeboy and left the area

[42] Piers to Burghley, 26 Jan. 1574, SP 63/44/17; 'Extracts from letters of the earl of Essex, 6 Sept. 1573 to 24 Nov. 1574', SP 63/48/58.
[43] Piers to Walsingham, 12, 20 June 1580, SP 63/73/54, 59; James Dowdall and Piers to Irish council, 6 Aug. 1580, SP 63/75/20; Piers to Walsingham, 18 Aug., SP 63/75/58; Waterhouse to Walsingham, 25 Jan. 1581, SP 63/80/28; for Piers' 'Plot', see HMC, *De Lisle and Dudley MSS*, II, pp. 87–91.
[44] Essex's 'Instructions to Mr Ashton', June 1575, SP 63/52/17.

temporarily without a Gaelic leader of any significant force or influence. An even more vicious attack upon the MacDonnells almost drove them from the north-east altogether, and in the autumn of 1574, when he moved to Farney, Essex launched the largest punitive campaign ever conducted against Turlough Luineach in Tyrone.[45] But the ends to which this new ruthlessness were directed were strikingly moderate. Almost immediately after the massacre of Sir Brian Mac Phelim, Essex offered the leadership of the entire territory to a successor of his own choosing, Brian Mac Fertagh. He was willing also to make generous terms to Sorley Boy Mac Donnell on the basis of a personal submission. And early in 1575 he entered into a treaty with Turlough Luineach which the Dublin administration thought to be far too liberal.[46] But Essex himself was unconcerned by the precise terms of his treaties. What mattered in all cases was that these personal arrangements depended for their validity on the continuance of good relations between the earl and the other party. After Sidney's reappointment Essex was prepared to accept office from the deputy as lord president of Ulster. But whatever his title, the reality of Essex's newly established position in the province would remain the same. At the time of his sudden death in 1576, Essex, like Bagenal and Piers was poised for ready absorption into the bastard feudal politics of Gaelic Ulster.

The gradual submergence of a plantation effort under the predominant pressures of the surrounding environment traced in the above instances is most apparent in the largest colonising enterprise launched by the crown in the mid-sixteenth century, the plantation of Laois–Offaly. There, the ordered settlement which Sussex claimed to have instituted in 1556 never existed. In reality the area had never been at rest: a continuous guerrilla war had waged between the native clansmen and the settlers which sometimes exploded in eruptions of ferocious violence. A major insurrection in 1564–5 almost razed the plantation, and though the settlers succeeded in rooting out the strongest pockets of resistance, the colony remained vulnerable to damaging raids throughout the decade. In 1573 serious rebellion broke out again in Laois and in the following year spread to Offaly under the leadership of Rory Og O'More, grandson of Callough, the chief of the clan who had been executed under questionable circumstances in 1557. Between 1573 and 1576 Rory, in alliance with groups of the O'Connors, wreaked havoc in both counties. A ruthless campaign of attrition waged by the government

45 Essex to Fitzwilliam, 14 Nov. 1574, SP 63/48/52 enclosure (iii); *AFM* sub anno; Essex to Eliz., 22, 31 July 1575, SP 63/52/67 and *Lives and letters of the Devereux earls*, I, pp. 113–17; Essex to Burghley and to Privy Council, 8 Oct. 1574, SP 63/48/3–4.
46 Waterhouse to Walsingham, 9 July 1575, SP 63/51/51; Essex to Eliz., 22 July, SP 63/52/67; Essex to Walsingham, 23 July, SP 63/52/70 and enclosures; Essex's 'Articles with Turlough Luineach', 27 June 1575, SP 63/52/45; Malby to Walsingham, 5 July, SP 63/52/46.

gradually eroded Rory's support, but the rebellion continued to smoulder until 1578 when Rory himself was captured and killed by Sir Barnaby Fitzpatrick.[47]

Chronic warfare left the plantation exhausted. In 1574 one of the greatest planters in Offaly believed his country to be in a worse state than it ever had been since the beginning of the plantation and gloomily predicted the utter extinction of the entire settlement.[48] Even after the suppression of Rory's rebellion, the settlers declared that the country had been left so utterly waste by his spoiling 'and brought into such poverty that they could never recover themselves'.[49]

There were, however, other consequences to Sussex's failure to maintain his carefully planned experiment in the midlands. First, the settlement ceased to grow. In 1564 there were 88 grantees in the combined territories with some 262 soldier-tenants. Under Sussex's scheme, freeholders and tenants were expected to increase rapidly, but by 1571 the number in both cases had actually fallen slightly. This stagnation was accompanied by a strong tendency for land to become concentrated in the hands of a few large owners.[50] By 1570 Elizabeth was sufficiently alarmed by developments to warn Sidney 'to have good regard that the inhabitants there [Laois–Offaly] do not engross many farms unto few hands', but by then the process was already far advanced.[51] By 1571 the Cosbys had increased their holdings in Laois from 2,000 acres in 1562 to 4,200 acres. In the same period, the Colleys almost trebled their holdings in Offaly. The earl of Kildare had acquired some 5,400 acres in the plantation by 1571 while the Gaelic Irishman, Owen Mac Hugh O'Dempsey, who had been granted only a modest holding at the outset, enjoyed an estate of more than 3,300 acres by the same time.[52] The process of concentration was to continue in the 1570s when late arrivals like Robert Harpole grew to rival the great by displacing lesser settlers.

Engrossment was accompanied by a rising demand for a revision of the terms on which the original grants had been made. The planters sought to have their tenures converted from fee-tail to fee-simple not only because the greater freedom of conveyance allowed thereby would facilitate the process of engrossment, but because their responsibility for the early decay of the

---

47 On the early history of the plantation generally, see Dunlop, 'The plantation of Leix–Offaly', pp. 61–96 and John O'Hanlon and E. O'Leary, *History of the Queen's County* (2 vols., London 1907), II, chs. 15–17.
48 Henry Colley to Burghley, 22 Jan. 1574, SP 63/44/14.
49 'Petition of the gentlemen in Queen's County', SP 63/62/32–4.
50 See White, 'The Tudor plantations', II, chs. 12, 20, and appendices 2 and 3.
51 Eliz. to Sidney, 17 May 1570, *Sid. SP*, no. 75.
52 See White, 'The Tudor plantations', appendices (ii) and (iv).

plantation's objectives would be greatly lessened.[53] It was, indeed, the government's fear that such enlargements would accelerate the return of the native Irish as freeholders in officially proscribed areas that determined its unfriendly responses to the request. But by the early 1570s the extent of Gaelic infiltration into hitherto prohibited areas was already very great. Native labourers had never been excluded from the English and Anglo-Norman zones of the settlement, but in the original scheme their numbers were to be strictly limited. By the early 1560s, however, a notable relaxation had occurred: the grants then issued specifically prohibited subinfeudation only to such Irish 'as have estates of inheritance within King's County and Queen's County'.[54] Native tenants were admitted in large numbers in the restricted zones, however, throughout the 1560s and protected from the full force of law by their own landlords. Native Irishmen, like Sir Barnaby Fitzpatrick and Owen Mc Hugh O'Dempsey, moreover, attained positions of major importance in the governance of the plantation. Under Sidney, Fitzpatrick became lieutenant of Laois, thus enjoying a title which Sussex had once specifically reserved for his own brother.[55] O'Dempsey was recognised by the government as one of the greatest defenders of the plantation in Offaly; and, for a time, under Fitzwilliam's recommendation, the crown seriously considered granting him the lordship of Galin to the west of the county on condition that he banish the outlawed O'Connors and establish an independent colony of his own there in the classical style.[56] That the idea of granting such autonomous powers to a Gaelic Irishman should be seriously considered as late as 1573 is a striking indication of the extent to which the plantation had diverged from the objectives which Sussex had laid down.

Engrossment and the infiltration of Gaelic freeholders and tenants, however, led to an even more serious source of decay within the plantation. The few who grew great in these circumstances did so by adopting the political and social mores of the clansmen who surrounded them. Kildare's use of Gaelic kerne over whom he had been given charge by the government for his own personal and quite illegal purposes has already been noticed.[57] But his neighbours in the plantation were hardly more restrained. Sir Francis Cosby, Fitzpatrick, O'Dempsey, Henry Colley, the government's chief officer in Offaly, and his successor, Edward More, all extended their patronage to delinquent septs of the O'Mores and O'Connors for their own

---

[53] 'Memorial for . . . Ireland causes', Apr. 1570, SP 63/30/40; Elizabeth to Sidney, 6 June 1569, *Sid. SP*, no. 65.
[54] *Fiants Eliz.*, no. 474.
[55] Ibid., *Fiants Eliz.*, no. 2844.
[56] Fitzwilliam to Burghley, 7 Apr. 1571, SP 63/32/3, 'Note of Ireland suits', 1571?, SP 63/34/45; Fitzwilliam to Burghley, 10 Aug. 1573, Bodl., Carte MSS, 56/204.
[57] See ch. 4 above.

purposes and ignored the clansmen's disorders and flagrant disregard of English law. When a personal feud broke out between Fitzpatrick and More, each set about recruiting additional kerne without any regard for the welfare of the settlement, 'the Lieutenant retaining one sort of the O'Connors and Mr. More another so as through their overthwart dealings the country is utterly spoilt and become waste for the most part, and the rebels enabled thereby'.[58] Cosby and O'Dempsey also employed kerne to their own purposes. O'Dempsey made much use of some septs of the O'Mores in a feud with the O'Molloys and as a means of foisting a protection racket upon the smaller freeholders of Laois. Cosby alleged that O'Dempsey was intent upon driving the settlers to ruin.[59] Despite his indignation, however, Cosby himself closely emulated O'Dempsey's practices. For he too was notorious as 'a great devourer of Englishmen', and he too formed an alliance with a leading sept of the O'Mores in order to serve his purposes.[60] From the late 1560s, Cosby had been a friend and protector to Rory Og O'More 'until he had grown out into a great, great force' in Laois.[61] His friendship with Rory not only gave Cosby's own property immunity from attack, but also enabled him to mount awesome pressure upon his neighbours. On at least one occasion, Cosby's attempts to intimidate lesser freeholders led him into serious trouble with the privy council.[62] Rory's defiance in 1573, however, severed this particular alliance for good: after this it was war to the death on both sides.

Yet even the highly energetic response of Cosby and his fellow grandees to Rory's rebellion tended only to underline the degree to which they had departed from the original aims of the plantation. As the rebellion dragged on the grandees and the lesser freeholders came to agree that their mutual security could be guaranteed only by the utter extirpation of all the landless septs in the plantation. In 1576 a number of Offaly planters some of whom were themselves Gaelic Irishmen proposed the most ruthless of strategies for dealing with the chronic troubles of the area. The clansmen, they urged, should be driven to 'straight corners in the country and there cut short by those appointed to go there'.[63] Cosby and the other big planters in Laois had already come to the same conclusion. The ruthless retribution they visited on any who offered Rory succour was intended to stamp out potential

---

[58] 'Complaint of the Offaly freeholders', 1576, NAI, MS 2552; see also Irish council order, 3 Mar. 1573, Bodl., Carte MSS, 56/58.
[59] Cosby to Fitzwilliam, 16 Dec. 1573, Bodl., Carte MSS, 56/248; Fitzwilliam to Cosby, 10 Jan., ibid., 56/206.
[60] Malby's(?) 'Notes on Ireland', BL, Add. MSS, 48015, fo. 191. N. White to Burghley, 17 July 1573, SP 63/41/180; 'Petitions of Offaly freeholders', NAI, MS 2552.
[61] 'Petitions of Offaly freeholders', NAI, MS 2552.
[62] Privy Council to Fitzwilliam, 6 July 1573, Bodl., Carte MSS, 56/300–1.
[63] 'Petition of Offaly freeholders', NAI, MS 2552.

pockets of resistance for ever.[64] Even Rory's own death did not curb their rage: they were determined to forestall the possibility that his mantle should ever fall to a successor. To that end, sometime in 1578, Cosby and Robert Harpole summoned Lysagh Mac Conall the remaining leader of the O'Mores and several septs of the clan to a parley at Mullaghmast on the borders of Kildare. The ostensible reason for the meeting was the settlement of all disputes outstanding on the death of Rory O'More, but 'as they entered that place they were surrounded on every side by four lines of soldiers and cavalry who proceeded to shoot and slaughter them without mercy'; few escaped.[65] The killing was a preface to no renewed programme of reform. Like Essex's conduct in Ulster, the violence was simply a fearful revenge on insolent subordinates who had deigned to withstand the ruling powers. Thereafter, Cosby could look for due respect among natives and settlers alike.

The massacre at Mullaghmast gave lurid proof of the failure of the reform objectives of the original project to plant in the midlands. Yet it was also the inevitable consequence of a process which had begun many years before. The reasons behind the planters' ready adaptation to their local environment were mixed. In part their conversion had been a matter of sheer expediency: having been abandoned by a government incapable of fulfilling its obligations towards them, they had little other means of survival. Yet their reaction was also greatly influenced by their realisation that the Gaelic ways were the surest avenues to power and profit. The 'very sweetness' of the Gaelic system, as Tremayne would have put it, offered newcomers like Cosby, More, Bagenal and Piers opportunities which they could never have enjoyed had they fulfilled their duties strictly as officers of the crown. Thus the central government's loss of control over colonisation at a time when so many individual projects had been sanctioned resulted not only in the failure of the attempt to introduce English law and custom by way of practical example, but also in an intensification of the existing methods of Gaelic political action. In the midlands as in Ulster, colonies did not as was envisaged reform the evils of Gaelic political culture: they merely compounded them.

The degeneration of the enterprise of colonisation would not of itself, however, have been a source of dismay to the promoters of reform. Had it occurred in isolation, the reformers would have been capable of discovering some acceptable rationale or even particular explanations for the loss.

---

[64] For a general account, see O'Hanlon and O'Leary, *History of Queen's County*, ch. 16.

[65] 'Account of the massacre of Mullaghmast', RIA, MS 12.0.12; *AFM s.a.*, see O'Donovan's extensive note on the affair, vol. V, pp. 1694–7; *Dowling's Annals* (Irish Arch. Soc., 1849), pp. 42–3.

Genuine bewilderment arose only when the very same process began to afflict a quite different policy which, far more than colonisation, they regarded as the central means of pacifying Ireland: the internal reform of the Gaelic lordships.

THE REFORM OF THE LORDSHIPS

(i)

By the early 1550s St Leger's policy of effecting the peaceful reform of the native lordships from within had undergone significant development. The hurried formal agreements, the passing of patents, the visits to court and the ceremonial endowment of titles that had marked the first propagandist phase of the policy had now ceased and a series of *ad hoc* treaties securing short-term understandings, but deferring permanent settlement had taken their place. The changes were in part a response to the serious problems which the policy had encountered. But they did not constitute a withdrawal from the ultimate objectives of the policy. St Leger, Bellingham and Crofts, as we have seen, continued to work for the extension and consolidation of reform, and despite their criticisms of their predecessors, neither Sussex nor Sidney contemplated the abandonment of internal reform as a central government policy. The chief aim of his policy towards the Gaelic Irish, Sussex professed, was to ensure that 'every one possessed of the captaincy of his nation should be induced to leave that tenure and to take the same from the prince to him and his heir male'.[66] In 1565 Sidney's declared aim was no different: the 'Irish captains should be induced as they have heretofore offered to take estates of their land by way of inheritance to them and to their heirs male'.[67] Both also adopted the traditional techniques of establishing preliminary relations with the Irish captains. Like Grey and St Leger before them, they made frequent and extensive tours of the provinces with the intent of impressing the Gaelic lords with their power and authority. Sussex had plans to bring his parliament of 1556 to Limerick in order to allow the Munster Irish to participate and Sidney sought to gain the attendance of as many gaelic captains as possible at his projected parliament of 1566.[68] These, admittedly, were unrealised ambitions. But the practical achievements of both men elsewhere were by no means insignificant.

Sussex's and Sidney's shared antagonism towards Shane O'Neill, Sussex's

---

[66] Sussex's 'Opinion', 1562, Lambeth MSS, 609, fo. 1.
[67] Sidney's 'Instructions', 5 Oct. 1565, SP 63/15/4.
[68] 'A present remedy for the reformation of the north'. ? 1556, SP 62/1/13; Sidney to privy council, 13 Apr. 1566, SP 63/17/8.

deep dislike for Desmond and Sidney's for Thomond, have given rise to the false impression that neither was in sympathy with the general conciliatory spirit of internal reform. Alternative explanations have already been offered above to account for these particular cases, but no matter how they are to be interpreted, they have unnecessarily distracted attention from the far more numerous, if less well known, instances in which the ends of reform were enthusiastically pursued by both governors. Sussex, for instance, was particularly anxious to establish a peaceful settlement with MacCarthy More whom he considered to be one of the most powerful and yet friendly men in Munster, and one 'very desirous' to have his estates confirmed to him by surrender. Sussex knighted MacCarthy in 1558 and repeatedly urged Elizabeth to raise him to the peerage, until, at length, the captain completed the formal process of surrender at Westminster in 1565 and had the title, earl of Clancar, conferred upon him.[69] Sussex also secured similar surrenders in Munster from O'Sullivan Beare and MacCarthy of Muskerry.[70] But his main interest lay in Ulster. He was quick to renew relations which St Leger had already established with the lesser captains of the province who sought to be free of pressure from the O'Neills. Early in his first term of office, Sussex toured the province outside Tyrone, settling what disputes had arisen amongst the captains and confirming the arrangements they had made with St Leger. Before he departed he had gained their agreement to attend upon hostings and to supply victuals to the government's troops on campaign. Typically, Sussex exaggerated the importance of these initial agreements. Yet they proved to be more resistant to pressure from Tyrone than might have been expected. The services he had demanded continued to be erratically acknowledged by the captains and Sussex was able to preserve tenuous diplomatic links with most of their number throughout his period in office.[71]

Even his least successful liaison with the MacMahons of Fermanagh was not without some result. MacMahon promised allegiance only if Sussex would 'kill none of his people', and the lieutenant was once compelled to spoil the territory in order to prevent the captains' withdrawal to O'Neill. But throughout, MacMahon yielded up supplies and paid a fitful attendance upon hostings against Shane, and Sussex conveyed the conventional

[69] 'Journey made by the earl of Sussex', June to July 1558, Lambeth MSS, 621/23; Sussex's 'Instructions', 16 July 1559, SP 63/1/60; 'Memoranda for Sussex', May 1561, SP 63/3/76; Eliz. to MacCarthy More, 28 Feb. 1565, SP 63/12/41; 'Oath of MacCarthy More . . . earl of Clancar', 24 June 1565, SP 63/13/76; GEC, Peerage, III, p. 214.
[70] 'Matters to be ordered with Desmond', 20 May 1562, SP 63/3/11; privy council to Lord Justice Arnold, 22 June 1565, SP 63/13/69; H. W. Gillman, 'Sir Cormac McTeig MacCarthy', Jn. Cork Hist. Arch. Soc., ser. 1, 1 (1892), pp. 192–200.
[71] Irish council book, HMC, Haliday MSS, pp. 8–9; 'Journey made by Sussex', June to Aug. 1556, Lambeth MSS, 621/15 ff.

recommendations of his service to the queen.[72] Matters were better with the O'Reillys. In 1558 Sussex arbitrated a series of disputes between the chief Maolmordha and the borderers of the Pale. Having convinced O'Reilly of the crown's good-will and induced him to join in the alliance against O'Neill, Sussex placed an exceptional confidence in the chieftain, reporting his good service to the privy council and recommending that he be created earl of the Brenny. O'Reilly, he argued was already so civil and so bound to the government that no president or intermediary official would be required to monitor his activities for the crown: he should be allowed to deal directly with the chief governor.[73] Sussex, however, established his closest personal links with a lesser chief who had attained an unusually high degree of formal education, Shane Maguire. Maguire, who corresponded in English with Sussex and with Lady Sussex, was the lieutenant's chief confidant in Ulster, and Sussex was particularly anxious to have him confirmed in his title and elevated to the peerage.[74] Less intimate, but more strategically important, was Sussex's alliance with Callough O'Donnell. Callough was less attractive and more insecure in his own territory than most of the other Ulster chieftains with whom Sussex dealt. But his claims to succeed to his father's title were undeniable and Sussex was determined to complete the process of assimilation begun years previously with Manus even to the point of concluding a formal, if rapid, surrender of Tyrconnell at a time when the unfortunate Callough had little authority left in his territory to offer up.[75]

As in every other sphere, Sidney did not depart from Sussex's practice; he simply did more. On his first tour of Connacht he received the assent of several lesser chieftains to preliminary demands similar to those which Sussex had made on the Ulster Irish. Like Sussex, he was confident that these initial arrangements would in time give way to the more normal processes of surrender and regrant, since many of the captains, like O'Hara, had fallen 'in such love of Englishmen and English government as he vowed to go into

---

72 Sussex and Council to Eliz., 16 July 1561, SP 63/4/22; Sussex and council to privy council, 26 May 1563, SP 63/8/50; Sussex to P. Mac Rory, 5 Nov. 1562, BL, Cotton MSS, Vespasian F XII, no. 74.

73 'Memoranda for Ireland', 13 Mar. 1561, SP 63/33/36; 'Memoranda for Sussex', May 1561, SP 63/33/76; Eliz. to Sussex, 27 May, SP 63/33/83; Sussex to Cecil, 17 July 1561, SP 63/4/23; O'Reilly et al. to Sussex, Oct.–Nov. 1562, BL, Cotton MSS, Vespasian F XII, nos. 25, 63, 64, 75; Sussex's 'Opinions', *c.* June 1562, Lambeth MSS, 609, fo. 14 and his 'Relation', *c.* Dec. 1562, ibid., 614/225 ff.

74 Sussex's 'Opinion', Lambeth MSS, 609, fo. 14 and his 'Relation', 614, fos. 225 ff., Sussex and Council to privy council, 26 Oct. 1562, enclosing Maguire to Sussex, 20 Oct., SP 63/7/34 and enclosure (i); Maguire to Sussex, 25 Nov., SP 63/7/48 and 15 Aug., 20 Oct., 9 Dec., BL, Cotton MSS, Vespasian F XII, nos. 46, 92 and 42; Sussex to Maguire, 9 Nov., ibid., no. 88; Sussex's 'Relation', *c.* Dec. 1562, Lambeth MSS, 614, fos. 225 ff.

75 *DNB*, s.v., 'Callough O'Donnell'; Eliz. to Sussex, 22(?) May 1561, SP 63/3/76; Sussex to Cecil, 17 July, SP 63/4/23; *Fiants Eliz.*, no. 602.

England and to behold the majesty of our sovereign'.[76] In 1567 not only O'Hara, but O'Connor Sligo and the son and heir of O'Reilly, departed with Sidney to conclude formal surrenders at court.[77] In his second tour of duty, Sidney entered into further preliminary arrangements with the O'Rourkes and the MacGeoghans and successfully completed a division of the Annaley amongst the O'Farrells, who had recognised no single chieftain.[78]

It has sometimes been suggested that such general encouragement of the lesser chieftains was no more than a Machiavellian attempt to undermine the power of the great lords. But the degree to which these exercises deviated from the original purposes of reform should not be exaggerated. St Leger's attempt to establish a settlement among the O'Tooles and his plans for the partition of Thomond indicate that he was willing to recognise political divisions within the lordships wherever it seemed necessary; and he clearly envisaged the eventual release of all the vassals from their overlords even though he could see no means of accomplishing the work at once. This strategic orientation, then, appeared to originate with Sussex and Sidney only because they employed it on a large scale. In this as in everything else, they were simply more energetic and audacious, deeming to be immediately feasible what their predecessor had merely regarded as desirable.

The governors' attitude towards the great lords was never in any case one of unrelieved hostility. Both Sussex and Sidney recognised that the overlords would have to be compensated in some measure for their loss of authority, and in practice displayed a surprising tolerance of the overarching claims of provincial powers. Sussex's determination to defend a settlement in Thomond that was unrealistically favourable to the earl has already been discussed, but Sidney was also capable of generous concessions, as his agreement with Turlough Luineach O'Neill in 1567 testifies.[79] Sidney's plans for Turlough were forestalled by events in England; but though he never achieved his aim and though he seemed at times to be willing to abandon it, the establishment of Turlough as a stable power in Ulster remained central to Sidney's northern policy. Even in 1575 after innumerable indications of Turlough's undependability, Sidney still hoped for a permanent settlement. He persuaded Turlough to withdraw the inflated demands he had made on Essex and to petition for a renewal of the 1567 terms. Sidney promoted

---

[76] Sidney to Elizabeth, 20 Apr. 1567, SP 63/20/66; 'Memoranda of the division of O'Connor Sligo's co etc', Dec. 1567, SP 63/22/60; Sidney's 'Memoir', *UJA*, 1st ser., 3 (1855), p. 97.

[77] Sidney and council to Eliz., 12 Nov. 1566, SP 63/14/43; Eliz. to lords justice, 25 Jan. 1568, SP 63/23/17; Eliz. to lords justice, 24 Feb. 1568, SP 63/23/51; *Cal. pat. rolls Henry VIII–Eliz. I*, pp. 495, 507; Indentures of O'Donnell and O'Reilly, 24 Oct., 28 Nov., 1566, Lambeth MSS, 614, fos. 155–7.

[78] 'Indentures with O'Farrells', 11 Feb. 1571, Lambeth MSS, 611, fos. 170 and 175.

[79] 'Memorial delivered by Mr Knight', 15 June 1567, SP 63/21/20, 'Submissions' of Turlough, 18 June 1567, SP 63/21/22: 'Note of Sidney's letters', 5 July, SP 63/21/48.

the suit enthusiastically, recommending that Turlough be made earl of Clanconnell and his sons barons 'of some one place'.[80] In 1578 Sidney renewed his promise to secure a satisfactory settlement for Turlough and when he left Ireland the patents making Turlough an earl and a baron had already been drawn up.[81]

Neither in theory nor in practice did Sussex or Sidney abandon the policy of gradual reform. It remained for both as it had been for St Leger the centrepiece of the project to establish the English government's authority in Gaelic Ireland. But if the alteration of government after 1556 entailed no fundamental change in policy, the particular pressures placed upon these administrations committed to the execution of specific programmes seriously influenced the way in which the policy was to be implemented. Neither Sussex nor Sidney could afford the leisurely approach required by St Leger's delicate process of acclimatisation. The terms of their service precluded the possibility of allowing final settlements to mature slowly from within; they had rather to be arrived at quickly, and imposed, moreover, from without. This demand for tangible results, hastily achieved, exercised a malign influence on two levels. In general it introduced a rigidity into the diplomatic process which St Leger's subtle manoeuvrings had sought to evade. The achievements of the governors had to be expressed in concrete ways through legitimate lineages safely established, through allegiance constantly reaffirmed, through revenues gained: the quieter success of a developing relationship, well supervised, was not enough. Much more was promised, much more undertaken, and so, as in the case of colonisation, much more was placed at risk. The rush towards stability produced, however, a second, less obvious but extremely difficult problem. How, during the course of their administrations, were the governors to handle those areas where conditions did not allow of rapid assimilation or an easily imposed solution, but promised instead to degenerate into dangerous factional strife?

The first of these problems was the most obvious. Sussex's commitment to uphold all existing settlements which had been confirmed by royal treaty led him to adopt an attitude which was wholly inappropriate to conditions in Thomond and Tyrone. Thus, despite the remarkably sensitive appreciation of the difficulties involved in introducing reform in the lordships which he displayed in his lengthy memoranda on the subject, Sussex's actual

---

[80] 'Lord Deputy Sidney's requests', 22 Dec. 1575, SP 63/54/22; Turlough Luineach to Eliz., 16 Nov., SP 63/53/61; Sidney to Privy Council, 15 June 1576, SP 63/55/58; for a detailed discussion of Turlough's relations with the English government throughout his career, see Joseph Costello, 'Turlough Luineach O'Neill: the urrithe and the central government', unpub. MA thesis (UCD, 1973).

[81] 'Patent creating Turlough Luineach . . . earl of Clanconnell', 10 May 1578, SP 63/60/60.

dealings in Gaelic Ireland degenerated rapidly into confrontation and interminable war. The circumstances of Sidney's appointment allowed him to be more flexible in these matters of succession, yet he too had incurred extraneous obligations which levelled an equal burden on the prospects of reform. In promising to govern Ireland not only more efficiently but also more economically, Sidney was compelled to look upon surrender and regrant both as a way of producing political stability and as a means of raising revenue. The idea that surrender and regrant could be profitable was not new. St Leger and Sussex both believed that a substantial rental might eventually be raised from the reformed lordships. Sussex had made detailed estimates of potential gains and had actually begun to collect a fraction of the sum.[82] But Sidney set out with the clear intention of realising Sussex's projections as soon as possible. Far from being a late stage in the process, the collection of a rent should be the very first; by 1571, however, Sidney had received only £593 in such payments and even this small sum was uncertain.[83] Yet when Sidney returned to office to implement his policy of composition in 1575, he made it clear that the immediate payment of a tax was the essential prerequisite to any further development of reform.[84]

The effects of this narrowing and intensification of the reform objective that had occurred under the Elizabethan viceroys were several. Inevitably demands for unswerving allegiance or the payment of a rent made the native lords wary of entering too quickly into close relations with the government or of pursuing those agreements they had already made with great enthusiasm. Thus, however much they may have valued the long-term benefits of reform, the immediate incentives presented to them were far from attractive. Inhibitions of this kind, moreover, were considerably strengthened by a second, rather different consequence of the Elizabethan governors' programmatic innovations: that is, the successive decline and failure of their administrations. As their inability to discharge their specific undertakings led to their discredit and recall, so their larger ambitions for a general reform remained frozen as mere aspirations with little relevance to immediate realities. Sussex's carefully considered proposal to establish mixed constitutions in the Gaelic lordships during the process of transition never bore fruit, and the benefits which Sidney was confident would rapidly follow upon the acceptance of his composition scheme were never realised.

---

[82] Sussex's 'Opinion', *c.* June 1562, Lambeth MSS, 609; 'A brief declaration of the revenues ... 1564', SP 63/17/8 enclosure (ii).

[83] See, for instance, Sidney's 'Indentures with O'Farrells', 11 Feb. 1571, Lambeth MSS, 611/170 and 175.

[84] Note of revenues received by Sidney, SP 63/64/1.

The repeatedly abortive character of Elizabethan reform projects profoundly disturbed the pattern of relationships between the government and the native lordships in a manner that paralleled the failure of so many contemporaneous colonial schemes. Within the lordships themselves, the repeated interruption of the reform process was the cause of greatly increased political tensions, multiplying the difficulties of those lords and freeholders who had declared a willingness to support the government and encouraging those who opposed them to redouble their efforts at subversion. In their efforts to maintain their authority in these troubled times, several chieftains such as O'Reilly, Maguire and O'Donnell sought to contain these internal tensions by allowing them to find representation from within their own immediate family, encouraging some of their sons to maintain good relations with Dublin, while permitting others to act as leaders of the military opposition. This fissuring of the ruling dynasties was progressive, and it was to exert catastrophic effects on Irish politics in the wake of the collapse of the last great reform effort launched by Sir John Perrot.[85] But even before that crisis emerged, the expedients to which Perrot's predecessors were driven in order to maintain some presence in troubled areas over which they could exert no directly effective influence powerfully assisted the enemies of reform. For, as in the case of colonisation, the greatest disturbance arose not in those regions where the failure of reform was total, but where the agencies of English law, having survived after a fashion, began to function in a way far different from that for which they had originally been intended.

As their energies became increasingly absorbed by the demands of their specific undertakings, the immediate problem faced by Sussex and Sidney in regard to Gaelic Ireland as a whole was to find a means of exerting some influence in the affairs of the troublesome lordships which if it did not reform them would at least prevent them from presenting an unexpected embarrassment to their overcommitted administrations. The solution happened on by both men was the same, and it was not in conception at any rate novel: this was the seneschal system.

(ii)

Originally denoting the chief officer in a feudal lord's household, the office of seneschal gradually acquired larger administrative responsibilities. In late medieval Ireland, seneschal was the title normally given to the chief

---

[85] For further discussion of these issues see Brady, 'The O'Reillys of East Breifne', pp. 233–62, and 'Sixteenth-century Ulster and the failure of Tudor reform' in Brady, O'Dowd and Walker (eds.), *Ulster: an illustrated history*, pp. 77–103.

administrative figure of the great palatine liberties.[86] In the early sixteenth century the Dublin administration assumed responsibility for appointing seneschals in liberties no longer under the direct rule of a feudal lord. To begin with, the procedure was innocuous: local families like the Synotts in Wexford or the Savages in the Ards continued to occupy the office under the crown as they had done under their lord. The act against absentees (1536), however, which granted the crown title to abandoned seignories paved the way for major change.[87] In 1553 the appointment of Francis Agard as seneschal in Wexford marked the first occasion when a government servitor was preferred over a local figure for the office.[88] This transfer of the feudal powers of the seneschal to an officer of the crown was of immense political significance. But it was not until Sussex came to Ireland that the larger possibilities of the office were explored.

Under St Leger a number of border forts to defend the Pale and other English areas from attack had been erected. By mid-century, however, several of the wards had been abandoned, and some like Dungarvan and Wicklow were in the hands of local families. St Leger made some attempt to assert the government's authority in Leinster, but only one of his appointees, Brian Jones at Carlow, remained after his departure.[89]

It was Sussex who instituted genuine reform. He not only reconstructed Bellingham's forts in the midlands, but also undertook the rebuilding of the wards at Ferns, Leighlin and Athlone, placing men of his own appointment in each.[90] He renewed Agard's appointment in Wexford and removed Dungarvan from the Walshes.[91] Sussex also extended the powers and responsibilities of the new warders. They were now charged to keep order among the native septs against whom they had hitherto maintained only a defensive posture. Jacques Wingfield, the constable of Dublin Castle, was given responsibility for the O'Byrnes and O'Tooles, and Nicholas Heron at Leighlin 'the keeping of the Kavanaghs'. Seneschal Agard was made constable at Ferns and given charge of certain septs of the same

[86] *OED*, s.v.; T. B. Butler, 'Seneschals of the Liberty of Tipperary', *Irish Genealogist* 2–3 (1955–7), see note by 'Kevin' (R. C. Simington), *Catholic Bulletin* III (1923), pp. 203–4; see also R. F. Frame, 'The Dublin administration and the Gaelic Irish in the later middle ages', unpub. PhD thesis (Dublin University, 1974).

[87] *Irish Statutes*, 28 Henry VIII, c. 3, p. 84.

[88] *Fiants Eliz.*, no. 24; other Englishmen had held the office previously, but they were local landowners, not servants of the crown.

[89] For Dungarvan, see *Fiants Eliz.*, no. 558; Wicklow, ibid., no. 138; HMC, *De Lisle and Dudley MSS*, I, p. 304.

[90] 'Sidney's Accounts 1556–9', HMC, *De Lisle and Dudley MSS*, I, p. 378; *Fiants Eliz.*, nos. 171, 251; Sussex's 'Relation of service', *c.* Dec. 1562, Lambeth MSS, 614/225 ff.

[91] HMC, *De Lisle and Dudley MSS*, I, 'Sidney's Accounts', 1556–9, pp. 372–9; *Fiants Eliz.*, no. 39.

clan.[92] The constables were issued with impressive commissions of peace and array which allowed them to billet and victual their men at their discretion, to imprison, fine and 'prosecute by fire and sword those enemies and rebels who should attempt any evil against the crown'.[93] In addition, they were given command over Gaelic contingents from their area on general hostings and allowed to exercise martial law over the conscripted clansmen. By the time he left Ireland. Sussex's revitalised constables were firmly in place in Leinster, and he recommended strongly that his system be extended throughout the country.[94]

Sidney took the advice. On his first tour of Leinster, he confirmed Heron in his position, appointed Robert Pipho over the septs of west Wicklow, replaced Wingfield by Agard as controller of the O'Byrnes and recommended Stuckley for Agard's place in Wexford. Sidney also made one further advance. He confirmed the constables in the enlarged powers which Sussex had bestowed upon them by extending to some of them the other title enjoyed by the constable at Wexford: he called them seneschals.[95]

In the years following 1566, the seneschal system was gradually extended throughout the country and the powers of the office were formally ratified. Seneschals appointed in Westmeath, Clare and Galway were made responsible for the payment of all new rents and services and were required to oversee the conversion of Gaelic military service, or 'bonnaught', into a cash payment. They were authorised to undertake the 'booking' of the clansmen and were held responsible for the apprehension of proclaimed rebels and outlaws in their territories through the use of martial law. Yet the exemplary and educative purposes which characterised the presidential idea were absent from their brief. They were given no instructions to observe the procedures of common law where possible: their task was simply to maintain order and raise a revenue by whatever means they might. The appointment of seneschals, of course, marked no deliberate withdrawal from the assimilative objectives represented by a presidency. The office was regarded as a temporary expedient. Seneschals were intended to stabilise the lordship during the delicate opening phases of its contact with English government. As the lordship gradually became more accustomed to the ways of English governance, the seneschalship was expected to be replaced by the conventional sheriff. Reality, however, was to belie these hopes. The presence of English government officials amidst the Gaelic lordships was in time

---

[92] Irish council book, HMC, *Haliday MSS*, p. 20; *Fiants Eliz.*, no. 218; HMC, *De Lisle and Dudley MSS*, I, p. 82.
[93] Irish council book, HMC, *Haliday MSS*, pp. 20–2; Commission to Cosby and Strafford, 23 Jan. 1558, *Cal. pat. rolls Henry VIII–Eliz.*, p. 408.
[94] Sussex's 'Opinion', *c.* June 1562, Lambeth MSS, 609, passim.
[95] Sidney and council to privy council, 13, 15 Apr. 1566, SP 63/17/8 and 13, and 13 (i).

expected to exercise a powerful cultural influence over the clansmen, but the process worked in reverse.[96]

The Englishmen who filled the post of seneschal were a varied group. They had not all come to Ireland at the same time and they were not all connected with the same affinity. But they did display some collective characteristics. All were men of some previous military experience: few had any expertise in law.[97] They showed, moreover, little enthusiasm for religious reform. Only one, Francis Agard, was noted to be a promoter of the reformed church but at least two others were alleged to be papists. Most were indifferent, preferring, like the constable of Dungarvan, to surround themselves with men who enjoyed the company of 'a hawk, a whore and a hound' to men who read their bibles.[98] Some, like Cosby and Agard, were related by blood before they came to Ireland, but many more established such connections by marriage.[99] Robert Harpole's son and heir married Henry Davells' daughter, and another Harpole son married Francis Cosby's daughter, Cosby's eldest son reciprocated by marrying Harpole's daughter. Another of Cosby's daughters married into Sir Henry Sidney's family, while Henry Harrington became Sidney's son-in-law. Mary Agard was betrothed to Sir Warham St Leger. A son of Nicholas Heron married a daughter of Marshal Bagenal. Through these interlinkages and connections with influential figures in Irish government, the seneschals established themselves collectively as part of a national power elite.[100]

Interaction amongst them however, was not always harmonious. Harpole, the constable at Carlow, greatly distrusted Robert Pipho, the seneschal of west Wicklow. Thomas Masterson, the seneschal of Wexford quarrelled first with Henry Davells at Dungarvan and later with Harrington, the seneschal of the O'Byrnes. Harrington collided seriously with the earl of Kildare and Masterson carried on a long feud with the wealthy English

---

[96] *Fiants Eliz.*, nos. 1409, 1564, 1618, 2415; see powers conferred upon the seneschal of the O'Farrells, 11 Feb. 1571, Lambeth MSS, 611/170–5; see also Kevin (R. C. Simington), 'Note on powers of seneschal'.

[97] Stucley, *DNB*, sv; Heron, *LP Henry VIII, 21 (1545)*, pt. II, p. 79; John Hooker, *Life of Sir Peter Carew*; White to Cecil, 9 Feb. 1570, SP 63/30/12.

[98] Gerrard's 'Notes on the Irish officers, lawyers, etc.', Oct. 1576, SP 63/56/45–6; the papists were Stuckley and Wingfield, 'Bishop Gardner's true disciple' (see Fitzwilliam to Burghley, 18 June 1573, Bodl., Carte MSS, 56/171–3); 'Charges against the Constable of Dungarvan', 30 Jan. 1569, ibid., 58/775.

[99] 'Genealogy of the Cosbys of Stradbally', G.O. MS 161, pp. 54–6, 61, 'Genealogy of the Cosbys of Stradbally', compiled by W. Fitzgerald, *Jn. Kildare Arch. Soc.* 5 (1906–9), pp. 316–17; 'Genealogy of the Harpoles', ibid., 4 (1903–5) between pp. 300–1.

[100] Fitzgerald, 'Genealogy of the Harpoles', A. Collins, *Letters and memorials of state*, I, pp. 79–82, 97; Waterhouse to Walsingham, 17 July 1581, SP 63/84/24; 'Note of Ireland suits', May 1582, SP 63/92/124; Henry Sheffield to Burghley, 29 Mar. 1587, *Cal. State Papers (Ire.) 1586–8*, pp. 288–9.

settlers in Wexford, the Colcoughs.[101] Thus, though they may be seen to have formed a coherent social group, the English seneschals did not constitute an administrative unit bound by a common *esprit de corps*. The characteristics they shared were those of personal background and a common personal interest in the future; they bore little relation to the general purposes of government.

As might be expected, then, their execution of their responsibilities was erratic and negligent. Their wards were often inadequately furnished. Robert Harpole, it was alleged, kept no more than half of the assigned complement of troops at Leighlin Bridge. Despite Sussex's efforts, the fort there was declared by a survey of 1574 to be almost beyond repair.[102] Dungarvan was noted by Sidney in 1576 to be in dire need of reconstruction; by 1581, Ferns was an abandoned ruin.[103] This general decay, however, was by no means a symptom of apathy; for even as they allowed their official residences to decay, the seneschals were busy acquiring extensive personal holdings in the areas under their authority.[104]

Similarly, the seneschals had no qualms in departing even from the loose guidelines laid down for their conduct. Their sessions and the laws applied in them were dubious: pledges and restitutions were accepted, open pardons were frequently granted. They took bribes and exacted perquisites. They became immersed in the prevailing factionalism, making alliance with certain septs in their areas and sometimes taking their allies into formal government service. Few, however, went so far as Pipho, who married into the chief sept of the O'Byrnes. Their governmental responsibilities were soon blurred by these informal alliances. Complaints of the despoiled were ignored, known outlaws were sheltered, witnesses intimidated and the country was not infrequently left a prey to the extortions of the seneschal's favoured group.[105] Along with the abandonment of any pretence at

---

101 Examination concerning Harpole, 1 May 1573, Bodl., Carte MSS, 56/139, Pipho to Walsingham, 18 July 1580, SP 63/74/47; 'Petition . . . of Pipho', June 1581, SP 63/83/64; Grey to Walsingham, 7 Jan. 1582, SP 63/88/9; 'Submission of Hugh McShane O'Byrne', 1 Oct. 1578, SP 63/63/1' Malby to Walsingham, 24 July 1579, SP 63/67/50; Harrington to Burghley and Walsingham, 7 May 1580, SP 63/73/3–4; Wallop to Walsingham, SP 63/81/2.

102 'The book against R. Harpole', 21 Aug. 1571, SP 63/33/39; Carew to Burghley, enclosing note of Harpole's exactions, 28 Aug., SP 63/33/47 and 47 (i); 'Survey of Leighlin', 6 Aug. 1574, Bodl., Carte MSS, 56/472.

103 Sidney to privy council, 27 Feb. 1576, SP 63/55/19: Wallop to Walsingham, 8 June 1581, SP 63/83/41.

104 See leases of crown lords given to several of their number in *Fiants Eliz.*, Masterson, nos. 1577, 3294, 3786, 4242; Harpole, nos. 533, 612, 808, 1235, 1599, 1600, 2838, 3164, 3173; Harrington hos. 2566, 2599, 2626, 3334.

105 'Charges against Harpole', 1, 12 May 1573, 26 Oct. 1574, 15 Jan. 1575, Bodl., Carte MSS, 56/139, 57/529, 56/536, 55/133; Malby to Walsingham, 24 July 1579, SP 63/67/50; Wallop to Walsingham, 19 May 1580, SP 63/73/19.

impartiality came a habit of resorting at will to extravagant and unwarranted violence. When Henry Harrington wanted to rid his territory of the troublesome Lucas O'Toole, he travelled to Dublin, raided a tavern in which O'Toole was lodging and had him hanged before morning: there was no warrant, no indictment, and no trial. In 1580 when Thomas Masterson grew exasperated with the unruliness of one of the septs of the Kavanaghs, he laid ambush for them and slaughtered over sixty. Harrington laid a similar plot for Fiagh Mac Hugh O'Byrne, but without success. Later in the 1580s, Dudley Bagenal, then seneschal at Ferns, repeated Masterson's exploit against the Kavanaghs with like results.[106]

Massacre is an impressive way to assert authority. But as in the case of degenerate colonisation, the readiness of the seneschals to employ violence against any resistance they encountered did not result in any significant advance for English law in the Gaelic areas under their charge. During the regimes of Stuckley and Masterson, north Wexford remained in a state of continual disorder. Throughout the 1570s, intermittent warfare continued between the settlers and the Kavanaghs, and though Sidney sought to make the best of Masterson's service, he was forced to make a personal intervention into the affairs of the country in 1577.[107] In 1579, Drury was less concerned to protect the seneschal's reputation. The entire responsibility for the waste state of the country, he declared, lay entirely with Masterson. Lord Deputy Grey confirmed Drury's opinion. By his negligence, extortion and corruption, Masterson, he believed, had alienated more loyal subjects than had been won by his severity. He had the seneschal dismissed from office and placed under arrest. But the disgrace was only temporary, and Masterson was soon permitted to resume his office unhampered by further scrupulous interference from Dublin.[108]

The countries of the O'Tooles and the O'Byrnes proved even less susceptible to progress. Despite Brian O'Toole's experience as a sheriff, despite repeated requests from the O'Byrnes that they might complete the process of surrender and regrant, and despite the fact that both areas were believed to be ripe for full absorption into the Pale in the early 1560s, no

[106] Kildare to Walsingham and to Eliz., 3, 4 May 1580, SP 63/73/42; Masterson to Knollys, 23 May 1580, SP 63/73/66 enclosures (i) and (ii); 'Masterson's declaration', Apr. 1580, SP 63/72/1–2; J. P. Prendergast, 'The plantation of Idrone', *Jn. Kilkenny and S.E. Ireland Arch. Soc.*, 2nd ser., 3 (1860–1), pp. 20–44, 69–80.

[107] 'Report of James Dowdall and other commissioners', 22 July 1573, Bodl., Carte MSS, 55/310; Eliz. to Fitzwilliam, 3 May 1572, Carte MSS, 57/487; Sidney's 'Proclamation against disorders in Wexford', 1577, Lambeth MSS, 628/347–8.

[108] Drury to Walsingham, 6 Mar. 1579, SP 63/66/2; Wallop to Walsingham, 8 June 1581, SP 63/83/41; Grey to privy council, 10 July 1581, SP 63/84/12.

progress was made under either Sussex or Sidney. The lack of success was due in good part to the conduct of the seneschal, Francis Agard, who, it was said, was too prone to leave the Irish to their own devices. Agard's successor, Harrington, was also accused of diffidence, but a mere insouciance was not the underlying cause of their laxity. Both men remained friendly with Hugh Mac Shane O'Byrne who was engaged in a long-standing succession dispute with the lesser septs of the clan. Agard enjoyed remarkable personal influence over the otherwise ungovernable Hugh, and on most occasions was able to bring him and his allies amongst the O'Tooles to order when required without force. After an early and difficult period of adjustment, Harrington too acquired a similar understanding with Hugh's son and heir, Fiagh. Rather than attempting to suppress the dispute between Hugh and his rivals, the seneschals aided and abetted its development, for its continuance allowed them to assume a position of power and influence amongst the clansmen which would otherwise have been impossible. Not as the agents of English law, but simply as third parties in the configuration of Gaelic politics, they became sought after, feared and honoured, and came to acquire also the material benefits that inevitably followed. They could have no interest in seeing their special position suddenly undermined by assimilation into the Pale. All the incentives were on the side of leaving things as they were.[109]

Agard's and Harrington's conduct amongst the O'Byrnes illuminates the general position occupied by the English seneschals throughout the Gaelic territories. The Gaelic practices of restitution and compensation were not only the easiest legal procedures to adopt, they were also the most lucrative. The Gaelic system's ready acceptance of force offered simple means of operation and provided an attractive avenue to personal power. The perquisites available to them as brokers within the Gaelic polity were considerably more remunerative than those enjoyed by orthodox executives within the English administration. By the early 1580s, the seneschals had begun to explicitly justify their behaviour. Harrington conceded that he operated a protection system and accepted restitutions, yet he asserted that this was the way he had come to command respect amongst the natives. In

---

[109] Malby's 'Notes on Ireland', BL, Add. MSS, 48015, fos. 190–1; 'State of the provinces of Ireland', *c.* 1576, SP 63/56/62–3; Harrington to Burghley, 14 Nov. 1583, SP 63/105/65; 'Memorial of . . . Harrington's service', Nov. 1585, SP 63/121/20. On general history of the O'Byrnes in the sixteenth century, see Liam Price, 'The Byrne's Co. in Co. Wicklow in the 16th Century', *Jn. RSAI*, 7th ser., 3 (1933), pp. 224–42 and 6 (1936), pp. 41–66 and 'Notes on Fiagh Mac Hugh O'Byrne', *Jn. Kildare Arch. Soc.* 11 (1930–1), pp. 134–75; for a different interpretation from that presented here, see Brendan Bradshaw, 'Native reaction to the Westward Enterprise: a case study in Gaelic ideology', in K. R. Andrews, N. P. Canny and P. E. H. Hair (eds.), *The Westward Enterprise: English activities in Ireland, the Atlantic and America* (Liverpool, 1978), pp. 66–80.

view of the influence he had begun to assert over Fiagh Mac Hugh, he had a strong case.[110]

The seneschals' real power, then, rested upon their continuing willingness to ignore or to condone a certain level of violence within their territories. Raids upon other rival septs or upon their allies, an inordinate incidence of highway robbery and the chronic extortion of coyne and livery was the price which Agard and Harrington paid for their alliance with the dominant sept of the O'Byrnes. Within this alliance, moreover, a continuous process of bargaining went with each side measuring the extent of its power over the other. Occasional blood-letting formed part of this pattern, but at times it could result in serious embarrassment for the seneschals themselves, as when Hugh Mac Shane raided Dublin itself and Fiagh visited a punishing raid upon Seneschal Masterson.[111] The net result of all this interaction, however, was simply to accentuate the existing lawlessness. The price of the seneschal's survival was the demise of the government's aims.

Yet the more the governors pressed those aims, the more they were compelled to recruit and to depend upon these semi-autonomous regional agents. Because he was desperate to find some means of keeping the Leinster Irish in some semblance of order and yielding some token revenues, while he set about the more ambitious objectives of his programmes, Sidney was willing to leave Agard and Harrington to their own devices. For the same reason, Sidney greatly preferred the unscrupulous, but effective, Thomas Stuckley as seneschal in Wexford to the conscientious common lawyer Nicholas White. And for this reason also, he welcomed unreservedly the unsolicited appearance in Ireland of one of the most ambitious of would-be seneschals, Sir Peter Carew.

After an ostentatious waiver of his claim to the lands of Sir Christopher Cheevers, Carew proceeded immediately with his suit against the Kavanaghs.[112] The clansmen's defence was so weak that it was regarded as no plea at all, and on 1 June 1569, Carew was granted full title to the barony of Idrone. Sidney had even larger plans for Carew. After his failure to have Stucley's appointment as seneschal in Wexford ratified by the queen, Sidney had deliberately kept the constableship at Leighlin vacant. In February 1569 he placed Carew unofficially in the fort, and immediately

---

[110] Weston to Eliz., 23 Mar. 1571, SP 63/31/33, and Harrington to Burghley, 14 Nov. 1583, SP 63/105/65.

[111] 'Examination on plunder of O'Byrnes', 20 May 1574, Bodl., Carte MSS, 56/356–8; Sidney to privy council, 15 Dec. 1575, SP 63/54/17; Harrington to Walsingham, 1 July 1580, SP 63/74/1.

[112] On Carew generally, see John Hooker, *Life of Sir Peter Carew*, ed. John MacClean (London, 1857).

thereafter Carew petitioned to have his appointment as constable confirmed.[113]

White objected and Carew remained unrecognised, but as with Stucley Sidney continued to invest Carew with the reality of the seneschal's powers. In March he was joined with the sheriff of Carlow on a commission which empowered him to prosecute, suppress, vanquish and utterly destroy all enemies, rebels and traitors by fire and sword and by all politic means that shall seem best to their discretion.[114] He was authorised to cess, to billet, to conscript men for service and to negotiate agreements with whom he thought fit. Carew quickly adapted to his semi-official role – he did Sidney good service in defending the country against the attacks of the rebel Butlers – but he was primarily concerned to use his new position as a means of stabilising his relations with his Gaelic tenants in Idrone. Whatever hostility the Kavanaghs may have felt towards the interloper at the outset was soon dissipated by Carew's judicious mixture of coercion and flamboyant goodlordship. After some early disputes he quietly confirmed the chief members of the clan as freeholders and granted easy leases to the remaining groups. He kept a house at Leighlin 'which was so liberal and bountiful as none [was] like unto him in that contry'. He extended a full pardon to all who had first resisted him. By the early 1570s the Kavanaghs had grown accustomed to their new overlord and his greatest opponent, Brian Mac Cahir Kavanagh, had taken to the English language and dress under Carew's friendly tutelage. It was even said that Carew's success with the Kavanaghs had encouraged other clans to seek his lordship.[115] Carew himself soon became immersed in the traditional feud between the Kavanaghs and the Wexfordmen. He refused to deliver persons indicted for theft in Wexford and quarrelled sharply with Seneschal Masterson. He became the leading opponent of the government's attempts to impose cess in Carlow, complaining strongly against the extortions of Harpole's troops and offering to enter into a composition arrangement similar to those being made by Gaelic chieftains with seneschals elsewhere.[116] Carew was so pleased with his achievement in Idrone that he proposed, though without success, to repeat his experiment in other lands to which he had made a claim in County Cork.

The early deviation of seneschals and constables like Agard, Masterson

[113] *Fiants Eliz.*, no. 1302; Carew to Cecil, 23 Feb. 1569, SP 63/27/33.
[114] *Fiants Eliz.*, nos. 1417–18, 'Articles of instruction for Sir Peter Carew', Lambeth MSS, 105/15.
[115] J. Hooker, 'Chronicle of Ireland', in Holinshed, *Chronicles*, pp. 372, 377; Hooker, *Carew*, pp. 84–6; see also James Hughes, 'The fall of Clan Kavanagh', *Jn. Royal Hist. Arch. Soc.*, 4th ser. 2 (1873), pp. 282–305.
[116] Masterson to Fitzwilliam, 27 Jan. 1575, Bodl., Carte MSS, 55/166; Carew to Fitzwilliam, 29 Aug. 1572, ibid., 57/399; Carew's 'Petition against Cess', 1570 or 1571, Lambeth MSS, 605/19–20; Carew's 'suits', 1573, ibid., 605/40, 45.

and Carew into the prevailing modes of Gaelic politics inevitably attracted criticism. A particularly acute observer was himself a former but rather exceptional seneschal, Sir Nicholas White. In his time White had had occasion to attack most of the seneschals individually, but his strictures on the system were general. 'I wish the country were more governed by law than by discretion', he wrote to Burghley in 1574. The seneschals, he warned, had been corrupted by the wide powers allowed to them. For the most part they made no attempt to reform the worst abuses of the Gaelic Irish and when they did assert their authority it was only through the most brutal violence 'which will sooner consume away the people than alter their way of life'. Burghley, he urged, should persuade the queen by all possible means 'not to be committed to those who cannot govern themselves but seek to make quarrell with her people, delivering them injustice instead of justice and causing their own will to be holden for laws'.[117] White undoubtedly spoke for the Anglo-Irish group which felt particularly threatened by these powerful and irresponsible interlopers. But similar criticisms were voiced against the system by Englishmen of very different dispositions. Sir Henry Wallop, no lover of the Gaelic Irish, nor of the Anglo-Irish administrators, agreed that the seneschals were wasteful and corrupt; and sought repeatedly to have Masterson and Harrington removed from office.[118] Writing from afar, Sir James Crofts perceptively argued that the appointment of these military men to places of responsibility within the Gaelic territories was the outstanding cause of the natives' continuing distrust of the government.[119] Sir John Perrot believed that the seneschals' exploitation of coyne and livery had severely retarded the progress of English law in Ireland and recommended that they should be allowed to take up supplies only with the prior permission of the viceroy.[120] But perhaps the most consistent critic of the system was Edmund Tremayne. In his series of memoranda he emphasised that his objections to this form of government were not limited to the evils it visited upon the native Irish, but extended also to the corrupting effects which it exerted upon those Englishmen who had taken up places of government amongst the Irishry. The new officers, Tremayne perceived, had so rapidly accommodated themselves to the Gaelic environment 'as we have . . . for the most part as Irish as the rest'. He concluded that progress could be made in the Gaelic areas only when the demands which the government

---

[117] White to Cecil, 26 Feb. 1569, 18 Apr., 15 May 1571, 23 Dec. 1581, HMC, *Cecil MSS*, I, pp. 400–1; SP 63/28/6, 32/31, 87/55.
[118] On Masterson, see Wallop to Walsingham, 1 Mar. 1581, SP 63/81/2 and 8 June, SP 63/82/41; on Harrington, Wallop to Walsingham, 19 May 1580, SP 63/73/19, and 28 Aug. 1581, SP 63/85/27.
[119] Treatise by Sir James Croft, *c.* 1584, NRO, Fitzwilliam MSS (Irish), no. 68.
[120] Perrot's 'Plat for Ireland', *c.* 1581, BL, Add. MSS, 48017, fos. 86–91.

made upon the community were equitably rated and systematically imposed by the central authority, and when no favour was given to any, English or Irish, above the law.[121]

These were acute observations in so far as they went, but they were rather narrowly conceived. English law had failed to progress, the seneschals had become immersed in Gaelic politics not simply because some people were negligent and some corrupt, but because the chief governors themselves, acting under the constraints of their own declared programmes, had unwittingly determined that it should be so. It was, therefore, an irony, but one that reflected the underlying paradox of the governmental structure, that Sidney, the man to whom Tremayne addressed his arguments, should, through the failure of his own overarching ambitions, have been responsible for the installation of the chief example of the type against whom Tremayne had railed – Sir Nicholas Malby, the governor of Connacht.

In 1576 few men had more experience of service in Ireland than Nicholas Malby.[122] He had first come to Ireland in 1556, and though he left in the early 1560s, he returned again in 1567 to be joined with William Piers as joint constable at Carrickfergus.[123] In the north Malby soon acquired a reputation for harsh and forceful dealing that commanded the respect of the Scots and the Irish; even Lord Deputy Fitzwilliam was afraid of him.[124] He dabbled in colonisation and in 1571 received a grant of MacCartan's Country in Co. Down on condition that he establish settlement there before the end of the decade.[125] He seems, however, to have made no attempt at all to fulfil his obligations, and by 1576 he was at court petitioning to be released from the grant.[126] It was while he was at court that he came to the attention of Secretary Walsingham as a possible candidate for presidential office in Sidney's new composition government. Malby's appointment was delayed, however, and by the time he arrived in Connaught to take up his duties, the province was already in rebellion.

The Clanrickard rebellion which destroyed Sidney's attempt to enforce his centrally controlled composition laid the foundation for the formidable,

121 See ch. 4 above, and Tremayne's largest tract in BL, Add. MSS, 48015, fos. 274–9.
122 On Malby generally, see *DNB*, sv; G. W. Lambert, 'Sir Nicholas Malby', *Jn. Galway Arch. Soc.* 23 (1948–9), pp. 1–13, and Thomas Churchyard, *Churchyard's choice* (London, 1579), passim.
123 'Consignation of Leix', 1556, SP 62/1/21; he was appointed sergeant of the army by Sidney in 1566, NRO, Fitzwilliam MSS (Irish), no. 49; *Fiants, Eliz.*, no. 1191; Weston and Fitzwilliam to Eliz., 30 Oct. 1567, SP 63/22/16.
124 Malby to Cecil, 19 Mar. 1568, SP 63/23/73.
125 Malby to Cecil, 12 Feb. 1568, SP 63/23/37, and 9 Oct. 1571, SP 63/34/25; Burghley's 'Memoranda', 1571, SP 63/34/41; *Cal. pat. rolls (England) Eliz. I (1569–72)*, p. 313.
126 Malby's 'Petitions', 2 June 1575, 7 Mar. 1576, SP 63/52/14, 55/23–4; privy council to Sidney, 23 Jan. 1576, 63/55/5 and 10 July, 63/56/7.

semi-autonomous position which Malby was to establish for himself in Connacht. By the end of 1577 he had managed to get the military situation under control and had begun the process of converting the president's cesses into a fixed rent. He had established informal relations with the officially outlawed Burkes and had made firmer connections with the lesser families of Clanrickard and with the O'Kellys and O'Flahertys of West Connacht. By the middle of 1578 he was extracting a small, but steady revenue from the province and could realistically promise greater gains in the future.[127] Thus, when the privy council chose to jettison Sidney's plan in favour of Gerrard's, they decided to make a singular exception of the president of Connacht. Malby was now to be appointed governor of the province by letters patent. He was to be given entirely autonomous charge of the administration of law and order in Connacht and of the collection of its revenues. No sheriff was to be appointed without his recommendation and he was to be responsible for the upkeep of all civil and military offices. The costs of the Connacht administration were to be met entirely from the composition money, and Malby was to pay the surplus, 'if any be', into the exchequer. No provision was made, however, for the regular inspection of his accounting procedures. In the following year, Malby's jurisdiction was extended southward into Thomond and northward towards the ancient boundaries of Connacht against Ulster.[128]

These formal instructions merely gave official sanction to a personal campaign which Malby had already set in motion throughout the province. As soon as he had asserted his authority in Clanrickard, he marched northward, gradually establishing relations with the Gaelic clans of Lower Connacht. He negotiated agreements with O'Conor Roe and Mac Dermot, carefully encircling the other major power in his jurisdiction, the Mac William Burke. In the winter of 1577–8 he entered O'Connor Sligo's country, expelling O'Donnell who had recently revived a claim to suzerainty, and forcing O'Connor to enter into a composition and to recognise an English sheriff. Next he invaded O'Rourke, 'the proudest man living this day on earth', and received his submission. Finally he returned to the lordship of MacWilliam, exploiting a succession struggle that was currently raging there by compelling the most powerful claimant, Richard 'an Iarann', to recognise his right to decide the issue.[129]

[127] Malby to Walsingham, 30 Aug., 10 Nov. 1577, 3 May 1578, SP 63/59/3 and 43 and 50/55; 'Abstract of rents due within Connaught', c. 1577, 63/59/71.
[128] 'Queen's Instructions to lords justice', 31 Mar. 1579; Walsingham letter-book, pp. 46–7; privy council to Drury, 21 Dec. 1579, SP 63/63/59; 'Instructions to Malby', 31 Mar. 1579, Lambeth MSS, 614/112–17.
[129] See Malby's detailed reports of his proceedings, 10 Nov. 1577, 12 Apr. 1578, 26 July 1578, 8 Apr. 1580, SP 63/59/43–4, 63/60/37, 63/61/41, 41 (i) and 63/72/39.

By the outbreak of the rebellion in Munster, Malby could boast that his own province was so peaceful that he could leave it unguarded and travel south with a force of 600 raised from the country.[130] The boast was somewhat exaggerated, for as the rebellion dragged on discontents in his province began to make themselves apparent. But the trouble was in most cases temporary: traditional displays of insubordination against an absent lord which disappeared immediately upon his return. Later absences produced no further opposition, and when he returned from a visit to court early in 1582 Malby himself was overwhelmed by the reception he received from the clansmen. His sudden death on 4 March 1584 was said to have been genuinely mourned in the province; and in a peculiar way his memory was enshrined: 'There came not to Connacht a better gentleman of the foreigners than he, and he placed all Connacht under bondage'.[131]

Malby himself was the first to reflect upon the curious nature of his success in Gaelic Ireland. He wrote to Burghley,

I did think myself before the province of Connacht was committed unto me I could very well have judged of Ireland government, but I assure your honour that I was but a novice in the very department of government which I have I think always attained unto . . . [but now] the imitation of the Irishman's policy hath won unto me that advantage over them as now they find I am a good schoolmaster over them in their own art that they are contented to be in such obedience in every way as I must assure your honour that for general obedience and commodity . . . this province is now the best in the land. The Irishman [he declared with astonishing frankness] has taught me to try him with his own law.[132]

Malby certainly demonstrated a readiness to indulge in fierce and often redundant violence. He made it clear from the outset that he wanted the old earl of Clanrickard dead by fair means or foul, and he contemplated with equanimity the prospect of liquidating his entire kinship group. In 1578 he secured O'Rourke's submission by besieging his chief castle and slaughtering all within, women and children without quarter. When he attacked Richard 'an Iarann' Burke he brought him to heel by a scorched earth policy that left miles of countryside barren, and when Burke finally surrendered he and his followers were left to starve for days on an isolated island before Malby relented. Malby justified these terrorist tactics with ease. They enabled him, he argued, to meet the clansmen on their own terms, they won for him a respect that otherwise he would never have attained, and

130 Malby to Walsingham, 20 Aug. 1579, SP 63/68/45.
131 Malby to Walsingham, 17 June 1582, SP 63/93/30; AFM sa 1584, the quotation is from *The Annals of Loch Ce*, W. M. Hennessy (ed.), (2 vols., London, 1871; IMC, Dublin, 1939), II, p. 459.
132 Malby to Walsingham, 12 Apr. 1578, 3 May, SP 63/60/37, 55.

in the long run, he calculated, they saved more lives than they cost. It is impossible to tell.[133]

But there were other aspects of Malby's adaptation to local folkways which he was far less eager to publicise. Despite the formal appearance of his composition arrangements, Malby's rule remained highly arbitrary. He never abandoned coyne and livery. He retained a large army of up to 800 men which he billeted on the country. He governed by martial law (or without regard to legal form at all), and issued similar commissions to his subordinates. He shielded his special servants by general pardons; charges against them were quashed or simply ignored. Uncompliant sheriffs were dismissed, arrests were made and prisoners retained entirely at his discretion.[134] The governor, however, was sufficiently sensitive to the delicacy of his position to recognise the need to make more positive ties with O'Madden, O'Flaherty and the elder Mac William. He was even on good terms with the famous Grace O'Malley.[135] It was these groups which provided the body of his personal army, and in return Malby issued them with protections and pardons when necessary. He was, indeed, so free in his dispersal of pardons and safe-conducts to favoured groups that they were said to be on sale to the highest bidder. His arbitration of disputes and assessment of fines were also made subject to considerations of favour and paid little heed to the requirements of formal procedure.

Malby's adaptability to the demands of local politics is clearly evidenced in the often brazen inconsistency of his reports to London. O'Connor Sligo, once one of the most dangerous of the queen's enemies, became one of the soundest men in the province, and Richard 'an Iarann', whom he had so relentlessly pursued, became the legitimate successor to Mac William, whose title Malby was ready to defend against all challenges.[136] The clearest instance of the governor's flexibility is provided by his relations with the Mac an Iarlas. Though once eager for both their heads, Malby began to manoeuvre between the two sons, recommending one and then the other for the favour of the crown, while at the same time negotiating with both in order to preserve his own position. He gave them protections; they gave him

---

[133] Sidney to privy council, 20 Sept. 1576, SP 63/56/31 and 20 Apr., 63/60/42; Malby to Walsingham, 31 May 1579, 63/66/68; Malby's 'Discourse', 8 Apr. 1580, 63/72/39.

[134] Malby to Walsingham, 10 Nov. 1577, SP 63/69/43 and 29 Feb. 1580, 63/81/64 and 23 Mar. 1581, 63/81/43; 'Note of certain abuses ... of Malby', *c.* Mar. 1580, SP 63/72/24–5, and Dec. 1580, SP 63/79/41.

[135] Malby's 'Discourse', 8 Apr. 1580, SP 63/72/39; Malby's 'Note of Connaught hostings', 18 Jan. 1582, 63/88/34; Anne Chambers, *Granuaile: the life and times of Grace O'Malley, c. 1530–1603* (Dublin, 1979).

[136] Malby to Walsingham, 10 Nov. 1577 and to Burghley, 8 Apr. 1580, SP 63/59/43 and 72/38; Malby's 'Discourse', 8 Apr. 1580 and Malby to Walsingham, 30 Apr. 1583, SP 63/72/3, 101/46.

castles. He ceased to pursue them; they desisted from attacking his allies. He offered them pardons; they promised their allegiance. In the end, he negotiated a peace with them that, during Malby's lifetime at least, seemed to satisfy both.[137]

In matters of religion the governor was equally flexible. Despite his frequent declamations against popery, Malby showed little enthusiasm for the reformation. During his regime some twelve monasteries 'stuffed with friars' enjoyed his protection.[138] He recommended clerics of dubious allegiance to vacant benefices and he negotiated with papal appointees to episcopal sees.[139] Most important of all, he attempted to establish himself and his family as major independent landholders in the province. Malby accepted restitution for crimes against his own property and fostered out his children amongst the natives.[140] He gained a grant and refurbished the fortress town of Roscommon and began to extend his holdings by acquiring monastic sites in the surrounding countryside. His greed for land was such that it was given out that he would allow no grants of property to be made to others anywhere near his own settlement. Malby also undertook the construction of a second grand residence at Meleek on O'Madden's country, and he sought to have both of his holdings granted to him and his heirs in tail.[141]

Malby eventually overreached. Not content with Thomond and Sligo, he sought to extend his jurisdiction in Munster and Ulster, and presented the privy council with detailed propositions for both.[142] But the council demurred, and Malby was summoned to London to answer charges of misconduct preferred against him by his fellow English administrators.[143] Like Masterson and Harrington, however, his discomfiture was short-lived.

---

[137] Cf. Malby to Eliz., 20 Sept. 1576, SP 63/56/34; to Walsingham, 17 Mar. 1577, SP 63/57/40, and 12 Apr. 1578, 63/60/37, 10 Aug. 1579, 63/68/33. 4 Nov., 12 Dec., 63/70/2, 55; 'Articles to be observes of Ulick and John Burke', 5 June 1580, SP 63/73/52 (i).

[138] 'Note of abuses', c. Mar. 1580, SP 63/72/24–5 and Malby's and R. Fowle's replies to such allegations, Apr. 1582, 63/81/24 and 40.

[139] Abuses and replies, as in n. 138 above, and see Malby to Walsingham, 16 Apr. 1582, forwarding suit of Malahy O'Malone 'popish bishop of Killaloe', SP 63/101/29 and enclosure (i), and Malby's 'Requests', Jan. 1582, 63/88/59.

[140] See note 138 and also Malby to Burghley, 26 May 1580, SP 63/73/28.

[141] 'Receipt by Clanrickard's agent', 23 June 1580, SP 63/73/61; Malby to Walsingham, 6 Apr. 1581, SP 63/82/12; Malby's 'Offers for Roscommon and Meleek', Dec. 1581, SP 63/87/74; his 'Requests', Jan. 1582, SP 63/88/59–60; 'Notes of . . . lands held by Malby', May 1582, SP 63/92/60.

[142] Malby's 'Notes for Connaught', c. 1576, SP 63/56/64; Malby to Walsingham, enclosing notes for Munster, 22 Aug. 1579, 63/68/41, 41 (i); Malby to Walsingham, enclosing his 'Plot for Ireland', 27 Nov. 1579, 63/70/31 and 31 (i); Malby's 'Plot', 26 Sept. 1579, 63/69/63 (i).

[143] 'Note of abuses' and Malby's 'Replies' as in note 138 above. Edward White's 'Petition', May 1582, SP 63/92/17; White to Walsingham, 23 May, SP 63/92/58–9.

He had after all delivered the promised modest revenues, and kept a peace of his own in the province. The council's loss of control over their agent may have been regrettable, but the cost of dismissing him and replacing him was unthinkable. He returned to Connacht and his powers undiminished and died there in the full exercise of his office.

The corollary of the gaelicisation of English local and regional officials was the gradual cooption of existing Gaelic figures into the ranks of English provincial government. Neither Sussex nor Sidney sought to restrict appointment to positions of governmental authority within Gaelic areas to Englishmen alone. Both had accepted the necessity of confirming the existing powers in certain localities by *de facto* recognitions of their positions as 'captains' under certain conditions. Recognised captains, according to Sussex, were to undertake the booking of their men. They were to attend upon hostings, pay for the upkeep of an agreed number of galloglas and supply beeves to the viceroy's army. In time they were to apply English law to felonies and crimes against property committed in their lordship.[144] In practice, however, the procedure remained informal under Sussex, and the demands he made upon his recognised captains were determined by the exigencies of his war against O'Neill. But in the late 1560s Sidney embarked on a deliberate extension of the practice. The legislation of 1569 included an act by which captaincies were recognised by letters patent only.[145] And grants of captaincies made thereafter made explicit reference to the legislation's terms. As Sussex had recommended, the new captains were recognised not merely as Gaelic leaders, but as crown servants. Thus Brian O'Rourke was confirmed as a captain and simultaneously appointed sheriff of his country.[146] Elsewhere, however, Sidney was conscious that such a conventional title was inappropriate to the conditions of Gaelic lordship, and so he conferred on them the title he had already granted to English officials in similar circumstances: he made them seneschals.[147]

Whatever their long-term significance, the new titles of sheriff or seneschal made little immediate difference to the chieftain's position. His patent confirmed his traditional right over his subjects, and no means other than personal connection was provided to ensure that these new royal officers would be any more loyal or dependable than the old chieftains had been. Sidney in fact displayed a remarkable facility in establishing good personal relations with influential figures in Gaelic Ireland. His 'gossiprick'

---

[144] Sussex's 'Opinion', *c.* June 1562, Lambeth MSS, 609; for Sussex's grants of captaincies, see *Fiants Eliz.* passim.
[145] *Irish Statutes*, 12 Eliz. I, c. 4, p. 367.
[146] *Fiants Eliz.*, no. 1512; see also appointment of McHubert as 'chief sergeant' of his county, no. 1605.
[147] *Fiants Eliz.*, nos. 1760, 1817, 2090, 3212.

with Shane O'Neill and his initial warmth towards Desmond and his Gaelic allies are the best known instances of this talent, but he employed it also in less prominent ways. The key to his success, for example, in persuading MacGeoghan to accept the reorganisation of his territory in accord with English reform lay in his personal friendship with the chieftain's eldest son, Ross. Ross MacGeoghan was a man of some education and experience: he could write English fluently while his father and brother left only their mark, and he had served as a captain and purveyor to the royal army since the days of Sussex's administration.[148] Under Sidney he was retained permanently in military service and received a generous grant of crown lands from the deputy as well as an unusual appointment as sheriff of Westmeath. In 1571 Sidney endorsed Ross' removal of his father from the chieftainship without scruple and bolstered his position by appointing him royal seneschal of the MacGeoghan's territory. Such favour, however, proved little more than a liability to Ross. In 1572 he was compelled to surrender the chieftainship and seneschalship to his father, and lived thereafter in constant mistrust with his family until he was murdered by his brother Brian in 1580. Nothing had changed: the new title of seneschal which MacGeoghan had appropriated from his son was merely old captain writ large and the change of nomenclature had done little more than compound the MacGeoghan's existing dynastic problems.[149]

Sidney's personal influence with the Fitzpatricks of Upper Ossory was more successful. Once again, his connection with the family was through the son and heir of the existing chieftain, Sir Barnaby. After he had returned in 1554 from his especially favoured position at the court of King Edward, Sir Barnaby found himself seriously estranged from his own family, but he quickly attached himself to the Dublin administration. Like Ross MacGeoghan he supplied the government with men and received the customary favours in return. In 1560 he was knighted by Sidney and was thereafter regarded as the government's chief agent in Upper Ossory. In 1569 Sidney officially recognised his deposition of his father, and confirmed him as captain of his people. In 1576 he made him lieutenant of the king's and queen's counties, a title held by none since Sussex's brother, Henry Radcliffe.[151]

The only surviving son of his father's first marriage, Sir Barnaby, unlike

148 'Sidney's accounts, 1556–9', HMC, *De Lisle and Dudley MSS*, I, pp. 365–7, 370.
149 *Fiants Eliz.*, nos. 965, 1391, 1833, 1760; 'Note of Ireland suits', *c.* 1571, SP 63/34/45; Fitzwilliam and Council to Eliz., 18 Feb. 1572, 63/39/27 and enclosures (i) and (ii); Wallop to Walsingham, 9 Sept. 1580, 63/76/21.
150 *DNB*, sv; on Fitzpatrick's early life, see *Chronicle . . . King Edward VI*, ed. W. K. Jordan (London, 1966), passim; GEC, *Complete Peerage*, XII, pp. 184–7.
151 GEC, *Peerage, Fiants Eliz.*, nos. 953, 1329, 1437, 2843.

Ross MacGeoghan, suffered no direct threat to his succession. But he confronted serious trouble from his step-mother's family, the O'Carrolls who were determined to preserve their recently won influence in the territory. His difficulties were further increased by the interference of the earl of Ormond who claimed ancient rights of jurisdiction in the lordship. As the threats to Sir Barnaby increased on Sidney's departure in 1571, he expelled his father and the O'Carrolls who surrounded him and propagated the elaborate rumour that his step-mother was plotting the destruction of the Fitzpatricks by witchcraft.[152] When the Graces, Ormond's chief henchmen, kidnapped his wife and children, holding them 'in most miserable captivity and like to die', Sir Barnaby was compelled to resort to more desperate measures.[153] He found new allies among some of the discontented O'Carrolls, and even hired some of the mercenary Graces. He gave succour to Geraldine refugees from the Munster rebellion of 1569–72 and encouraged their attacks on the Butlers. Ormond was so alarmed by Sir Barnaby's conduct that he secured the queen's order for his arrest. Lord Deputy Fitzwilliam patched up a temporary truce, but by the time of Sidney's reappointment war had again broken out between the two lords. And it was only following his father's death in 1576 that Sir Barnaby's position in Upper Ossory was secured.[154]

Sir Barnaby's survival, however, did little to further the anglicisation of his lordship. Despite his title and his office he did little to establish the instruments of English administration in his country and after Sidney's departure he resumed the feud with the Butlers. On the outbreak of the Desmond rebellion allegations that he had colluded with the rebels mounted until he was placed under arrest. As in so many cases, however, his disgrace was temporary: the Dublin administrators decided that his possible disloyalty was of lesser importance than his service as a foil to the powerful earl of Ormond, and he was soon released. He died in his lordship shortly afterwards and was succeeded by his half-brother, Florence, who had spent most of his previous career on the wrong side of the administration. Florence was duly recognised as captain by the government, but he too made no effort to advance the cause of reform and the country remained unshired until 1602.[155]

152 Upper Ossory to Fitzwilliam, 3 May, Sir Barnaby to Fitzwilliam, 4 May 1573, Bodl., Carte MSS, 57/30–3.
153 Fitzpatrick to Sidney, 6 May 1573, SP 63/40/27.
154 Elizabeth to Fitzwilliam, 18 May 1574, SP 63/46/21; 'Names of malefactors . . . maintained by Fitzpatrick', SP 63/46/22; Ormond to Fitzwilliam, 16 July 1574, SP 63/47/16; Fitzwilliam to Walsingham, 11 Oct. 1574, SP 63/48/7; Sidney to Ormond, 24 June 1576; to Richard Buckley, 9 Sept. 1580, HMC, *De Lisle and Dudley MSS*, II, pp. 38, 94.
155 Ormond to Walsingham, 28 May 1580, SP 63/73/30 and 30 (i), and 28 July, 63/74/72; Wallop to Walsingham, 14 Jan. 1581, SP 63/80/5 and 23 Apr. 63/82/47; on Florence Fitzpatrick, see GEC, *Peerage*, XII, pp. 187–8; *Fiants Eliz.*, no. 6610.

The cases of MacGeoghan and Fitzpatrick provided only further examples of what was fast becoming a general rule: that recognised government agents in Gaelic areas either abandoned the pretence of reform and accommodated themselves rapidly to the prevailing political and social norms, or did not survive at all. But the disappointment which was the result of the failure of such *ad hoc* arrangements throughout the country was to be dwarfed by the calamitous effects produced by the same process in the most troublesome of provinces, Ulster.

In spite of all Sidney's efforts to reach a final settlement with him, Turlough Luineach O'Neill remained a difficult man to deal with. He clung tenaciously to his claims over several lesser lords in the province – his *urrithe* – and seemed determined to retain rights of vassalage over at least some of them as a guarantee against his decline in old age.[156] It was indeed their continuing suspicion of Turlough's long term intentions that persuaded the privy council to defer ratification of Sidney's last treaty with him and by the time of the Desmond rebellion they still had made no decision on what to offer him. Characteristically, Turlough sought to exploit the crisis in order to increase his demands. He sued now to be granted military and political control over all Ulster, 'as it were by some commission of lieutenancy'. In return he promised to keep the province in general peace and to find an annual revenue of £3,000 for the royal exchequer.[157] He sought in short to take all Ulster to farm in the same way that Connacht had been granted to Sir Nicholas Malby and in the way he believed Sidney himself had once sought to have all of Ireland. Turlough remained too untrustworthy for the government to contemplate his offer. Yet the general attractiveness of the proposal, coupled with their awareness of Turlough's declining position in Tyrone prompted the councillors to look with increasing favour on his more promising and rather more dependable rival for power among the O'Neills and in the province as a whole, the baron of Dungannon.

Few men wholly trusted Hugh O'Neill. His dual origin made him suspect both to the government and to his own countrymen.[158] But the baron did win the confidence of a number of influential friends, notably Sir Henry Sidney, with whom it seems he spent some part of his early life. It was Sidney who

---

156 On Turlough's later relations with the government, see Joseph Costello, 'Turlough Luineach O'Neill: the "urrithe" and the central government', chs. 3–5.
157 'O'Neill's offers', 4 July 1579, SP 63/67/21; Gerrard to Grey, 30 Aug., SP 63/75/77; Fenton to Burghley, 30 Sept. 1580, enclosing Turlough's petitions, SP 63/76/77 and 77 (i); Turlough's Petition, 6 Oct. 1580, *Tanner letters* (IMC, 1943), pp. 32–3; Costello, pp. 206 ff.
158 On Dungannon generally, see J. K. Graham, 'Hugh O'Neill, 2nd Earl of Tyrone', unpub. MA thesis (QUB, 1938) and Sean O'Faolain, *The Great O'Neill* (London, 1942); and most recently, Hiram Morgan, *Tyrone's rebellion: the outbreak of the Nine Years War* (Woodbridge, 1993), ch. 5.

established him securely in his inheritance in 1568 and who made the earliest recommendation that he be allowed to succeed his grandfather as earl of Tyrone.[159] To the end, he never lost confidence in the baron's promise. Further support came from Essex who regarded him as the most dependable government servant in Ulster, from Malby and even (until the mid-1580s) from Marshal Bagenal.[160]

Until then, however, the actual role allotted to Dungannon in the politics of the province was necessarily secondary: he was a useful generally self-sufficient check upon the dangerous Turlough Luineach. As in so much else it was the Desmond rebellion that profoundly altered his fortunes. Impressed by his energetic service in Munster, Lord Deputy Grey considerably extended his military responsibilities in the north. He was joined with Marshal Bagenal in a commission to protect the Pale from invasion from Ulster which empowered him to use martial law throughout the province at his discretion.[161] It was at this point that the idea of formally appointing Dungannon to permanent government office in the province which had sometimes been raised in a general way in the past began to receive serious consideration. As yet it was considered that the responsibility of the task was too great and Dungannon's standing in the province too uncertain to confer such high office on him alone. He was instead to be joined with Turlough Luineach and Marshal Bagenal in a triumvirate which would share a common commission of lieutenancy for Ulster.[162] Yet the appointment of Dungannon along with these older men whose political careers were for different reasons now in the process of decline marked a recognition of the great potential which awaited him in the near future. The greatest of all those twilight figures of regional politics which had emerged from the wreckage of successive national programmes, he was to embody all the ambitions and ambiguities of that group in a uniquely intense manner, and to supply the nemesis of that benign but incoherent reform effort that had shaped his life.

[159] 'Extract of Sidney's letters', 11 Apr. 1570, SP 63/30/38.
[160] Essex to Privy Council, 20 Oct. 1573, SP 63/42/55; Malby to Walsingham, 13 May 1583, SP 63/102/28; lords justice to Walsingham, 14 May 1583, SP 63/102/30; Grey to Walsingham, 9 Dec. 1580, 63/79/5.
[161] Lords justice to Walsingham, enclosing Dungannon's suits, 6 June 1583 and 23 Aug., SP 63/102/71, 104/28; 'Commission for the government of Ulster', 7 Oct. 1584, HMC, *Cecil MSS*, III, pp. 67, 142.
[162] Morgan, *Tyrone's rebellion*, esp. pp. 38–9, 94–5; 'Plot for the government of Ulster', Hatfield House, Cecil MSS, 163/48–9.

Epilogue: reform in crisis: the viceroyalty of Sir John Perrot, 1584–1588

Me thinks it is now out of season to make any . . . discourse of a general reformation. (Sir Henry Sidney, 1580)

It is vain to speak of the planting of laws or the plotting of policies till . . . [the Irish] be altogether subdued. (Edmund Spenser, 1596)[1]

The perception that the mounting difficulties encountered by the Tudor reform policy could be traced to the character of the administrations chosen to implement it appeared in a variety of guises in the 1560s and 1570s. It could be found in the later writings of Edward Walshe, in the disillusioned commentaries of Sir Nicholas White and in the detached reviews of the experienced Sir James Crofts.[2] And for a brief period it gained official recognition in the government established on Chancellor Gerrard's advice in the autumn of 1578. But the practical relevance of such criticism was limited. Neither Walshe nor Crofts nor even White was in a position to exert a guiding influence over policy; and even if they were, their arguments had little to offer in the way of a positive alternative. Similarly, the establishment of 1578 was a reactionary reflex. Having discovered what had gone wrong under Sussex and Sidney, it merely sought to go back before their time: its model was the plan formulated, but never implemented, under Sir William Skeffington in 1531.[3] It showed little appreciation of the constellation of problems which had emerged since that time, and it offered no serious prescription for their resolution. Such intellectual poverty is understandable: had they pressed further, the critics would soon have encountered awkward questions about the value of the English political and legal system as a bulwark against encroaching anarchy. But before these doubts could

---

[1] Sidney to Grey, 27 Sept. 1580, Collins, *Letters and memorials of state*, I, 279–83; Spenser, *View of the present state of Ireland*, ed. W. L. Renwick, p. 12.

[2] Walshe, 'A detection of errors', BL, Cotton MSS, Titus B XII, no. 48; White, 'A plat', c. 1574, Lambeth MSS, 614/165–70; White to Burghley, 23 Dec. 1581, SP 63/87/55; Crofts' 'Discourse for the reformation of Ireland', NRO, Fitzwilliam MSS (Irish), no. 68.

[3] Gerrard papers', *Anal. Hib.*, 2 (1931), pp. 93–8, 183–7, 194–9.

develop, they were mercifully dispelled by the general crisis which erupted upon Fitzmaurice's return and the rebellion of the Desmonds.

The Desmond rebellion functioned as a marvellously simplifying agency in the later sixteenth century. It helped deflect critical introspection about governmental deficiency and the limitations of English law, and focused attention instead on the manifest treachery of the Irish. This change of emphasis was of immense importance ideologically and strategically: for in any later reflections on the failure of English reform in Ireland its seeming inevitability made it less important to examine the weaknesses of government policy than to explain the treachery and fundamental incorrigibility of the Irish.

This reorientation in political thinking encouraged a more uninhibited defence of a policy of simple coercion. But it did not automatically produce a new consensus on the way in which the island was to be ruled. The complexities that remained were illustrated in the reaction to the spectacular conduct of Lord Arthur Grey de Wilton who held the viceroyalty for a brief but fiercely repressive term of office in 1580–1, in the early days of the Desmond rebellion. The source of much contemporary discussion, Grey's viceroyalty was to be interpreted in a number of ways.[4] To some, still only a minority, it seemed to serve as an example of the only way in which Ireland could be brought to order. For others, most notably the leading Anglo-Irish administrators, it constituted a scandalous departure from the normal methods of government and a betrayal of the aims that had guided Tudor policy in Ireland for decades. But for others the matter was more complex. Grey's brusque and arbitrary decisions in Munster and in the Pale demonstrated how far a viceroy might succeed in freeing himself from the trammells of convention and local interest and set about the task he had allotted himself as briskly as possible. Yet the limitations of Grey's narrowly forceful approach were revealed in his complete inability to exploit initial success in the interests of some long-term political objectives. He made no gains for English rule in Leinster and he manifestly failed to suppress the rebellion in Munster. Grey's ambiguous record thus helped rekindle confidence in the idea that England's troubles in Ireland might still be tackled by a full programme of reform which should now be executed with a little more firmness and a little less regard for constitutional and political niceties which had hampered such efforts in the past. A new Sidney, sustained by a stiffened resolve at court, was what was required. This late flowering of Tudor reform thinking was embodied most fully in the

---

[4] H. S. V. Jones, 'Spenser's defence of Lord Grey,', *University of Illinois Studies in Language and Literature* 5 (1919), pp. 151–219; Ciaran Brady, 'Arthur Grey de Wilton', in A. C. Hamilton et al. (eds.), *A Spenser encyclopedia* (Toronto, 1990), pp. 341–2.

programme devised by the first viceroy to assume office in Ireland after the suppression of the Desmond rebellion, Sir John Perrot.

Perrot was in many ways the apotheosis of the programmatic governor. Having badgered the privy council throughout the 1570s with proposals for the better government of Ireland, he was finally invited in 1581 (the year of Grey's fall from grace) to present his plan for the final settlement of Ireland after the rebellion had been suppressed. Though it contained some original propositions, Perrot's project of reform was strikingly similar to those which had gone before.[5] He presented a detailed estimate of costs, gave a favourable prediction of revenues to be gained and committed himself to a limited time-table. His proposed methods of operation were also similar. Like Sussex, he sought to establish a centrally controlled group of administrative subordinates, and proposed to bring over a new cadre of military officers to serve under him. Like Sidney, he undertook to supervise the implementation of a wide range of policies, but planned to integrate these diverse issues in one legislative programme which he was to present before a specially summoned parliament in Dublin. Like his predecessors, he isolated some outstanding problems of governance for his own attention. He would expel the Scots from the north-east, and make a final settlement in Ulster. He would end rebellion in Munster and establish an extensive plantation on the attainted lands of the province. But the central element of his programme was the same as that which Sidney had attempted to introduce in 1575. He proposed to negotiate and complete a general composition for cess throughout the land.

Once appointed in 1584, Perrot began his work with the energy characteristic of men of his type.[6] He toured the country, establishing his composition presidents (John Norris in Munster and Richard Bingham in Connacht) and leading a major expedition against the Scots. Characteristically also, he trumpeted his actions loudly, promising an early and permanent success in all his undertakings.[7] But Perrot epitomised the programmatic style in its more negative aspects also. His promises

[5] Perrot's 'Plat for Ireland', *c.* 1581, BL, Stowe MS 159; other copies, BL, Harl. MSS, 3292 and Sloane MSS, 2200; his other principal proposals are SP 63/54/39, 112/22, 23, 41, 45; BL, Add. MSS, 48015, fos. 291–5, 313–18; see also Perrot's instructions, Dec. 1583, SP 63/106/43 and his comments thereon, SP 63/107/37.

[6] On Perrot's administration generally see Bagwell, *Ireland under the Tudors*, III, chs. 40–1, and more controversially Mathew, *Celtic peoples and renaissance Europe*, ch. 11; the best modern account of Perrot's Ulster policy is to be found in Morgan, *Tyrone's rebellion*, ch. 3; an important near contemporary but anonymous memoir is Richard Rawlinson (ed.), *The history of Sir John Perrot* (London, 1728).

[7] For examples of his self-advertisements see Perrot's 'Instructions to Mr Edward Norris', Aug. 1584, Lambeth MSS, 614/257; Perrot to privy council, 15 Sept. 1584, ibid., fos. 72–4; Perrot to Walsingham, 20 Oct., and to privy council, 25 Oct. 1584, SP 63/112/22, 41.

notwithstanding, all his hastily executed work started to come apart almost immediately after it had been completed, as the individual weakness of his separate undertakings began to combine against him.

In Munster his plans to establish viceregal authority over the new plantation failed from the very outset, as his demand that the entire province should contribute equally to the composition settlement rapidly alienated the newly arrived settlers.[8] At the same time, Perrot's refusal to acknowledge the provincial influence of the earl of Ormond by honouring the earl's promises of patronage and his suits for favourable treatment under the composition rapidly alienated the great earl who, though he had once been a close ally, began to employ the same court-centred intrigues against Perrot which had worked so well against Sidney.[9]

In the Pale things were worse. The summoning of the parliament which Perrot had hoped would secure the support of the Palesmen for his projects in a manner that had evaded Sidney in 1575 merely provided the Pale leaders with the opportunity to express their revulsion at Grey's conduct towards the country at the time of the Baltinglas conspiracy five years before. Determined to proclaim their defiance of coercive government, the well-organised Pale opposition not only rejected Perrot's composition scheme and mangled his entire parliamentary programme, but asserted their right to dissent from the government on one matter of high principle: they declared themselves to be recusants.[10]

But in Ulster Perrot's difficulties were most serious of all. The Scots, to begin with, refused to be so easily despatched from the north-east. Evading his onset, as they had once evaded Sussex, they returned to their settlements once he had departed, and compelled him at length to accept their presence as a permanent element in Ulster's politics.[11] More importantly, his elaborate plan to reorganise the structure of the Gaelic lordships in the province failed drastically. His schedule of closely linked phases, moving from the establishment of a military presence through the negotiations of composition agreements with the great lords to the final commutation of all feudal dues obtaining between the lords and their freeholders, fell into

---

[8] Michael MacCarthy-Morrogh, *The Munster plantation* (Oxford, 1986), pp. 52, 76–7; Bodl., Perrot MSS, 1, fo. 164.

[9] 'Petitions of Henry Shee' (Ormond's steward), 14 Apr. 1587, SP 63/129/10; Perrot to privy council, 28, 30 Apr. 1587, SP 65/12/, fos. 13–15, 63/129/41; Perrot and council to privy council, 20 May 1587, 65/12/89.

[10] Victor Treadwell, 'Sir John Perrot and the Irish parliament of 1585–6', *Proc. RIA 85* (1985), sect. c, pp. 259–308; Ciaran Brady, 'Conservative subversives: the community of the Pale and the Dublin administration, 1556–86', in P. J. Corish (ed.), *Radicals, rebels, and establishments, Historical Studies XV* (Belfast, 1985), pp. 28–30.

[11] 'Indenture with Sorley Boy', 'Division of the Route', SP 63/124/83, 85; Morgan, 'Outbreak of the nine years war', pp. 34–5.

disarray. In the first instance, Perrot's small garrisons received a highly uneven reception in the lordships in which they were introduced, with some meeting open resistance and others fitting gradually, like so many before them, into the traditional factional politics of their environment.[12] The effects of Perrot's second phase were similarly uneven. He renewed earlier treaties with the provincial lords and negotiated new terms with lesser figures. But the agreements remained for the most part formal and the arrangements which Perrot promised failed to materialise. Perrot's plans to introduce internal compositions were even less successful: for though several lords displayed an interest, only O'Reilly made a sustained effort to implement the change and his efforts remained inconclusive.[13] Most seriously of all, Perrot's ambitious plan to establish a regional government in the province through a division of authority between Turlough Luineach O'Neill, Marshall Bagenal and the baron of Dungannon (whose accession to the earldom of Tyrone he had conceded in 1585) proved abortive and resulted only in the intensification of rivalries between each of the three protagonists.[14]

The consequence of these multiple failures for Perrot's administration was similar to that which had attended his predecessors in office. Overspending and the absence of promised results produced an increasingly hostile attitude at court which was fuelled by the criticism and complaints of the Palesmen and the earl of Ormond. Within eighteen months of his assumption of office Perrot was under heavy attack from the queen and council and in receipt of directives demanding immediate response to criticism and the suspension of central parts of his programme. All of this would have been painfully familiar to Sussex and to Sidney.

Yet there was one further element in the deputy's sea of troubles which the others had been spared. Within a year of taking office Perrot had encountered sharp opposition to his programme from his own advisers on the Irish council and soon he had lost the confidence of the bulk of the English administrators in Ireland. He quarrelled first with Chancellor Loftus and Treasurer Wallop, and one by one he made enemies of Secretary Fenton, Marshal Bagenal and Presidents Norris and Bingham until he could depend only on a small group of Pale counsellors, most notably Sir Luke Dillon and Sir Nicholas White. The councillors' criticism of Perrot's conduct was harsh and surprisingly consistent. The viceroy's authoritarian

---

12 D. B. Quinn (ed.), 'Calendar of the Irish council book, 1 March 1581–1 July 1586', *Anal. Hib.* 24 (1967), pp. 91–180, p. 175; Wallop to Burghley, 26 Apr. 1586, SP 63/123/52; Morgan, *Tyrone's rebellion*, pp. 38–46.
13 Morgan, *Tyrone's rebellion*, ch. 3; Brady, 'The O'Reillys of East Breifne', pp. 233–62.
14 Hatfield House, Cecil MSS, 163, fos. 48–9; Perrot to privy council, 25 Oct. 1584, SP 63/112/41; Morgan, *Tyrone's rebellion*, ch. 3.

style, they alleged, was politically irresponsible and financially wasteful. The difficulties he had encountered in Munster, Connacht, in the Pale and in Ulster, they said, were largely of his own making and his actions were storing up major problems for the future. In his pursuit of personal ambition the governor, they claimed, was systematically undermining the fundamental interests of the English crown in Ireland.[15]

Perrot's isolation in Dublin Castle can be partly explained in terms of his highly abrasive personality: his high-handed and arbitrary dealings with his colleagues featured strongly among the charges that were later to ruin him. But the fact that such general opposition should have been so rapidly provoked against a political and administrative strategy that was essentially the same as Sussex's and Sidney's was a sign that a major change in outlook was taking place within the ranks of the Dublin administration. Not since the very beginning of the reform policy, in the days of Lord Leonard Grey, had such a sharp division arisen among the English administrators in Ireland. St Leger, as we have seen, had coped masterfully with internal opposition, isolating his critics and carefully constructing a loyal following of his own; and when he was at length dislodged from office, it was not through internal discontent but by external assault. Sussex and Sidney in their turn had suffered their share from malicious intrigues at court and in the country at large; but throughout their travails they had at least enjoyed the unswerving allegiance of their own administrative and executive subordinates, and it was only in his last days that Sidney was exposed to the unexpected attack of his own lord chancellor. The re-emergence of conciliar strife was, therefore, a symptom of more than a clash of personalities. It was, rather, an indication that thinking about the problem of Irish governance within the Dublin government was undergoing a crucial revision in the light of which the methods of Sussex and Sidney, and those currently being applied by Perrot were now perceived as increasingly irrelevant.

This gathering disillusion with the underlying assumptions of the traditional reform strategy varied considerably in extent and in the depth of its sophistication. On different grounds and to different degrees observers such as Andrew Trollope, Sir William Herbert and later Richard Beacon and Edmund Spenser began to express the view that English government could be maintained in Ireland not by peaceful, diplomatic persuasion, but only by a massive reassertion of English military might. A large standing army

---

[15] 'Articles' for Perrot, Feb. 1586, SP 63/122/92; Loftus to Burghley, 26 Apr., 4, 12 Dec. 1586, SP 63/123/24, 127/25 and enclosure (i); Bingham to Burghley, 26 Feb. 1587, SP 63/128/60; Perrot to Leicester, 18 Apr. 1587, Lambeth MSS, 618/68–71, and to Walsingham, 7 Mar. 1588, SP 63/124/7; Irish council to privy council, 15 May 1587, SP 63/129/83; Nicholas White to Burghley, 23 May, SP 63/129/93, enclosure (i); Wallop to Walsingham, 5 July, 63/135/72.

would be required to coerce the people into orderliness and suppress their natural rebelliousness. Extensive plantations were to be established in every province and a systematically repressive structure of local and regional government was to be established throughout the island.

Such demands for a radical departure in Irish policy were not, it should be said, the products of some political ginger group: important differences of analysis and intent may be discerned between their various arguments which cannot be ignored.[16] Yet for all their significant differences these critics shared a common concern to come to terms with the most pressing question raised by the Tudor experience in Ireland over the previous half-century. Why, they asked, had English law failed to take root in the island; why, after so much effort, had their demonstrably superior civilisation failed to improve the Irish? The case of Ireland raised a fundamental challenge to humanist assumptions concerning the reformability of mankind and to specifically English assumptions concerning the inestimable value of the common law upon which they had all been trained. Thus it is not surprising that in their attempts to address this disturbing problem they paid exceptional but generally unacknowledged attention to Machiavelli whose *Discourses on Livy* provided the most elaborate defence of the use of coercion and even tyranny in the governance and rehabilitation of decayed or corrupted polities. The use of colonies, the maintenance of a standing army and the firm regimentation of the populace by extra-legal methods all featured among Machiavelli's suggestions concerning the ways in which a degenerate commonwealth could be coerced into health. But more importantly than any specific recommendation, Machiavelli offered a justification in terms of a higher political morality for the use of any means, however forceful, that would bring order out of chaos.[17] To reflective Englishmen, mystified by the apparent intractability of the Irish problem, Machiavelli not only explained the failure of English law in Ireland in a manner that exonerated English government from the burden of guilt, he also justified the abandonment of the discredited policy of gradualist reform and the adoption where necessary of the more ruthless alternatives.

---

16 Nicholas Canny and Ciaran Brady, 'Debate: Spenser's Irish crisis', *Past & Present* 120 (1988), pp. 201–15; Brendan Bradshaw, 'Robe and sword in the conquest of Ireland', in Claire Cross, David Loades and J. J. Scarisbrick (eds.), *Law and government under the Tudors* (Cambridge, 1988), pp. 139–62.

17 On Machiavelli's influence over late Elizabethan writers, see Felix Raab, *The English face of Machiavelli* (London, 1964), chs. 1–2; and on Spenser in particular, E. A. Greenlaw, 'The influence of Machiavelli on Spenser', *Modern Philology* 7 (1909), pp. 187–202, and R. A. McCabe, 'The fate of Irena: Spenser and political violence' in Patricia Coughlan (ed.), *Spenser and Ireland* (Cork, 1989), pp. 109–25; for an illuminating discussion of Machiavelli's attempts to construct a higher political morality, see Sheldon Wolin, *Politics and vision* (London, 1961), ch. 7.

In the late 1580s and early 1590s, however, such a radical analysis was attempted by only a few. The massive increases in expenditure of treasure and effort which these arguments demanded, as well as their profoundly disturbing implications concerning the past conduct of English policy-makers in Ireland, rendered them, in the receding climate of the late Elizabethan era, politically quite unrealistic. Amidst the crisis years of the later 1590s, they would gradually assume a greater significance: and by the middle of the next century they had achieved the status of orthodoxy.[18] But at the time of their inception, they were for the most part ignored. Few men cared to analyse the causes of reform's failure in so rigorous a manner; and most administrators experienced its decline at the level of emotion only, as a source of disappointment, frustration and failure. The lessons of the century's defeats were etched most sharply on the mind of the man chosen to replace Perrot as viceroy in 1588, Sir William Fitzwilliam.

A man of long experience in Ireland who had witnessed the destruction of the two great reform governors under whom he had served and who had himself been a victim of Sidney's desire to regain office, Fitzwilliam resumed the viceroyalty with no great plan for Ireland and no ambition other than to maintain his administration in the cheapest possible manner, to defend himself against the slanders which Perrot, like Sidney before him, was now spreading in London, and to deal with whatever problems confronted him by the quickest and simplest means available. The principal events of Fitzwilliam's last term of office – his seizure of Brian O'Rourke, his settlement of Monaghan, his failure to control Sir Richard Bingham's ambitions in the north-west and his release of Hugh O'Donnell and Philip O'Reilly those notorious opponents of the Ulster composition whom Perrot had imprisoned in Dublin Castle – fit into no pattern other than the deputy's instinctive desire to avoid a commitment to any specific programme. But their cumulative effect was to bring to a head those processes which had already been developing slowly towards the point of crisis under Sussex's, Sidney's and finally Perrot's abortive regimes. The blatant opportunism of his intervention in Monaghan, coupled with his arbitrary execution of Hugh MacMahon the leading claimant for the title of chieftain, coming only months after his arrest of Brian O'Rourke on a charge of treason, severely disturbed the province's political elite. Among the MacMahons themselves the settlement turned out to be remarkably successful, but Fitzwilliam renounced all intention of maintaining the composition negotiations which Perrot had instituted for the reform of the province. Instead his probable

---

[18] Nicholas Canny, 'Identity formation in Ireland: the emergence of the Anglo-Irish' in Nicholas Canny and Anthony Pagden (eds.), *Colonial identity in the Atlantic world, 1500–1800* (Princeton, 1987), pp. 159–212.

connivance in the escape of O'Donnell and O'Reilly greatly encouraged the enemies of reform within the Ulster lordships while his bland toleration of the increasingly ambitious designs of the new earl of Tyrone rapidly disillusioned those who had supported composition as a means of freeing themselves from external influence and intimidation.[19]

Fitzwilliam's similarly inconsistent management of his own administration was equally damaging. In his concern to assert himself against Perrot, he consumed much time and much patronage in mounting a false and rather shabby allegation of treason against the former deputy. This malicious preoccupation and the sordid intrigues with dubious figures in which it embroiled him compromised Fitzwilliam's status as the Irish viceroy; but even more serious was his related campaign to destroy the remnants of Perrot's administrative support group. The allegations against Perrot led to the disgrace and in the latter case to the imprisonment of Sir Luke Dillon and Sir Nicholas White, the last remaining Anglo-Irish counsellors of influence, whose work as mediators between the country and the government had done so much to facilitate the introduction of many reform proposals in the past. Even more critically, Fitzwilliam's dismissal of Perrot's captains in Ulster and their replacement by new men who had no interest in promoting the composition greatly exacerbated tensions throughout the province, while at the same time his obvious ineffectualness in dealing with the more powerful Binghams in Connacht only confirmed their confidence that they need no longer have regard to Dublin.[20]

Behind all these blunders and provocations there lay no sinister device on the part of Fitzwilliam, but rather a silent repudiation of the high ambitions that had guided his three great predecessors in the viceregal office. Recognising the pressures under which they had buckled – their inability to control the effects of their own initiatives and their vulnerability to subversion and betrayal by their own supposed allies – Fitzwilliam by a very different route came to the conclusion now being articulated by Perrot's most radical critics: that the central administration could never function as

---

19 On Fitzwilliam's last viceroyalty, see in general Bagwell, *Tudors*, III, chs. 43, 44; on Ulster in particular Morgan, *Tyrone's rebellion*, ch. 4; 'Extradition and treason trial of a Gaelic lord: the case of Brian O'Rourke', *The Irish Jurist* 22 (1987), pp. 285–301; on Monaghan, Peadar Livingstone, *The Monaghan Story* (Enniskillen, 1980), ch. 4; and on Breifne, Brady, 'The O'Reillys of East Breifne'.

20 Charges and countercharges of Fitzwilliam and Perrot, *c.* 9 May 1589, SP 63/144/6, 7; Fitzwilliam to Burghley, 16 Feb., 30 Apr., 23 June, 28 July, 24 Sept. 1590, SP 63/150/144, 151/93, 153/24, 153/54, 154/38; White to Burghley, 7 May 1590, SP 63/152/26; Dillon to Walsingham, 13 Oct. 1589, SP 63/147/19, and to Burghley, 26 June 1590, SP 63/153/28; the fullest contemporary attack on Fitzwilliam is Thomas Lee, 'A brief declaration of the government of Ireland', *c.* 1594, in John Lodge (ed.), *Desiderata curiosa Hibernica* (2 vols., Dublin, 1772), II, pp. 87–150.

the means of constructing a reformed polity in Ireland. The old governor's preferred administrative style was, therefore, reactive and defensive, determined by the need to protect himself from external attack and utterly heedless of the cumulative implications of his apparently unrelated opportunist decisions. In this disavowal of responsibility in relation both to the objectives of his predecessors and to the long-term consequences of his own actions, Fitzwilliam embodied the disillusionment of Englishmen in Ireland with the reformist assumptions that had guided their actions over the previous fifty years, in a manner no less profound than the more articulate analyses of men like Spenser and his fellows.

Thus, under the eyes of a viceroy who renounced all responsibility for the problems he had inherited, the spirit of Tudor reform expired. And as conditions in Ulster rapidly deteriorated and everywhere else Irish lords and English captains confronted each other in an atmosphere of increasing hostility, the idea of establishing a model English kingdom in Ireland fell from sight – a victim neither of ideological change nor political convulsion, but of exhaustion, disillusion and neglect.

BIBLIOGRAPHY

SOURCES
MANUSCRIPT MATERIAL

Except where otherwise stated, the manuscript sources listed here are large collections of miscellaneous letters and papers concerning sixteenth-century Ireland.

Archivio Segreto Vaticano

Nunziatura di Fiandra, vol. 2 (Extract on microfilm in National Library of Ireland, N 2905, P 2526)

Bibliothèque Nationale, Paris

Fonds français, MSS 15971–3; MS 17832

Bodleian Library, Oxford

Carte MSS, 1, 55, 56, 57, 58, 131
Perrot MSS
University College MS, 103

British Library, London

Additiona, MSS 4763, 4767, 4797, 4823, 15914, 17520, 32091, 25830–2, 40061, 48015, 48017
Cotton MSS Titus B II
  Titus B X
  Titus B XI
  Titus B XII
  Titus B XIII
  Vespasian F IX
  Vespasian F XII
Harleian MSS 35, 2090, 3756, 6991–2, 7004
Lansdowne MSS 19, 35, 102, 159
Stowe MSS 159

Essex County Record Office, Chelmsford

Smith Papers MS D/Dsh 01/1–10

Genealogical Office, Dublin

MSS 161, 162, 169, 172, 200

Hatfield House, Hertfordshire

Cecil Papers 150–60, 201–2, 207

Henry E. Huntington Library, San Marino

Ellesmere MS E.L. 1701

Lambeth Palace Library, London

Carew MSS 600, 603, 605, 607, 609, 611, 614, 621, 624, 628

Marsh's Library, Dublin

Z.3.2.7, Annals of Dudley Loftus

National Library of Ireland, Dublin

MA 669, MS 2301, MS 8065

Northamptonshire Record Office, Northampton

Fitzwilliam MSS (Irish)
Fitzwilliam MSS (Correspondence)

National Archive of Ireland, Dublin

Ferguson MSS
Frazer MSS
Lodge's MSS
M2440
M2552
M2753
M2759
M5037–9
Record Commissioners' Reports
    R.C.1/1–6, Manuscript calendar of patent rolls, 1547–1588
    R.C.5/1–15, Chancery Inquisitions, transcripts
    R.C.9/10–11 Exchequer inquisitions, transcripts
    R.C.10/7–12 Transcripts of deeds and wills from exchequer inquisitions

Public Record Office, London

Exchequer Accounts E 101/248/22, E 101/520/1, E 101/532/2
State Papers Domestic, Edward SP 10
   Domestic, Mary SP 11
   Domestic, Eliz. SP 12
   Domestic, Addenda SP 15
   Ireland, Henry SP 60
   Ireland, Edward SP 61
   Ireland, Mary SP 62
   Ireland, Eliz. SP 63
Ireland Accounts SP 65; SP 66 Case A, No. 4
Transcripts 31/16/70

Royal Irish Academy, Dublin

MS 12.0.11. Account of the massacre of Mullaghmast

Trinity College, Dublin

MSS 581, 669, 842, 1087

PRINTED MATERIAL

Record publications

Acts of the Privy Council of England 1542–1631 (APC), 46 vols. (1890–1964).
Calendar of the Carew MSS preserved at Lambeth, 6 vols. (London, 1867–73).
Calendar of Fiants, Henry VIII–Elizabeth I (7th–22nd Reports, Deputy-Keeper of the Public Records of Ireland).
Calendar of the Patent Rolls, Edward VI, 6 vols. (1924–9).
Calendar of Patent Rolls, Mary I, 4 vols. (1937–9).
Calendar of Patent Rolls, Elizabeth I to 1575, 6 vols. (1939–73).
Calendar of Patent and Close Rolls of Chancery in Ireland, Henry VIII–Elizabeth, 2 vols. (1861–2).
Calendar of State Papers, Domestic, 1547–1603, 8 vols. (1856–72).
Calendar of State Papers, Foreign, 1547–1603, 25 vols. (1863–1950).
Calendar of State Papers, Ireland, 1509–1603, 11 vols. (1860–1912).
Calendar of State Papers, Rome, 1558–78, 2 vols. (1916–26).
Calendar of State Papers, Scotland, 1547–1603, 13 vols. (1898–1952).
Calendar of State Papers, Spanish, 1485–1603, 17 vols. (1862–1954).
Calendar of State Papers, Venetian, 1509–1603, 9 vols. (1867–98).
Letters and Papers, foreign and domestic, Henry VIII, 21 vols., and addenda (1862–1932).
Liber Munerum publicorum Hiberniae, ed. R. Lascelles, 2 vols. (London, 1852).
State Papers during the Reign of Henry the Eighth, 11 vols. (1830–52), vols. II–IV.
The Statutes at large passed in the parliaments held in Ireland 1310–1800, 20 vols. (1786–1801).

Publications of the Historical Manuscripts Commission

9th Report, appendix II (a) Leinster MSS; (b) Morison MSS
15th Report, appendix III, Haliday MSS
Bath (Longleat) MSS, V (1980).
De Lisle and Dudley MSS, I, II (1925–34).
Egmont MSS, I (1905).
Ormond MSS, I (1895); new ser., I (1902).
Pepys MSS (1911).
Salisbury (Cecil) MSS, I, II, III, XIII, XXIII (1883–1973).

Publications of Irish Manuscripts Commission (IMC)

Analecta Hibernica 2 (1931), 'Gerrard Papers: – Sir William Gerrard's notes of his report on Ireland, 1577–8', ed. C. McNeill, pp. 93–291.
Analecta Hibernica 4 (1932), 'Fitzwilliam MSS at Milton', ed. C. McNeill, pp. 287–326.
Analecta Hibernica 10 (1941), Guide to English financial records for Irish history 1461–1558, ed. D. B. Quinn, pp. 3–69.
Analecta Hibernica 24 (1967), Calendar of the Irish Council book, 1 March 1581 to 1 July 1586, ed. D. B. Quinn, pp. 91–180.
Analecta Hibernica 26 (1970), Additional Sidney State Papers, ed. D. B. Quinn, pp. 89–102.
The Compossicion Booke of Conought, ed. A. M. Freeman (Dublin, 1936).
Irish Monastic and Episcopal Deeds, A.D. 1200–1600, ed. N. B. White (Dublin 1936).
Calendar of Ormond Deeds, vols. iii–iv (1413–1603), ed. Edmund Curtis (Dublin, 1935–43).
Extents of Irish monastic possessions, 1540–41, ed. N. B. White (Dublin, 1943).
The Tanner Letters, ed. C. McNeill (Dublin, 1943).
The Walsingham Letter book or Register of Ireland 1578, ed. J. Hogan and N. McNeill O'Farrell (Dublin, 1959).
Dowdall Deeds, ed. Charles McNeill and A. J. Otway-Ruthven (Dublin, 1960).
Fitzwilliam Accounts 1560–65 (Annesley Collection), ed. A. K. Longfield (Mrs H. G. Leask) (Dublin, 1960).
Patentee officers in Ireland, ed. J. L. J. Hughes (Dublin, 1960).
Sidney State Papers 1565–70, ed. Tomás O'Laidhin (Dublin, 1962).
Crown surveys of lands 1540–41; with the Kildare rental begun in 1518, ed. Gearóid MacNiocaill (Dublin, 1992).
Herbert, Sir William, *Croftus: sive de Hibernia Liber*, eds. Arthur Keaveney and John A. Madden (Dublin, 1992).

Other documentary material

Bagenal, Sir Nicholas, 'The description and present state of Ulster, 20 Dec. 1586', *Ulster Journal of Archaeology* 2 (1854), pp. 137–60.
Collins, Arthur, *Letters and memorials of state – from the De Lisle and Dudley papers*, 2 vols. (London, 1746).
Croft, Sir James, 'The autobiography of Sir James Croft', ed. R. E. Ham, *Institute of Historical Research, Bull.* No. 50 (1977), pp. 48–57.

Devereux, W. B., *Lives and letters of the Devereux earls of Essex in the reigns of Elizabeth, James I and Charles I*, 2 vols. (London, 1853).

Edward VI, *The chronicle and political papers of King Edward VI*, ed. W. K. Jordan (London, 1966).

Fasti Ecclesiae Hibernicae: the succession of the prelates and members of the cathedral bodies of Ireland, ed. Henry Cotton (2nd edn, 6 vols., 1845–78).

Fenelon, Bertrand de Salignae de la Mothe, *Correspondance diplomatique 1578–75*, ed. J. B. A. Teulet, 7 vols. (Paris and London, 1838–40).

Fitzgerald, C. W., *The earls of Kildare and their ancestors, 1057–1773*, 2 vols. (Dublin, 1858–62, 2nd edn with addenda).

Fitzgerald, Walter (ed.), 'The will of Sir John Alen', *Jn. Kildare Arch. Soc.* 4 (1903–5), pp. 164–6.

Gerrard, William, 'Discourses on Wales', ed. D. L. Thomas, *Y Cymmrodor* 13 (1899), pp. 154–63.

Gilbert, Sir Humphrey, *The voyages and colonising enterprises of Sir Humphrey Gilbert*, ed. D. B. Quinn, 2 vols. (London, 1940).

Harris, Walter (ed.), *Hibernica: or some ancient pieces referring to Ireland*, 2 vols. (Dublin, 1747).

Hayman, Samuel, *Unpublished Geraldine documents*, 2 vols. (Dublin, 1870–81).

Haynes, Samuel, *A Collection of State Papers . . . 1542 to 1570* (London, 1740).

Hore, H. F. (ed.), 'The rental book of the Earl of Kildare', *Jn. RSAI* 5 (1858–9), pp. 266–80, 301–10; 7 (1862–3), pp. 110–37; 8 (1864–6), pp. 501–18, 525–46.

Hore, H. J. and Graves, J., eds., *The social state of the southern and eastern counties of Ireland in the sixteenth century* (Dublin, 1870).

Hughes, P. L. and Larkin, J. F. (eds.), *Tudor Royal Proclamations*, 3 vols. (New Haven, 1964–9).

Maxwell, Constantia, *Irish history from contemporary sources, 1509–1610* (London, 1923).

Paget, Sir William, 'The letters of William Lord Paget of Beaudesert, 1547–1563', ed. B. L. Beer and S. M. Jack, *Camden Society*, 4th ser. 13 (1974), pp. 1–141.

Phillips, J. R. S., *The justices of the peace in Wales and Monmouthshire, 1541–1689* (Cardiff, 1975).

Sidney, Sir Henry, 'Memoir or narrative addressed to Sir Francis Walsingham, 1583', *Ulster Journal of Archaeology*, 1st ser., 11 (1855), pp. 33–52, 85–109, 336–57; 5 (1857), pp. 299–322; 8 (1866), pp. 179–95.

White, Rowland, 'Discors touching the reformation of the realm of Ireland', ed. N. P. Canny, *Irish Historical Studies* 20 (1976–7), pp. 439–63.

'Dysorders of the Irisshery, 1571', ed. N. P. Canny, *Studia Hibernica* 19 (1979), pp. 147–60.

Annals, pamphlets and other contemporary or near contemporary writings

A letter sent by I.B. gentleman unto . . . Mayster R.C. esquire wherein is conteined a large discourse of the peopling and nhabiting the cuntries called the Ardes (London, 1571, STC, 1048).

Annála Connacht, ed. A. M. Freeman (Dublin, 1944).

Annála Rioghachta Eireann: Annals of the kingdom of Ireland by the four masters, ed. and trans. John O'Donovan, 7 vols. (Dublin, 1851).

Annála Uladh, ed. W. M. Hennessy and B. McCarthy, 4 vols. (Dublin, 1887–1901).

The Annals of Loch Ce: a chronicle of Irish affairs, 1014–1590, ed. W. M. Hennessy, 2 vols. (London, 1871).

Bale, John, 'The vocacyon of John Bale to the bishoprick of Ossorie in Irelande, 1553', *Harleian Miscellany*, VI (nd).

Beacon, Richard, *Solon his follie* (Oxford, 1594).

Boemus, Johan, *The fardel of facions* (London, 1555, STC, 3197).

'Book of Howth', ed. J. S. Brewer and W. Bullen, in *Cal. Carew MSS*, V, pp. 1–260.

Boorde, Andrew, *The fyrst boke of the Introduction of knowledge*, ed. F. J. Furnivall for the Early English Text Society, extra ser., 10 (1870).

Camden, William, *The history of Queen Elizabeth* (London, 1608).

Campion, Edmund, *Two bokes of the histories of Ireland* (1571), ed. A. F. Vossen (Assen, 1963).

Opuscula omnia nunc primum e M.S. edita, ed. R. Turner (Milan, 1625).

Churchyard, Thomas, *The miserie of Flaunders, calamitie of Fraunce, misfortune of Portugall, unquietness of Irelande, troubles of Scotlande and the blessed state of England* (London, 1579).

Churchyarde's choise, a general rehersall of warres (London, 1579, STC, 5235).

Cox, Richard, *Hibernia Anglicana or the history of Ireland from the conquest thereof by the English to this present time* 2 pts. (London, 1689–90).

Davies, Sir John, *A discovery of the true causes why Ireland was never entirely subdued* (London, 1612), in H. Morley, ed. *Ireland under Elizabeth and James I* (London, 1890).

Derricke, John, *The image of Ireland* (London, 1581).

Dowling, Thaddeo, *Annales Breves Hiberniae*, ed. Richard Butler (Irish Arch. Soc., 1849).

Herbert, Sir William, *Croftus: sive de Hibernia liber*, ed. W. E. Buckley (Roxburghe Club, 1887).

Holinshed, Raphael, *Chronicles of England, Scotland and Ireland*, ed. H. Ellis (London, 1808).

Hooker, J. alias J. Vowell, 'The chronicle of Ireland, 1547–83' in R. Holinshed, ed., *Chronicles* (1587 edn), VI, 32–461.

Life of Sir Peter Carew, ed. John McClean (London, 1857).

Lombard, Peter, *De regno hiberniae*, ed. P. F. Moran (Dublin, 1868).

Moryson, Fynes, 'Of the commonwealth of Ireland', in *Shakespeare's Europe*, ed. Charles Hughes (London, 1903), pp. 185–260.

Nichols, J. G. (ed.), Diary of Henry Machyn, citizen of London 1550–1563, *Camden Society*, 1st ser., 42 (1847).

O'Daly, Dominic, *Initium, incrementa et exitus familiae Geraldinorum . . .* (Lisbon, 1655); translated by C. P. Meehan as *The rise, increase and exit of the Geraldines* (1847, 1878).

O'Sullivan Beare, Philip, *Historiae Catholicae Iberniae Compendium* (1621); translated by M. J. Byrne as *Ireland under Elizabeth* (Dublin, 1903).

Perrot, Sir James, *The chronicle of Ireland, 1584–1608*, ed. Herbert Wood (Dublin, IMC, 1933).

Rawlinson, Richard (ed.), *History of that most eminent statesman, Sir John Perrot* (London, 1727).

Rich, Barnaby, *A new description of Ireland* (London, 1610).

Spenser, Edmund, *A View of the present state of Ireland in 1596*, ed. W. L. Renwick (London, 1934, repr. Oxford, 1970).

Stanihurst, Richard, 'Description of Ireland' in R. Holinshed, *Chronicles*, ed. Henry Ellis (London, 1808), pp. 1–69.
'Chronicle of Ireland to 1547', ibid., pp. 73–320.
De Rebus in Hibernia Gestis libri quattuor (Antwerp, 1584).
Walshe, Edward, *The office and duety in fighting for our countrey* (London, 1545).
Ware, Sir James, *Rerum hibernicarum annales* (Dublin, 1664).
Whole Works, ed. Walter Harris, 2 vols. (1739–64).

LATER WORKS
PUBLISHED BOOKS AND ARTICLES

Alsop, J. D., 'Government, finance and the community of the exchequer', in *The reign of Elizabeth I*, ed. C. Haigh (London, 1985), pp. 101–24.
'The structure of early Tudor finance, c. 1509–1558', in *Revolution reassessed: revisions in the history of Tudor government and administration*, ed. C. Coleman and D. R. Starkey (Oxford, 1986), pp. 135–62.
Andrews, K. R., *Elizabethan privateering; English privateering during the Spanish war 1585–1603* (Cambridge, 1964).
Andrews, K. R. et al. (eds.), *The westward enterprise: English activities in Ireland, the Atlantic and America, 1480–1650* (Liverpool, 1978).
Aylmer, Sir Fenton, 'Sir Gerald Aylmer, knight and baronet', *Journal of the Kildare Archaeological Society* 11 (1930–3), pp. 367–85.
Aylmer, G. E., *The king's servants: the civil service of Charles I 1625–42* (London, 1961, 2nd edn, London 1974).
Bagenal, P. H., 'Sir Nicholas Bagenal, Knight Marshal', *Journal of the Royal Society of Antiquaries of Ireland*, 6th ser., 5 (1959), pp. 5–26.
Bagwell, Richard, *Ireland under the Tudors*, 3 vols. (London, 1885–90).
Ball, F. E., *A history of County Dublin to the close of the eighteenth century*, 6 pts. (Dublin, 1902–20).
The judges in Ireland, 1221–1921, 2 vols. (London, 1926).
Barnewall, S. B., 'The family of Barnewall in the sixteenth and seventeenth centuries', in *The Irish Genealogist* 3: 4, 5, 7, 8, 10 (1956–67).
Bean, J. M. W., *The estates of the Percy family, 1416–1537* (London, 1958).
The decline of English feudalism, 1215–1540 (Manchester, 1968).
Beckett, J. C., *Confrontations: studies in Irish history* (London, 1972).
Beckingsale, B. W., *Elizabeth I* (London, 1963).
Thomas Cromwell, Tudor minister (London, 1978).
Berleth, Richard, *The twilight lords* (London, 1978).
Bindoff, S. T., J. Hurstfield and C. Williams (eds.), *Elizabethan government and society: essays presented to Sir John Neale* (London, 1961).
Bossy, John, 'The counter-reformation and the people of catholic Ireland, 1596–1641', in *Historical Studies VIII* (1971), pp. 155–69.
Bottingheimer, K. S., 'Kingdom and colony: Ireland in the westward enterprise', in K. R. Andrews et al. (eds.), *The westward enterprise* (Manchester, 1978), pp. 45–65.
Boynton, L. O., *The Elizabethan militia* (London, 1967).
Bradshaw, Brendan, 'The opposition to the ecclesiastical legislation in the Irish reformation parliament', *Irish Historical Studies* 16 (1969), pp. 285–303.
'George Browne, first reformation archbishop of Dublin, 1536–54', *Journal of Ecclesiastical History* 21 (1970), pp. 301–26.

'The beginnings of modern Ireland', in *The Irish parliamentary tradition*, ed. Brian Farrell (Dublin, 1973), pp. 68–87.

The dissolution of the religious orders in Ireland under Henry VIII (Cambridge, 1974).

'Cromwellian reform and the origins of the Kildare rebellion', *Transactions of the Royal Historical Society*, 5th ser., 27 (1977), pp. 69–93.

'The Edwardian Reformation in Ireland', *Archivium Hibernicum*, 34 (1976–7), pp. 83–99.

'The Elizabethans and the Irish', *Studies* 65 (1977), pp. 38–50.

'Sword, word and strategy in the reformation in Ireland', *Historical Journal* 21 (1978), pp. 475–502.

'Native reaction to the Westward Enterprises: a case study in Gaelic ideology', in K. R. Andrews, N. P. Canny and P. E. H. Hair (eds.), *The Westward Enterprise: English activities in Ireland, the Atlantic and America* (Liverpool, 1978), pp. 66–80.

The Irish constitutional revolution of the sixteenth century (Cambridge, 1979).

'The Elizabethans and the Irish: a muddled model', *Studies* 70 (1981), pp. 233–44.

'Edmund Spenser on justice and mercy' in Tom Dunne (ed.), *The writer as witness: Historical Studies XVI* (Cork, 1987), pp. 76–89.

'Robe and sword in the conquest of Ireland', in Claire Cross, David Loades and J. J. Scarisbrick (eds.), *Law and government under the Tudors: essays presented to Sir Geoffrey Elton on his retirement* (Cambridge, 1988), pp. 139–62.

Bradshaw, Brendan (ed.), 'A treatise for the reformation of Ireland, 1554–5', *Irish Jurist*, new ser. 16 (1981), pp. 299–315.

Brady, Ciaran, 'Faction and the origins of the Desmond rebellion of 1579', *Irish Historical Studies* 22 (1981), pp. 289–312.

'The killing of Shane O'Neill: some new evidence', *The Irish Sword* 15 (1982), pp. 116–23.

'The O'Reillys of East Breifne and the problem of surrender and regrant', *Breifne*, 6 (1985), pp. 233–62.

'Conservative subversives: the community of the Pale and the Dublin administration, 1556–86' in P. J. Corish (ed.), *Radicals, rebels and establishments: Historical Studies XV* (Belfast, 1985), pp. 11–32.

'Spenser's Irish crisis: humanism and experience in the 1590s', *Past and Present* 111 (1986), pp. 17–49.

'Thomas Butler, tenth earl of Ormond (1531–1614) and reform in Tudor Ireland' in Ciaran Brady (ed.), *Worsted in the game; losers in Irish history* (Dublin, 1989), pp. 49–60.

'The road to the view: on the decline of reform thought in Tudor Ireland', in Patricia Coughlan (ed.), *Spenser and Ireland* (Cork, 1989), pp. 25–45.

'Ulster and the failure of Tudor reform' in Ciaran Brady, Mary O'Dowd and Brian Walker (eds.), *Ulster: an illustrated history* (London, 1989), pp. 77–103.

Brady, Ciaran and Gillespie, Raymond (eds.), *Natives and newcomers: essays on the making of Irish colonial society* (Dublin, 1986).

Burkes Irish Family Records, 5th edn (London, 1976).

Bush, M. L., 'The Lisle-Seymour land disputes: a study in power and influence in the 1530s', *Historical Journal* 9 (1966), pp. 255–74.

The government policy of Protector Somerset (London, 1975).

Butler, George, 'The battle of Affane', *The Irish Sword* 8 (1967–8), pp. 43–51.
Butler, T. B., 'Seneschals of the Liberty of Tipperary', *Irish Genealogist* 2–3 (1955–7).
Butler, W. F. T., *Gleanings from Irish history* (London, 1925).
Canny, N. P., 'Hugh O'Neill, earl of Tyrone and the changing face of Gaelic Ulster', *Studia Hibernica* 10 (1970), pp. 7–35.
'Changing views on Gaelic Ireland', *Topic* 24: *Themes in Irish culture* (Washington, 1972), pp. 19-28.
'The ideology of English colonization: from Ireland to America', *William and Mary Quarterly* 30 (1973), pp. 575–98.
The formation of the Old English elite in Ireland, National University of Ireland. O'Donnell Lecture (Dublin, 1975).
The Elizabethan conquest of Ireland: a pattern established, 1565–76 (Hassocks, 1976).
'Dominant minorities. English settlers in Ireland and Virginia 1550–1650' in A. C. Hepburn (ed.), *Minorities in history: Historical Studies XII* (London, 1978), pp. 51–69.
'The permissive frontier: social control in English settlements in Ireland and Virginia' in K. R. Andrews et al. (eds.), *The Westward Enterprise* (Manchester, 1978), pp. 17–44.
'Edmund Spenser and the development of an Anglo-Irish identity', *The Yearbook of English Studies* 13 (1983), pp. 1–19.
From reformation to restoration: Ireland 1534–1660 (Dublin, 1987).
Kingdom and colony: Ireland in the Atlantic world, 1560–1800 (Baltimore, MD, 1988).
'Identity formation in Ireland: the emergence of the Anglo-Irish' in Nicholas Canny and Anthony Pagden (eds.), *Colonial identity in the Atlantic world, 1500–1800* (Princeton, 1987), pp. 159–212.
Challis, C. E., 'The Tudor coinage for Ireland', *British Numismatic Journal* 40 (1971), pp. 97–119.
Chambers, Anne, *Granuaile: the life and times of Grace O'Malley, c. 1530–1603* (Dublin, 1979).
Chieftain to knight, Tibbot Bourke, 1567–1629, first Viscount Mayo (Dublin, 1983).
Clark, Peter, *English provincial society from the reformation to the revolution: religion, politics and society in Kent, 1500–1500* (Hassocks, 1977).
Clarke, Aidan, *The Old English in Ireland, 1625–1642* (London, 1966).
'Colonial identity in early seventeenth-century Ireland', in T. W. Moody (ed.), *Nationality and the pursuit of national independence: Historical Studies*, XI, pp. 57–71.
Coburn-Walshe, Helen, 'The rebellion of William Nugent, 1581', in R. V. Comerford, Mary Cullen, Jacqueline R. Mill and Colm Lennon (eds.), *Religion, conflict and coexistence in Ireland* (Dublin, 1990), pp. 26–52.
Coleman, Christopher and David Starkey (eds.), *Revolution reassessed: revisions in the history of Tudor government and administration* (Oxford, 1986).
Coleman, C., 'Artifice or accident? The reorganization of the exchequer of receipt, c. 1554–1572',in *Revolution reassessed*, ed. C. Coleman and D. R. Starkey (Oxford 1986), pp. 163–98.
Complete Peerage of England, Scotland, Ireland, Great Britain and the United Kingdom, ed. G. E. Cokayne (rev. edn, 13 vols., London, 1910–49).

Conway, Agnes, *Henry VII's relations with Scotland and Ireland, 1485–98* (Cambridge, 1932).

Corristine, Laurence, *The revolt of Silken Thomas: a challenge to Henry VIII* (Dublin, 1987).

Cosgrove, Art (ed.), *A new history of Ireland (ii), Medieval Ireland, 1169–1534* (Oxford, 1987).

Crawford, John C., *Anglicising the government of Ireland: the Irish privy council and the expansion of Tudor rule, 1556–1578* (Dublin, 1993).

Cregan, D. F., 'Irish Catholic admissions to the English Inns of Court, 1558–1625', *Irish Jurist*, new ser., 5 (1970), pp. 95–114.

Cruikshank, C. G., *Elizabeth's army* (1946; 2nd edn, Oxford, 1966).

Cunningham, Bernadette, 'The composition of Connaught in the lordships of Clanrickard and Thomond, 1577–1641', *Irish Historical Studies* 24 (1984), pp. 1–14.

Curtis, Edmund, *A history of mediaeval Ireland, 1110–1513* (London, 1923).

Davies, C. S. L., 'Provisions for armies, 1509–1550: a study in the effectiveness of Tudor government', *Economic History Review*, 2nd ser., 17 (1964), pp. 234–48.

Peace, print and Protestantism 1450–1558 (London, 1976).

Dewar, M., *Sir Thomas Smith: a Tudor intellectual in office* (London, 1964).

Dictionary of National Biography (DNB), ed. L. Stephen and S. Lee, 2nd edn., 22 vols. (London, 1908–9).

Dolley, Michael, 'Anglo-Irish monetary policies, 1172–1637', in J. C. Beckett (ed.), *Historical Studies VII* (1969), pp. 45–64.

Dunlop, Robert, 'The plantations of Leix and Offaly, 1556–1622', *English Historical Review* 6 (1891), pp. 61–96.

'Some aspects of Henry VIII's Irish policy', in *Owens College Historical Essays*, eds. T. F. Tout and J. Tait (London, 1902), pp. 279–305.

'Sixteenth-century maps of Ireland', *English Historical Review* 20 (1905), pp. 309–37.

'Sixteenth-century schemes for the plantation of Ulster', *Scottish Historical Review* 22 (1924–5), pp. 51–60, 115–26, 199–212.

Edwards, David, 'The Butler revolt of 1569', *Irish Historical Studies* 28 (1992–3) pp. 228–55.

Edwards, R. Dudley, *Church and state in Tudor Ireland* (London, 1935).

'Ireland, Elizabeth I and the counter-reformation' in S. T. Bindoff, Joel Hurstfield and C. H. Williams (eds.), *Elizabethan government and society* (London, 1961), pp. 315–39.

'The Irish reformation parliament of Henry VIII, 1536–7', in T. W. Moody (ed.), *Historical Studies VI* (London, 1968), pp. 59–84.

Ireland in the age of the Tudors: the destruction of Hiberno-Norse civilisation (London, 1977).

Edwards, R. Dudley and T. W. Moody, 'The history of Poynings's Law, 1495–1615', *Irish Historical Studies* 2 (1941), pp. 415–24.

Edwards, R. D. with Quinn, D. B., 'Thirty years' work in Irish history (ii): sixteenth-century Ireland', *Irish Historical Studies* 16 (1968–9), pp. 15–32.

Edwards, R. D. and O'Dowd, M., *Sources for early modern Irish history, 1534–1641* (Cambridge, 1985).

Ellis, S. G., 'The Kildare rebellion and the early Henrician Reformation', *Historical Journal* 19 (1976), pp. 807–30.

'Tudor policy and the Kildare ascendancy in the lordship of Ireland', *Irish Historical Studies* 20 (1976–7), pp. 235–71.

'Taxation and defence in late medieval Ireland: the survival of scutage', *Journal of the Royal Society of Antiquaries of Ireland* 107 (1977), pp. 5–28.

'Thomas Cromwell and Ireland', *Historical Journal* 23 (1980), pp. 497–519.

'England in the Tudor state', *Historical Journal* 26 (1983), pp. 201–12.

'John Bale, bishop of Ossory, 1552–3', *Journal of the Butler Society* 2 no. 3 (1984), pp. 283–93.

Tudor Ireland: crown, colony and the conflict of cultures 1470–1603 (London, 1985).

Reform and revival: English government in Ireland, 1470–1536 (Woodbridge, 1986).

'Economic problems of the church: why the reformation failed in Ireland', *Journal of Ecclesiastical History* 41 (1990), pp. 239–65.

Elton, G. R., *The Tudor constitution* (2nd edn, Cambridge, 1982).

Reform and renewal: Thomas Cromwell and the common weal (Cambridge, 1973).

Studies in Tudor and Stuart politics and government (3 vols., Cambridge, 1974–83).

Empey, C. A. and Simms, M. K. 'The ordinances of the White Earl and the problem of coign in the later middle ages', *Proceedings of the Royal Irish Academy 75*, sect. C (1975), pp. 161–87.

Evans, F. M. G., *The principal secretary of state: a survey of the office from 1558 to 1680* (Manchester, 1923).

Falls, Cyril, *Elizabeth's Irish wars* (London, 1950).

'Black Tom Ormonde', *Irish Sword* 5 (1961–2), pp. 10–22.

Ferguson, A. B., *The articulate citizen and the English renaissance* (Durham, NC, 1965).

Finch, M. E., *The wealth of five Northamptonshire families 1540–60* (Northampton, 1956).

Fitzgerald, Walter, 'Kilkea Castle', *Journal of the Kildare Archaeological Society* 2 (1896–9), pp. 3–32.

'Genealogy of the Harpoles', *Journal of the Kildare Archaeological Society* 4 (1903–4), pp. 300–1.

'Genealogy of the Cosbys of Stradbally', *Journal of the Kildare Archaeological Society* 5 (1906–9), pp. 316–17.

Fletcher, Anthony, *Tudor rebellions*, 3rd edn (London, 1983).

Fox, A. and J. A. Guy, *Reassessing the Henrician Age: humanism, politics and reform, 1500–1550* (Oxford, 1986).

Frost, James, *The history and topography of the county of Clare* (1st edn, reprint Cork, 1978).

Greenlaw, E. A., 'The influence of Machiavelli on Spenser', *Modern Philology* 7 (1909), pp. 187–202.

Hammerstein, Helga, 'Aspects of the continental education of Irish students in the reign of Queen Elizabeth I', in T. D. Williams (ed.), *Historical Studies VIII* (1971), pp. 137–54.

Hampson, C. P., *The Book of the Radclyffes* (priv. pr., Edinburgh, 1940).

Hawkins, Michael, 'The central government: its role and its aims', in Conrad Russell (ed.), *The origins of the English civil war* (London, 1973).

Hayes-McCoy, G. A., *Scots mercenary forces in Ireland, 1565–1603* (Dublin, 1937).

'Gaelic society in Ireland in the late sixteenth century', in G. A. Hayes-McCoy (ed.), *Historical Studies IV* (1963), pp. 45–61.

Irish Battles (London, 1969).

Henley, Pauline, *Spenser in Ireland* (Dublin, 1928).

Hill, George, *An historical account of the MacDonnells of Antrim* (Belfast, 1873, reprint Ballycastle, 1976).

Hoak, D. E., *The king's council in the reign of Edward VI* (Cambridge, 1976).

Hogan, James, 'Shane O'Neill comes to the court of Elizabeth', in S. Pender (ed.), *Feil-Scribhinn Torna* (Cork, 1947), pp. 154–70.

Hore, H. F., 'The Clan Kavanagh, temp. Henry VIII', *Journal of the Kilkenny and South-East Ireland Archaeological Society*, new ser., 2 (1858–9), pp. 73–92.

History of the town and county of Wexford, 6 vols. (London, 1900–11).

Hoskins, W. G., *The Age of Plunder: the England of Henry VIII, 1509–47* (London, 1976).

Hughes, James, 'Sir Edmund Butler of the Dullough, Knt.', *Journal of the Royal Historical and Archaeological Association of Ireland*, 4th ser., 1 (1870–1), pp. 153–92, 211–31.

'The fall of Clan Kavanagh', *Journal of the Royal Historical and Archaeological Society*, 4th ser., 2: 2, (1873), pp. 282–305.

Hurstfield, Joel, *The Queen's Wards: wardship and marriage under Elizabeth I* (London, 1958).

Elizabeth I and the unity of England (London, 1960).

Freedom, corruption and government in Elizabethan England (London, 1973).

Ives, E. W., 'Faction at the court of King Henry VIII', *History* 57 (1972), pp. 169–88.

Faction in Tudor England (Historical Association pamphlet, 1979).

Jackson, Donald, *Intermarriage in Ireland, 1550–1650* (Montreal, 1970).

James, M. E., 'The concept of order and the northern rising, 1569', *Past and Present* 60 (1973), pp. 49–83.

English politics and the concept of honour, 1485–1642 (Past and Present supplement 3, Oxford, 1978).

Jones, W. R. D., *The mid-Tudor crisis 1539–63* (London, 1973).

Jordan, W. K., *Edward VI: the threshold of power. The dominance of the duke of Northumberland* (London, 1970).

Lambert, G. W., 'Sir Nicholas Malby', *Journal of the Galway Archaeological Society* 23 (1948–9), pp. 1–13.

Lander, J. R., *The crown and the nobility, 1450–1509* (London, 1976).

Lehmberg, S. E., *Sir Walter Mildmay and Tudor government* (Austin, 1960).

Lennon, Colm, 'Recusancy and the Dublin Stanihursts', *Archivium Hibernicum* 33 (1975), pp. 101–10.

Richard Stanihurst: the Dubliner 1547–1618 (Dublin, 1981).

'The counter-reformation in Ireland 1542–1641', in Brady and Gillespie (eds.), *Natives and Newcomers*, pp. 75–92.

The lords of Dublin in the age of reformation (Dublin, 1989).

Levine, Mortimer, *The early Elizabethan succession question* (Stanford, 1966).

Livingstone, Peadar, *The Fermanagh story* (Enniskillen, 1969).

The Monaghan story (Enniskillen, 1980).

Lloyd, H. A., 'The Essex inheritance', *Welsh Historical Review* 7 (1974), pp. 13–39.

Loach, J. and R. Tittler (eds.), *The Mid-Tudor polity c. 1540–1560* (London, 1980).

Loades, D. M., *The Tudor conspiracies* (Cambridge, 1965).

The reign of Mary Tudor: politics, government and religion in England, 1553–8 (London, 1979).

The Tudor court (London, 1986).

Lydon, J. F., *The lordship of Ireland in the Middle Ages* (Dublin, 1972).

Lytner, H. L., 'The family of Alen of St. Wolstan's', *Journal of the Kildare Archaeological Society* 4 (1903–5), pp. 95–110.

McCabe, Richard, 'The fate of Irena: Spenser and political violence', in Patricia Coughlan (ed.), *Spenser and Ireland* (Cork, 1989), pp. 109–25.

MacCaffrey, Wallace, 'Place and patronage in Elizabethan politics', in S. T. Bindoff et al. (eds.), *Elizabethan government and society* (London, 1961).

'Elizabethan politics: the first decade 1558–1568', *Past and Present* 24 (1963), pp. 25–42.

The shaping of the Elizabethan regime (London, 1969).

Queen Elizabeth and the making of policy, 1572–8 (Princeton, 1981).

Mac Carthy-Morrogh, M., *The Munster Plantation: English migration to southern Ireland 1583–1641* (Oxford, 1986).

McConica, J. K., *English humanists and renaissance politics* (Oxford, 1965).

MacCurtain, Margaret, *Tudor and Stuart Ireland* (Dublin, 1972).

Madden, A. F. McC., '1066, 1776 and all that: the relevance of English medieval experience of empire to later imperial constitutional issues' in *Perspectives of empire*, ed. J. E. Flint and Glandwyr Williams (London, 1973), pp. 9–26.

Martin, F. X., *Friar Nugent, agent of the counter-reformation* (Rome and London, 1962).

Mathew, David, *The Celtic peoples and renaissance Europe* (London, 1933).

Mayer, T. F., *Thomas Starkey and the commonweal* (Cambridge, 1989).

Moody, T. W., 'The Irish parliament under Elizabeth and James I', *Proceedings of the Royal Irish Academy* 45, section C. no. 6 (1939), pp. 41–81.

Moody, T. W., F. X. Martin and F. J. Byrne (eds.), *A new history of Ireland: iii early modern Ireland* (Oxford, 1976).

Morgan, Hiram, 'The colonial venture of Sir Thomas Smith', *Historical Journal* 28 (1985), pp. 261–78.

'The end of Gaelic Ulster; a thematic interpretation of events between 1534 and 1610', *Irish Historical Studies* 26 (1988), pp. 8–32.

'Extradition and treason trial of a Gaelic lord: the case of Brian O'Rourke', *The Irish Jurist* 22 (1987), pp. 285–301.

Tyrone's rebellion: the outbreak of the Nine Years War in Tudor Ireland (Woodbridge, 1993).

Morton, R. C., 'The enterprise of Ulster', *History Today* 17 (1967), pp. 114-21.

Neale, J. E., 'The Elizabethan political scene', in *Essays in Elizabethan history* (London, 1958).

The Elizabethan house of commons, revised edn (London, 1963).

Elizabeth I and her parliaments, 2 vols. (London, 1953–7).

Nicholls, K. W., *Gaelic and gaelicised Ireland in the Middle Ages* (Dublin, 1972).

Land, law and society in sixteenth century Ireland (O'Donnell Lecture, 1976).

ÓCorráin, Donncha, *Ireland before the Normans* (Dublin, 1971).

O'Donoghue, John, *Historical memoirs of the O'Briens* (Dublin, 1860).

O'Dowd, Mary, 'Gaelic economy and society', in Brady and Gillespie (eds.), *Natives and newcomers*, pp. 120–47.

O'Hanlon, J. and O'Leary, E., *History of the Queen's County*, 2 vols. (Dublin, 1907, 1914).

O Laidhin, T., 'Sir Henry Sidney's first lord deputyship', *Bulletin of Irish Comm. of Hist. Sciences* 80 (1957).

O'Sullivan, M. D., 'Irish lawyers in Tudor times', *Dublin Review* 179 (1926), pp. 1–11.

O'Toole, P. L., *History of the Clan O'Toole* (Dublin, 1890).

Otway Ruthven, A. J., *A history of medieval Ireland* (London, 1968).

Piveronus, P. J., 'Sir Warham St. Leger and the first Munster plantation, 1568–9', *Eire/Ireland* (Summer 1979), pp. 15–36.

Powicke, F. M. and Fryde, E. B., *Handbook of British chronology* (2nd edn) (London, 1961).

Prendergast, J. P., 'The plantation of the barony of Idrone', *Journal of the Kilkenny and South-East Ireland Archaeological Society*, ser. 2, 2: 2 (1859), pp. 400–28.

Prestwich, Michael, *War, politics and finance under Edward I* (London, 1972).

Price, Liam, 'Notes on Feagh McHugh O'Byrne', *Journal of the Kildare Archaeological Society* 11 (1930–5), pp. 134–75.

'The Byrnes' country in County Wicklow in the sixteenth century', *Journal of the Royal Society of Antiquaries* 63 (1933), pp. 225–41, 64 (1936), pp. 42–66.

Pugh, T. B., *The marcher-lordships of South Wales, 1415–1536* (Cardiff, 1963).

Pulman, M. B., *The Elizabethan privy council in the fifteen seventies* (Berkeley, 1971).

Quinn, D. B., 'Anglo-Irish Ulster in the early sixteenth century', *Belfast Natural Historical and Philosophical Society Report and Proceedings* (1935), pp. 56–78.

'The Irish parliamentary subsidy in the 15th and 16th centuries', *Proceedings of the Royal Irish Academy*, 35, sect. c (1935), pp. 219–46.

'Anglo-Irish local government, 1485–1534', *Irish Historical Studies* 1 (1939), pp. 354–81.

'The early interpretation of Poynings' Law, 1494–1534', *Irish Historical Studies* 11 (1941), pp. 241–54.

'A Discourse on Ireland (circa 1599): a sidelight on English colonial policy', *Proceedings of the Royal Irish Academy* 42, sect. c (1942), pp. 151–66.

'Government printing and publication', *Proceedings of the Royal Irish Academy* 42, sect. c (1942), pp. 45–129.

'Parliaments and Great Councils in Ireland, 1461–1586', *Irish Historical Studies* 3 (1943), pp. 60–77.

'Agenda for Irish history, 1461–1603', *Irish Historical Studies*, 4 (1945), pp. 258–69.

'Sir Thomas Smith and the beginnings of English colonial theory', *Proceedings of the American Philosophical Society* 89 (1945), pp. 543–60.

'Edward Walshe's "Conjectures" concerning the state of Ireland, 1552', *Irish Historical Studies*, V (1947), pp. 303–33.

'Ireland and sixteenth-century European expansion', in T. D. Williams (ed.), *Historical Studies I* (1958), pp. 20–32.

'Henry VIII and Ireland, 1509–34', *Irish Historical Studies* 12 (1961), pp. 318–44.

Raleigh and the British Empire, 2nd edn (London, 1962).

The Elizabethans and the Irish (Ithaca, 1966).

'The Munster plantation: problems and opportunities', *Journal of the Cork Historical and Archaeological Society* 71 (1966), pp. 19–41.

'Renaissance influences in English colonization', *Transactions of the Royal Historical Society*, 5th ser., 25 (1976), pp. 73–93.

Raab, Felix, *The English face of Machiavelli* (London, 1964).

Rae, T. I., *The administration of the Scottish frontier, 1513–1603* (Edinburgh, 1966).

Read, Conyers, 'Faction in the privy council under Elizabeth', *Annual report of American Historical Association* (1911).

'Walsingham and Burghley in Queen Elizabeth's Privy Council', *English Historical Review* 43 (1928), pp. 195–9.

Mr Secretary Walsingham and the policy of Queen Elizabeth, 3 vols. (Oxford, 1925).

'Profits on the re-coinage of 1560–1', *English Historical Review* 6 (1936), pp. 186–93.

Mr Secretary Cecil and Queen Elizabeth (London, 1955).

Lord Burghley and Queen Elizabeth (London, 1959).

Reid, Rachel, *The king's council in the north* (London, 1921).

Ronan, M. V., *The reformation in Dublin, 1536–1558* (Dublin, 1926).

The reformation in Ireland under Elizabeth, 1558–80 (Dublin, 1930).

Round, J. H., 'The earldom of Kildare', *The Genealogist*, new ser., 9 (1892–3), pp. 202–6.

Simmington, R. C. (Kevin), 'Note on powers of a seneschal', *Catholic Bulletin* 13 (1923), pp. 203–4.

Smith, A. G. R., *The government of Elizabethan England* (London, 1967).

The emergence of a nation state: the commonwealth of England, 1529–1660 (London, 1984).

Smith, A. H., *County and court; government and politics in Norfolk 1558–1603* (Oxford, 1974).

Starkey, D., D. A. L. Morgan, J. Murphy, P. Wright, N. Cuddy and K. Sharpe, *The English court from the wars of the roses to the civil war* (London, 1987).

Stone, Lawrence, 'The anatomy of the Elizabethan aristocracy', *Economic History Review*, 18 (1948), pp. 1–41.

Taffe, D. J., *An impartial history of Ireland*, 4 vols. (Dublin, 1809–11).

Titler, Robert, *Sir Nicholas Bacon: the making of a Tudor statesman* (London, 1976).

Treadwell, Victor, 'The Irish parliament of 1569–71', *Proceedings of the Royal Irish Academy* 65, sect. c (1966), pp. 55–89.

'Sir John Perrot and the Irish parliament of 1585–6', *Proceedings of the Royal Irish Academy* 85 sect. c (1985), pp. 259–308.

Tyrrell, J. H., *Genealogical history of the Tyrrells* (Dublin, 1904).

Tytler, P. Frazer, *England under the reigns of Edward VI and Mary*, 2 vols. (London, 1839).

Weikel, Ann, 'The Marian council revisited', in J. Loads and R. Titler (eds.), *The mid-Tudor polity* (London, 1980), pp. 52–73.

White, D. G., 'The reign of Edward VI in Ireland: some political, social and economic aspects', *Irish Historical Studies* 14 (1965), pp. 197–211.

'Henry VIII's Irish kerne in Scotland and France', *Irish Sword* 3 (1957–8), pp. 213–25.

Williams, Neville, *Thomas Howard, fourth duke of Norfolk* (London, 1964).

Williams, Penry, *The council in the marches of Wales under Elizabeth I* (Cardiff, 1958).

'The council in Munster in the late sixteenth century', *Bulletin of the Irish Comm. of Historical Sciences* 123.

The Tudor regime (Oxford, 1979).

Wilson, Charles, *The revolt of the Netherlands* (London, 1970).

Wilson, Philip, *The beginnings of modern Ireland* (Dublin, 1912).

Wolin, S. S., *Politics and vision* (London, 1961).

Wood, Herbert, 'The court of Castle Chamber', *Proceedings of the Royal Irish Academy* 32 sect. c (1914), pp. 152–70.

'The office of chief governor of Ireland, 1172–1509', *Proceedings of the Royal Irish Academy* 36, sect. c (1923), pp. 206–38.

'The secretary of state for Ireland', *Proceedings of the Royal Irish Academy* 38, sect. c (1928), pp. 51–68.

Woodworth, Allegra, 'Purveyance for the royal household in the reign of Queen Elizabeth', *Transactions of the American Philosophical Society* new ser., 35 (1945), pp. 1–86.

Zeeveld, W. G., *The foundations of Tudor policy* (Cambridge, MA, 1948).

UNPUBLISHED THESES

Costello, Joseph, 'Turlough Luineach O'Neill: the urrithe and the central government', MA (University College, Dublin, 1973).

D. P. Dorrian, 'The cockpit of Ireland: north-east Ulster in the late sixteenth century', BA thesis (Trinity College, Dublin, 1984).

Empey, C. A., 'The Butler lordship to 1509', PhD (University of Dublin, 1970).

Hanrahan, M. C., 'Gerald, the eleventh earl of Kildare', MA (University of Manchester, 1974).

Kennedy, D. J., 'The presidency of Munster', MA (University College, Cork, 1973).

Lyons, T. B., 'Shane O'Neill: a biography', MA (University College, Cork, 1947).

Morgan, Hiram, 'The outbreak of the Nine Years War in Ulster', PhD (University of Cambridge, 1987).

Simms, Katharine, 'Gaelic Ulster in the late middle ages', PhD (University of Dublin, 1976).

White, D. G., 'Tudor plantations in Ireland to 1571', PhD (University of Dublin, 1967.

INDEX

act for the kingly title, the, 25, 30, 50, 71, 79, 160, 209
Agard, Francis, 39, 117, 214, 274
Agard, Mary, 274
Agard, Thomas, 32, 36–7, 38, 39, 61, 65, 67, 117
Alen family, 238
Alen, Sir John, chancellor, 9, 18, 19, 20, 21, 23, 24, 27, 33, 41, 42–3, 50, 61, 65, 67, 81–2, 88, 250
Alen, John, 192–3, 236
Alen, Thomas, 82
Alford, Launcelot, 83
Anglo-Irish, 9, 40, 68, 73, 84, 91–3, 113, 122, 207, 208, 212
Argyle, earl of, *see* Campbell, Archibald
Arnold, Sir Nicholas, lord justice, 104, 106, 107–11, 114, 116, 118, 119, 121, 123, 189, 216, 224
Aylmer, Sir Gerald, C.J., 18, 20, 21, 23, 24, 48, 83
Aylmer, Gerald, 240
Alymer, Richard, 67

Bacon, Francis, 159
Bacon, Sir Nicholas, 103, 193
Bagenal, Dudley, 276
Bagenal, Sir Nicholas, 67, 116, 121, 225, 257–60, 264, 290, 295
Bagwell, Richard, xi, 106, 113
Bale, John, 56
Baltinglas, Viscount, *see* Eustace, James and Rowland
Baltinglas Abbey, 36
Barnewall family, 214, 238
Barnewall, Sir Christopher, 181
Barnewall, James, 82, 83, 84
Barry James Fitzrichard (Viscount Barrymore), 194, 200
Bathe, ?James, 19
Bathe, Thomas, 249

Beck, Edward, 16
Bellingham, Sir Edward, 46, 48–9, 50, 51, 52, 59, 60, 61, 62, 63, 69, 215, 217, 219–21, 222, 249, 265
Bermingham family (Carbery), 39
Bermingham, Patrick, 237, 238, 240
Bermingham, Wm., 103–4, 235, 236, 237, 238, 241, 243, 252
billeting, statistics for, 223, *see also* cess, soldiers' conduct
Bingham, Richard, 293, 295, 298
Body, Wm., 18
Boleyn, Anne, 14
Brabazon, Mary, 32
Brabazon, Sir Wm., 9, 19, 21, 32, 33–36, 37, 38, 39, 41, 56, 62, 65, 66, 67, 83, 117
Bradshaw, Brendan, ix, 8, 25–6, 30, 39–40
Brady, Hugh, 121
Brasier, Richard, 65–6
brehon law, 74
Brett, Jerome, 132, 250
Browne, Valentine, 66–7, 86
Bryan, Sir Francis, 58, 215
Burghley, baron, *see* Cecil, Wm.
Burke family (Clanrickard), 49, 109, 172, 180, 186, 189, 200, 201–2, 207
Burke, Richard (2nd earl of Clanrickard), 75, 98, 109, 137, 144, 151, 169, 172, 174, 175, 176, 179, 182, 183, 184, 187–9, 201, 283
Burke, Richard 'an iarann', 282–3
Burke, Ulick (1st earl of Clanrickard), 38, 179
Burke, Ulick (3rd earl of Clanrickard), 201
Burnell, Henry, 149, 236–7, 240, 241
Butler (Cahir), 39
Butler (Dunboyne), 39
Butler family (Ormond), 3, 9, 17, 19, 21, 24, 29, 30, 40, 41, 57, 72–3, 109–10, 122, 124, 128, 160, 163, 173, 178, 179,

Butler family (*cont.*)
 180, 182, 185–6, 187, 188, 194, 201,
 207, 288
Butler, Sir Edmund, 134–5, 181–3, 184, 188
Butler, Sir Edward, 181, 183, 184, 188
Butler, James (9th earl of Ormond), 20, 21,
 38–9, 41–3, 57, 61, 169
Butler, Sir Piers (8th earl of Ormond and
 earl of Ossory), 4, 17, 20, 24, 181
Butler, Thomas (7th earl of Ormond), 179
Butler, Thomas (10th earl of Ormond), 73,
 109–10, 122–3, 135, 142, 171, 172,
 175, 176, 178–84, 185, 186, 188, 190,
 191, 193, 196, 202, 235–6, 288, 295

Calvinism, ix
Campbell, Archibald (5th earl of Argyle), 58
Campion, Edmund, 211, 215
Canny, Nicholas, ix, 118
Cantwell, Wm., 61
Carew, Sir Peter, 128, 132, 134, 135, 163,
 173, 182, 191, 214, 278–280
Cecil, Wm. (baron Burghley), 81, 103, 121,
 123, 125, 128, 134, 145, 148, 149,
 151, 170, 213, 232, 242, 280, 283
'Celtic fringe', ix
cess, 88–9, 134, 146–9, 151, 152, 153–4,
 216–17, 220, 222, 226, 227, 230, 231,
 232, 233, 234, 235, 237, 242, 243
 statistical tables, 221, 228–9
 petitions against, 238
Chatterton, Christopher, 132, 255, 256
Chatterton, Thomas, 132, 256
Cheevers, Sir Christopher, 134, 214, 235,
 236, 238, 278
Church of Ireland, 56
Churchyard, Thomas, 242
civic humanism, 26
Clancar, earl of, *see* MacCarthy More,
 Donal
Clanrickard, earls of, *see* Burke
Coccerell, Ralph, 83
Colcough family, 275
Colley family, 261
Colley, Henry, 84, 116, 262
common law, x, 137, 141, 155
composition, 114, 141, 142–143, 148,
 149–54, 157, 162, 171, 198, 214, 293
Cosby family, 261
Cosby, Sir Francis, 84, 116, 262–4, 274
council government, 9
counter-reformation, 210
Cowley, Robert, 9, 17, 20, 41, 42, 249
Cowley, Walter, 9, 20, 21, 31, 43, 49–50,
 61, 249–50, 252

coyne and livery, 4, 6–7, 52, 74, 75, 131,
 139, 141, 142, 155, 173–5, 177
Creagh, Richard, 210
Croft, Gabriel, 83, 86
Crofts, Sir James, 46, 48–9, 51, 52, 59, 60,
 62, 63, 64, 69, 87, 98, 220, 221, 255,
 265, 280, 291
Cromwell, Thomas, x, 2, 5, 8, 13–18,
 20–21, 23, 24, 25, 29, 32, 33, 54
crown lands, 34–6, 38, 39, 43–4, 53, 66
Curwen, Hugh, 83
Cusacke, Sir Thomas, 21–2, 31, 32, 37, 38,
 48, 51, 61, 67, 81, 82, 105–6, 109, 110,
 111, 116–17, 121, 213, 214

Dalton, E. A, 113
Danyell, Terence, 121
Davells, Henry, 200, 274
Davies, Sir John, 245
debasement of coinage, 63–4, 87
Delvin, baron, *see* Nugent, Christopher
Devereux, Walter (1st earl of Essex), 144–6,
 149, 163, 196, 251, 252, 256, 257,
 259, 260, 264
Dillon family, 236
Dillon, Luke, 214, 295, 299
Dillon, Nathaniel, 214
Dillon, Robert, 83, 84, 117, 204, 214
Dillon, Thomas, 214
Dixe, Wm., 108
Dowdall, George, 90–1, 102, 163, 224, 239
Dowdall, James, 84, 213
Draycot family, 238
Draycot, Henry, 84
Drury, Sir William, 151, 173, 189, 197–8,
 200–1, 202, 204
Dudley, John (duke of Northumberland),
 47, 54, 55, 59, 60, 64, 65, 87, 104
Dudley, Robert (earl of Leicester), 102–4,
 106–7, 112, 114, 119–120, 122, 124,
 136, 144–5, 151, 180, 189, 193, 194,
 197, 199
Dungannon, baron of, *see* O'Neill, Mathew
dynastic crisis, 54–56, 160

Edward VI, 45, 54, 55, 56, 62, 287
Elizabeth, ix, 55, 72, 78, 93, 97, 100, 104,
 110, 111, 114, 119, 120–1, 122, 124,
 127, 131, 132, 134, 142, 143, 144,
 152, 158, 164, 169–70, 175, 187, 193,
 196, 200, 211, 217, 241, 242, 243,
 252, 261, 266
Essex, earl of, *see* Devereux
ethnology, ix
Eustace family, 236

Eustace, James (3rd viscount Baltinglas), 204–6, 209–12
Eustace, Rowland (2nd viscount), 225

Fenton, Geoffrey, 202, 204, 205, 295
Ferguson, Adam, ix
feudalism, bastard, xi, 4, 170, 173, 260
financial management, 9, 14, 15, 29, 33–4, 42, 47, 55, 62–3, 65–7, 68, 69, 71, 85–6, 104, 118, 119, 131, 134, 144, 150, 151, 157–8, 159, 162, 233–4, *see also under* cess, crown lands, debasement of coinage
Finglas, Patrick, 248–9, 252
Fitton, Edward, 75, 137–8, 140, 141, 142, 144, 172, 182, 183, 184, 185, 186, 189, 233
Fitzgerald family (Desmond), 2, 16, 17, 23, 30, 40, 72, 78, 109–10, 135, 163, 182, 207
Fitzgerald family (Kildare), 1, 2, 3, 9, 16, 17, 19–20, 29, 30, 40, 57, 72, 78, 109, 122, 163, 189, 207
Fitzgerald, Sir Edward, 196
Fitzgerald, Gerald (9th earl of Kildare), 4, 5, 7
Fitzgerald, Gerald, (11th earl of Kildare), 23, 73, 75, 78, 79, 83, 91–3, 102, 106, 109, 116, 121, 127, 142, 149, 169, 172, 173, 174–5, 180, 189–93, 196, 203–207, 235–6, 237, 261, 262
Fitzgerald, James FitzJohn, (13th earl of Desmond), 2–3, 16, 22, 31, 38, 39, 41, 46, 51, 57, 62, 75, 90–1, 169
Fitzgerald, James FitzMaurice (12th earl of Desmond), 16, 18
Fitzgerald, James Fitzmaurice, *see* Fitzmaurice
Fitzgerald, Sir John (of Desmond), 124, 126, 127, 128, 193, 199–200, 206, 254
Fitzgerald, Sir Maurice, 194
Fitzgerald, Thomas (baron Offaly), 18
FitzJames, Gerald (14th earl of Desmond), 105–6, 109, 110, 123–4, 126, 127, 144, 149, 151, 169, 170, 171, 172, 173, 174, 175, 176, 178–9, 193–202, 204, 266
Fitzmaurice family (Kerry), 18
Fitzmaurice, James, FitzMaurice (FitzGerald), James, 128, 173, 181, 182, 183, 194–6, 198–200, 204, 215, 292
Fitzpatrick sept, 39, 41, 178, 184
Fitzpatrick, Sir Barnaby, 171, 203, 261, 262, 263, 287, 289

Fitzpatrick, Florence, 288
Fitzsimons family, 214
Fitzwalter, Lord Thomas, *see* Radcliffe, Thomas
Fitzwilliam, Michael, 84
Fitzwilliam, Sir Wm., 66–70, 75, 83, 92, 100, 107–8, 116, 117, 127, 136, 144, 145, 151, 154, 184, 185, 186, 188, 189, 191, 193, 195, 196, 222, 232–3, 238, 239, 247, 258–9, 262, 281, 288, 298, 299, 300
Fleming, Thomas, 126
forts and fortification, 59–60, 62, 63, 83, 88, 219, 222, 228, 237, 248–9, 251, 257, 272

Gaelic Ireland, 7–8, 27, 39, 40, 46, 49, 50, 58, 59, 68, 73, 74, 90, 97, 108, 113, 126, 140, 143, 156, 166, 185, 210, 212, 220, 230, 245–90 *passim*, 294
garrison, size of, 85, 103, 119, 120, 129, 135–6, 141, 145, 156, 218–21, 226–8
see also under presidency
Gerrard, Gilbert, 86, 118, 159
Gerrard, Wm., 146, 148–9, 152, 154–8, 159, 166, 187, 204, 217, 282, 291
Gilbert, Humphrey, 135, 137, 139, 140, 141, 250
Goldsmith, John, 32, 83
Gormanston, Viscount, *see* Preston
Grace family, 288
Grey, Lord Leonard, xiii–xiv, 10, 13–14, 18–25, 29–30, 31, 32, 33, 40–1, 42, 50, 57, 60, 61, 64, 84, 160, 176, 190, 191, 218, 265
Grey, Thomas (1st marquis of Dorset), 24
Grey de Wilton, Arthur, lord, 202, 209, 210, 215, 290, 292, 293, 294

Harpole, Robert, 261, 264, 274, 275
Harrington, Henry, 204, 274, 276, 280, 285
Henry II (of France), 57
Henry VIII, ix, 2, 5, 8, 20–1, 23, 25, 33, 40, 43, 45, 54, 55, 62, 63, 69, 114, 249
Herbert, Francis, 16, 33, 61
Heron, Nicholas, 84, 116, 227, 272, 273
Howard, Thomas, (earl of Surrey, and 3rd duke of Norfolk), 4, 5, 24, 215, 218
Howard, Thomas (4th duke of Norfolk), 121, 181

Jenyson, Thomas, 83, 117, 234
Jones, Brian, 272
judicial circuits, 156–7, 159, 166

Kavanagh sept, 17, 18, 27, 41, 203, 249, 272, 276, 279
Kavanagh, Brian Mac Cahir, 279
Kavanagh, Cahir MacArt, 28, 46, 49, 51
Keating family, 192
Kells Abbey, 39
Kildare, earls of, *see* Fitzgerald
Kilkenny, Statutes of, 74
Knollys, Sir Francis, 120, 127

Laois (Leix) and Offaly plantation, 74, 76–7, 82, 85, 94–6, 97, 104, 118, 144, 189, 250, 255, 260–4
Larkin, Edward, 83
Leicester, earl of, *see* Dudley, Robert
Loftus, Adam, 206, 295
Lynn, Hugh, 16

Mac an Iarlas, 151, 186, 187, 199
Mac Carthy sept (of Muskerry), 200, 266
Mac Carthy, Sir Cormac, 194
Mac Carthy More sept, 18, 254
Mac Carthy More, Donal (earl of Clancar), 51, 57, 197, 200, 255, 266
Mac Conall, Lysagh, *see* O'More
Mac Dermot sept, 282
Mac Donagh sept, 254
Mac Donnell clan, 111, 128, 260
Mac Donnell, Alexander, 124
Mac Donnell, James, 58, 79
Mac Donnell, Sorley Boy, 260
Mac Geoghan, Brian, 287
Mac Geoghan, Ross, 287–8, 289
Mac Mahon sept, 22, 49, 266, 298
Mac Neill More, Hugh, 127
MacWilliam Burke sept, 17, 18, 284
Machiavelli, N., 297
Magennis sept, 18, 39
Maguire sept, 49, 130, 134, 271
Maguire, Shane, 267
Malby, Sir Nicholas, 187, 189, 201–2, 205, 255, 281–5, 290
Margaret Tudor (queen dowager of Scotland), 58
Mary, 45, 54, 55, 60, 61, 64, 68, 72, 77, 87, 90, 91, 93, 96, 104, 116, 163
Mary, queen of Scots, 54
Masterson, Thomas, 203, 274, 276, 278, 280, 285
Mellifont, 36
Might, Thomas, 232
Mills, C. Wright, x
monastic lands, 14, 32, 33–4, 36–9, 41, 43, 53, 178, 214
More, Edward, 262, 263, 264

Morton, Ralph, 116
Moryson, Fynes, 245
Mullaghmast, 264
Multifarnham, 37

Netterville, Richard, 149, 153, 236, 240
Norris, John, 293, 295
Northumberland, duke of, *see* Dudley, John
Nugent family, 205, 236
Nugent, Christopher (baron Delvin), 205, 238
Nugent, William, 205, 209–10, 212

O'Brennan sept, 49
O'Brien clan (Thomond), 16, 22, 27, 28, 52, 67, 100, 138, 180
O'Brien, Conor (3rd earl of Thomond), 98, 99, 109, 179, 182, 183, 184–5, 266
O'Brien, Cormack, 18
O'Brien, Donough (2nd earl of Thomond), 98
O'Brien, Sir Donnell, 77, 98–9, 105, 109, 110
O'Brien, Murrough (1st earl of Thomond), 38, 39, 98
O'Byrne sept, 57, 98, 192, 205, 249, 272, 275, 278
O'Byrne, Fiagh Mac Hugh, 276, 278
O'Byrne, Hugh Mac Shane, 278
O'Callaghan sept, 254
O'Carroll sept, 184, 288
O'Carroll, Calough, 49
O'Carroll, Teig, 49
O'Connor sept, 2, 17, 22, 23, 33, 49, 56, 57, 67, 77, 79, 94, 96, 108, 110, 192, 249, 260, 262–3
O'Connor, Cahir, 2–3
O'Connor, Donough, 95
O'Connor, Ferganim, 18
O'Connor Sligo, 268, 282
O'Conor Roe, 282
O'Dempsey, Own MacHugh, 261, 262, 263
O'Donnell clan, 2, 111, 271, 282
O'Donnell, Calough, 111, 267
O'Donnell, Hugh, 129, 130, 298–9
O'Donnell, Manus, 2–3, 17, 51, 57
O'Flaherty sept, 22, 282, 284
O'Hara sept, 267
O'Kelly sept, 282
O'Madden, 284
O'Malley sept, 17
O'Malley, Grace, 284
O'More sept, 2, 17, 18, 46, 49, 56, 57, 67, 77, 94, 108, 110, 184, 192, 249, 262
O'More, Callough, 260

O'More, Connell, 95
O'More, Lysagh MacConall, 264
O'More, Rory Og, 192, 260–1, 263–4
O'Neill clan, 2, 22, 27, 99, 126
O'Neill sept (Clandeboye), 51, 258
O'Neill, Brian MacFertagh, 259–60
O'Neill, Sir Brian MacPhelim, 258–60
O'Neill, Con Bachach (1st earl of Tyrone),
   2–3, 17, 18, 28, 46, 49, 51, 57, 99, 111,
   258
O'Neill, Hugh (2nd earl of Tyrone), 257,
   289–90, 295
O'Neill, Mathew (baron of Dungannon), 28,
   51–2, 67, 99–100
O'Neill, Phelim, 49
O'Neill, Shane, 28, 52, 67, 78–9, 85, 97,
   99–102, 105–6, 110–11, 116, 118, 120,
   123, 124–5, 126, 127, 130, 131, 163,
   190, 215, 220–1, 228, 231, 256, 265,
   266, 287
O'Neill, Turlough Luineach, 126, 127, 128,
   130, 132, 134, 135, 257, 259, 260,
   268–9, 289
Ordinances for the government of Ireland, 4,
   5
O'Reilly sept, 18, 74, 130, 134, 267, 268,
   271, 295
O'Reilly, Philip, 298–9
Ormond, earls of, see Butler
O'Rourke, Brian, 282, 286, 298
O'Sullivan sept, 254
O'Sullivan Beare, 266
O'Toole sept, 27, 28, 57, 98, 249, 268, 272
O'Toole, Brian, 28, 276
O'Toole, Lucas, 276

Pale, the (and Palesmen), 2, 5, 7, 19, 23, 38,
   39, 40, 43, 50, 51, 63, 64, 67, 82, 83,
   84, 87, 88–9, 90, 92, 94, 96, 103, 104,
   105, 106, 113, 126, 128, 134, 142,
   144, 146, 148, 149, 153–7, 166, 173,
   204, 205, 206, 208, 255–6, 276, 290,
   294, 295
   law students' grievance, 102–3, 222, 224,
      236 (quoted), 241
   agents' mission to court, 149, 152, 153,
      154, 157, 241
   reform and, 209–44 *passim*
   petitions against cess, 238
Parker, John, 31–2, 33, 37, 38, 39, 61, 66,
   67, 84, 106, 214, 224
Paulet, George, 21
Paulet, Wm. (1st marquis of Winchester),
   127
Peppard, Walter, 32, 37, 38, 61, 67, 214

Perrot, Sir John, xii, xv, 172, 195, 196, 241,
   246, 291–300 *passim*
Philip II (of Spain), 54, 68, 76
Piers, Wm., 83, 125, 250, 252, 258–9, 260,
   264, 281
Pipho, Robert, 273, 274
Plantagenet, Arthur (viscount Lisle), 24
plantation, 52–3, 68, 73, 96–7, 128, 145,
   251, 254; *see also* Laois and Offaly
Plunket, Sir John, 83, 84, 213
Pollard, A. F., 45
Portas, Wm., 83
Poynings, Sir Edward, 218
presidency and presidential councils, 73–4,
   90–91, 117–18, 131–2, 134, 137–41,
   145, 146, 149–50, 170–1, 172, 173,
   176, 293
   troops of, 171
Preston family, 236
Preston, Jenico, (viscount Gormanston), 205,
   238
prices, 232–3
print, 238
purveyance, 216–18

Quinn, David, ix

Radcliffe, Henry (2nd earl of Sussex), 69,
   108
Radcliffe, Sir Henry, 78, 83, 96, 116, 227,
   287
Radcliffe, Thomas (3rd earl of Sussex), xii,
   xiii, 31, 46, 52–3, 61, 62, 68–71,
   72–112 *passim*, 114, 115, 116, 117,
   118, 119, 120, 121, 122, 123, 130–31,
   137, 143, 163–6, 170, 178–81, 184,
   187, 188, 189, 190, 202, 207, 208,
   209, 210–11, 214, 215, 216, 217, 220,
   221, 222, 226, 228, 230, 231, 236,
   237, 238, 243, 255, 256, 257, 260,
   261, 262, 265–73, 275, 286
rebellion (Clanrickard), 151, 155, 281–2
rebellion (Kildare), xiii–xiv, 1–3, 8–9, 13,
   90, 160, 169, 177
rebellion (Desmond), 135–6, 143, 172, 190,
   200, 202, 207, 208, 254, 289, 292
religious policy, 46, 54, 55, 69, 104, 117,
   118, 137, 169, 210–11
Roche, David (Viscount Fermoy), 194
Rokeby, Ralph, 138
Rouse, Sir Edmund, 66, 82, 86
Ryan sept, 49

Sackford, Thomas, 232
St John's Hospital, 36

St Lawrence, Christopher (8th baron Howth), 83
St Lawrence, Thomas, Justice, 19
St Leger, Sir Anthony, xiii, xiv, 13, 20, 21, 24–34, 37–44, 45–6, 48–9, 50, 52–3, 56, 57, 59, 60, 61, 62, 63, 64, 65, 67–8, 69–71, 75, 79, 80, 81, 82, 83, 84, 87, 90, 91, 98, 102, 105, 107, 111, 112, 114, 115, 116, 117, 160–2, 176, 178, 190, 191, 215, 217, 219, 220, 226, 249, 255–6, 265, 268, 269
St Leger, Robert, 37, 42
St Leger, Warham, 117, 122, 126, 132, 172, 173, 180, 195, 254
St Mary's Abbey (Dublin), 37
St Thomas's Abbey (Dublin), 36
Savage family, 272
Scots (in Ulster), 51, 52, 58–9, 67, 68, 85, 96–7, 100, 111, 118, 125, 127–8, 134, 251, 252, 258, 259, 293, 294
Scurlocke, Barnaby, 83, 89, 149, 235, 236–7, 238
Selsker Abbey, 37
senechal system, 273, 278, 280
Seymour, Edward (duke of Somerset), 47, 54, 55, 59, 60, 65
Sidney, Sir Henry, xii, 31, 83, 89, 92, 99, 104, 112, 113–58 *passim*, 159, 162–6, 170, 172, 174, 176, 178, 181–91 *passim*, 193–4, 196, 197, 198, 199, 200, 202, 206, 207, 208, 209, 210–11, 214, 215, 216, 217, 220, 221, 222, 223, 224, 226, 230, 231, 232, 237, 238, 239–40, 243–4, 255, 256, 257, 260, 261, 262, 265–6, 268–70, 275, 278–9, 282, 286, 289, 291, 298
Sidney, Sir Philip, 152, 243
Skeffington, Sir Wm., 4–5, 9, 31, 32, 159
Skeyn, Mathew, 16

Smith, Sir Thomas, 250–1, 252–3, 256, 257
soldiers' conduct, 224–5, 230, 237
Somerset, duke of, *see* Seymour, Edward
Spenser, Edmund, 245, 291, 300
Stafford, Henry, 83, 116
Stanihurst, Richard, 212, 245
Stanley, George, 67, 82, 83, 116
Stuckley, Thomas, 121, 200, 273, 276, 278
surrender and regrant, 29, 52, 72, 73, 91, 97–8, 215
Surrey, earl of. *see* Howard, Thomas
Sussex, earl of, *see* Radcliffe, Thomas
Synott family, 272

Travers, John, 33, 84
Tremayne, Edmund, 140–3, 145, 146, 147, 150, 152, 264, 280–1
Tuite, James, 19
Tuite, Richard, 19

Wakely, John, 61
Wallop, Sir Henry, 202, 204, 205, 240, 280, 295
Walsh, Sir Nicholas, 212
Walshe, Edward, 81, 89, 250, 291
Walshe, James, 83
Walsingham, Sir Francis, 149, 151, 153, 170, 187, 281
Waterhouse, Sir Edward, 152, 158, 202
Weber, Max, x
Weston, Robert, 127
White, Sir Nicholas, 134, 148, 149, 213, 242, 280, 291, 295, 299
White, Rowland, 81–2, 89, 128, 252–3, 258
Wilson, Thomas, 158
Wingfield, Jacques, 82, 116, 132, 272
Wise, Andrew, 32, 66, 67, 69, 106–7
Wise, Sir Wm., 32
Wrothe, Sir Thomas, 104, 108, 224

Cambridge Studies in Early Modern British History

Titles in the series

*The Common Peace: Participation and the Criminal Law in Seventeenth-Century England**
CYNTHIA B. HERRUP

Politics, Society and Civil War in Warwickshire, 1620–1660
ANN HUGHES

*London Crowds in the Reign of Charles II: Propaganda and Politics from the Restoration to the Exclusion Crisis**
TIM HARRIS

*Criticism and Compliment: the Politics of Literature in the England of Charles I**
KEVIN SHARPE

Central Government and the Localities: Hampshire, 1649–1689
ANDREW COLEBY

John Skelton and the Politics of the 1520s
GREG WALKER

Algernon Sidney and the English Republic, 1623–1677
JONATHAN SCOTT

Thomas Starkey and the Commonwealth: Humanist Politics and Religion in the Reign of Henry VIII
THOMAS F. MAYER

*The Blind Devotion of the People: Popular Religion and the English Reformation**
ROBERT WHITING

The Cavalier Parliament and the Reconstruction of the Old Regime, 1661–1667
PAUL SEAWARD

The Blessed Revolution: English Politics and the Coming of War, 1621–1624
THOMAS COGSWELL

Charles I and the Road to Personal Rule
L. J. REEVE

George Lawson's 'Politica' and the English Revolution
CONAL CONDREN

Puritans and Roundheads: the Harleys of Brampton Bryan and the Outbreak of the English Civil War
JACQUELINE EALES

An Uncounselled King: Charles I and the Scottish Troubles, 1637–1641
PETER DONALD

Cheap Print and Popular Piety, 1550–1640*
TESSA WATT

The Pursuit of Stability: Social Relations in Elizabethan London
IAN W. ARCHER

Prosecution and Punishment: Petty Crime and the Law in London and Rural Middlesex, c. 1600–1725
ROBERT B. SHOEMAKER

Algernon Sidney and the Restoration Crisis, 1677–1683
JONATHAN SCOTT

Exile and Kingdom: History and Apocalypse in the Puritan Migration to America
AVIHU ZAKAI

The Pillars of Priestcraft Shaken: the Church of England and its Enemies
J. A. I. CHAMPION

Stewards, Lords and People: the Estate Steward and his World in Later Stuart England
D. R. HAINSWORTH

Civil War and Restoration in the Three Stuart Kingdoms: the Career of Randal MacDonnell, Marquis of Antrim, 1609–1683
JANE H. OHLMEYER

The Family of Love in English Society, 1550–1630
CHRISTOPHER W. MARSH

The Bishops' Wars: Charles I's Campaigns against Scotland, 1638–1640*
MARK FISSEL

John Locke: Resistance, Religion and Responsibility*
JOHN MARSHALL

Constitutional Royalism and the Search for Settlement, c. 1640–1649
DAVID L. SMITH

Intelligence and Espionage in the Reign of Charles II, 1660–1685
ALAN MARSHALL

The Chief Governors: the Rise and Fall of Reform Government in Tudor Ireland, 1536–1588
CIARAN BRADY

Politics and Opinion in Crisis, 1678–1681
MARK KNIGHTS

Catholic and Reformed: the Roman and Protestant Churches in English Protestant Thought, 1604–1640
ANTHONY MILTON

Sir Matthew Hale, 1609–1676: Law, Religion and Natural Philosophy
ALAN CROMARTIE

*Also published as a paperback

Malet Street, London WC1E 7HX
020-7631 6239
Items should be returned or renewed by the latest date stamped below.
Please pick up a Library guide or visit the Library website
http://www.bbk.ac.uk/lib/
for information about online renewals.

11/12/07

ONE WEEK LOAN

Printed in the United Kingdom
by Lightning Source UK Ltd.
121212UK00002B/94